The Naval Institute
Guide to Naval Writing

Robert Shenk

The Naval Institute
Guide to Naval Writing

Third Edition

Naval Institute Press   Annapolis, Maryland

Naval Institute Press
291 Wood Road
Annapolis, MD 21402

Library of Congress Cataloging-in-Publication Data
Shenk, Robert, 1943–
    The Naval Institute guide to naval writing / Robert Shenk. — 3rd ed.
        p.   cm.
    Includes bibliographical references and index.
    ISBN 978-1-59114-822-7 (alk. paper)
    1. United States. Navy—Records and correspondence.   2. United
States. Marine Corps—Records and correspondence.   3. Naval art
and science—Authorship.   4. Military art and science—Authorship.
5. Technical writing.   I. Title.
VB255.S54   2008
808'.066359—dc22
                                                        2007036843

14   13   12   11   10   9   8   7   6   5   4   3

Page 323 is a continuation of the copyright page.

*Mary K. Shenk, Stephanie Shenk,
Henry Shenk, and Peter Shenk—
professionals all.*

I was a math major. I was in the Navy twenty-one years, and I never solved a differential equation. But I wrote every day.

—Retired naval officer

Always remember: You write for the distracted reader.

—Naval writing expert, Naval Academy

Contents

Acknowledgments

In doing interviews this time around, I am again indebted to many naval professionals. Although sometimes even getting in to talk to people was difficult in this post-9/11 world, I was occasionally quite humbled by what I heard. One LDO said he had read an earlier edition of this book cover to cover when he was first commissioned; a lieutenant reported she had been given the book as a commissioning gift (and was a great fan of the text); and a captain reported that, when in command, he had procured the book for all his officers and chiefs. Such reports kept my spirits up in what turned out to be an unexpectedly difficult revision.

Thanks to the dozens of naval professionals who were so kind as to invite me to their offices, spend some time with me, offer words of wisdom, or show me documents. In particular, I'd like to thank Gregory Akers, Nancy Batten, CAPT Blakeney, Kevin Brooks, Hank Coates, Sandra Davidson, C. B. Davis, Rob Davis, Adolfo Demontalvo, Fred Federick, Tony Feliz, Al Foucha, Lane Heath, Yancey Lindsey, Chris Loundermon, Kelly Maksem, Tariq Rashid, James Taylor, and Harry White. Of course, any errors in this edition are mine, not theirs.

The Naval Institute
Guide to Naval Writing

Writing is another way of competing. *A lot of my impression of you is based upon what you write.*

—Commanding Officer, USN

1

Introduction

When interviewed, naval professionals of all ranks often commented on how important it is for them to write well.

WHO IS DOING IMPORTANT WRITING?

It is not surprising, perhaps, that the writing done by senior officers carries great weight. But it is rather remarkable how important writing can be for junior people. The duties of three lieutenants, a Marine major, two civil servants, a Marine staff sergeant, and a Navy chief stand out. These people's responsibilities demonstrate how important writing can be at almost any level.

For example, a lieutenant (junior grade) was made administrative officer of a destroyer late in his first shipboard tour because he was such a good writer. He ended up writing all of the award nominations, many evaluations, frequent press releases, and much of the command correspondence aboard ship. He felt he had gained invaluable perspective from working directly for the commanding officer (CO) and executive officer (XO). Like a civilian executive assistant (EA), he was at the living center of the organization and was being trained to step up.

The disbursing officer of a Naval Construction Battalion did a great deal of writing in addition to that required by his disbursing duties. This Navy lieutenant wrote letters of commendation; award justifications and citations; letters requesting new duties for himself and draft endorsements for others applying to special programs; and letters of condolence. Many of the documents he wrote were drafts for his commanding officer to sign.

In contrast, officers given independent duty often sign most or all of the documents that they draft. This was the case with a lieutenant when she became the officer in charge (OinC) of a Personnel Support Detachment. She had to compose enlisted evaluations, award justifications, instructions, correspondence, and messages with no one around except her first class yeoman to offer guidance and criticism.

Another officer had the opposite problem—working under many eyes. This Marine major was the EA to an O-6 division head at a school's command. Like many EAs, he wrote a good deal, but he edited and coordinated much more. Besides drafting messages, letters, memos, and performance evaluations for the colonel's signature, the major had a hand in JAGMAN Investigations and letters replying to congressional inquiries. He also coordinated award ceremonies, dining-ins, and other social functions—all of which required a good deal of writing. And he supervised a team of civilian secretaries.

It almost goes without saying that, today, officers like those mentioned above must daily read, respond to, forward, or otherwise deal effectively with dozens of official emails from every conceivable naval addressee. Many of the specific genres of documents mentioned in this and in later chapters are now sent via email, the understanding and use of which requires considerable craft of its own.

Civil servants can also have important writing responsibilities. At a fairly high rank, a civil servant in the Navy's budget-writing office was an unsung individual whose writing had major impact on the Navy. His ability to rewrite budget justifications ("POM issue papers") submitted from throughout the service—without time to query officials at major commands as to the exact meaning of their sometimes unclear terminology—had a vital effect on the success of Navy budget requests. At a somewhat lower level, another civil servant wrote Pentagon executive summary memoranda and accompanying correspondence. Her paperwork often reached up to and was signed off by two- and three-star admirals.

Among enlisted writers, a boatswain's mate chief found he had a big writing burden when he reported aboard ship. He was assigned as the first lieutenant on a frigate, duty that required writing many instructions and reports, recording some counseling sessions, and even putting together a JAGMAN Investigation, besides doing the evaluations and award write-ups that were already very familiar to him. Indeed as one of the vessel's dozen or so division officers, he found himself doing far more division paperwork than work in his own rating—not an uncommon experience for senior enlisted men and women.

And a Marine administrative chief spoke of the job he once had as a staff sergeant in the Secretary of the Navy's office. Although his position was in security, he happened to work alongside officers who drafted answers to service members who had written the President. When the officer staff suddenly got overloaded, the sergeant was asked to contribute. Guided by a senior civilian secretary, he learned the required style over many weeks of practice, and soon he was researching and drafting eight to ten letters a week, many for the signature of the President of the United States. This experience later served him well in the adjutant's office of a Marine division, where he supervised Marines writing responses to congressional inquiries and supervised many other kinds of correspondence and staff work.

Some service members have major writing responsibilities very early in their careers. Others do not—many junior enlisted aboard ship may not write very much, and some junior officers may not either (although virtually everybody has to write and respond to email). Junior Marine Corps officers assigned to a battery may never write a letter or report, and some naval aviators in squadrons may not have to write much in their initial tours.

Eventually most of these situations will change. When junior enlisted become senior they will at the very minimum have to draft enlisted evaluations and letters of commendation for their people and will contribute to letters and reports, most of the latter being forwarded via the Navy and Marine Corps Intranet (NMCI). Often they

"Few of my young lieutenants could write well. They had little concept of detail, style, spelling, or grammar. Duty in the Fleet Marine Force, particularly in staff billets, requires an ability to write."

—Marine Lieutenant Colonel

"Most of the paperwork falls on the shoulders of those who can—which usually means those individuals have lots of face time with the XO and CO."
—LDO, Admin Officer
on a carrier

will have much more writing to do. As for officers, sooner or later almost all of them will join staffs on which writing becomes a major personal responsibility. In short, virtually all naval professionals should learn the principles of good writing early in their careers.

WHAT ARE THEY WRITING, AND WHY?

The purposes of naval documents are multifold; a brief description of the uses of the major types of service writing can illustrate how vital they are. Of course, almost everyone writes emails in daily work—documents that serve virtually all the administrative functions you can name. In addition, ships, units, and staffs run themselves by directives, whether called instructions and notices (in the Navy) or orders and bulletins (in the Marine Corps).

Beyond that, personnel evaluations ensure that the services promote the best individuals and help place the right people in key positions, while award justifications, letters of commendation, and award citations recognize individuals for their achievements. In a related area, sooner or later service members all have to write letters to request changes of designator, entry into new programs, and so on. Such letters and their required endorsements allow service members to find good places to use their skills, and this helps the services to funnel talent into needed areas.

News features in base papers help keep up morale and spread the word about the good jobs people are doing. Hard news releases, letters responding to congressional inquiries, and formal position papers present news and naval perspectives to the public and to public officials. In a different area, JAGMAN Investigations and other legal writing efforts help ensure that justice is done both for service members and for the services they serve.

Point papers and briefing folders circulating internally on staffs, both electronically and in hard copy, articulate policies and procedures while budget justifications and technical reports help build and maintain the services. Staff reports and formatted messages feed and equip fleet units while reports sent by operational units back to a staff inform commanders of the situation in the field. Without the messages, after-action reports, lessons learned, logistics requests, and many other documents that originate from ships and Marine operational units, shore staffs would have precious little information with which to form impressions, solve problems, and make changes to guide the Navy and Marine Corps. Finally, documents such as war-fighting doctrine, night orders, battle orders, operation orders, and operational messages directly assist the naval services in fighting a conflict or war. Of course, emails sent to and from navy people everywhere—both horizontally and at every level and up and down the chain of command—have become the nerve networks of the modern navy as well as the transmitting mechanism for most of the other missives mentioned here.

This text presents guidance on most of the topics outlined above. However, the various kinds of actual writing situations beggar description. In interviews service members mentioned all sorts of occasions for writing about which they had no guidance at all. Such out-of-the-ordinary writing responsibilities only begin to suggest the great need for naval professionals to be generally good writers, good enough to adapt to greatly varied needs.

For example, one junior officer commented that hard as he might try to draft a personal letter to an admiral to invite him to the ship's change of command, he couldn't get to first base. His commander eventually had to write it. Another officer said that after writing so much navalese, addressing a civilian in a letter was like trying to change gears in her mind—and she couldn't do it. Such inability is unfortunate.

At the very least almost every officer has occasion to write recommendations for enlisted men and women leaving the service. If you don't know how to address civilians about the talents of your subordinates, your letter probably won't help your people very much.

No official guidance tells you how to communicate with a previous CO or other official on missing evaluations or fitness reports, or, more touchy yet, how to request evaluations be removed from your record. In a related area, whether to write to the selection board is often argued at happy hour but seldom discussed in print (it is discussed briefly in this text).

Senior officers also mentioned quandaries. A destroyer squadron staff officer pointed out that the budget reports he wrote for his boss were always freehand. No one told him how to write them or how to compose the "justification" section of a request to convince Commander, Naval Surface Force, Atlantic (SURFLANT) to augment the staff's OPTAR ("Operating Target") by $100,000. A destroyer's XO said that letters of indebtedness were usually but not always pro forma. After two or three form letters to an individual you'd have to spell the situation out very clearly, or the problem might result in a congressional inquiry.

Enlisted service members' struggles with specialized writing tasks were similar. Besides situations like those described above, in which Sailors and Marines have to write evals, letters, point papers, technical descriptions, and so on, many a command master chief or top sergeant has tried to offer written words of wisdom to Sailors or Marines about to go ashore in the Far East or in the Mediterranean. Often the content of their advice as to what to do (and, sometimes more important, what *not* to do) is very good. But if it is not written well, or isn't written or placed so as to catch people's attention, it may have little effect.

Clearly, if a person has confidence in writing, he or she can adapt to a great many writing situations and can master all kinds of documents that neither this nor any writing text can discuss individually. You cannot prepare for anywhere near all the specific documents you'll have to compose in a naval career, nor can this text offer instruction on every possible eventuality. What you can do is master the principles of good writing, practice them in all the kinds of writing situations that are covered here, and with these same principles to guide you, adapt to other circumstances by using your head.

PRINCIPLES OF GOOD WRITING—A WRITER'S TRIANGULATION

As in navigation, good writers look for fixed points of reference from which to plot their positions and ideal headings. The classic writer's (or speaker's) triangle looks like this:

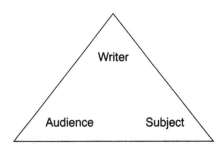

Knowing your audience, your subject, and yourself (including how others will see you in the writing situation), you can gauge your position with respect to any particular communication.

"As you proceed up the ladder of seniority, the need to write effectively increases greatly."
—Marine Colonel

"I teach this course to help make you not look like an idiot in front of your CO."
—Retired Commander, instructor of professional writing, U.S. Naval Academy

"Sometimes engineers who are briefing a general have trouble because what interests them, what they think important, or how they think does not match the general or the general's needs."
—Marine Colonel

Know Your Audience

To start with, the nature of your *audience* is obviously important, beginning with its rank, position, or billet. Whether you're writing to someone senior or junior to you makes a difference in how you'll pitch a letter or memo. Also critical is the position your correspondent holds—is he or she higher up in the organization, at your same level but in a different branch, or in a different organization altogether? The possible complexities in organizational relationships beggar description, especially on staffs in Washington, D.C.

You should also consider how important the *boss* of the person you're writing to is, "politically" speaking. Knowing the standard policy positions of the organization he or she works in can be vital, too. Your attention to such things can affect whether your letter or memo receives standard routing, gets put on the back burner, or merits immediate command attention (for better or for worse).

Besides the organizational and "political" realities of your communication, you have to recognize the personality of the person you're writing to, or your correspondent's known opinions on the issue you're bringing up. For instance, knowing an admiral's personal preferences and normal way of working can be vital if you have to get the admiral on your side. Remembering the principle of audience will also help you adjust your style. Unless your readers will all be aviators, for example, you'll do well to forgo terms like "painting bogies," "out of knots," "losing a hop," and "strapping on the jet." Even when writing to aviators, you probably won't want to use such jargon for official correspondence that leaves your command—you don't know who is likely to read those terms and view them as too informal to be used outside the briefing room. Nor do you know which of your informal emails (with your jokes and gossip) is going to be forwarded at the touch of a key to third parties you never thought of addressing.

In addition, writing down the chain of command in response to a personal request requires special care. It's easy to fall into the habit of patronizing a service member, saying things like "Perhaps you don't realize that the regulations require . . . ," or speaking in stilted, bureaucratic terms. YNCM Charles E. Miller, Jr. (who often taught the Action Officer's course at BUPERS) regularly recommended that with such an audience you should "write like you talk—explain things at the reader's level. Don't sound like a Navy Regulation." Actually, he thinks you ought to write like that all the time. Particularly in responding to a personal letter, a writer should go out of his or her way to be natural, even personable. In such circumstances, the master chief suggests that one consider including a couple of personal references, like "I'm so glad to hear your son is doing well" or—as one admiral likes to say—"I have a son in the Navy myself. I know what you're going through."

Writing to nonmilitary audiences requires even more adjustment and some simplification. As a naval official writing to a civilian, you'll usually have to explain more than you do to fellow service members and do without all those Navy-specific or bureaucratic terms we all use so widely in-house. In short, *know to whom you're writing*—that's the very first principle of good writing awareness.

Know Your Subject

Second, you must make adjustments for *the subject matter* with which you are dealing. Those who live or die by whether what they write is actually read—recruiters, for example—know this principle very well. "As a recruiter I learned that as soon as my recruiting document went beyond a paragraph or a paragraph and a half, it was thrown away" said a Navy chief. "So I had to get a reader's attention in that opening

"Nobody reads at a desk in a quiet room."
—Retired Commander, naval writing expert

"When you get to be an E-7 or O-4, God installs an automatic bullshit detector."
—Master Chief Charles E. Miller, Jr.

"There's a culture difference between our students and us. They think we keep the same hours they do, and have a similar great need to stay connected electronically."
—Commander of an NROTC detachment

paragraph." Depending on the subject, a writer doesn't always need to be so immediate with the message. Almost all of us will study discussions of changes in pay and benefits with some care because such subjects arouse natural interest.

Knowing the way readers usually treat a document can also be valuable. Naval directives are typically scanned, not read word for word—so headings can help alert readers to key information. On the other hand, extremely technical material requires great patience on the part of readers, and a manual writer must be careful to go slow and give readers many aids—summaries, headings, visuals, section reviews, and so on. The large number of emails handled daily by naval offices everywhere suggests the critical importance of accurate and descriptive email subject lines. Obviously, there are many other such considerations.

It should go without saying that you should know your argument inside out. Lapses in logic or in documentation, failures to explain or exemplify, or omissions of crucial details can all sink your recommendation before you get out of harbor. Because of space limitations, very little of your knowledge may show up in a briefing memo. But in tabs, appendixes, links, or material held in reserve you should be able to support any position. Make use of examples, statistics, pertinent testimony, comparison and contrast, definition and analysis—all the furniture of standard argument.

Know Yourself

Third, you should always remember who *you are* and the self-image you want to project when composing your letter, message, or speech.

Some service members forget this principle when they compose letters to selection boards, criticizing the service or their superiors to explain away some low rankings. The writers come across as malcontents to board members, who just as quickly vote "no confidence" in the tank.

Clearly, deference and respect are always good qualities in juniors speaking to seniors. But keep your wits about you here. You are sometimes in a position to speak *for the command,* not just for yourself. Even if you're relatively junior, if you're representing your command at a conference you can be very forceful in your expressions of opinion. E-7s or E-8s from a staff may speak decisively and with strong credibility even among senior officers, for they know the admiral will back them up.

Naturally, seniors are expected to be forceful. In a recent inspection, a senior Navy inspector often heard the commanding officer criticized for not taking charge or giving strong direction. "He didn't act like a Navy captain," commented one of his officers, and this complaint was widespread. That impression hurt the captain's credibility both with enlisted and officer members of his command—and in turn with the inspecting party. The point: *Act so as to be believed and respected* whenever you speak or write.

Being aware of the impression you make can have wide application. If you are appearing before Congress to support a budget request, you'll be expected to wear your uniform proudly and speak forcefully to the needs of the service. On the other hand, if as a base commander you have to address civilians in the local community about projected school closings that could affect service members' children, you might consider toning down your customary military manner to meet the civilians halfway.

To be sure, one's purposes in all circumstances will affect that adjustment—one may or may not want to be conciliatory; one may or may not want to portray a strongly military image in any particular case. The point is to remember that the way you come across to others in manner and tone can influence how they receive your message. If you know what you sound like when you speak or write, you can make use of that knowledge to help get your message across.

A Special Case of Knowing "Yourself": Writing for the Boss

One other aspect of speaking with credibility, or of remembering who you are when you write, is especially important in naval service. Many times (*most* times aboard ship) you don't write for your own signature but for someone else's. In many an email, letter, directive, or report, the drafter disappears, and the only name that appears (or is assumed) is that of the commanding officer. This principle is even truer of major staffs where staff action officers are writing for very senior officers.

Writing for seniors can require considerable adjustment. A chief yeoman was given special training to be a flag writer. His whole work was writing for the signature of a two-star admiral. When interviewed, he commented that even after his schooling, he needed *six months* to learn to write like the admiral before his work began progressing smoothly.

Whatever time it takes, sooner or later not only specialists like flag writers and staff action officers but almost all naval professionals must learn to write for their superiors. A lieutenant commander, executive officer of a helicopter squadron, often encountered difficulty in writing for "the command." Once he finally mastered the process, he made this suggestion: "Keep the facts in, and leave the adverbs out. Let the Old Man put in the modifiers." He also advised giving the skipper *more* than needed, to allow the CO to decide how much is necessary and just chop out any extra parts. Not giving him enough makes him come back to you to complete the paperwork; if all he has to do is chop something out, he can give the document to the yeoman immediately, thereby cutting out an extra step. However, the XO continued, you must not assume such a review. The letter or message should be ready to go out as written, for many times there will be no change.

The situation sounds complex—and writing for the boss or bosses can be extremely complex. After working in a high-level office in the Office of the Chief of Naval Operations (OPNAV), a commander reported, "I became somewhat frustrated in my previous job because the deputy director and director had radically different writing styles from myself and each other. The result was an awful lot of 'wordsmithing.'"

Then she went on: "I think that every new tour puts you in the position of writing for a new senior who has his own writing style—good or bad. You have to learn the basics of expressing yourself clearly and succinctly in writing, but you have to learn to be flexible and not to take the rewriting/reediting by your seniors too personally. The bottom line is to find the best way to communicate your points effectively so that you get the support or approval you're seeking."

Not everyone finds writing for a senior an aggravation. A limited duty officer found a special usefulness in a senior's signature: "My biggest problem is electrical safety. But who will listen to me? My working for the engineering officer carries weight; I use the boss's signature for added authority." And a lieutenant on a surface division staff advised that junior service members try to imitate the boss: "Work at writing like the Captain writes; learn his key phrases," he advised. He thought this practice had improved his own writing, for by doing so he had learned another style.

Indeed, seniors should assign juniors to write for them not only to reduce the workload but to help juniors learn. This type of writing not only helps a junior master naval style but also teaches a commander's perspective. Drafting night orders for a destroyer's commanding officer while the ship is under way can become an exercise

"The major requirement for contact with senior officials is the ability to write."
—NAVY COMMANDER

"Becoming a member of a staff is like learning a language: you have to learn how the admiral writes. *For instance,* this *admiral wants the writing brief but also personable."*
—FLAG SECRETARY, SURFLANT

"I had to learn that, particularly as a junior officer, it wasn't about writing as an individual —but writing for the command. *You had to learn to speak in the generic:* 'This is the USS Maine *speaking.'"*
—NAVY LIEUTENANT

GHOSTWRITING FOR THE ADMIRAL

The personal correspondence that you will draft for the admiral presents a new and interesting problem. You must write in your admiral's style and vocabulary. You'll have to learn what tone and level your admiral would use in different situations and with different people. You must be able to convey a portion of the admiral's personality.

— Naval Flag Writers Handbook

"By the nature of your position on an admiral's staff, you will become familiar with many other admirals and senior officers. At times they may become extra friendly, belly-ache, share confidences, and generally let their hair down. Do not treat this as an invitation to reciprocate."

—Advice to Flag Writers, *Naval Flag Writers Handbook*

"I like to route a copy of a document back to the action officers after the admiral signs it. They'll be able to see what was cut and what was kept— how to do it the next time. If they're good, they'll pick it up."

—Commander

in thinking as the commander has to think, in seeing through the Old Man's eyes, as it were. If you see how the commanding officer modifies what you've written, then you've shared a CO's general outlook and operational perspective.

Another surface line officer thought that drafting messages and letters from a ship to a staff offered great opportunities for learning. His ship was the test platform for a new sonar, and the testing required lots of free-flowing status reports. When an apparatus didn't work, he found he had to choose words carefully so as not to blame anyone. He wanted to avoid putting a senior in a tight spot or stepping on anyone's toes, but still he always had to get his message across.

He learned that there are subtle ways of presenting a case—hints, hidden bottom lines, etc.—that are the fruit of strong "political" awareness, tricks that you normally pick up on staff tours as you get more senior. He didn't have that awareness, but seniors did. So his standard way of operating was to present the facts as he saw them. Then the XO wordsmithed the document, and the CO polished it. He found this process very educational, for the CO had the political awareness to know exactly how to say what had to be said.

This officer had made a point of comparing the smooth copy of documents the CO had signed with his own rough drafts. Other drafters would also find this practice educational. Seniors are typically glad to share the reasons for substantive revisions, and they appreciate juniors showing the interest. But such individual initiative isn't enough, and executive officers and others in the chain of command would do well to incorporate this kind of feedback into formal training programs. At the very least, seniors can make a policy of routing a copy of outgoing correspondence back down to the person who first drafted it.

NAVAL WRITING—THE BASIC STEPS

Knowledge of the basic communication triangle outlined above—the three fixes from which to plot your course—gives you good perspective for any particular writing situation. But there is a great deal more to understand, particularly about the steps we take or *processes* we go through in writing—researching, brainstorming, drafting, revising, and editing. Although you may take only a few moments for each particular step or process when you compose any particular document, you can inform your whole perspective on naval writing if you consider each step in some depth.

Check the Basic Reference

Before proceeding with any kind of writing assignment, take one essential preliminary step—*become thoroughly familiar with the basic reference.* In the service we're too accustomed to going by "the gouge," whether official or not. Don't let patterns laid out in this book or any other unofficial writing guide govern your writing exclusively. Regulations change often, and no published text (including this one) can keep up with all the changes. Remember, you're accountable to what is official—know the official instruction, and use it.

When you write Navy enlisted evaluations or officer fitness reports, for example, first get thoroughly acquainted with BUPERSINST 1610.10 (of course, as with any directive, always make sure it's the effective version and that it incorporates the latest changes). You can then use the enlisted evaluation guidance found in this or any other text to help you describe key accomplishments or craft an effective summary statement. Similarly with letters, briefing memos, other staff papers—above all, get the basic reference down first.

Follow the Prescribed Formatting

Even if the Navy or Marine Corps has no particular format for a certain document, your own command may have. Most letters, correspondence folders, and formal reports require a standard format, especially at major commands. (If a local format differs from any format outlined in this book, follow the local practice.) The quickest way to get a piece of correspondence on a ship or a staff sent back to you is to make simple technical errors that a YNSN or PFC admin clerk can catch.

In fact, if funding is scarce or time is short, harassed senior officials on staffs may use simple errors in formatting or documentation to reduce the number of substantive decisions they have to make. If they find a minor error, say, in a POM issue paper or other funding request, they may simply cancel your request with a stamp: "Standard Procedures Not Followed." This matter is not a joke; budget requests of major monetary proportions (and *months* in the processing) have failed simply because the format or documentation was not exactly right.

Use Informal Guidance, as Available

Make use of any informal guidance that is available, either personal help from experts or written guidance such as comes later in this book. You can learn a great deal from such informal material. For example, the "bullet format" that we have become so accustomed to now was almost entirely an *unofficial* development. We learned to write that way from seeing and talking about others' innovations. Used judiciously, unofficial guidance—word of mouth from selection boards, good examples of a point paper you've seen, semiformal writing guides put out by major staffs—can give a writer invaluable help.

Can you sometimes plagiarize in the Navy or Marine Corps? To an extent, you can, for some written material really constitutes "boilerplate"—that is, material usable in a variety of contexts with little variation. For example, as a senior officer pointed out recently to new action officers in OPNAV, one seldom has to create PowerPoint slides completely from scratch; usually an existing slide can be adapted for your own briefing needs. Moreover, not only do award citations typically begin and end with standard terminology, but an award justification can be built partly out of bullets from eval or fitrep drafts.

Nevertheless, think twice before taking phrases from a pamphlet or book like this one and planting them in an argument without adaptation. In some cases it's dishonest. Beyond that, it usually doesn't work and comes across as foreign matter in the midst of your thoughts. Typically use writing guides to give you *perspective,* not to replace your own thoughts.

"Do not take anything in this handbook as directive in nature; it is only to give you a first place to look. . . . Remember: 'If you live by the gouge, you'll die by the gouge.'"

—NAVAL FLAG
WRITERS HANDBOOK

"The very best writers I know are those who cheat the most. *They find out what works, and then they copy that."*

—XO, NAVAL
AIR STATION

Do the Necessary Research

Take account of all the notes, documents, directives, messages, and other written information you already have on hand, and consider what more you require. Then *do the required research.*

When writing messages aboard ship or ashore, the standard means of research is to search message and other shipboard files. When writing naval letters, one often looks to directives, office files, regulations, manuals, policy letters, and operating instructions. Writing a performance evaluation, on the other hand, primarily requires knowledge of a service member's performance. Similarly with award nominations—the research required is to get the facts about what an individual has done. JAGMAN Investigations can call for a variety of kinds of research, from conducting interviews to looking into regulations, to evaluating procedures and logs, and so forth.

Library research such as one learns in high school or college is *occasionally* called for in naval writing—when writing a professional article or drafting a speech, for example. Guided by a standard tool such as the *Air University Library Index to Military Periodicals* (now available online), you can look into past articles to see what has already been said about your subject. There are many other guides to periodicals, and much naval information is available online. Base or station librarians can guide you in this research.

The point is that your situation and writing task govern the kind of research you must do. Be sure to talk to experts at your command or nearby about new writing tasks. For example, see the executive officer or a senior yeoman about writing letters and directives; consult a local staff judge advocate on JAGMAN Investigations; and see members of the local staff "secretariat" or civilian consultants when you work on major staffs. Don't forget to consult past files of reports of the same kind you have to do, and the people who once put those reports together if still on station or reachable by email inquiry or by phone. These sources can offer invaluable suggestions on where to start and how to proceed.

Draw Up an Outline

Once convinced you have enough material (admittedly, sometimes hard to tell), prepare to write. At this point, unless you have only a short memo to draft, pause long enough to *write out a rough outline.* Don't make it so formal that you focus more on outlining than on writing, but use it to set your sights.

By going through your notes and listing specifics in an outline, you're checking the road map and putting the car in gear. Use this organizing as a starting technique whereby you review all the material you have, getting it fresh in mind. As you read through your material, your mind will unconsciously begin structuring beyond what you've put down on paper; the engine will be revving up more than you realize. Once you've got an outline down on paper, you can usually begin writing.

Of course, there are other "brainstorming," "freewriting," or "first-drafting" techniques, all of them methods of what used to be called "rhetorical invention," of finding the important things to say, and then beginning to say them on paper. These launching techniques have been studied in depth by modern rhetoricians, and if you've been taught a particular method in a composition class, go to it. Use whatever launching technique works best for you. Outlining is simply one of the classic ways to begin.

Incidentally, there's no magic to that first outline. If it proves faulty later, you can change it. And sometimes it will be premature. If you see holes in your argument and realize you haven't done enough spade work, stop and do further research, but then come back and rework the outline.

SEA LANGUAGE

There seems to be an idea abroad that Secretary Josephus Daniels abolished *starboard* and *port* in the United States Navy. That is not true. Even with the enormous infiltration of landsmen in World War II, the Navy, like the Merchant Marine, still uses *forward* and *aft, starboard* and *port, above* and *aloft* and *below.* Ships still have *bulkheads,* not walls; *cabins* or *compartments,* not rooms (except in composition like wardroom, storeroom, etc.); *overheads,* not ceilings; and *decks,* not floors. What Mr. Daniels did change (and it was all to the good) was the form of orders to helmsmen, who no longer have to translate "port your helm!" into a right turn on the wheel, or "starboard helm!" into a left turn. Orders are now given as "left" or "right" so many degrees, or "left" or "right standard rudder" with variations, assuming the helmsman to be facing forward.

It will be a sad day when sea language leaves English literature. . . .

—From Samuel Eliot Morison, "Notes on Writing Naval
(*not* Navy) English," *The American Neptune* 9 (January 1949): 10.
Reprinted by permission of S. E. Morison, Jr.

Write the First Draft

Once begun, go ahead and *draft as much as you can* of the point paper, letter, or email that you're composing. Try not to let anything stop you from getting the bulk of your argument down on paper. You can always go back and alter what you've written, but there's a momentum to writing, a "heat of composition," and if you stop the momentum, you may not be able to get back into the mood.

That is, bulling your way through a rough draft is always better than getting sidetracked by looking up dates, figures, names, or other technical details. Don't consider grammar, spelling, punctuation, or style while writing the basic draft. You may have learned that you tend to write in the passive voice, and that using passive verbs keeps you from speaking forthrightly and adds needless bulk (good advice)—but don't worry about that problem now. You can go back and fix the passives and other errors later, when you're tired, for example, or between watches, musters, phone calls, meetings, or inspections. Getting a draft of an important document on paper is not easy to do in hassled minutes late in the day.

Even if you know your organization is faulty, don't stop short to fix it, but keep writing the sections you find on the tip of your tongue. You'll usually find some place for what you're writing now, or at least for what you'll eventually get into by not stopping now. Ideas can come and go very quickly. Get them down on paper, and wait to polish and revise them. *Capture the raw material,* and leave the finished product till later.

Once you've got a pretty full draft on paper, take a bit more time to go back and clean it up. Fill in the names and figures (always double check the figures), flesh out passages you left sketchy, correct the errors, add needed transitions, and look up whatever you need to. In other words, fill out your draft and smooth it a bit. Make that first draft a *complete* draft. Once you've gotten that far, the rest is all revision.

Let It Rest a While

One of the keys to a good revision is rest—a time for your composition to stew. A limited duty officer working for a three-star in OPNAV remarked in frustration, "If they'd only let the paper ferment *a half hour,* anyway. But they're caught up in the rush, and as a result they don't get to the major topic until page three."

On a large writing project, *let your first draft sit for a day or two,* if you can, before you come back to it. If you simply don't have the time, at least try to *wait thirty minutes* before proceeding. You'll often be surprised how different your text will look with just that much time separation. Even short emails can often profit by a short period between drafting and sending.

Begin to Revise or Redraft

When you come back to look again at the document, you'll usually find it needs obvious work. It's time to do a thorough revision, and then to have someone else edit your work. These processes (which are similar) require a full section in themselves.

RULES FOR NAVAL EDITING

Confident that your content is correct and your organization straightforward, you have yet to check for correctness of format, correctness of details, and overall effectiveness. We usually term this process *revision* if you work with your own document, or *editing* if you work with someone else's. For convenience, we'll term the process *editing* throughout this section.

Many people edit others' documents more often than they write their own. Division officers typically draft more than they edit while executive officers usually edit much more than they write (and spend a great deal of time proofreading documents). All should know the basic principles of editing. Those principles include, first, the Naval Writing Standards, referred to earlier and outlined later in this chapter, and second, the naval editing rules, discussed below.

Of course, not all these rules will apply to any particular document. On shorter documents, you can look for several problems at once. With written material several pages long or with a document that is extremely important, you may want to go through the writing several times, looking for different problems each reading. Seldom should you check all ten items in the following section one by one when analyzing any particular document. However, if you also master the ten rules discussed below, you can be pretty confident you know the basics for making writing both *correct* and *effective.*

1. Edit for Content—Ensure the Document "Answers the Mail"

Clearly, the most important thing is the content of your document. Have you gotten your point across? If you are writing an award justification, does it show off the special quality of the service member's performance? If it's a CASREP, will the addressees know exactly what equipment has failed and why (if you know why), what you are doing about the problem, and what your ship can and cannot accomplish?

If you don't think you've served your basic purpose, add information or revise the wording until you are sure the specific audience you're addressing will get the *very key points.*

2. Edit for Organization—Put the Main Point *Up Front*

Presenting your major points clearly is important, but putting them in a logical order is just as crucial. *Beginning quickly* and *writing short* are particularly vital to most naval documents. Usually keep background sections very brief, and get on to your key statement or argument very early on. Briefing memos throughout OPNAV, for

"What you submit to me forms my impression of you. Your goal ought to be that your document goes through with zero editing."

—SHIP'S XO

"Lots of staffers produce packages that look terrific and are formatted perfectly, but don't answer the original question.*"*

—NAVY CAPTAIN IN OPNAV

PAPERWORK REDUCTION?

We want your suggestions as to paperwork reduction. It may take some courage for us to say we don't need that piece of paper, but it will help all of us reduce our administrative burden. So give us your suggestions. In triplicate.

—Overheard at a staff briefing

---

example, are typically too lengthy and wait too long to express the point. With all kinds of documents, do your best to get your major request, answer, conclusion, or argument *at the very beginning* of your paper, leaving details and explanations to follow.

Of course, there can be other problems in structure besides not starting fast. See that all the paragraphs link with the ones before and after and that your overall structure is clear and easy to follow. Then make sure there's no extraneous material.

3. Edit for "Plain English"

Members of all bureaucracies tend to write "bureaucratese" after they have been around for a while. Over the years, naval writing has been as bureaucratic—unnatural, impersonal, and prolix—as the writing of any U.S. government agency. "Navalese" is a virus that clogs up official prose in all naval organizations, especially naval staffs. It infects writers of all kinds—officers, enlisted, and naval civilians.

Calls for "plain English" appeared in the "Naval Writing Standards" of the 1983 Correspondence Manual and in the pamphlet "Just Plain English," originally written in the CNO's office in 1981, reissued by the Vice Chief of Naval Operations in 1996, and regularly handed out to action officers in the Pentagon as late as 2006—it's perennially apt guidance. Nevertheless, bureaucratic prose persists, and any good editor must learn to deal with it. Besides getting to the point quickly (step 2, above), there are many other ways to modify naval writing so it is *well organized, natural, personal, and active.* See the section on "Just Plain English" later in this chapter, which outlines specific ways to cut down on navalese and write documents in plain English.

4. See if You Can Use Bullets, Lists, or Other Visual Signposts

All naval authors know the usefulness of "bullet" format. A "bullet" is a piece of type used to introduce each element of a list or series; it is shaped like a bullet seen head-on: •. Bullets should be grammatically parallel in form and in sentence order, like this:

- Bullets help a reader to skim.
- Bullets emphasize key ideas.
- Bullets often enliven a text.

If you use sentence fragments instead of complete sentences, head them with an introductory statement. Ensure each such bullet

- completes the clause,
- contains the same basic structure, and
- expresses its content concisely.

Many typewriters and some word processors don't have bullets, in which case

- hyphens (-),
- asterisks (*), or
- small "O"s (o)

will do just as well.

Other means of drawing attention to particular data visually are boxes, →pointers←, <u>underlining</u>,

> vertical spacing,

bold print, larger type, or ALL CAPS. Of course, there are stars, pointing hands, and many other devices.

The degree to which you can freely use such visual formatting devices varies with the formality of the document you're writing and for whom you're writing. Bullet format, of course, has now gained wide acceptance and can be used in all except the most formal documents (hardly ever in award citations or letters to Congress members but almost anywhere else).

Remember to use *strategic placement* in any list of information. Normally the *first* item in a series of bullets (and to a lesser extent the last) will attract the eye and be much more obvious than an item buried in the middle. Of course, don't overdo your use of typographic devices or you'll make your document more difficult to read (rather than less), and you'll be accused of being "cute" too.

"There's a time and place for bullets, but they don't work when you have to express complex ideas."

—Navy Captain

5. Add Headings for Readability, and Make Subject Lines Genuinely Informative

Headings can greatly help readers skim a text, find material, and simply comprehend. Consider using them on any documents longer than a couple of paragraphs (including reports, staff documents, and directives). Use them even on emails of more than a paragraph or two if you need to catch a reader's eye.

Also make them as interesting and pointed as possible, to draw readers' attention. Make sure they're grammatically parallel—match a full sentence with a full sentence, a noun phrase with a noun phrase, and so on, within each level of heading. See the headings in this text as examples.

As for the special kind of heading called a subject line (standard to emails and many other naval documents but especially important on NMCI), it can be crafted well or poorly. Make your subject line a sentence fragment that announces the specific subject of your communication. Without using more than ten words or so, make it as genuinely informative as possible.

For example, instead of "Engine Failure" as a subject line for an email, write "H-3 Engine Failure Data" or, better yet, "Request for H-3 Engine Failure Data." That phrase is more specific but still brief.

Be careful with acronyms in subject lines. Remember, there are thirty to forty uses for some abbreviations (like "IT" or "EIC") in the government; several acronyms have many meanings even within the naval services. Don't lose or confuse your readers.

Try to avoid long noun strings ("hut-2-3-4 phrases") here. The subject line "Approved Joint Air Defense Operations Manual Position Reporting System" is very hard to follow, stringing together as it does some nine adjectives and nouns in a row. Is the subject a Position Reporting System for an Operations Manual on Approved Joint Air Defense? Or is it a Manual Position Reporting System for Approved Joint Air Defense Operations? Strung together in this way, no one but an insider will know.

CHECK THAT SPELLING—AGAIN

Spell-checking also has its pitfalls, most of which center on homophones [sound-alikes] such as they're/there/their, your/you're, site/cite/sight, to/too/two, and the like. . . . All documents, no matter how short they may be, should be computer spell-checked by the writers, of course. But writers should also not allow themselves to be lulled into a false sense of security, since spell-checkers are not perfect. They will not notify the writer of the errors in a sentence such as "*Their maybe two many problems to site before the counsel at it's meeting.*" <u>Six</u> errors lurk among those words!

—William K. Riley, College Editor,
Armed Forces Staff College

---

6. Preface Long Documents with Summaries

Regulations require that writers use summaries to preface technical reports, research reports, correspondence packages, and many staff documents—but we could use summaries more widely still. This text discusses several common methods of summarizing that are highly useful for naval writers. *Briefing memos, executive summaries,* and *abstracts* find wide use at commands and staffs, for they help busy senior officials quickly get the gist of any particular document. And *letters of transmittal* are helpful in pointing out key information in the complex documents or the thick correspondence packages that they introduce.

Also useful are the standard ways of organizing what follows the summary. For example, consider the *inverted pyramid* used by news writers to organize material following the news lead (discussed in chapter 11). This technique accustoms journalists to state the vital facts first, then to add other information in descending order of importance, a habit that can be useful in naval documents as diverse as operational reports (OPREPS), performance evaluations, briefing memos, and longer documents sent by email.

7. Add Visuals, if Appropriate

Charts, graphs, and drawings may help explain your topic or convince your audience. They're normally most appropriate in oral briefings, technical reports, and professional articles rather than correspondence. However, they may find places as appendixes to correspondence packages and occasionally in instructions. Make sure they are simple and clear in presentation—cluttered visuals only confuse and slow the reader.

8. Proof for Errors in Spelling, Punctuation, Capitalization, and Grammar

Computer spell-checkers can pick up spelling errors, but those programs won't find homonyms and technical terms not in their files. A good dictionary (a collegiate dictionary, not a pocket one) will help. The "Handbook" at the end of this text provides a short guide to punctuation, capitalization, and proper use of numbers, with naval examples (pp. 295–321).

In the process of reading, we all naturally anticipate and skip a great deal. We skip even more while editing our own writing. When editing you should work to break this habit, and learn to proof rather than just read.

"Here's an editing device practiced by many naval staffers when you literally have no time and yet have to make a document effective:

- *Have one person draft the document.*
- *Have two others immediately edit."*

—Staff Action Officer

"The spell checker will not only miss homophones, but will also miss some vital transpositions and typos. Some that immediately come to mind:

• *from and form ('Form: Operations Officer'; 'Too: CIC Officer')*
• *the and thee, be and bee*
• *it/if/is/as*
• *add/ass (this could be a great one!)"*

—PENTAGON STAFFER

How to proof? One way is to use a pointer (such as a letter opener) and systematically move it from word to word while you read, pausing to look at each punctuation mark. This method will ensure you don't inadvertently skip over any word, number, or mark on the page. A second method is to read *out loud* as you edit —that will also help you pay close attention to the text. A third way is to work backward sentence by sentence through each paragraph, purposely upsetting your ordinary reading custom. This process will help you look at each sentence with a fresh eye.

As for grammar, computerized grammar- and style-checkers will signal overused words or phrases and can catch errors such as incomplete sentences and problems in pronoun agreement. Learn to use these aids. However, realize that they can be mistaken, and they seldom have a navy "ear." You can best check for errors in grammar if you have a good knowledge of the subject. Second best is to keep at hand a standard grammar handbook and use it often to check your writing. A good yeoman or secretary can also help, but you may not always have such an expert to consult. So have a handbook on hand, and know it well.

9. Check the Visual Impression Your Document Makes

Make sure the type is clean and dark and the margins are reasonable—normally one inch on all sides (but you can adjust the margins to center short documents on the page). The sharp appearance of paperwork—whether actually printed out or sent by email from computer screen to computer screen—can make as much of an impression as a sharp uniform and be even more important in its impact.

10. Notwithstanding All of the Above—*Get the Work Out*

As a commander advised, "Before you order a revision, count the cost. 'A few minutes' on a single document easily becomes 30; a 'few minutes' on everything works into hours. You end up taking three or four days before you get a document on its way." Even Naval Writing Standards (described later in this chapter) are not sacred compared to getting work through the top of an organization. As a limited duty officer who once worked in the office of the Vice Chief of Naval Operations commented, mild problems of passive voice, doublings, and the like in a briefing memo or letter for signature would not stop a package from going forward for signature if everything else was right.

"Don't fine-tune all you write, but only the most important things. Get the *work* out. *Adapt existing documents to your purposes—don't reinvent the wheel."*

—LIEUTENANT COMMANDER

At sea, this penchant for getting the job done is perhaps even more pronounced. As one senior captain commented, "Those who really operate don't overedit; those who really edit don't operate." To *operate* is naval jargon for to *perform;* and almost everywhere in the naval services, performance is what really counts. Of course, bad writing can profoundly inhibit performance. That's why editing is so important. But everything has its season—and sometimes meticulous editing is out of season.

THE MODE OF WRITING: A COMMENT ON WORD PROCESSING

Word processing has revolutionized naval paperwork. Formats are regularly loaded into word processing programs, which reduces the need for yeomen, secretaries, and clerks. Networks and electronic bulletin boards have replaced the printed memo at some offices, and "paperless ships" have become possible in conception. Of course, many questions have yet to be sorted out, and computers can't do everything. Later on we'll discuss problems that occur with the use of email on naval staffs. Right now, though, let's look at the general limitations of word processing programs.

Limits That Computers Have

- They will not solve all your problems. "Garbage in, garbage out" remains a standard rule. Service members must still learn composition, research, editing, drafting, revising, and all manner of other communication skills. Word processing software remains a *tool* and can't substitute for thorough research, clear expression, and good reviews.
- They will not find all common errors. As mentioned above, both spell-checkers and grammar programs have many limitations. Overconfidence in these computer aids can lead to embarrassment when obvious errors show up in important documents.
- They still take time to use. Though revising is much easier on a computer than by hand or typewriter, the time to type a document into the machine hasn't changed appreciably from standard typing. Initializing discs, saving text, numbering and naming documents, or a myriad of other standard word-processing operations can all consume minutes or hours of the day.
- They invite over-revision. "The word processor is a two-edged sword," an XO remarked. "A CO would like to see things different ways, so you'll run a document three, four, five, six times, even if it's a POD that circulates only within the command. We easily become subjugated to the word processor." The XO was right.

"With word processing, the final quality of writing has improved. But at what cost? With a typewriter, you only did it once. Now, we end up tweaking a document again and again and again."

—LIEUTENANT COMMANDER

Procedures You Should Follow

Because we all have computers, and because secretaries and clerk-typists are a fast-disappearing species throughout government, more and more of us have become our own word processors. Advice on details of word processing should be taken to heart by everyone who manages, edits, writes, or otherwise uses computers for writing. Follow this advice:

- Save files frequently and make both disk and hard-copy backups. A power surge can erase hours of work, and poor labeling, an inadvertent misstroke, or a computer gremlin of some sort can delete a whole file from a disk and sometimes destroy the disk as well. Intermittently print out hard copy when engaged in long projects, and make backup copies of files at least once a week.
- Revise on hard copy. Spelling and other typos tend to be more noticeable on paper copies than on computer screens. Moreover, some features of a programmed document do not appear on the screen but only become obvious when printed.
- *Use* but *don't overuse* typographical features such as formatting, underlining, bold print, font style, etc. Used judiciously, such functions can help a busy reader get the key points. Overuse of fancy type styles and changes in size of type can make a page resemble an old-time billboard advertisement for a circus rather than a professional document.
- Finally, refrain from changing "happy" to "glad" just because you have a computer. While you should reprocess documents with major content or typographical errors, *count the cost* of revisions for superficial or minor stylistic improvements. For example, often seen these days are fancy invitations sent by email, documents that announce a party via a clever document that dances and waves and sings,—and takes two to three minutes to load! In thirty seconds, long before the email has gotten to who, what, when, and where, you've already lost several invitees.

GENDER IN WRITING: SOME QUICK POINTERS

Naval directives suggest that, where possible, we use pronouns and titles that include either sex. As one manual pointed out, "Such [gender-free] language fosters mutual understanding and demonstrates the Navy and Marine Corps' commitment to equal opportunity for all members." However, the same manual also recognized some complexity when it advised the writer to "avoid creating curiosities such as 'freshwomen' for 'freshmen' and 'seaperson' for 'seaman.' Such awkward terms only invite ridicule."

Legal issues further complicate this subject. For instance, a Joint Chiefs of Staff directive stipulates that titles established in directives or law, such as "airman" or "Chairman, Joint Chiefs of Staff," should be used as is (though the directive counsels selecting sex-neutral titles when establishing new positions). On the other hand, while laws originally limited all combat roles to men, those laws have now changed somewhat, and the exclusive use of male pronouns in reference to Navy combat personnel (on ships, say, or in aircraft) is no longer appropriate. Even in the case of ground combat forces for which the combat-exclusion rule still applies (as with Navy SEALs or Marine Corps infantry units, for instance), women often serve in support forces nearby, and a writer must choose terms with care.

One other important factor is tradition. Tradition reaches deep in the naval services, and naval authorities wisely foster tradition, knowing the great part it plays in human communities. Partly from tradition, no doubt, when women first entered the Naval Academy the Superintendent decided that the term "midshipman" would not be changed but that the proper terms to use would be "male midshipman" and "female midshipman." Kindred decisions are even now being made throughout the services. At last report, "helmsman" and "man overboard" were still standard terms even on ships with women permanently assigned, although those same ships warned of "personnel working aloft." Clearly, universal rules are hard to come by.

In the face of such complexities, *keep your wits about you.* Realize that certain choices of pronouns or titles may offend, thereby proving obstacles to effective communication. Remember also that the specific way they offend may differ, depending on the situation and the audience. Both males and females can take offense—rightly and wrongly in either case, depending on the situation.

Follow the advice outlined below (based on the Correspondence Manual, among other sources) when you need to change single-gender references to gender-neutral ones.

- Write directives as if talking to a group of readers, or one typical reader. Use "you," stated or implied. Instead of "The young officer must take his training seriously," write "Take your training seriously" or just "Take training seriously."
- Choose plural pronouns such as "they" "their," or "them." Replace "A chief can submit his request to his division officer" with "Chiefs can submit their requests to division officers." Note, however, that the use of "their" with a *singular* antecedent, as in "Anyone can take their laundry off base for cleaning," is technically incorrect ("anyone" is singular). Usage is changing and many of the most recent guidebooks actually say this is ok. However, don't be surprised if your XO or CO or admin chief (who's been taught differently) objects! In formal writing you will be safer to say, "All Sailors can take their laundry off base for cleaning."
- Reword sentences to eliminate pronouns. In place of "The private should return to his barracks," say, "The private should return to barracks." Instead of "None of the Marines was proud of his performance in the exercise," say, "None of the

---

FAMOUS PHRASES IN *NAVALESE*

Here are five famous phrases, as some naval bureaucrats would have written them. See p. 21 for the original phrases.

1. Argumentative contesting by originator has not yet commenced.
2. May the metallic underwater explosive devices be execrated. Let maximum velocity in a forward direction be achieved forthwith.
3. When the subordinates desire, permission is hereby authorized for the expeditious emission of ordnance.
4. Upon arrival in the theater of operations, an overview of the environment was conducted, and the conflict situation was subsequently resolved in my favor.
5. Expenditure of ammunition is to be withheld pending the detection of whiteness in the ocular organs.

"Gender no longer has the importance it once did in the Navy. Sex has become irrelevant. More important, we don't talk a lot with the first name—the rank is a first name. Even the last name, orally, often goes away, and one is called by the billet as in 'XO,' 'Master Chief,' etc."
—FEMALE COMMANDER, SUMMER OF 2006

Marines was proud of the exercise." (Be alert, though, to subtle shifts of meaning, as in this revision.)

- Substitute articles for possessive pronouns. As an alternative to "Every petty officer must be assigned her watch station by Friday" write, "Every petty officer should be assigned a watch station by Friday."
- Use terms referring to a particular sex in reference to a particular person. Although it is often wise to use job titles that include both sexes, such as "service member" instead of "serviceman," "chair" rather than "chairman," and so on, you may still refer to "Spokeswoman McCarthy" and "Chairman Jones" in reference to the actual sex of the person cited.
- Occasionally write "he or she," as in "He or she must choose a place of duty carefully." Don't overuse this method. Repeated reference of this kind, as in "He or she should take his or her seabag with him or her," becomes very awkward and tiresome.

One final note: don't allow concern over the gender issue to interfere with your rough drafts—wait until you edit to adjust all such references.

NAVAL WRITING STANDARDS, OR "JUST PLAIN ENGLISH"

As mentioned above, naval writers must often edit to cut out "navalese"—bureaucratic prose. The following guidelines are drawn from a workbook for the Correspondence Manual (it was originally titled "Better Naval Writing"—OPNAV 09B-P1-84). They are essentially the same as those found in "Just Plain English," a small pamphlet drafted in 1981 and distributed in OPNAV as late as 2006. These guidelines outline excellent means for cutting back deadly bureaucratese, which still plagues official Navy language.

Rules for Organized Writing

Start Fast, Explain as Necessary, Then Stop

When you write a letter, think about the one sentence you would keep if you could keep only one. It should appear by the end of the first paragraph. The strongest letter highlights the main point in a one-sentence paragraph at the very beginning. Put requests *before* justifications, answers *before* explanations, conclusions *before* discussions, summaries *before* details, and the general *before* the specific. Avoid mere chronology.

Delay your main point to soften bad news, for example, or to introduce a controversial proposal. But don't delay routinely. In most cases, plunge right in.

To end most letters, just stop. When writing to persuade rather than just to inform, you may want to end strongly—with a forecast, appeal, or implication. When feelings are involved, you may want to exit gracefully—with an expression of good will. When in doubt, offer your help or the name of a contact.

Downplay References

Reading slows down with every glance from the text to the reference caption. Justify such distractions by using only references that bear directly on the subject. Avoid unnecessary or complicated references. Many letters need no references at all while others are complete with a reference to only the latest communication in a series.

When you respond to an earlier communication, subordinate it to your main point. Don't waste the opening—the strongest place in a letter—to merely summarize a reference or say you received or reviewed something.

Be sure to mention in the text any reference cited in the reference block. List references in the reference block by following the order of their appearance in the text.

Use Short Paragraphs

Long paragraphs swamp ideas. Cover one topic completely before starting another, and let a topic take several paragraphs if necessary. But keep paragraphs short, down to roughly four or five sentences. Call attention to lists of items or instructions by displaying them in subparagraphs.

Now and then use one-sentence paragraphs to highlight important ideas.

Take Advantage of Topic Sentences

A paragraph may need a topic sentence, a generalization explained by the rest of the paragraph. Then again, it may not. In a short paragraph a topic sentence may be unnecessary if a reader can follow the writer's thinking without it.

Be alert to the advantages of topic sentences, for they help shape masses of information. Without them, some paragraphs make readers shrug and say, "So what?"

Write Disciplined Sentences

Here are four ways to write sentences that call attention to important ideas:

- Subordinate minor ideas. Subordination clarifies the relationship between ideas and prevents the overuse of *and,* the weakest of all conjunctions.
- Place ideas deliberately. An idea gains emphasis when it appears at either end of a sentence. To mute an idea, put it in the middle.
- Use more parallelism. Look for opportunities to arrange two or more equally important ideas so they look equal. Parallelism saves words, clarifies ideas, and provides balance. Go by the first words of the series; all should use the same parts of speech (verbs in the previous sentence).
- Try some minisentences. An occasional sentence of six words or less slows down readers and emphasizes ideas.

Rules for Natural Writing

Speak on Paper

Make your writing as formal or informal as the situation requires, but do so with language you might use in speaking. Because readers *hear* writing, the most readable

> *"If you were to put the word 'Motherhood' at the heading of every instruction, you could eliminate 'Background,' 'Purpose,' and 'Discussion' altogether and go right to 'Action.' As currently written, instructions and notices never get to the point."*
>
> —Commander

> *"Junior officers have lived and breathed their project through great mounds of detail, and they want to share their knowledge . . . whether or not their audience needs all that detail!"*
>
> —Naval Academy Professional Writing instructor

THE FAMOUS PHRASES KEY

1. I have not yet begun to fight.
2. Damn the torpedoes; . . . Go ahead, Jouett—Full speed.
3. You may fire when ready, Gridley.
4. I came, I saw, I conquered.*
5. Don't fire until you see the whites of their eyes.

*The navalese version was used as epigraph to
CAPT Carvel Slair, USN, "Effective Writing, Navy or Civilian."
U.S. Naval Institute *Proceedings* (July 1968):131.

"Though we're the Bureau of Naval Personnel, we try not to be bureaucratic."

—MASTER CHIEF
CHARLES E. MILLER, JR.

writing sounds like people talking to people. Begin by imagining your reader is sitting across from your desk. Then write with personal pronouns, everyday words, and short sentences—the best of speaking.

Use Personal Pronouns

Though you needn't go out of your way to use personal pronouns, you mustn't go out of your way to avoid them. Avoiding natural references to people is false modesty. Speak of your activity, command, or office as *we, us, our.* These words are more exact than the vague *it.* Use you, stated or implied, to refer to the reader. Use *I, me, my* less often, usually in correspondence signed by the commanding officer and then only to show special concern or warmth.

Rely on Everyday Words

The complexity of our work and the need for precision require some big words. But don't use big words when little ones will do. For example, deflate *utilize* to *use, commence* to *start,* and *promulgate* to *issue.* Prefer short, spoken transitions over long, bookish ones. Use *but* more than *however* and *still* more than *nevertheless.* Avoid the needless complications of legalistic lingo; let a directive's number or a letter's signature carry the authority. Use *here's* for *herewith is* and *in spite of* for *notwithstanding.* Write to express, not to impress.

"Sometimes the writing itself is almost inconsequential. Was I prepared for the way writing is done in the Navy? No. As an English major, I expected to do lots of analysis and to cloak words and correspondence in lots of style. I had to relearn all that."

—NAVAL ACADEMY
GRADUATE

Use Some Contractions

Contractions link pronouns with verbs (*we'd, I'll, you're*) and make verbs negative (*don't, can't, won't*). They are appropriate in less formal writing situations. Day-to-day naval writing should be informal enough for contractions to fit naturally. If you are comfortable with contractions, your writing is likely to read easily, for you will be speaking on paper. If contractions seem out of place, you may need to deflate the rest of what you say.

Keep Sentences Short

For variety mix long sentences and short ones, but keep the average under twenty words. Though short sentences won't guarantee clarity, they are usually less confusing than long ones. Try the eye test: average fewer than two typed lines. Or try the ear test: break up most of the sentences you can't finish in one breath.

Ask More Questions

A request gains emphasis when it ends with a question mark. Do you hear how spoken a question is?

BANNED BOMBAST

The Terrible Ten Bureaucratic Verbs

Instead of	Try
commence	begin, start
disseminate	give, issue, pass, send
facilitate	ease, help
implement	carry out, start
necessitate	cause, need
obligate	bind, compel
prioritize	rank
promulgate	issue, publish
terminate	end, stop
utilize	use

The Awful Eight Long-Winded Phrases

Instead of	Try
at the present time	at present, now
due to the fact that	due to, since, because
for a period of	for
for the purpose of	for, to
in accordance with	by, following, per, under
in the amount of	for
in the event that	if
until such time as	until

For a comprehensive list of overdressed, bookish, and legalistic language to avoid, see the pamphlet "Just Plain English."

Be Concrete

Without generalizations and abstractions, lots of them, we would drown in detail. We sum up vast amounts of experience when we speak of dedication, programs, hardware, and lines of authority. But lazy writing overuses such vague terms. Often it weakens them further by substituting adjectives for examples: immense dedication, enhanced programs, viable hardware, and responsive lines of authority. Don't use a general word if the context allows for a specific one; be as definite as the situation permits. Work to avoid vague, high-sounding language in job descriptions and personnel evaluations.

Listen to Your Tone

Tone—a writer's attitude toward the subject or readers—causes few problems in routine letters. You may pay special attention to tone, however, when the matter is delicate. The more sensitive the reader or issue, the more careful you must be to promote good will. Tactlessness in writing suggests clumsiness in general. When feelings are involved, one misused word can make an enemy. To avoid tactlessness, use positive language.

Rules for Compact Writing

Cut the Fat

Give your ideas no more words than they deserve. The longer you take to say things, the weaker you come across and the more you risk blurring important ideas.

"Economy in use of words is always important. Bare bone facts . . . in the right format . . . with the right header . . . to the right person."
—Naval Academy instructor, just back from a fleet tour

NATURALLY WRITTEN NIGHT ORDERS

Seldom is there more need for clarity than in drafting night orders. The set of night orders shown below, which dates from World War II, is admirably terse and clear.

Thursday Night 23–24 December

1. On the Truk-Rabaul line.
2. Course 100°T
3. Speed: About 10.2 kts (Aux load and propulsion on #4 main eng.)
4. At 2130 CC to 190°T (this should put us right along the line).
5. Stop and listen each half hour, as last night.
6. This is a hot spot! Men of war are making the transit. They have radar. We do not. We *must* see or hear them. I will be in the fish grotto. Wallop me at any suspicion of contact.
7. Moonrise 0354. Zig Zag if it is bright.
8. Call me at 0530.

Respy
R. J. Foley

—Transcribed from the Night Order Book of 23–24 December 1943 of USS GATO (SS 212), commanded by Robert Joseph Foley. Used by permission of the Nautilus Memorial Submarine Force Library and Museum.

Suspect wordiness in everything you write. When you revise, tighten paragraphs to sentences, sentences to clauses, clauses to phrases, phrases to words, words to pictures—or strike the ideas entirely. To be easy on your readers, you must be hard on yourself.

Avoid "It Is" and "There Is"

No two words hurt naval writing more than *it is*. They stretch sentences, delay meaning, hide responsibility, and encourage passive verbs.

Like *it is* constructions, forms of *there is* make sentences start slowly. Don't write these delayers without trying to avoid them.

Prune Wordy Expressions

Wordy expressions don't give writing impressive bulk; they clutter it by getting in the way of the words that carry the meaning. *In order to* and *in accordance with,* for example, are minor ideas that don't deserve three words.

Free Smothered Verbs

The most important word in a sentence is the verb, the action word, the only word that can *do* something. Weak writing relies on general verbs, which take extra words to complete their meaning. When you write a general verb such as *is* or *make,* check to see if you can turn a nearby word into a verb (not *is applicable to* but *applies to,* not *make use of* but *use*).

Splice Doublings

As the writer, you may see some differences between *advise* and *assist, interest* and *concern,* or *thanks* and *gratitude.* But your readers won't. Repeating a general idea can't make it any more precise.

"For the most part, the JOs are pretty sharp. They are weakest in writing skills, especially newly commissioned officers. Specifically, they still try to write like 'college students,' with flowing paragraphs and big words that impress English professors but not evaluation/ correspondence receivers."

—COMMANDING
OFFICER, USN

CUTTING THE FAT

Here's a memorandum that one naval office sent to another, along with a revision of that memorandum by someone fed up with "budget-speak."

Original Memorandum:

1. Your request for $750, as stated reference (a), is approved. Contact Mr. John Jeffries, X4442, to coordinate the appropriate procedures for utilization of funds from Account 15B of the Foundation Support Fund.

2. Liaison with the Foundation Support Committee Associate Budget Officer indicates that this item will be supported out of departmental funds in the future, and, therefore, is not considered a routine budget item for Foundation Support Funds.

Revised Memorandum:

1. You can have the $750. John Jeffries at X4442 will tell you how to get the money.

2. In the future, though, your department will have to pay for this, instead of the Foundation Support Fund.

Comment:

Problems of passive voice, long words, and officialese plague the original memorandum. The writer should shorten it, make it more direct, and speak more naturally.

"They'll come to see the Admin Officer. Sheepishly they say, 'I have to write this thing.' It's almost like they're coming to see the priest. They come quietly. They show me this document, this piece of. . . . After a while, with some work and criticism, they get a little better."

—LDO, ADMIN OFFICER
ON A CARRIER

Shun "The –ion of" and "The –ment of"

Most words ending in *–ion* and *–ment* are verbs turned into nouns. Whenever the context permits, change these words to verb forms (not *for the accomplishment,* but *to accomplish;* not *for the development of,* but *for developing*).

Prevent Hut-2-3-4 Phrases

Though you should cut needless words, sometimes you can go too far. Avoid hut-2-3-4 phrases, long clots of nouns and modifiers. Readers can't tell how the parts fit together or where they all will end.

We must live with some established hut-2-3-4 phrases such as *standard subject identification codes* for *subject codes,* but you can keep them out of whatever you originate by adding some words or rewriting entirely.

Avoid Excessive Abbreviating

Excessive abbreviating is false economy. Use abbreviations no more than you must with insiders and avoid them entirely with outsiders. Spell out an unfamiliar abbreviation the first time it appears.

If an abbreviation would appear only twice or infrequently, spell out the term every time and avoid the abbreviation entirely. Put clarity before economy.

NAVAL TRADITION VERSUS BEAUTY

Yellow-journalist Robbie Dunn had grown up in Newport among prominent naval personalities and had accompanied the world tour of the Great White Fleet as a correspondent. He was always eager to experience things first-hand. Hence when America was about to enter the war in Europe in early 1917 and he heard of some tincans heading for Ireland, Dunn enlisted in the Navy.

Though he was just shy of forty, the Navy let him in, and he had great fun standing lookout in the North Atlantic off Europe and, as a yeoman, changing "commences" to "begins" every time the first word occurred in several months' worth of engineering logs.

His boss caught him doing it, and objected. "'Commences' is a vulgar Latinism, sir,'" Dunn replied. "Well, you put it back on every damned page," said the officer, characteristically valuing naval tradition above beauty.

—Robert Shenk, unpublished manuscript, citing an incident from Robert Dunn's posthumous autobiography, *World Alive,* p. 268.

Rules for Active Writing

Avoid Dead Verbs

Passives cause problems. They make writing wordy, roundabout, and sometimes down-right confusing. To avoid this infectious disease, learn how to spot passives and make them active. Most of your sentences should use a who-does-what order. By leading with the doer you automatically avoid a passive verb.

Learn the Symptoms of Passive Voice

A verb in the passive voice uses any form of *to be* plus the past participle of a main verb:

am   is   are   was   were   be   being   been

PLUS

a main verb usually ending in *–en* or *–ed*

Sentences with passives don't need to show who or what has done the verb's action. If a doer appears at all, it follows the verb. But most passives in naval writing only imply the doer, which is sometimes a severe problem when the context doesn't make the doer clear.

Know the Three Cures

- Put a doer before the verb:
    The part must have been broken by *the handlers.*
    The handlers must have broken the part.
- Drop part of the verb:
    The results *are listed* in enclosure (2).
    The results *are* in enclosure (2).
- Change the verb:
    Letter formats *are shown* in the Correspondence Manual.
    Letter formats *appear* in the Correspondence Manual.

ON REVISING TO NAVAL WRITING STANDARDS

Here's a method of revision designed for making sure a document conforms to Naval Writing Standards. This short, step-by-step method of revision helps to enliven your writing, unburdening it of navalese:

1. Read through the writing quickly.

2. Circle the main point and make sure it's early.

3. Flag unnecessary words and ideas:
   - "it is," "there are"
   - smothered verbs
   - doublings
   - excessive abbreviating
   - wordy and unnatural expressions
   - hut-2-3-4 phrases
   - "the *–ion* of" and "the *–ment* of"
   - passive constructions

4. Revise ruthlessly, editing out what you've flagged.

5. Read through for continuity and smooth flow, checking for topic sentences and clear transitions.

6. Use visual guideposts—subject lines, subparagraphs, white space, parallelism—to highlight key ideas and their relationships.

7. Read the writing out loud. Does it sound like people talking to people? Have you used personal pronouns and an occasional contraction or question?

8. Put the writing down and come back later for a final edit.

—From Better Naval Writing, OPNAV 09B-P1-84, p. 56.

Write Passively Only for Good Reason

Write passively if you have good reason to avoid saying who or what has done the verb's action. This situation may occur when the doer is unknown, unimportant, obvious, or better left unsaid:

Presidents are elected every four years.
(doer obvious)

The part was shipped on 1 June.
(doer perhaps unimportant)

Christmas has been scheduled as a work day.
(doer better left unsaid)

When in doubt, write actively, even though the doer may seem obvious or unimportant. You will write livelier sentences (not, livelier sentences will be written by you).

2

Letters, Memos, and Directives

Good guidance on naval correspondence format can be found in the Naval Correspondence Manual. If that manual is not already on your desk, get your command to order you a copy or photocopy short parts of it for your own use. Also consult its wide-ranging advice on writing and on paperwork management.

This chapter presents advice and examples following the guidance of the Correspondence Manual but focuses on subjects not given thorough discussion there. A short treatment of the style, content, and format of a standard naval letter begins this chapter. Advice on particular kinds of naval letters follows. Then comes a discussion of business letters of several types, succeeded by some pointers on memos. A short section on naval directives ends the chapter.

The naval examples shown here are based on actual documents (as they are throughout this text), although some individual and ship names have been changed for privacy and some examples have been edited slightly. These examples incorporate principles of plain English, as do examples in other chapters in this book. The advice presented here has been gathered from wide interviewing and research.

Standard Naval Letters

Use standard naval letters to write to organizations within the Department of Defense. Both commands and individual service members write standard naval letters, the marks of which are formality, the use of standard naval terminology and abbreviations, and a businesslike tone.

STANDARD NAVAL LETTER—ITS FORMAT, STYLE, AND USE

Here's some advice on how to compose the standard naval letter.

5216
N13
1 Jun 07

From: Author, USNI Textbook
To: Navy and Marine Corps Officers (All Codes)

Subj: HOW TO COMPOSE THE STANDARD NAVAL LETTER

Ref: (a) SECNAVINST 5216.5, Dept. of the Navy Correspondence Manual

1.   Follow the excellent advice of "plain English" experts: *Jump right in* with the main point in a *brief* opening paragraph.

2.   Put your chief request or conclusion somewhere in the opening three or four lines to help get the attention of the right people from the very first. As reference (a) puts it,

> When you write a letter, think about the one sentence you would keep if you could keep only one. Many letters are short and simple enough to have such a key sentence. It should appear by the end of the first paragraph. The strongest letter highlights the main point in a one-sentence paragraph at the very beginning. Put requests <u>before</u> justifications, answers <u>before</u> explanations, conclusions <u>before</u> discussions, summaries <u>before</u> details, and the general <u>before</u> the specific.

3.   After the opening, spell out the details. Write in relatively brief paragraphs—normally no more than four or five sentences apiece. Writing short paragraphs and punctuating them by white space makes reading easier; long paragraphs can discourage the reader and encourage skimming.

4.   Keep most letters down to a single page. Try using enclosures to spell out additional material, if more than a page is necessary. In longer letters use headings to keep the reader oriented and to help in ready reference (see paragraph 6, below).

5.   Use the standard naval letter to correspond with DOD activities, primarily, but also with the Coast Guard and some contractors. Send business letters to other external addressees. Of course, before you even write the letter, <u>make sure some other means won't suffice.</u> Telephone calls documented by emails or memos for record can often take the place of formal correspondence.

6.   Follow this additional guidance:

   a.   <u>Show Codes and Titles in Addresses.</u> Whenever practical, indicate the office that will act on your letter by including a code or person's title in parentheses right after the activity's name.

   b.   <u>Compose a Good Subject Line.</u> Craft the subject line to make it genuinely informative. Try to limit it to 10 words or less. In a reply, normally make the subject line the same as that of the incoming letter.

   c.   <u>On Paper, Make Pen-and-Ink Changes.</u> Rarely redo correspondence already in final form just for a rare typo, an omitted word, or other minor error. Unless the importance of the subject or addressee or the high visibility of the document justifies the time of retyping, make neat pen-and-ink changes—up to two per page, and to all copies—and send the correspondence on.

   d.   <u>Reply Promptly.</u> Answer most received correspondence within 10 days. If you don't anticipate being able to answer within that time, inform your correspondent of the expected delay by email or phone.

"Tell young ensigns: 'Get to the ship, and take note of other people's correspondence. Figure out who's doing it right, and who's not.'"

—XO, NROTC UNIT

"Give them guidance on use of letterhead stationery. Only the CO—or anyone signing 'by direction' for the CO—is authorized to use letterhead. Letterhead is not appropriate for personal correspondence."

—SENIOR CHIEF YEOMAN

e. <u>Get All the Other Details Right.</u> See reference (a) for further details as to standard-letter format, serial numbers, markings on classified letters, and joint letters.

7. Always include your phone and fax numbers and email address when your correspondence might prompt a reply or inquiry, and make sure you include your own office code. Use no complimentary close ("Sincerely," etc.) on a standard naval letter. For rules on signatures (on who signs the letter, on "by direction" authority, on how to put together a signature block, etc.), see reference (a).

R. E. SHENK

Copy to:
USS ALLHANDS (NAV 1)

OFFICIAL PERSONAL LETTER

The technical details of communicating with higher commands on personal matters (such as enlisted applications for warrant officer or LDO, officer applications for augmentation or change of designator, and so on) are spelled out pretty clearly in the Correspondence Manual. It recommends this procedure for Navy people:

"The Admiral should only have to see most paperwork once."
—*NAVAL FLAG WRITERS HANDBOOK*

> prepare your letter on plain bond paper in standard letter format. . . . Address the letter to the higher authority and send it via your chain of command. Each via addressee prepares an endorsement and forwards the correspondence to the next addressee.

Marine Corps personnel use NAVMC 10274, Administrative Action (AA) Form, as prescribed in MCO 5210.2. Sometimes an office will authorize submission by email.

Normally, the format to use in such letters is thoroughly specified by the responsible authority. In all blocks requiring precise data, the only way a person can go wrong is to leave something out, supply faulty information, or make errors in grammar or spelling. Any such mistakes might admittedly call into question the administrative ability of the person applying. If you pay attention, it's difficult for you to go wrong in supplying that information.

However, what gets said in the "remarks" section, if there is one, can influence those who take action on your request. How well you write this paragraph (or paragraphs) can be crucial to your letter's success.

Writing a Good Remarks Section

Usually you craft this section to add key information and express the nature of your interest or desire. There are several possible approaches. One approach is to recount, in brief summary form, what special qualifications or interests make you well suited for the position for which you are applying.

For instance, in the following excerpt a Surface Warfare Officer justifies his request for a change of designator to Supply by emphasizing his strong academic background, his experience and course work in business, and his operational experience. He manages to work into this paragraph many of the pertinent highlights of his naval service. True, these highlights might be picked up by board members in their review of his service record, but he *makes sure* the board sees them by mentioning them in his letter.

Having completed nearly four years of service as an Unrestricted Line Officer, I strongly desire to broaden my career by transfer to the Naval Supply Corps. My civilian experience includes a strong academic background:

- B.A. (summa cum laude, Phi Beta Kappa), Univ. of Pennsylvania
- M.A., Cambridge University, England
- Several positions in the business and arts management fields, often involving considerable fiscal responsibility

Following graduation with honors from Surface Warfare Officer School I began a tour of duty aboard USS MCCAMPBELL (DDG-85), holding demanding billets in engineering and operations. As both Auxiliaries Officer and Administrative Department Head, I have worked closely with the ship's Supply Department and have gained much insight into Supply procedures.

The officer might have made his background even more impressive by naming the positions he held in business and arts management, or perhaps by specifying the fiscal responsibility he has had ("I was responsible for a $ —— budget," etc.).

Besides mentioning your own accomplishments as in the letter above, you can also cite *command* accomplishments to which you've made a significant contribution. The lieutenant who authored the "closing statement" below thought his command's good maintenance record reflected well on his own performance as Maintenance Material Control Officer and enhanced his request for augmentation.

During my tenure as Maintenance Material Control Officer (MMCO), Fighter Squadron THIRTY-THREE has been recognized as one of the top commands in Fighter Wing One. Functioning during a post-deployment period with the lowest requisition priority in CFW-1, the oldest F-14A aircraft in the naval inventory, and substantial Fleet Maintenance Fund reduction, VF-33 has aggressively pursued operational commitments rivaling those of any deployed unit. Significant accomplishments while I have been MMCO include:

(a) 100% sortie completion rate during FFARP.
(b) Best missile expenditure record in fighter community for FY 1987.
(c) Overall FY 1987 sortie completion rate of 97.2% during 3657.6 flight hours, with mission capability rate high of 87.2% (CNAL average is 74.4%).
(d) Achievement of zero NMCS/PMCS requisitions on three occasions, and maintenance of zero FOD rate during CY 1987.
(e) Lowest XRAY message error rate CY 1987 (highest in CY 198G), and finest aircraft logbooks in Fighter Wing One.

These achievements reflect my commitment to aviation maintenance duty. I am resolute in my career intentions and respectfully request augmentation to the regular Navy.

Although perhaps somewhat more technical than it need be (not all the members of the augmentation board will be aviators, nor will everyone understand all the abbreviations), this closing statement does spell out impressive specifics, accomplishments that stemmed in part from this officer's own work. He even supplies comparative data for the board's information, and his closing comments sound forthright.

Figure 2.1 is an example of a complete letter of application, written a few years back. As the writer explains, he was originally rejected for pilot training because his

Figure 2.1 Official Personal Request. The writer expresses a good attitude while narrating many pertinent details. Note that NMPC in the "To" line has since changed its name to BUPERS.

26 June 1987

From: Lieutenant _____, USN, XXX-XX-XXXX/1320
To: Commander, Naval Military Personnel Command (NMPC-432N)
Via: Commanding Officer, Attack Squadron SIXTY-FIVE

Subj: REQUEST FOR BOMBARDIER/NAVIGATOR TO PILOT TRANSITION

Ref: (a) BUPERSMAN 6610360

Encl: (1) Current Flight Physical (forms 88 and 93)

1. I hereby apply for Pilot Training, under the provisions of reference (a).

2. Enclosure (1) is forwarded per reference (a). The date of my birth is 14 May 1958.

3. I certify that I have not been previously separated from any Flight Training Program of the Army, the Navy, or the Air Force.

4. Throughout my childhood I made every effort to follow in my father's footsteps and pursue a career in Naval Aviation. My strongest desire throughout my Naval Career is to become a Naval Aviator. After graduating from the United States Naval Academy in May 1981, I reported to Flight School at Pensacola in January 1982. I was not physically qualified for Student Naval Aviator because my visual acuity was less than 20/20; however, I aggressively accepted training as a Naval Flight Officer. Upon completion of my training I received my first choice of communities because of my class standing. In April 1983 I reported to Attack Squadron FORTY-TWO, home of the A-6 Intruder. I completed the training syllabus at the top of my class and also as the number four CAT I Bombardier/Navigator for FY 1984. I again received my first choice of orders and reported in June 1984 to Attack Squadron SIXTY-FIVE, the "World Famous Fighting Tigers." I complete my tour with Attack Squadron SIXTY-FIVE in August 1987, and I am in receipt of orders back to Attack Squadron FORTY-TWO as an instructor for replacement aircrews.

5. I have accumulated 1080 hours of total flight time, of which 920 are in the A-6. I have 235 carrier landings on four aircraft carriers. I qualified and was designated a Post-Maintenance Functional Check Flight Crew Member within 18 months of reporting to Attack Squadron SIXTY-FIVE. I was designated as a Mission Commander as a junior LTJG. My experience and accomplishments in both my ground job and role as a crewmember increased rapidly, and I was rewarded with added responsibilities. Based on my proven aeronautical abilities and superb knowledge of the A-6 Intruder flight and weapon systems, I have been assigned to fly with the inexperienced replacement pilots as well as visiting senior Naval Aviators.

6. The "All Weather Attack Community" in my mind is the most important and exciting branch of U.S. Naval Carrier Aviation. There is nothing more rewarding to me than to fly the Intruder in its environment, the way it is meant to be flown, and put bombs on target, on time. I have tremendously enjoyed the A-6 Intruder as a Bombardier/Navigator. I feel that the Co-Pilot and Mission Commander experience that I have obtained in the A-6 Intruder have prepared me well and would greatly facilitate my transition to the pilot program. I am a proven performer. I have excelled at every challenge presented to me and am confident that, if selected for transition, I will be able to do the job exceedingly well. I will continue to be an asset to the U.S. Navy and to the A-6 community after completion of flight training.

[signed]

eyesight, while good, was less than perfect. Now, having been a Naval Flight Officer for several years, he is applying for pilot training in a "transition" program that did not require quite the same degree of visual acuity as the original program. This officer's letter does well both in listing specific details supporting his request and in expressing the desire and aptitude for the requested program.

ENDORSEMENT TO A PERSONAL REQUEST

In official requests, sometimes only a paragraph or two is for general remarks. In contrast, the endorsement to such a request is usually free-form. A commander can write endorsements as a few short paragraphs or can use bullet form (as adapted to standard naval letters). The endorsement does best when it begins with an overall opinion, then sketches specifics, and ends with a recommendation.

However, the endorsement will usually have a much stronger impact than any single performance evaluation. Rather than being filed away in the service record with all the other fitreps or evaluations, the recommendation remains attached to the request while it is being processed. Although the service record may be on hand for those who make the decisions, the command's recommendation will usually be the only evaluative document on hand to comment on the *specific request* being made.

Clearly, it is very important to craft the endorsement well. Not only commanders but also juniors who make requests should know how to write endorsements. Juniors should normally submit a draft endorsement along with the request letter.

What steps should you take in composing an endorsement? First of all, **speak specifically to the particular request being made.** Specific comments are relatively easy to make if the member's past service has been related to the request at hand. The paragraph below endorses an unrestricted line officer's application for redesignation as an intelligence officer (163X). Because the officer has been the squadron's intelligence officer, the endorser can speak directly to the officer's intelligence-related duties:

> He is the proven performer who has substantially enhanced the squadron's intelligence and radar identification training program. In his role as an intelligence instructor, he has provided positive, aggressive leadership and technical guidance during the intelligence/mission-planning phase of fleet replacement aircrew training. He has also performed expertly during the Medium Attack Tactical Employment School and during weekly intelligence training briefs to staff and replacement aviators.

In many other cases—applications for subspecialty, requests for entry into technical programs, and so on—a commander can, with profit, cite specific experience directly related to the request.

At other times, **try to connect the individual's general qualities with the particular request.** Below, in an endorsement to the letter cited earlier in which a surface line officer requested a change of designator to Supply, the ship's captain points out aspects of the lieutenant's past performance that make him particularly apt for a Supply career:

> A recent squadron command inspection rated his Admin Department OUT-STANDING, with Lieutenant ——— receiving special praise for his superb

organizational skills, close attention to detail, and dedication to the concept of "service to the crew." All these qualities should serve him well in the Supply community.

Another possibility is to **make specific comparisons to others.** This technique is used well in the following endorsement to an officer's request for selection to civilian postgraduate school:

> Although Lieutenant ———— is ninth in seniority among thirteen talented lieutenants in this command, he is this squadron's number three lieutenant, a rating all the more remarkable since the two officers rated above him are board-eligible for lieutenant commander this fall while Lieutenant ———— has only recently been promoted to lieutenant.

Then you might **try other ways to state the degree of your support,** for these statements can also help the selection board. Here, a commander endorses a chief's request to be considered for limited duty officer:

> I would be pleased to have Chief ———— under my command as a commissioned officer, proud to have her in my wardroom, and gratified to know that the support establishment was in the hands of someone as capable as she.

Finally, it may be important to **let the board know the length and closeness of your observation** of the person in question, if not already obvious. For instance, although the Marine lieutenant colonel writing below was not in the direct chain of command, the officer making the request for augmentation called him and asked for a letter. He gladly responded, speaking in the first sentences of the circumstances of his knowledge of the lieutenant:

> During my recent tour as the Consolidated Public Affairs Officer in Okinawa, Japan, I observed 2nd Lt ————'s performance of duty—as Media Operations Officer for one of the Corps' largest and most complex public affairs offices—for over six months.

Examples of a Complete Endorsement

Overall, the best endorsements are ones in which the *facts themselves speak.* The endorsement in figure 2.2, of the request for pilot transition shown earlier in figure 2.1, doesn't depend just on the commander's reputation and expressed opinion. Instead, at crucial moments the writer adduces strong evidence that the officer possesses qualities appropriate to a pilot. Because of the presence of convincing details, the readers can *see for themselves* both the quality of the person being recommended and the fit between the person and the qualification being sought.

Here's another well-written endorsement. In the original letter, a gunnery sergeant had requested a local transfer to avoid an upcoming six-month unit deployment of the construction battalion to which he was currently assigned. He argued that a major family crisis (specified in detail in the original letter) required that he be at home. In the endorsement, the CO points to the gunnery sergeant's highly professional performance as a major reason to approve the request.

Figure 2.2 Endorsement to a Personal Request. This endorsement—to the officer's letter in figure 2.1—provides a commander's perspective on the officer making the request; again, NMPC has since changed to BUPERS.

DEPARTMENT OF THE NAVY
ATTACK SQUADRON SIXTY FIVE
FPO NEW YORK 09501-6212

```
                                              1542
                                              Ser 00/272
                                              13 JUL 1987
```

FIRST ENDORSEMENT on LT _____, USN, XXX-XX-XXXX/1320 ltr of
              12 July 87

From: Commanding Officer, Attack Squadron SIXTY-FIVE
To: Commander, Naval Military Personnel Command (NMPC-432N)
Via: Commander, Carrier Air Wing THIRTEEN

Subj: REQUEST FOR BOMBARDIER/NAVIGATOR TO PILOT TRANSITION

1. Forwarded, most strongly recommending approval.

2. LT _____ has been assigned to Attack Squadron SIXTY-FIVE throughout my entire tour as Executive Officer and Commanding Officer. From the start he set the standard for professional excellence in this command. He has consistently ranked as one of the top lieutenants since reporting to the "Fighting Tigers." He has held nearly every major junior officer billet, producing flawless results. He was handpicked by Commander, Medium Attack Wing ONE to augment VA-176 during deployed Mediterranean Operations in order to bridge aircrew manning shortages and experience. During this short-fuzed deployment, he exceeded every expectation. His performance and tactical acumen underscored his versatility and "comfort level" with the all-weather attack mission. He is a proven leader who produces under pressure, and he currently holds the VA-65 Austin-Inglis Award for professional leadership.

3. LT _____'s outstanding aeronautical skills coupled with his ardent desire make him a logical choice for selection as a student Naval Aviator. I have no doubt that he will maintain the highest levels of performance as a pilot. His enthusiasm, determination, and naval instincts will enhance the "competitive edge" he must maintain while under instruction. He is command material. In my eighteen years of naval service I can think of no finer candidate for this program. He has my strongest possible recommendation for Pilot Training and ultimate reassignment as an A-6 Pilot.

                                    _____
                                    [signed]

1900
Ser 00/

FIRST ENDORSEMENT on Gunnery Sergeant Frank L. Competent, USMC,
######-####/#### of 28 Mar 02

From: Commanding Officer, U.S. Naval Construction Battalion ONE
To: Commandant of the Marine Corps (MMEA-86)
Via: (1) Commander, TWENTIETH Naval Construction Regiment

Subj: REQUEST HUMANITARIAN TRANSFER

1.   Forwarded, most strongly recommending approval. Based on my review of this case, Gunnery Sergeant Competent's presence at home would be instrumental in resolving this hardship.

2.   Gunnery Sergeant Competent has been working with his chain of command, the Command Chaplain, and Navy Family Counselors to assist in his family's challenges. Due to his strong will and dedication to the Battalion, he has refused to allow these difficulties to affect his superior performance as NMCB ONE's Marine Advisor. He has used his leave to attend appointments, surgeries, and physical therapy treatments. Gunnery Sergeant Competent and his son are truly stoic men, but the Competent family has endured many extreme tragedies, and granting him a humanitarian transfer will be a great benefit to his son's mental, physical, and emotional well-being. Furthermore, if allowed to remain in the local area, Gunnery Sergeant Competent's son will maintain medical continuity, and he will greatly benefit from his current physician.

3.   Granting this request would allow Gunnery Sergeant Competent the opportunity to give his family increased stability and emotional support. Additionally, the Gunnery Sergeant's superb ability to work with Seabees would greatly benefit the Navy and the TWENTIETH Naval Construction Regimental Marine Advisors. Since this Battalion will be deploying to Japan in June for a 6-month, I recommend this humanitarian transfer take effect immediately.

4.   Gunnery Sergeant Competent is not pending any disciplinary action.

R. L. APPROVER

RESPONDING TO A PERSONAL REQUEST

Throughout the services, officials of various ranks must compose replies to personal letters from service members. In the Navy, the heaviest load of this kind falls on BUPERS (which must respond to lots of letters from parents, too). But many other offices must respond to service members who have made personal requests.

Being considerate, on the one hand, and being fair, on the other—at the same time remembering the "needs of the Navy"—is obviously no easy job. In a memo at BUPERS, Admiral David Harlow once specially outlined the need for *written* communication in this situation:

> Too frequently, correspondence crossing my desk indicates that in a telephone conversation, someone within BUPERS has reportedly made a commitment to an individual that has become difficult to support in terms of current policy. Sometimes the cause may be a sympathetic desire to make

a situation more acceptable to a constituent; sometimes a misconception can arise when the individual "hears what he/she wants to hear." When we try to reconstruct what was meant as well as said, there is often no record. It has happened to all of us. In any case, our credibility, if not integrity, can be severely damaged.

Admiral Harlow argued that often the best answer to questions asked by phone is to say one will research the problem and respond *in writing*.

Writing such letters can be a craft in itself. Here are some guidelines on how to write responses, closely adapted from those developed by YNCM Charles E. Miller, Jr., who taught the Action Officer course in BUPERS in the late 1990s.

Guidelines on Preparing Correspondence at BUPERS

1. **Answer the Mail**

   Consider all issues raised in the letter. Does the letter make sense? Is the request reasonable? Can we say "yes"?

2. **Write the Response**

   Write like you talk. Explain things at the reader's level (but don't talk down).

   - *Acknowledge the letter* (though realize that "thank you for your letter" is not always appropriate); also *restate the issue.* Putting it in your own words makes clear that you understand the author.
   - *Assume a basic validity to the writer's viewpoint.* If the writer is wrong or mis-informed, do not argue; proving your superiority is counterproductive. Stick with the facts. See if the needs of the writer can be accommodated.
   - *Put the good news or bad news as close as possible to the beginning.*
     — If this is bad news, try at least to offer a ray of hope—but not false hope.
     — If this is bad news, do not close with "all the best."
   - *Try to include one or two personal references.* For example, when writing for the signature of a particular official, one might say, "I'm so glad to hear that your son is doing well." Do not send form letters.
   - *End on a positive note.* Make a sincere offer of further help. Give a point of contact and a telephone number if possible.

3. **Proofread**

   Insist on spell check. Does your letter make sense? Is the tone of the letter friendly, people-oriented?

4. **Track the Package**

   Pay attention to due dates. Be proactive: shepherd your package through the various stops. If you absolutely cannot meet the due date, get an extension. Prepare an interim response, explaining the reason for the delay. *Call the writer.* (For instance, "I got your letter; I think this is the answer. Is there anything else we can do for you?")

5. **Do Your Best**

   Our Sailors deserve nothing else. If you have questions about how to proceed, get advice. Spend time to save time: get it right, first time through.

"Our motto at BUPERS:

- *We listen*
- *We care*
- *We try to say yes."*

—MASTER CHIEF
CHARLES E. MILLER, JR.

Master Chief Miller argues that a letter's tone is especially important. As he puts it, when we speak we have these advantages—tone of voice, facial expression, hand gestures, and eye contact. When we write, we must compensate by explaining things at the reader's level—and do our best not to sound bureaucratic.

Not only *sounding* bureaucratic but *being* so is a habit hard to escape. For instance, one office may have no problem with a certain request, but regulations require that another office also approve the request. Yet service members in the fleet often have no knowledge of the bureaucratic hoops their requests must go through.

A reservist requested a waiver for a medical condition so he could continue serving in a pay billet. BUMED issued an OK and sent it to the reservist, who believed his request was wholly approved. It came as a shock a few weeks later when BUPERS issued a negative response, and (despite BUMED's OK) the request was fully denied. The reservist lost his pay billet and (naturally enough) was angry in the bargain. *Give your correspondent a heads up about any other major hurdles down the line.*

Along a somewhat different line, a naval officer asked the disbursing officer of her unit to write a generalized "To whom it may concern" letter concerning her frustrating difficulty in getting the Montgomery GI Bill benefits to which she was entitled, a difficulty that had not been resolved upon the disbursing officer's reassignment. In that letter (reproduced below), the disbursing officer does his best to outline the problem clearly and competently:

---

24 Jul 03

From: LT Carroll B. Davis, SC, USNR
To: Whom It May Concern

Subj: ENTITLEMENT TO EDUCATIONAL BENEFITS

1. Formerly the Disbursing Officer for NMCB-1, I am writing to express my concern that LT Susan B. Frustrated may be denied her Montgomery GI Benefits as well as $2,400.00 of her pay due to a number of disbursing difficulties beyond her or any service member's ability to correct.

2. Dutifully aware of the requirement to pay $2,700.00 to convert from VEAP to Montgomery GI Benefits (MGIB), LT Frustrated completed an allotment form in May 2001 in my office to begin monthly deductions from her base pay starting in June 2001. Unfortunately, our computing systems rejected my Disbursing Clerk's numerous attempts to process the allotment.

3. I assigned LT Frustrated's allotment exclusively to one of my most diligent disbursing clerks to resolve, and with her almost daily attention the allotment took nearly three months to begin. Apparently (in the least disbursing-specific terms I can manage), the newness of the conversion program prevented the allotment from being recognized when it was released to the Defense Finance and Accounting Service (DFAS). Rigid bimonthly cut-off dates, unfulfilled promises of weekly resolutions from DFAS technicians, and operational commitments such as field exercises that removed my staff from the office delayed the start of her MGIB allotment until August of the same year.

4. Ultimately, the two- to three-month delay would prevent the $2,700.00 required for LT Frustrated's conversion benefits from being paid by October 2002, a deadline of which both she and I were unaware.

5. Finally, though an emotional plea has little place in a letter of this nature, I would kindly ask you to review LT Frustrated's MGIB account favorably, for I am beholden to her officership like few others in the U.S. Navy. I had already completed my undergraduate and graduate education when I arrived at my first duty station where LT Frustrated served as the Admin officer. Her guidance to me and every other junior officer in our battalion was inestimable. I can only imagine what she could do for the rest of the fleet with benefits afforded by higher education through the MGIB.

6.   Thank you for your consideration in this matter. If you require any additional information, please contact me at (410)293-6225 DSN 281-6225 or U.S. Naval Academy, English Department, 107 Maryland Avenue, Annapolis, MD 21402-5044.

Very Respectfully,

C. B. DAVIS
LT, SC, USNR

LETTER TO A PROMOTION BOARD

When there is no format to a particular "request" letter, you must do your best to write with the particular communication situation in mind. For example, neither in the Naval Military Personnel Manual (MILPERSMAN) nor in the U.S. Marine Corps Promotion Manual (MCO P1400.31, Vol. 1) is there any standard format prescribed for writing a letter to a promotion board. These references simply direct you to use a standard naval letter. MILPERSMAN article 2220110—the reference on Navy officer boards—does stipulate that any "third-party correspondence" must contain a written acknowledgment by the eligible officer that he or she desires it in the record. Besides setting out such standard procedures and listing an address, neither MILPERSMAN nor the Marine Corps order helps by telling you how or when to write such a letter.

In contrast to most evals or fitreps, letters to the board may be read by the whole board and not just by the briefers (there is no universality here; each board sets its own policy). Hence, such letters can make a very strong impression, pro or con. What governs the impression you make? Let's look at those three keys to any writing situation—to whom you're writing, who you are, and the nature of your message.

To whom are you writing? Remember, a promotion board is composed of individuals senior to those under consideration. These individuals have wide naval experience, so you don't need to explain to them how the service works. On the other hand, they will not all be experts in your particular career field. On a Navy chief's board, for instance, some rates will be unrepresented, and so a few technical details may have to be explained. But always remember that board members typically have a great deal to do in a very short time.

Who are you? Obviously you are someone under consideration, and junior to your audience. You are a member of the Navy or Marine Corps and should sound like one. Respectfulness is your proper demeanor. You must not appear to be looking for any advantages but just fair treatment. On the other hand, you have a right to your say, and from your firsthand knowledge may be able to contribute what no one else can.

Finally, what is your message? Your message is *not* that you should be promoted. That's the board's decision, and, in fact, only the board is in the best position to make that decision. Your goal, if you write, is to explain circumstances in your record that do not stand on their own. You really have no business writing at all unless there are some special circumstances or facts the board doesn't know or might overlook about your past performance, items not discoverable or not well explained in your service record. What kinds of circumstances? Unusual duty, for example, or an unusual pattern of career assignments. A logical explanation of broken service might be well received. Of course, there are many other possibilities.

The communication situation suggests a number of dos and don'ts, outlined below. No doubt your knowledge of the particular kind of board to which you are writing, your knowledge of yourself as an officer or enlisted person, and your knowledge of the particular case you need to make will suggest many additional points:

Do:

- Be as brief as the subject matter allows (long letters, regardless of content, are viewed dimly). Write a page or a page and a half at most.
- Write respectfully to the board members.
- Assume they are scrupulously fair.
- Get to the point quickly.
- Spell out explicitly and clearly the vital facts; put them in logical order.
- Explain unusual circumstances.
- Explain the positive aspects of any negative facts.
- Have your letter read by former selection board members, if you can, or other experts such as senior officers and leading chiefs.

Don't:

- Explain what board members will already know.
- Make grammatical or spelling errors.
- Express negative opinions or emotions either toward naval service or toward particular individuals.
- Write a letter to the board *at all* if you have no clear reason to do so.

Figure 2.3 is a letter submitted by a Navy lieutenant to a lieutenant commander board. He sent it because he had been out of the service for three years and wanted to explain the circumstances. Respectful, to the point, and clear, this letter spends its main effort explaining the unusual circumstances of the lieutenant's leaving, then returning to Navy duty. It makes the most of positive aspects of those circumstances—that he had stayed in the government even though he had left the Navy; that he returned to the Navy as soon as his three-year FBI obligation allowed; that he excelled even when in the FBI; and that he immediately began renewing his qualifications once he returned to Navy duty. Overall, the letter makes a very positive impression.

It is also possible for someone other than the service member to write the board on that individual's behalf. Below is a letter written by a Marine captain. A lieutenant who had once served with him (whom we'll call Lieutenant Bravo) asked the captain to write to the promotion board on his behalf. The lieutenant had received a poor fitness report from a Marine general during Desert Storm—unjustly, in his opinion. He worried lest he not be selected and then be dismissed from the Corps. Note that this letter, as required, was submitted to the board via the lieutenant himself.

---

12 Jan 94

From: Captain Herman S. Clardy, III
To: President, 1994 Captain Selection Board
Via: First Lieutenant J. R. Bravo xxx-xx-xxx/xxxx/xxxx

Subj: INFORMATION FOR CONSIDERATION: CASE OF FIRST LIEUTENANT JAMES R. BRAVO xxx-xx-xxxx/xxxx/xxxx

1. This letter is forwarded to the 1994 Captain Selection board for consideration in the promotion of Lieutenant Bravo. I was Lieutenant Bravo's company commander from 13 July

Figure 2.3 Letter to a Promotion Board. An officer explains the special circumstances of his leaving and then returning to active duty.

```
                                                    27 April 1987

From:  Lieutenant _____, USN, XXX-XX-XXXX/1320
To:    President, FY 88 Lieutenant Commander Line Promotion Board

Subj:  FY 88 LIEUTENANT COMMANDER LINE PROMOTION BOARD

1.  I would like to submit to the board the following information
for consideration in addition to my record on file:

    a.  I have faithfully served the U.S. Government since my original
commissioning in May 1974, having accumulated 13 years of consecutive
government service, uninterrupted by terminal leave of any sort.

    b.  I had a life-long desire to serve both in the U.S. Navy and as a
Special Agent in the Federal Bureau of Investigation (FBI).  Unfortunately, I
had to leave the employ of one to pursue the other.  I enjoyed a very
successful career with the U.S. Navy from May 1974 until January 1981.  It
was only after much vacillation that I elected to pursue a career in the
FBI.  Early during my three-year obligation to the FBI I decided that I wanted
to return to the U.S. Navy.  Throughout my FBI tour I continued to perform to
the best of my ability, receiving seven letters of commendation for my
performance, including two from the Director of the FBI, the Honorable William
H. Webster.  I point this out to show that my desire and ambition to
excel have never diminished.

    c.  The FBI restricts a Special Agent from participating in the military
reserve, making it impossible for me to retain a reserve commission with the
U.S. Naval Reserve during those three years.

    d.  In the spring of 1984 I received my reserve commission, which was
necessary to reapply for recall to active duty.  I was informed, though, that
there were no quotas for recall back to U.S. Navy (Regular).  However, the TAR
program was available, and I was subsequently selected for this program and
assigned to the Naval Air Reserve, Norfolk.  I immediately took it upon
myself to get refresher training and then NATOPS qualified in the F-14A
Tomcat, eventually receiving orders as a staff instructor to the F-14 FRS in
August 1985.

    e.  I applied for augmentation at my earliest qualification date, August
1985, and was selected in September 1985 with redesignation to the Regular
Navy on 3 January 1986.

2.  I sincerely believe my record speaks for itself.  I have maintained the
highest standards of excellence through both careers, and my goal is clear - to
SERVE, ADVANCE, and COMMAND in the U.S. Navy.  I feel I have demonstrated the
talents and abilities required for success in the U.S. Navy and respectfully
request the board deliberate these when deciding upon my selection for
promotion to lieutenant commander.


                              _____
                              [signed]
```

1992 to 1 November 1993 at Company x, xx Light Armored Infantry Battalion. I feel I can present an accurate picture of Lieutenant Bravo's value to the Marine Corps.

2.   Lieutenant Bravo served as a scout platoon commander, weapons platoon commander, fire support commander, and executive officer of my company. He performed his duties with distinction and enthusiasm. Lieutenant Bravo exhibited exceptional knowledge of light armored reconnaissance employment and fire support at both the platoon and company levels—knowledge superior to that of his peers. Additionally, Lieutenant Bravo inspired unparalleled devotion from his Marines, a loyalty, in fact, greater than I have ever witnessed. As acting company commander on several occasions, Lieutenant Bravo displayed maturity in dealing with higher headquarters, forethought in integrating training with maintenance, and determination to succeed at every task. His performance was equal to the challenge of command and irrefutably showed his potential for promotion.

3.   Lieutenant Bravo demonstrates the qualifications of leadership, knowledge, and professionalism. Based on my observations, his worth to the Marine Corps cannot be overstated. I enthusiastically endorse his advancement to the grade of captain. KEEP THIS MARINE OFFICER IN THE CORPS!

H. S. CLARDY, III

One more example follows. It is a letter written by a former commanding officer of a submarine to a selection board for master chief. It was written at the officer's own initiative in support of his former Chief of the Boat (COB), but as per regulation, he sent it via the senior chief. On receipt, the senior chief had to decide whether to send it on.

---

19 January 1994

From: CDR (CAPT SEL) Richard L. Virgilio, USN, xxx-xx-xxxx/1120 Senior Member, COMSUBPAC Tactical Readiness Evaluation Team, Commander Submarine Force, U.S. Pacific Fleet (N70) Pearl Harbor, HI 9G8G0-G550

To: President, FY95 Master Chief Petty Officer Selection Board

Via: STSCS(SS), USN

Subj: RECOMMENDATION FOR SELECTION

1.   This letter was <u>not</u> solicited by STSCS(SS) ———.

2.   I am submitting this letter because in my current assignment I have observed many MCPOs and COBs. I believe this broader perspective is an important aspect in my recommendation, and is valuable as input to the selection process.

3.   I most strongly recommend STSCS(SS) ———, USN for selection to Master Chief. I observed him closely while I was his commanding officer and he was my Chief of the Boat, and since have observed many other Chiefs of the Boat during Tactical Readiness Evaluations. He is clearly <u>at the top of the heap</u>.

4.   In my observation of other MCPOs and COBs, the factors which point out clearly why STSCS(SS) ——— is <u>far better than a large majority</u> of them are:

   — His ability to <u>motivate and lead</u> the crew in challenging times, such as ship-wide examinations.

   — His <u>enforcement of high standards</u> of performance and professionalism, apparent even when he's not around.

— His visible and <u>effective personal involvement</u> in all aspects of the command, giving excellent results in many areas.

5.   We need Master Chiefs like STSCS(SS) ———, particularly to become Command Master Chiefs throughout the Navy. He is doing a bang-up job now, and will do so when he is assigned even greater responsibilities. <u>We must take advantage of his superb talent</u>. But he cannot become a C/MC until he is selected for E-9. We need him <u>now</u>; I most strongly urge you to <u>SELECT HIM</u> now.

R. L. VIRGILIO

Copy to: Commanding Officer, USS SUBMARINE (SSN xxx)

LETTER OF INSTRUCTION

The personnel-related letter of instruction (LOI) is a nonpunitive warning to a service member about subpar performance (another letter of instruction is a preexercise directive—we won't cover that here). You can issue the LOI either to an enlisted person or to an officer. It amounts to very formal counseling, counseling combined with a "memo for record" kind of documentation. This letter is a variation of a Navy Page Thirteen or a Marine Corps Page Eleven entry in a service record, though the LOI is somewhat more formal than either since it is issued directly to the individual.

Some commanders issue an LOI only when it documents performance poor enough to lead to the service member's relief or transfer to other duties. Others prefer to issue the LOI as early as possible, when the service member's performance first begins to degrade. Those who issue LOIs early argue that issuing one at the eleventh hour is a way to get rid of a problem, not to solve it.

Composing an LOI serves two major purposes. (1) *Having to write one* forces superiors to determine and describe the specific behaviors that need to be corrected. (2) *Having to read one* requires the service member to direct attention to particular problem areas and to explicit methods of improvement. In the best case, the formality of such a written set of instructions, including very well-defined goals and final attainment dates, can help galvanize a service member into great effort.

The cardinal rule in writing an LOI is to *be specific.* To generalize in the comments, to say no more than "you're a poor performer and need to build up your character and to improve in discipline," just demeans the individual and offers no real assistance. But detailing both the particulars of past deficiencies and the specifics of the needed improvement can make the LOI a highly effective counseling tool.

To summarize, the LOI should outline these five matters:

1.   **The specific failures** in performance: **when, where, and what.**
2.   **Actions the command has taken** to correct this problem.
3.   **Steps to be taken** by the service member, **or goals to be met,** for each area of failing performance.
4.   **Individuals who can help.**
5.   **Not-later-than ("drop dead") dates** for each step.

If well thought out and accompanied by the right kind of personal counseling, an LOI can genuinely aid the service member, helping greatly to turn his or her performance around. On the other hand, if the service member refuses to be helped, or for some

"What's your drop dead date?"

"Yesterday?"

—OVERHEARD

AT OPNAV

other reason cannot meet the goals on the dates specified, this letter serves as specific documentation of the failure. It then becomes formal grounds for subsequent relief, separation, transfer, disenrollment, or other such proceedings.

Figure 2.4 is an example of an LOI in the form of a letter that assigns extra military instruction to a petty officer for generally poor performance. The executive officer who wrote this document said this was a "low-level" LOI, which, he hoped, would help round this service member into shape.

And below is an example of an LOI written to an officer who has gotten behind in his warfare qualifications, including division officer administration. To be most helpful in their specific guidance, letters must usually run at least a page and a half or two pages in length. The example below is a bit shorter than the usual LOI.

1611
21 Dec 96

From: Commanding Officer, USS VESSEL (DDG XYZ)
To: Ensign J. R. Officer, USN, XXX-XX-XXXX/1160
Via: (1) Executive Officer, USS VESSEL
  (2) Weapons Officer, USS VESSEL

Subj: LETTER OF INSTRUCTION TO CORRECT SUBSTANDARD PERFORMANCE

1. Your professional growth as a Surface Warfare Officer has been substandard. Specific deficiencies include:

  a. Lack of satisfactory progress toward surface warfare qualification.

  b. Inadequate knowledge of the 5"/54 gun system and its operation and maintenance requirements, despite your having attended Gunnery Officer School and Ammunition Administration School.

  c. Inadequate knowledge of the 3-M system, manifested by improper planned maintenance scheduling and performance.

  d. Inability to develop, plan, and execute a basic division training program despite specific direction from your department head.

2. To improve your performance and help you become competitive with your contemporaries, I direct you to complete the following actions by the dates specified:

  a. Learn the mechanics, operation, and capabilities of the 5"/54 MK 42 MOD 10 gun, and be prepared to demonstrate that knowledge no later than 31 Jan 97 at an oral board composed of LCDR Howe, LT Soderman, and LTJG Griepentrog.

  b. Complete Basic 3-M PQS (NAVEDTRA 43241D1) prior to 31 Jan 97.

  c. Demonstrate significant progress toward Surface Warfare Officer qualification in the areas of division officer and warfare qualification. You will establish a qualification timetable and submit it to the Senior Watch Officer, the Weapons Officer, and the Executive Officer no later than 5 Jan 97.

  d. Complete the Gunner's Mate Guns (GMG) Petty Officer 3 & 2 correspondence course no later than 28 Feb 97.

3. These requirements constitute the bare minimum necessary to improve your SWO knowledge and skills. Completing these requirements will also help you gain a more confident demeanor when dealing with juniors and seniors.

Figure 2.4 Letter of Instruction. Repeated poor watchstanding prompted this Letter of Instruction (LoI).

19 Aug 94

From: Commanding Officer, USS HAMMERHEAD (SSN 663)
To: FT2(SS)   USN,

Subj: EXTRA MILITARY INSTRUCTION FOR WATCHSTANDING DEFICIENCIES

1. You have been assigned Extra Military Instruction as a result of your poor watchstanding practices and your lack of attention to detail. Accordingly, you must complete the following actions:

    a. Study the duties of the Below Decks Watch specified in the SSORM (Art. 2305), with particular attention to what the Below Decks Watch <u>must</u> and <u>must not</u> do. **DUE: 22 AUG**

    b. Read the following selected articles from Naval Reactors Technical Bulletin (NRTB) Volume B - Revision 2 - Book 1 (a copy of each article has been left in a folder with the Chief of the Watch for your convenience):

Article	Page(s)
(1) "Zero Defects"	B-1
(2) "Be Alert"	B-3
(3) "Violation of Proper Watchstanding Practices"	B-34, 35
(4) "Bilge Alarms"	B-42

    c. Complete an oral interview with your Department Head in which you discuss your duties and obligations as the Below Decks Watch and the lessons to be learned from the reading assigned in paragraph (b). **DUE: 27 AUG**

    d. Conduct a two-hour monitor watch of another Below Decks Watch, as specified on the watchbill generated by the Chief of the Boat, with emphasis on procedural compliance, attentiveness to irregularities or potential problems, "busy-ness" of the watchstanding routine, familiarity with the watchstation and accuracy and interpretation of logged readings. Turn in neatly written monitor watch comment sheets to the COB. **DUE: 8 SEP**

2. This remedial program is designed to make you think about the responsibilities and watchstanding practices of the ship's Below Decks Watch, with the long-term goal of enhancing your BDW watchstanding performance as well as that of other BDWs who may be similarly deficient.

J. C. MICKEY
By direction

4.   Individuals in your chain of command are always ready to assist you or provide additional guidance. Request help from me, from the Executive Officer, or from the Weapons Officer, whenever you need it.

D. D. SKIPPER

Business Letters

"Do learn how your boss opens and closes correspondence with different people. You may be given case-by-case guidance, but know who warrants first name salutations and a 'Warm Regards' close. Also remember 'the system'; know who is senior to whom."

—NAVAL FLAG WRITERS HANDBOOK

The business letter should really be called "the business or personal letter," for besides sending it to businesses, you can also use it for sending thanks, congratulations, or condolence. As the Correspondence Manual points out, it can even be used "for official correspondence between individuals within the Department of Defense when the occasion calls for a personal approach."

You can vary the format of a business letter somewhat so that, say, a letter of condolence isn't encumbered with serial numbers, or so the text of a very short letter fits in the middle of the page. The main variations, however, result from the differing uses of a business letter. We'll discuss several cases beginning with what is probably the most common use.

BUSINESS LETTER TO A BUSINESS OR OTHER ORGANIZATION

Here is guidance on how to write a business letter—in the form of a business letter.

Department of the Navy
USS HALEAKALA (AE 25)
FPO SAN FRANCISCO 96667-3004

5216
Ser AE 25/28
January 10, 1997

Business or Company Name
Attn: Person within the Company
Street Address
City, State ZIP

THE FORMAT, STYLE, AND USE OF A BUSINESS LETTER

State the purpose of your business letter in the first paragraph unless the occasion calls for delay to soften bad news or you are introducing a controversial proposal. Don't delay routinely.

See to it that your paragraphs are no longer than about 10 lines each—the first much shorter than that. Work at writing even more clearly in letters to civilian audiences than in standard naval letters. In particular, avoid all unfamiliar military terminology, including acronyms. If you must use such specialized language, make sure to explain each term the first time you use it. A great deal that we take for granted in our internal correspondence is unfamiliar to a civilian audience.

Other things that differentiate a business letter from a standard naval letter:

1.   You don't number main paragraphs. You may number subparagraphs (like this one).

2. There is no "From" line on a naval business letter, so you **must use a letterhead** (printed, stamped, or typed) to show the letter's origin.

3. You can express dates in month-day-year order if your readers are likely to be most familiar with that format. Whatever the order, always **spell out or abbreviate the month** rather than designate it by number. (If you express the date as 3/4/95 or 11/12/96 some readers may mistake the day for the month, or vice versa.)

4. If writing to a company in general but directing the letter to a particular person or office within it, **use an attention line** between the name and address. See above.

5. You may use either a salutation or a subject line in a business letter. If you use a salutation, be alert to the gender of your audience, and follow the Correspondence Manual's specific guidance. On routine administrative matters you may replace the salutation with a subject line (as above). Used this way, a subject line orients readers to the topic and avoids the stiltedness of "Dear Sir or Madam."

6. Business letters typically use the complimentary close "Sincerely," whereas standard naval letters omit the complimentary close entirely. If you wish to show special deference to a high public official, you may replace "Sincerely" with "Respectfully" or the like.

Sincerely,

O. H. PERRY Lieutenant,
U.S. Navy Administrative Officer
By direction of the Commanding Officer

Encl:
(1) Correspondence Manual (sep cover)

Figure 2.5 is a good example of a business letter—and it gives clear and classic guidance on the relationship of the Department of the Navy, the Navy, and the Marine Corps.

GOOD WILL LETTER

You will often want to express thanks to a person in or outside the military who has done you a favor. You might be thanking someone for a talk, for a personal favor of some kind (such as an introduction), for hospitality, or for a number of other services.

Whatever the circumstances, *be genuine.* Avoid form letters in this kind of writing, and strive especially to express real gratitude. The latter takes some care. Sometimes informality will help you write genuinely, the degree of informality depending on your relationship with the correspondent and the particular situation. Recount some of the details of the service rendered or what specific good it did, if you can.

Make sure your letter doesn't appear to have been written just to conform to the rules of service etiquette. To this end, *avoid the passive voice.* Saying "it was appreciated" instead of "we appreciated" will communicate aloofness, not gratitude. Of course, be timely in thanking someone; write quickly so you won't forget to write—at least within forty-eight hours of the occasion.

Here's the text of a letter of thanks written to a Japanese restaurant owner by the officer in charge of a small Navy unit. The writer speaks her gratitude warmly and simply.

Figure 2.5 Example of a Business Letter. A senior Marine Corps official outlines to a civilian the relationship of the Department of the Navy, the Navy, and the Marine Corps.

DEPARTMENT OF THE NAVY
HEADQUARTERS UNITED STATES MARINE CORPS
WASHINGTON, D.C. 20380-0001

IN REPLY REFER TO
1.11
HD:EHS
29 Dec 86

Ms. Fran Lazerow
Vice President
Toborg Associates, Inc.
1725 K Street, NW, Ste 803
Washington, DC 20006

Dear Ms. Lazerow:

Thank you for your letter of December 23.

Adjusting the program to make it read "Navy and Marine Corps" wherever it now reads "Navy" and then insuring that "Naval representation" includes Navy and Marine Corps representation will probably take care of my earlier misgivings.

If the conference accomplishes nothing more than an understanding of the Marine Corps as a service within the Department of the Navy and how that affects its role in joint operations, the conference, from my point of view, will have accomplished a good deal.

Permit me to elucidate a bit:

It is not merely that the Marine Corps "may consider itself somewhat of a separate branch of the service" as you state in your letter; it is a matter of law. The Marine Corps is a separate service within the Department of the Navy. "Department of the Navy" (nor, for that matter "Navy Department") is not synonymous with "U.S. Navy." The U.S. Navy is a separate service within the Department of the Navy.

Nor is it correct to say that "administratively the Corps is attached to the Navy." There are many linkages, both administrative and operational, between the Navy and Marine Corps, but in no sense is the Marine Corps "administratively attached" to the Navy. These relationships have been hammered out in law and practice over nearly a two-hundred year period, and the well-indoctrinated Marine does not regard them lightly.

"Naval," properly used, does subsume both the Navy and the Marine Corps; as for example, a Marine aviator is a Naval aviator, and Marine Corps aviation forms part of Naval aviation.

All of this is well understood by Dr. Christopher Jehn, the Vice President, Marine Corps Programs, Center for Naval Analyses. Dr. Jehn is immediately subordinate to Dr. DePoy and directs CNA's Marine Corps Operations Analysis Group.

Figure 2.5 (*continued*)

Now that we have cut away the underbrush and have good clear fields of fire, I will be pleased to help with your conference in any way I can, including the suggestion or nomination of participants, if you will let me know at what levels and with what groups you want Marine Corps participation.

From looking at your tentative agenda, I would suggest we participate in the following work groups:

1) Military History Data Availability and Accessibility;

2) Uses of Military History for Operational Planning;

3) Military History Education.

I myself would like to attend the plenary sessions.

With all best wishes for the success of the conference,

Sincerely,

E. H. SIMMONS
Brigadier General
U.S. Marine Corps, Retired
Director of Marine Corps
History and Museums

Dear Mr. Narita:

On behalf of the men and women of the Personnel Support Activity Detachment, I want to thank you for your gracious hospitality on Saturday, October 10.

From the moment you met us at the train station until our departure from your lovely restaurant, we knew we were in excellent hands. We will never forget the warmth of your reception. As a result of this trip, we are all eager to visit more places in your beautiful country.

Please extend our gratitude to your family, especially your son who so willingly took us to our destination. The day was truly blessed with good weather, good food, and good memories.

Sincerely,

And figure 2.6 is a letter clearly expressing thanks to the representative of a company who has done important work for the Naval Meteorology and Oceanography Command. With a ghostwritten letter of this kind, if the flag writer has done his job well, all the admiral has to do is to sign the letter and pen in a personal note.

Figure 2.6 Letter of Appreciation. An admiral sends a letter of appreciation to a civilian via the civilian's boss, to whom the admiral actually speaks.

DEPARTMENT OF THE NAVY
COMMANDER
NAVAL METEOROLOGY AND OCEANOGRAPHY COMMAND
1100 BALCH BOULEVARD
STENNIS SPACE CENTER MS 39529-5005

1650
Ser 0/213
29 NOV 2001

From: Commander, Naval Meteorology and Oceanography Command
To: Mr. Mike Quin
Via: Mr. Lee Johnston, Environmental Systems Research
      Institute, Inc.

Subj: LETTER OF APPRECIATION

1. Please extend my sincere appreciation to Mr. Mike Quin for
his contribution during our recent Fleet Battle Experiment
(FBE-I).

2. Faced with the Oceanographer of the Navy's challenge to
integrate METOC products in operator systems, the Naval Pacific
Meteorology and Oceanography Command, San Diego, California
needed to rapidly integrate Meteorology and Oceanography (METOC)
information into the Naval Fires Network (NFN). NFN is a new
but critical system. Completing the task required accomplishing
twelve months of work in four months.

3. Mr. Quin's team allowed us to satisfy 100 percent of our
short-fused customer requirements, an accomplishment thought to
be impossible. As a result, Commander Third Fleet has asked us
to expand our efforts, in addition to delivering this level of
support on a continuous basis.

4. Mr. Quin was, without question, one of the key reasons for
our unprecedented success. He is an outstanding individual, an
enthusiastic professional, and a true asset to any organization.
He is welcome here any time!

5. You have my sincerest thanks.

Well done and
well deserved!

T. Q. DONALDSON, V
Rear Admiral, U.S. Navy

LETTER TO PARENTS AND OTHER FAMILY MEMBERS

One of the most rewarding and successful parts of my command was, surprisingly, the form letters I sent to parents. I wrote each parent of the fifty people up for awards and promotions, modifying each letter slightly. The parents fired back letters to their kids, and morale zoomed up. It was a building block for success.

Such letters don't have to be long, or sexy, or even grammatically correct, but they have a great payoff.

—Navy Commander, after a command tour

Parents of Sailors and Marines are an interesting audience. Supportive of their children, usually patriotic, and also very understanding of the scrapes their children get into, parents will usually be very responsive if commanders treat them well. A Navy commander who reviewed an earlier edition of this book commented about his own efforts in this area:

> Writing letters to family members helps more than you can imagine. When I was OIC of Naval Security Group Detachment Diego Garcia, I wrote letters to parents, spouses, adult children, or whoever was listed as next of kin in the service record. Promotions, awards, and when the member first checked into the command were the occasions that generated my letters.
>
> Many of the parents wrote me back. One mother demanded to know why there had never been an article in the local paper about her daughter's many promotions, awards, and achievements in the Navy. A former Navy dad congratulated me on being an LDO (although I'm not) since no "real" officer would have the leadership to write letters home. Many Sailors thanked me personally for this minimal effort. Many more thanked my assistant OIC.
>
> One Sailor told me that his parents were so proud that they framed the letters and hung them on the wall next to his high school graduation picture. Sailors felt more connected to the rest of world. It is hard to prove these things empirically, but I believe we had significantly fewer discipline problems than other detachments/commands of similar size because of this letter writing effort.

"Personal correspondence still cannot be beat. The warm, happy, fuzzy feelings. My current command does lots of personal letters; it builds morale. Sometimes the admiral just calls to ask, 'How are things going?'"

—Chief of Staff, reflecting on the email age

Write to parents and other relatives of your people often. Welcome them to the unit's family. Praise their young service members on their promotions and awards. Always assume in your writing that your audience is mature, intelligent, and understanding.

These letters will help keep up morale, and it's simply a good thing to do. It will begin to establish a relationship. On more difficult subjects that might come up later, it is always easier to write to a familiar audience, one with whom you have already established contact.

Here are three good examples. To begin with, figure 2.7 is a letter from the commanding officer of a Coast Guard cutter; it congratulates the parents of a petty officer on his recent promotion to second class.

Figure 2.7 Letter to Parents. The commanding officer of a Coast Guard vessel informs parents of their son's recent advancement.

COMMANDING OFFICER
USCGC HARRIET LANE (WMEC-903)
4000 COAST GUARD BLVD.
PORTSMOUTH, VIRGINIA
23703-2199

October 12, 1988

Dear Mr. and Mrs. Kempton:

I would like to take this opportunity to inform you of your son Mark's recent advancement to Boatswain's Mate Second Class (E-5). He has demonstrated exceptional initiative and personal effort in reaching this goal on the advancement ladder.

His appointment as a Second Class Petty Officer carries with it the obligation of exercising increased responsibility. I have every confidence that he will discharge the duties of his new position with the same dedication to duty he has displayed in the past.

Mark is an outstanding HARRIET LANE sailor who has set an excellent example for the junior personnel. The Coast Guard needs men of his caliber. I am sure you are as proud of Mark's achievement as we are. Best wishes to you.

Sincerely,

B. B. STUBBS
Commander, U. S. Coast Guard

The second letter is more personalized and comes from the pen of a Master Chief Yeoman who was writing for a three-star (MC Charles E. Miller, Jr., mentioned in chapter 1). The master chief adjusts the style well to the level of the audience, several small children (their names have been changed from the original):

---

6 October 1994

Dear John, Freddy, Carol, and Stephi,

I wanted you to know how proud we are of your dad, who works for us here in the Bureau of Naval Personnel. Not only does he do a very good job every day but he also spent a lot of his own time, after work, putting together and watching over a group of 26 people during the trouble we had in Guantanamo, Cuba, last month. Because of your dad's hard work and careful planning, somebody from that group was always here to answer questions and solve problems for our Navy families in Cuba as they all got ready to leave. That wasn't a very easy job, but your dad rolled up his sleeves and made sure the job was done right.

Your dad did such a good job that I gave him a special award (called the Navy Achievement Medal) during a big ceremony here at the Bureau. I wish you could have been there.

Because your dad's in the Navy, that makes you special—but then, you always were and always will be special. I hope you'll come to visit the Bureau sometime, so you can see where your dad works. It would be great to meet you.

Your friend,

R. J. MURPHY
Vice Admiral, U.S. Navy

Master John L. Sailor
Master Freddy W. Sailor
Miss Carol B. Sailor
Miss Stephi A. Sailor
8222 Housing Place
Manassas, VA 22110

The third example is based on one written to a serviceman's parents in a difficult period (the 1970s). It does pretty well with a tough subject.

Dear Mr. and Mrs. A ———:

I am writing to inform you that your son John has petitioned the government for discharge as a conscientious objector.

Petitions such as John's are handled in a prescribed manner. First, John will be interviewed by a chaplain and Navy doctor, preferably a psychiatrist, if available. Then a lengthy, formal hearing will be conducted by an officer, usually a lieutenant commander, to consider the merits of the application. A final determination will be made by the Chief of Naval Personnel in Washington, D.C.

If successful in his petition, John will be discharged, but he will be ineligible for any veterans' benefits. If unsuccessful, he will be required to serve out the full term of his enlistment. As these cases require a substantial amount of documentation, it will be some months before a final decision is rendered. Additionally, I should point out that the burden of proving the case will be John's. He must show that the ethical convictions he holds have directed his life in the same manner as traditional religious convictions, and that the belief upon which the conscientious objection is based has been the primary controlling force in his life. Further, he must show that he gained his ethical convictions through training, study, contemplation, etc., comparable in rigor and dedication to the processes by which traditional religious convictions are formulated.

Until final resolution, John will be assigned duties other than those in the Electronics Technician rating for which he was trained. These duties will mostly consist of general cleanup and maintenance here at the naval facility.

I have talked with John at some length about the probabilities of success for his petition and about his driving philosophical outlook. In this day of an all-volunteer military, the success rate for this sort of petition is not very high. I am concerned about John because his strong aversion to participate in war (or, for that matter, even to assist a war effort) was present prior to his enlisting in the Navy. I find him a very confused young man who is frustrated with his present assignment as an Electronics Technician and quite upset with what the future holds for him. He does not appear to realize that his contract with the Navy was voluntary on his part and is a two-way one and that, to date, the Navy has completely made good its side. After reflecting on our conversation, I find John extremely idealistic and am doubtful that the world will ever be capable of meeting his expectations.

I hope this letter will assist you in understanding the process John will be undergoing. It is a difficult path he has chosen, and one that will require him to bare his soul if he is to be convincing at his hearing. If you have any questions, please write me.

Sincerely,

LETTER OF CONDOLENCE

Few will go through a career without the loss of a person in a unit—a friend, a shipmate, or a subordinate. The parents, spouse, and children may have very little to comfort them; sometimes a sincere letter that expresses what the loved one meant to another will be treasured. But expressions of insincerity may be worse than not being heard from at all.

—Navy Captain

If a service member has died and you must write to express your sympathy to a spouse, parents, or children, how do you go about it? There are no places for formulas here—no form letters, no canned phrases. Don't copy an example from a book, including this one. Anything that sounds insincere will be worse than writing nothing at all.

Express sympathy, sadness, or compassion. Say what you can say about the dead; say what you can in the way of sympathy with the living. You might mention the loss that shipmates feel. Perhaps the best guide is to search your own feelings and to remember your experiences with the person who has died. Reflecting on something you've shared with their loved one or something you know of the family might provide you a subject to speak on.

Be brief. Don't philosophize on the meaning of life and death; quote scripture or poetry *only if you know your particular audience will receive it well.* Service to country or shipmates might be appropriate subjects—or the service member's cheerfulness, dedication, good deeds. Use your best judgment. You might express your willingness to do whatever you can to help. Usually your own sympathy for the bereaved, your shared knowledge of their loved one, and your understanding of their pain are the chief expressions that might be of comfort.

Keep your tone familiar. Speak in the first person and use first names where appropriate. Show the letter to others, if you have any doubts, to see how what you have written strikes them. Sometimes chaplains can help with the writing. Pay particular care to the preparation of the letter, whether you type it or write in longhand. Keep the format simple; don't include a serial number or otherwise clutter the letter with bureaucratese.

Besides your letter there will probably be an official one from the command discussing funeral arrangements, shipping of personal effects, a command memorial service, and so on. The person who writes that letter will have to pay scrupulous attention to the accuracy of all of the details and should express sympathy too. But as a commander, leader, or friend, take the extra step of writing a personal letter. Don't mix up your genuine condolence with mere officialdom.

Some examples follow. First is an actual letter written by a lieutenant commander to an admiral with whom the younger officer had some official acquaintance. Although written over a half century ago, it still carries conviction on a difficult subject.

January 4th, 1935

Admiral Joseph M. Reeves, U.S.N.
USS Pennsylvania
San Pedro, California

Dear Admiral Reeves:

Mrs. Gallery and I send our deepest sympathy to you and Mrs. Reeves in the loss of your splendid boy. As the years go by, our chief interest is in our children. They make life worth living. They give us a new pleasure our earlier years never knew. We glory more in their success than in any that may have come to us. You have attained the highest place in the service, a place few indeed reach, but the promise of your boy gave you just pride and joy beyond any brought to you by the rewards gained by your brains and industry.

We understand what grief is yours. But know that we and your wide circle of friends grieve with you.

Yours truly,

Daniel V. Gallery, Jr.

Lieutenant Commander Gallery's presenting himself as a "friend" to such a senior officer may seem unusual. However, Gallery had a knack of gracefully dealing with very senior officers. While in flight training in the late 1920s, CAPT (later Fleet Admiral) Ernest J. King was in Gallery's aviation training squadron. During that short period, Gallery briefly got the famously dour King to crack a smile and even answer to the nickname "Ernie."

However, at the end of flight training, the Captain quickly reverted and became "E. J. King" once again (C. Herbert Gilliland and Robert Shenk, *Admiral Dan Gallery: The Life and Wit of a Navy Original* [Annapolis: Naval Institute Press, 1999], p. 44).

The second letter is a fictional passage from *Flight of the Intruder* (Naval Institute Press, 1986), in which LT Jake Grafton expresses his condolence to the wife of LT (jg) Morgan McPherson.

Jake began to write. After three drafts he had the semblance of an acceptable letter. It wasn't really acceptable, but it was the best he could manage. Two more drafts in ink gave him a letter he was prepared to sign.

Dear Sharon,

By now you have been notified of Morgan's death in action. He was killed on a night strike on a target in North Vietnam, doing the best he could for his country. That fact will never fill the emptiness that his passing leaves, but it will make him shine even brighter in my memory.

I flew with Morgan for over two years. We spent over six hundred hours together in the air. I knew him perhaps as well as any man can know another. We both loved flying and that shared love sealed our friendship.

Since I knew him so well, I am well aware of the depth of his love for you and Bobby and realize the magnitude of the tragedy of his passing. You have my deepest and most sincere sympathy.

Jake

Letters from those who have served with the person who has died can be uniquely valuable. The letter from which the paragraphs below were taken was written by the father of a young Marine to a columnist on the blog *Powerline;* the columnist published the letter on December 21, 2004. The writer points out the importance of friends and companions (rather than mere officials) writing letters to the family of a fallen serviceman.

If [our son] had been killed, we would have been first informed by a visit—in dress blues—from a condolence team typically consisting of two Marines and one Navy Chaplain. We know many families who've received that knock on the door. No letter is required. No words are required. A simple peek thru the view hole in the door and the sight of dress blue blouses, white covers, and white gloves tell you all you ever need to know. A letter of condolence from the SecDef is, honestly, not even worth opening. Families are much more interested in hearing from the men who served with their son and from their families. We share the constant knowledge and fear that it could be our door bell being rung. Sec. Rumsfeld doesn't know our son. He's a Lance Corporal. He directs a machine gun team. He is a vital link in the line that protects or way of life. He doesn't fight for his country, he doesn't fight for the SecDef, he doesn't even fight for his mom and dad. He fights for the guys on either side of him and for his team. He fights to secure his objective of the moment, which he may or may not understand or agree with. . . .

Don't get me wrong, we would appreciate the condolence letter from the SecDef, as well as one from the White House and from our Senator and Representative, from the Mayor and Governor. But none would bring back our son. And they are all form letters, signatures be damned. A letter from his 1st Sgt, [or] from the men we know in his unit would be a treasure and a comfort.

LETTER TO A NEW COMMAND

Good manners are never out of style.

—TRADITIONAL

"I wanted to know whether the new officers were married and/or prior enlisted so I could assign an appropriate sponsor. A married person would get a married sponsor; a prior enlisted of 32 years of age would not get a 21-year-old."

—COMMANDER

"Never tell the ship what you DON'T want; but rather, 'I'd love to be a gunnery officer.'"

—COMMANDER, USN

A type of business letter sometimes taught in senior enlisted or officer indoctrination classes is the letter to a new command. New ensigns or second lieutenants will often slave over their first such letters feverishly but later either will not spend much time on them or will fail to send them at all. Don't make that mistake; write a letter each time you transfer to a new command, and craft each letter with special care.

Such a letter is not just a courtesy but serves several distinct purposes. To start with, it alerts a ship or other station to the pending arrival of someone's relief. Normally, the command will have already heard through the personnel system of an assignment. However, even if they know your name, they usually won't have much information on your specific qualifications, background, or interests. Nor will they necessarily know anything about your family status, your need for knowledge of the area (for housing, schools, etc.), or your plans for leave and arrival dates.

If you can fill in your future senior and shipmates on this kind of information, it may help them fit you into billets, ensure for a contact relief, arrange an appropriate sponsor to help you find housing, and so on. They might be able to schedule various kinds of helpful temporary duty, if you give them enough information. Moreover, by penning such a letter, both officers and enlisted can create positive first impressions. Not long ago, a Navy lieutenant with orders to CINCLANTFLT Staff sent a short letter to the admiral, a letter very well crafted and professional in appearance. The letter impressed the deputy, who sent it on to his boss. The admiral responded: "I want to meet this lieutenant when he comes in. Give this officer an arrival call." This lieutenant's letter set him on a fast track.

Realize, however, that a letter can backfire if it is not well conceived. The commander of an aircraft squadron sent a message to another squadron, where he knew there was a young officer who had orders to his own command. The informal message read something like this:

TO LTJG SMITH: WELCOME ABOARD. VIOLA SENDS.

The young officer wrote back, and his response was quickly admired by all those with whom he would soon be working, something he probably would not have appreciated. Why not? The opening of his written response was

Dear Commander Sends: I'm looking forward to coming to your command. . . .

Clearly, here as elsewhere, it's often a good idea to have your drafts reviewed before you send them on.

Although emails may serve instead of letters in such correspondence (and often do), a letter is a bit more formal than an email, and is a bit less likely to be overlooked in the hundred-plus emails that a commanding officer typically receives each day.

The first example below is a fictional letter from a Navy ROTC graduate to his very first command.

1265 Kentucky St.
Lawrence, Kansas 66044
913-843-xxxx
cquinn@emailprovider.com
June 22, 2007

Commander Robert Jones, USN
Commanding Officer
USS Nitze (DDG 94)
FPO . . . .

Dear Commander Jones:

I recently received orders to the USS *Nitze*. I'm delighted to be assigned a fine destroyer like yours and greatly look forward to reporting aboard.

I will graduate from the University of Kansas in late July and am scheduled to report to Surface Warfare Officers School the first of September. While at Kansas I have been rush chairman, vice president and president of my fraternity chapter (Phi Gamma Delta), and captain of the fraternity's flag football team. I also sang in the University Concert Chorale, captained a quiz bowl team, and am a member of Sachem honor society. As you probably know, my major is history and I am minoring in English. In the NROTC unit here at Kansas, I was company officer my senior year; I had summer training on the USS *John C. Stennis* (CVN-74) and USS *Lassen* (DDG -82).

Just after graduation I will be getting married to Jeannette Ralph in Liberty, Missouri. Jeannette graduated from the University of Kansas in May and has done a good deal of work as a technical writer. We enjoy swimming, scuba diving, and biking.

I realize that the billet to which you assign me must be based primarily on need. However, my preference would be a first billet in either Operations or Weapons.

Thanks for the information you have sent me. However, it does not appear that I will be able to take advantage of your offer to visit the *Nitze* until after reporting to SWOS. If my plans change, I will let you know.

You can reach me at the above email address at any time till my reporting date. Also, I will continue to receive mail at the Lawrence address until leaving for SWOS in late August.

Very Respectfully,

Charles Quinn,
Midshipman First Class, U.S. Naval Reserve

The following letter is based on one written by a Coast Guard lieutenant commander to his prospective CO. Like the letter above, it includes important information that the command ought to know. But it's a bit more informal because the writer has met the commander before.

April 2, 1982

Dear Commander Yeaton,

As you know, I am under orders to be your executive officer. I am extremely pleased with these orders and look forward to serving in DAUNTLESS.

My previous afloat experience has been in USCGC WACHUSETT (WHEC 44), USCGC RUSH (WHEC 723), and USS HAROLD E. HOLT (FF 1070), all on the West Coast. This will be my first time in the Seventh District, and I can't wait!

I expect to detach from my present assignment on 1 July and report about mid-August. I cannot attend the Shipboard Helicopter Training Course at Mobile since its convening date conflicts with the PXO course. Unfortunately, that is the only week the course is offered. I have already passed the Rules of the Road test.

Patricia and Spenser are as excited about moving as I am. I suspect it's because Disney World is so close. Our baby, Joan, is too young to know. Once again, I am very happy with my orders and enthusiastically look forward to serving in DAUNTLESS.

Sincerely,

Harlan B. Badger
Lieutenant Commander, USCG

Commander H. Yeaton, USCG
Commanding Officer
USCGC DAUNTLESS (WMEC 624)
U.S. COAST GUARD BASE
MIAMI BEACH, FL 33139

Incidentally, the format shown in the Coast Guard letter above (with date centered at the top, comma after the salutation, address at the bottom left, no serial number, etc.) is known as personal correspondence format. This format is typically used by flag officers (and sometimes their aides, as was the case here) on personal flag stationery.

LETTER OF RECOMMENDATION OR REFERENCE

Very commonly, a commander, division officer, or chief will have to write a letter of recommendation to a corporation or school outside of the Navy. Someone may have retired or left the service and asked for a letter. Also, several naval programs exist that pay for an individual to attend a civilian college or training program that prepares them for further naval service. To gain entry into a civilian school the individual will have to ask for several letters of recommendation.

There's no mystery about writing letters of recommendation—all professionals have to do it. A writer should usually speak to the qualities being looked for in a specific program or profession, and in speaking to your knowledge of the individual, you may also want to mention the significance of your own credentials. In general, remember to translate military details into civilian terms, pointing out the importance of accomplishments or duties to one's reader that might not be clear to someone lacking naval experience.

The following letter was written for a naval officer applying for graduate study in engineering at the University of Florida. The author does well in making clear why the young officer is likely to succeed at graduate work—although much of what is said also pertains to the officer's likely success in his future naval career (also important). (Note: Ideally the drafter of such a letter would search out *the actual name* of the person to whom he is writing and would address that person, not "Dear Sir/Madam.")

22 January 2002

University of Florida
Civil and Coastal Engineering Dept.
124 Yon Hall
Gainesville, FL 32611

Dear Sir/Madam,

LTJG Charles Engineer carries my strongest personal recommendation for admission into your graduate school program. I have been his Commanding Officer for nearly two years, during which time he consistently exceeded my expectations.

LTJG Engineer is an intelligent and highly motivated Naval Officer who displays exceptional maturity and an inherent ability to lead. He gained my utmost confidence during his independent position as Officer in Charge of 26 enlisted personnel during a seven-month deployment to an isolated island over 1,500 miles away from my location. While deployed, he was engaged in two major construction projects that provided essential housing and quality of life improvements for the local population.

I recognized Charles early as a "quick study" and someone who easily retains large amounts of information relevant to his assigned duties. He completes all tasks on time and has uncanny attention to detail. Charles' ability to effectively prioritize large workloads and routinely produce creative solutions to complex problems suggest to me that he would be a proactive, competent student in a research-based program.

His Bachelor of Science in Ocean Engineering and his ability to work through tough, stressful situations provide a firm foundation capable of completing the most demanding Graduate School curriculum. His intense enthusiasm for ocean-related study is evident in his recent successful application into the Navy's Ocean Facilities Program. When he completes graduate school, Charles Engineer will be one of only a few Ocean Engineers providing valuable expertise to the Navy on countless coastal and ocean-related facilities.

Finally, as a Florida alumnus, I can assure you that he will continue to represent our fine institution with distinction.

Sincerely,

A. J. ENGINEER
CDR, CEC, USN

The fact that the commander signing the letter is an alum of the university to which he is writing is an interesting touch. Depending on the circumstances (say, if the commander had studied in the same school or remembers some of the professors there), even more might be made of this connection.

The document that follows is a character reference sent to an office *within* the Navy (which is perhaps why the drafter chose memo rather than letter format). The memo deals with a fellow officer's request for a security clearance. In this case, there had been some confusion of citizenship, and apparently the officer had been misled by a recruiter to take a shortcut of some kind—which had backfired. Of course, failure to get a security clearance would effectively end an officer's naval career, so this matter was quite important.

08 February 2005

MEMORANDUM

From: LCDR R. A. Ducent, USN
To: Personnel Security Appeal Board

Subj: CHARACTER REFERENCE ICO LT GEORGE R. APPEALING, USN

Ref: (a) DOD 5200.2-R

I have known LT George Appealing since I returned from deployment in January 2003. As squadron-mates we have interacted both professionally and off duty on a daily basis since then. In addition to evaluating his tactical performance while I was a squadron tactical instructor, I have also observed his general professionalism as a Naval Officer and Aviator.

LT Appealing is dedicated to his profession and has achieved every qualification commensurate with his time in the Navy. Despite the uncertainty and frustration created by the ongoing appeal process, he continues to show this dedication as Division Officer for Detachment Two. I can confirm that he is a man of integrity.

I have observed his dedication to his family at numerous times both on and off duty. This is not irrelevant. Loyalty to family is a character trait that extends to other areas of life.

Reference (a) Sec. C.2 states that the standard for access to classified information or assignment to sensitive duties is: "The person's loyalty, reliability, and trustworthiness are such that entrusting the person with classified information or assigning the person to sensitive duties is clearly consistent with the interests of national security [and] there is no reasonable basis for doubting the person's loyalty to the Government of the United States." In my estimation, there is no reasonable basis for doubting LT Appealing's loyalty.

For your information, I am currently assigned to Helicopter Antisubmarine Squadron Light Four Six as Detachment Seven Officer-in-Charge. I have over 1,956 hrs of flight time in 5 different aircraft types. At HSL-48 I completed 2 deployments as well as serving as acting Squadron Weapons and Tactics Instructor, Safety Officer, and Quality Assurance Officer.

R. A. Ducent
LCDR USN

LETTER TO ANSWER A CONGRESSIONAL INQUIRY

Anyone with a 32-cent stamp can provoke a congressional inquiry.

—Marine Corps General

A special kind of letter that virtually all commands must write sooner or later is the response to a congressional inquiry. Being able to write such a letter quickly and fluently is obviously a very important skill, and not just for senior officers. Commands of all sizes can receive such letters, and they must respond in very short order. While the final letter is usually honed by the XO or CO, a senior enlisted person or a junior officer could be assigned the first draft.

The Typical Situation

Most congressional inquiries to commands outside Washington, D.C., have to do with personnel. Ships' captains or unit commanders will not have to defend large issues of naval policy to members of Congress. Instead, they will normally have to handle inquiries about particular individuals' complaints.

Perhaps a Sailor has been turned down for the Navy diving program and has written a letter of complaint to his local congressman about that refusal. A petty officer may have complained to her representative about not being able to strike for a particular rating, or a Marine may have written his senator, contending that he hasn't received the correct pay.

In such cases, a congressional staffer will send a letter of inquiry either directly to the service member's command or the Navy Office of Legislative Affairs (OLA) or Marine Corps Headquarters, which will then write to the command. (BUPERS alone gets many hundreds of congressional inquiries each year.) Sometimes the complaint originally sent to the member of Congress is vague, emotional, and clouded in perception. Indeed, the service member may not even have been the prime mover in the letter's being written. A spouse or parent may have convinced the Sailor to write and may even have ghostwritten the letter.

Whatever the circumstances of the service member's writing, the senator or representative normally is simply asking for information with which to respond to the complaint. True, such correspondence can have great visibility. But typically the Washington official simply needs some perspective as to the problem, and the ship or station need not be on the defensive.

In nine out of ten cases, all that has to be done is to fill in all the missing information and the command's perspective, to give the Congress member what he or she needs for a reply.

Follow a few simple rules when receiving a congressional inquiry (typically abbreviated "CONGRINT," signifying that someone in the U.S. Congress—either the House or Senate—has "interest" in the matter at hand). Follow the same procedures when receiving a letter of inquiry from the White House—people write the President too, and the same kind of response is required. The situations considered here are mainly the most common, those involving personnel—but with only slight modifications the guidelines below will apply to other cases too.

Respond Quickly

After receiving a letter, the Congress member's staff has to write to the naval command. When it gets the letter, the naval command must investigate and write back to the Congress member; then the staff must write back to the constituent. (If there is an intermediate step via a liaison office in Washington, D.C., even more time is lost.) You can see that *months* could easily elapse were each stage not executed quickly. The rule is for a command to respond within five workdays of receipt of the inquiry (respond with an "interim" reply within forty-eight hours if you anticipate not being able to respond within five days). Many commands get most of their "final" replies out within *a day* of receipt.

Be Factual

Research the facts and then lay out in order the actions that both sides have taken—as well as the rationale behind the command's actions. If the problem is a long-standing one, a history of actions on the ship's or unit's part may exist, and you can catalog those actions. Often the XO and CO have been involved with the issue before and

"In writing for the signature of the President (who represents all Americans), any position you take—on women in combat, or whatever—can be seen as a position statement—as the position of the President himself on the subject.

"So you have to be very careful. Often the best thing to do is to find previous correspondence on the same subject that has been blest and approved—and paraphrase that."

—Lieutenant Commander, assigned to write letters on behalf of SECNAV and the President

will have lots of information on hand. Maybe the division officer has recorded some information in a division officer's notebook, or perhaps someone has written a memo for record about a particular Sailor's request or complaint or about a key counseling session. The files may contain past inquiries on the same or similar topics.

Whatever the situation, *be accurate, research and re-research the facts,* and *be sure of what you're writing.*

Explain the Command's Perspective

A Sailor may have written out of concern for his rights. The command certainly respects those rights, but it is also the custodian of the service's rights—the Sailor's obligations. Usually those obligations will not have been spelled out in the original letter. The Congress member will want to see the command's perspective on *all sides* of the issue.

To show that perspective in full, you may need to explain some key regulations or procedures, and also to outline exactly what violations of procedures may have occurred. Don't overexplain. Your correspondent is usually a very busy person who may handle more congressional inquiries in a day than your command does in a year. But remember to delineate the service-specific information needed to understand this particular problem.

Start with the facts, and proceed to explain the rationale for the command's actions. As you write, account as best you can for the service member's point of view and feelings. Admit forthrightly any mistakes that the command has made. Being straightforward, evenhanded, unemotional, and factually oriented are good ways to keep the tone right, to shun being overly defensive on the one hand and to avoid negative attitudes toward a service member on the other.

Incidentally, don't hide the matter from the implicated Sailor or Marine. Instead, tell the service member that you have received the congressional inquiry and that you plan to respond.

Try Seeing the Problem from the Congress Member's Point of View

The member of Congress will, of course, want to do whatever he or she can to address the service member's valid concerns. How can you aid the Congress member in that task? Here's one way: quite often, whether a complaint is justified or not, all the means for redressing that complaint within the service have not been exhausted. You can be very helpful by explaining to the Congress member exactly what the service member's options are, including the service member's very next move. Moreover, you might be able to provide a point of contact (with phone number) or send along forms the service member may need to pursue a further option, thus giving the member of Congress *specific aid* in responding helpfully to the original complaint.

Write in Civilian

Be careful not to confuse your reader with naval jargon or acronyms. Switch gears, step back a bit, and speak to an intelligent civilian, not a service member. Explain any acronyms you must use, but try to do without them. Use civilian-style dates (month-day-year) in the heading and throughout the letter. But mainly, try to write as if you were talking *face to face* with the individual to whom you're writing.

Check with the Right People to Review the Situation

Occasionally, the command may need to consult a naval lawyer, officers up the chain of command, or the respective office that handles legislative liaison in Washington,

D.C. Again, sometimes congressional inquiries will come via the Washington office in the first place, and a ship or unit will be asked to respond to that office instead of writing directly to the Congress member. (This procedure is standard in the Marine Corps; it is somewhat less standard for Navy units, which most often have to write the member of Congress directly.)

Once you have written your response, have it reviewed by your command's writing experts. Should anyone look at it beyond the command? Aboard a ship or squadron, although a commanding officer is often required to let the commodore know you have received a congressional inquiry, there is usually no formal requirement that the correspondence be routed through the group or squadron staff. Still, on sensitive issues, a prudent commander will ask if the boss wants to see a draft before it's sent out.

In the Marine Corps, normally a command's Office of the Inspector will prepare the smooth draft from the information it is given. In addition, as mentioned above, almost all responses are sent via the Congressional Inquiry Section of Headquarters, Marine Corps rather than going directly to the member of Congress from the command. Whatever the process, the responsible officer should ask to see a copy of the smooth draft before it leaves the command. That way he or she can make sure no errors have been made and can check to make sure the inspector's drafter has not taken too much license with the facts provided.

Get the Details Right

- Be sure to address the Congress member correctly:
  — Senator = "Dear Senator [last name]:"
  — Congress [man/woman] = "Dear Mr./Mrs./Ms./Miss [last name]:" (for a congresswoman, use "Ms." if in doubt)
  — Chairman or Chairwoman = "Dear Mr. Chairman:" or "Dear Madam Chairman:"
  See Appendix B of the Correspondence Manual for a comprehensive description of inside addresses and salutations.
- Normally begin a letter to a member of Congress with a thank-you phrase, such as "Thank you for your letter of February 21 concerning Petty Officer November's pay problem." This first thank-you paragraph serves the same function as subject and reference lines in a from-to letter. By stating here the subject the letter will discuss, the date of the Congress member's letter, and the constituent's name, you help the congressional staff to find the right file.
- Write the letter in *business-letter* style. (Some commands prefer you use a comma rather than a colon after the salutation.)
- Enclose an additional courtesy copy along with the original when you send it to the member of Congress.
- Navy commands replying directly to the Congress member are required to send a blind copy of the final reply and copies of all substantive interim replies to the Office of Legislative Affairs in Washington, D.C., and to the Bureau of Naval Personnel (PERS-3Q).

Example: Letter to a Congresswoman

Below is a fictionalized letter to a congresswoman. The congresswoman had inquired about the serviceman's loss of leave and asked why he had not been allowed to re-enlist, despite his receiving an honorable discharge. The person upon whose behalf Congresswoman Capitol has inquired is addressed as "Mr." in the letter since he is no longer in the Navy. (Note that current policies or regulations concerning illegal drug use may differ from those outlined below.)

LETTERHEAD STATIONERY

March 15, 2000

The Honorable Dorothy Capitol
House of Representatives
Washington, D.C. 20515

Dear Mrs. Capitol:

Thank you for your letter of March 10, 2000, concerning Mr. Charles Sailor's discharge from the Navy due to marijuana use.

Some details of Mr. Sailor's case may help clarify the circumstances of his discharge. The urine sample he submitted on June 18, 1999, tested positive for tetrahydrocannabinol (THC). The Navy Drug Testing Laboratory used radioimmunoassay for the initial sample screening and gas chromatography for confirmation. These tests yield results in which we have high confidence, with no false positives in over three years of quality-control testing.

After initially exercising his right for court-martial, Mr. Sailor changed his mind and requested his case be heard at a nonjudicial hearing under Article 15 of the Uniform Code of Military Justice. I found that he had committed the offense of illegal drug use with which he was charged, and I awarded punishment. Mr. Sailor did not exercise his right to appeal this punishment.

Care for due process and granting Mr. Sailor's requests, including a polygraph examination that he terminated prematurely, resulted in an adjudication period of July 1 to October 13, 1999. This period is longer than usual but is still within the 120 days required by the Manual for Courts Martial. During this period I did not allow Mr. Sailor to take leave because he was in a disciplinary status. (My command policy is not to grant leave to individuals awaiting disciplinary action, placed on restriction, or serving extra duty unless an emergency or hardship is involved.) As required by statute, Mr. Sailor lost all accrued leave in excess of 60 days at the beginning of the fiscal year.

We retested Mr. Sailor for drug use two days prior to his October 22 discharge, and his urine sample again tested positive for THC. We did not receive the results until after his discharge and therefore took no further action. Although he received an honorable discharge, we assigned an RE-4 (not recommended) reenlistment code because of drug use, in accordance with Navy policy.

Mr. Sailor has the right to petition the Board for the Correction of Naval Records (BCNR) regarding his reenlistment code and loss of accrued leave. I am enclosing the necessary forms should he desire to do so. We established the BCNR for the purpose of reviewing naval records and correcting possible injustices.

If I may be of further assistance, please let me know.

Sincerely,

L. N. OFFICER
Commanding Officer

Enclosure

Comments on This Letter

- The letter adduces strong evidence supporting the reasons for the "not recommended" reenlistment code, and it explains the apparent discrepancies clearly (honorable discharge but not recommended to reenlist; seemingly unjust loss of leave).
- The letter sketches the main details of the chronology, without going into every detail.
- The writer adds credibility by citing "three years of quality-control testing" (which suggests that the Navy is attuned to the possibilities of injustice) and by citing Navy rules (the assignment of a "not recommended" enlistment code; the statute on loss of accrued leave).
- The discussion of rights and of the ex-serviceman's logical next step manifests the command's concern for the individual's rights. Including the forms is also helpful.
- Overall, the letter is to the point, factual, and relatively brief.

Some Other Examples

Here are some passages from similar letters, illustrating various tacks you may want to take in a particular case.

Write to Explain the History of Events

We approved Petty Officer Unitas's request to work in Public Works at Naval Station, Long Beach, in the hope that he could receive better training and be more productive in a large, maintenance-oriented organization. However, he was apprehended in an attempted theft of government gasoline, and for this action he was subsequently awarded punishment at nonjudicial punishment ("Captain's Mast"). Because of this incident and his generally poor professional reputation, the Naval Station Public Works Officer disapproved his temporary transfer.

Petty Officer Smith's request for humanitarian reassignment certainly deserves consideration; however, until I received your letter of January 6, 1994, neither I nor anyone else in my chain of command was aware of his desires. He had not discussed humanitarian reassignment with his superiors, nor had he forwarded any written request for consideration. Petty Officer Smith has since stated that he wrote to you after discussing this issue with another shipmate (who is not in his chain of command) because his shipmate didn't feel that the request would be favorably endorsed.

Write to Explain How a Specific Policy Applies to an Individual's Situation

The 4th Marine Division's policy gives commanders authority to reduce Marines in grade administratively because of unexcused absences. The unit commander sent to Lance Corporal Doubletree via certified mail a letter of intent to reduce him in grade. That letter informed the service member that he had 20 days to respond to his officer in charge about the unexcused absence allegations, but he made no attempt in that period to appeal the reduction. Lance Corporal Doubletree was then reduced to his present grade.

Write to Explain What Options the Service Member Has Not Yet Pursued

Petty Officer Threefoot is not eligible for normal reassignment until March 1996. Until then he may consider a self-negotiated exchange of duty with another Sailor of identical paygrade and specialty who would like an assignment to Alaska. We have the necessary information if he is interested in pursuing this option.

Write to Explain the Command's Perspective

I wish to reiterate that we have made a concerted attempt to train Petty Officer Quarterman to perform satisfactorily at the first class petty officer level. However, he must be prepared to dedicate a large amount of effort to self-study and to learning the basic tenets of leadership if he is to pursue a successful naval career.

Write to Set the Facts Straight

We process enlisted performance evaluations through the division officer, department head, and executive officer; then they are signed by the commanding officer. Each level of leadership thoroughly examined Petty Officer Quintilla's performance record as did a review board of chief petty officers. He was, in fact, ranked as the worst 2nd class petty officer in this command, and his performance was judged unsatisfactory. Despite Petty Officer Quintilla's assertions to the contrary, he is the only Seabee to receive an unsatisfactory performance evaluation during my 20 months of command.

Checklist for Preparing Answers to Congressional Inquiries

Technical Details

- Have you written this response in business-letter format, omitting the originator's code and the letter serial?
- Have you double checked the addressee and address?
  — Did you use "The Honorable"? Have you addressed a Committee Chair properly?
  — Is the ZIP code correct?
- Is the salutation correct?
- Is the letter's opening stated properly?
- Have you included extra copies, as required?
- Have you checked for unnecessary jargon or acronyms?

The Substance

- Does the letter get to the point, stating the basic response right after the thank-you sentence?
- If the letter cites a chronology, does that chronology run smoothly and completely? Is the explanation sharp and pointed, rather than rambling?
- Is the letter fair to the service member, and does it also *appear* to be fair? Does it avoid a defensive tone?
- Is the letter fair to the needs of the service?
- If mistakes have been made, have you stated them forthrightly and apologized or stated future compensatory action, as appropriate?
- Does the letter raise any issues it doesn't have to raise?
- Does the letter obligate the service to do something? If so, have you checked to make sure that the service both *can* and will do it?
- Have you given the member of Congress sufficient perspective?
- Finally, does the letter answer all the Congress member's inquiries?

Memos

I wrote lots of memos as an XO and as a Department Head—but I seldom put "Memorandum" at the top of one. It's my style to understate and be less formal. I was

afraid to put "memo" at the top for fear of scaring my
subordinates (or boss) into thinking my notes were
always recorded to hang them with later.
Sometimes I did write (or type) "Memorandum"
—I was sure they'd read that one.

—Navy Commander

Memoranda range from brief notes to vital policy initiatives, and of course many modern emails are essentially memos. They are mainly for internal use aboard staffs and operational commands but can occasionally be used externally, between commands.

A preprinted form or a plain-paper memorandum is the least formal memo and is often handwritten. A memorandum on ship or station letterhead is about the same in structure but is somewhat more formal and can be sent from one activity to another (routine business only). A special memorandum is a memo for record, by which you record information that might otherwise be lost. It has wide potential usefulness—and could be used much more than it is. The memorandum-for is the most formal of all memoranda and is arguably the most important.

One other kind of memorandum, the briefing memo, is widely used on staffs in briefing folders. The chapter "Staff Writing" discusses the briefing memo, for staffs use it much more than anyone else.

Become familiar with all the formats and uses of memos, especially the common ones. Realize that although the Correspondence Manual does not so specify, common naval usage in the past was to add a complimentary close to many informal memos. That is, a senior would often close with "Respectfully" or "R" before signing or initialing a memo to a junior or someone of the equivalent rank, and a junior would pen "Very Respectfully" or "VR" before his or her signature when writing to a senior. This custom is not as widespread as it once was but still holds force in many circumstances.

THE INFORMAL MEMO
Below is guidance on an informal memo.

MEMORANDUM   10 January 1997

From: Writer's name, title or code
To: Reader's name, title or code

Subj: KEY POINTS ABOUT WRITING AN INFORMAL MEMO

1.   Plan Ahead. Whether using a preprinted form or a plain-paper memorandum, don't write thoughtlessly. Always plan out a memo; at least jot down a few points and then organize them before writing. On complicated matters, write up a full outline. A few seconds spent in planning will help make the writing go quickly and the correspondence effective.

2.   Get to the Point Quickly. Craft the subject line to state the essential matter briefly, and elaborate on your main point in the first paragraph. Normally, keep your memo to one page.

3.   Remember Your Audience; Watch Tone. Figure out, in light of your audience and purpose, what tone to adopt. Tone can be especially important in informal memos because memos are often very personal.

4. <u>Use Formatting as Needed</u>. Formatting helps in memos as in many other kinds of writing. Examples of such formatting include:

    a. Lists (in a, b, c order or in bullets).
    b. Headings (as in this memo).
    c. Occasional <u>underlining</u>, *italics*, **boldface,** or ALL CAPS.

5. <u>Remember These Shortcuts</u>. Very informal memos can be penned, and you need not keep a file copy if the matter is insignificant or short-lived. You can sign a memorandum without an authority line.

T. X. AUTHOR

Here's an informal memo on a routine matter, written in appropriately informal style.

---

20 February 1993

MEMORANDUM

From: Admin Officer
To: Department Heads

Subj: LETTERS OF DESIGNATION

1. There are numerous requirements laid on by this command and higher authorities to "designate in writing" individuals to perform certain tasks/responsibilities/accountabilities. It would behoove us to know exactly who all these folks are and "track 'em."

2. I'm requesting that each department review its working instructions, CVWR-30, and higher instructions (such as 4790.2) and forward a list of all such requirements to Admin NLT Friday, 28 February.

3. Admin will collate your responses into a notice, and we will thus be assured that all requirements to designate are met.

P. D. BRADY

Memos can of course be used for many purposes. Below an officer uses memo format to record a counseling session with a chief petty officer. In this well-written memo, the officer details very specific directions on how the chief should proceed (implicitly setting the standards by which he will be evaluated).

---

31 March 2004

MEMORANDUM

From: Maintenance Officer
To: ADC Romeo

Subj: PERIODIC PERFORMANCE COUNSELING, 10 Oct 03—31 Mar 04

1. This counseling is being held to document your performance from 10 Oct 03 to 31 Mar 04. This is your first periodic counseling since joining the department. You have

---

DON'T TRY TO LEAD BY MEMO (OR EMAIL EITHER)

You're following a gutless path if you try to lead by memo. Don't use memos in lieu of face-to-face discussions. You can write lots of bad stuff in memos that will become *permanent in impact,* the reaction to which *you cannot control.* A commanding officer of a ship was losing faith in his XO and therefore directed that all their communications be in writing, not face to face. But that "solution" helped to create the problem, not deal with it. Remember the old lines—

Say it with flowers,
Say it with mink,
But never, no never, say it in ink.

Memos within a shipboard command should be seen primarily as records, not communications—and *never as leadership.*

—Navy Captain

---

done an excellent job of integrating yourself into the Quality Assurance division. In addition to the numerous qualifications you already possess, you have progressed well towards additional qualifications.

2.   Training. Your attention to detail and training competence are evident. Your actions played a vital role in preparations for and conduct of the very successful March 04 CNAL AMMTI. As for the future:

   a.   I have counseled ATCS Murphy to work closely with you so that you learn the techniques and methods that he uses in the Quality Assurance process. You should be able to perform the bulk of his missions within 6 months. Obviously at least half the effort here will be yours.

   b.   Continue to train QARs and Detachment CDQARs with the objective of having others perform tasks except those which you are specifically required or uniquely qualified to perform.

   c.   Emphasize practical evaluations during DMPA and Weekly Maintenance training. Try to drive the training away from simple reading of written material. When able, personally oversee training for quality. I recommend you use CNAL AMMTI team technique where practical results drive the focus on program evaluation.

   d.   As you are the AVGFE, I expect you to maintain a flawless Aviation Gas Free program that is inspection ready at any time.

   e.   Quals: Safe for Flight within the next 30 days.

3.   Leadership. As an individual who went from E-5 to Chief in three years, you can provide lots of leadership to the First Class Petty Officers in the department. Use and create opportunities to influence and instruct them.

4.   You are a vital part of this department. You are a QAS in training and should see yourself that way. In addition, use your specific experience to lead the First Class POs.

Q. A. Officer

THE MEMO FOR RECORD

Do you want to ensure some key information is recorded, but are you afraid that because of the informal circumstances in which it came up, it won't be? Then pen a memorandum for the record (or memo for record or MFR).

The information might be from a meeting, a telephone conversation, or an informal discussion held on a staff. You can use the memo for record to record an agreement among several parties at a conference, or to record decisions made at decision briefings. The memo for record resembles the minutes of a meeting in some respects—and can be used for minutes—but is more the gist of the meeting than a formal set of minutes.

On a ship, in a squadron, or in a field unit, the memo for record can also be effective. Use it to document an informal investigation and its results or an important counseling session conducted with a subordinate along with the factors that led to the counseling. (Note, however, that some commands prefer to record such formal counseling in a letter of instruction. See pp. 42–45). Another common use of memos for record is to document information from a phone call or from the informal discussion that an investigator conducts in the process of a JAGMAN Investigation.

Usually you file a memo for record for future reference, but you can route it to your staff if everyone needs to know the information it contains. Staff officers can forward memos for record up the chain to keep seniors informed of what's happening down below.

Whatever you use it for, keep this memo informal. It's an in-house document, to help keep track of business. Do remember to sign and date it, but always keep it easy to use.

The example of a memo for record below is fictional, but it is based on MFRs that were used as exhibits in a JAGMAN Investigation. It documents a discussion that the investigating officer had with an expert about funds that had been stolen from a postal safe. Specifically, the officer wanted to know who had been assigned the responsibility for the safe's security.

---

11 August 2004

MEMORANDUM FOR RECORD

From: LT J. R. BLACK, USNR, Investigating Officer

Subj: RESPONSIBILITY FOR CHANGE OF POSTAL SAFE COMBINATIONS ON USS OVERHAUL (FFG 999)

1.   On 10 August 2004 I discussed this investigation with PCC Gray of the COMCENT-GULF Postal Assist Team. Specifically, I asked PCC Gray what the responsibility of the postal officer in this case would have been. He said that a postal officer must oversee the entire postal operation of the command. Therefore, ENS Brown did have a duty to make sure safe combinations were changed. However, he also pointed out that ENS Brown's responsibility was oversight only, and that the primary responsibility for changing the combinations remained that of the Custodian of Postal Effects (COPE) aboard USS OVERHAUL, that is, PC2 White.

J. R. BLACK

Clearly, it is important that such a discussion as is illustrated above be recorded right after the discussion takes place, and the memo for record provides a good way of doing that.

The next (again fictional) example is somewhat more formal than the one above. It resembles a memo for record that might be put out by an office in OPNAV or at another major staff. Rather than documenting information discovered in an investigation, here a division director sends cost figures on two major equipment procurements to individuals in the chain of command and to members of his own staff.

---

15 May 07

MEMORANDUM FOR THE RECORD

Subj: TARGET ANCHORS AND SALVO RETRIEVERS

1.   I have been asked the following questions by OP-88Z and by Mr. A. C. E. Shooter of SASC staff:

   a.   What are the quantity and funding profile for target anchors and salvo retrievers for FY 05 and prior through FY 07?

   b.   What would be the cost of 300 target anchors in FY 07?

2.   I provided the following information:

	FY 05 & Prior	FY 06	FY 07	FY 08
Target Anchors	150/$3.OM	300/$5.4M	400/$7M	50/$0.8M
Salvo Retrievers	250/$15M	400/$23M	550/$32M	800/$46M

The cost of 300 target anchors in FY 07 would be $4.8 million. The inventory objective for target anchors remains 1,500; the inventory objective for salvo retrievers is 3,000.

3.   This inquiry is probably the first of many on this subject. We should be consistent in our answers.

E. PREBLE
Director, Targeting Division

Copy to:
OP-OX
OP-OXA
OP-OXB

THE MEMORANDUM-FOR

Here is some guidance on the memorandum-for, common to OPNAV and other high-level staffs.

LETTERHEAD STATIONERY

5216
Ser 943D/345507
10 Jan 97

MEMORANDUM FOR THE DEPUTY CHIEF OF NAVAL OPERATIONS (OP-XX)

Subj: PROFESSIONAL PREPARATION OF THE MEMORANDUM-FOR—
       INFORMATION MEMORANDUM

Ref: (a) CNO Supplement to DON Correspondence Manual
       (b) HQMC Supplement to DON Correspondence Manual

1.   The memorandum-for is a very formal memorandum. Its normal use is to communicate with very senior officials such as the Secretary of Defense, the Secretary of the Navy, the Chief of Naval Operations, one of the Assistant Secretaries or Deputy Chiefs, or an Executive Assistant (EA) for any one of these officials.

2.   Take great care in the preparation of the memoranda-for. These documents have high visibility and require thorough staffing and tactful expression. Make sure each of them has:

— a subject line that best describes the memo's purpose;
— headings, if useful;
— brevity, always—normally keep the memorandum-for to *one page.*

3.   If you use tabs, be sure not to let those tabs substitute for good staffing. Do your best to pull the relevant information out of the references and weave it into your memorandum rather than asking a senior official to plow through the tabbed material.

4.   Protocol is important. List the addressees in the established order of precedence.

5.   Prepare the memorandum-for on letterhead stationery. Because it lacks a "From" line, show the signer's title below the typed name.

6.   Various offices have issued additional guidance on preparing this document. For example, the Secretary of Defense once asked that "ACTION MEMORANDUM" or "INFORMATION MEMORANDUM" be placed at the end of the subject line of each memorandum-for, and OPNAV offices have generally followed suit. See current versions of references (a) and (b) and other local information for up-to-date guidance.

J. MEMORANDUM
Deputy Chief of Naval Operations

"It is worth noting that the term 'memorandum' in no way lessens the formality of a document inside the Pentagon. Anything formal is a 'memorandum' and is treated the same as a formal naval letter is in the fleet."

—Pentagon staffer

Figure 2.8 is an example of an actual memorandum-for concerning a change of command at SURFLANT. Note the "Very Respectfully" complimentary close, and the "YES__ NO__" line at the bottom left. The latter is a very good staff device when all you want is a yes or no answer—the boss can give you the go-ahead with a simple stroke of the pen. See also the executive summary memorandum on page 99 for the version of a memorandum-for used in OPNAV as a briefing memorandum.

A document of the same family as the memorandum-for is a formal, multiple-address memorandum for a staff. This is usually called either a "MEMORANDUM FOR DISTRIBUTION" or a "MEMORANDUM FOR ALL HANDS (OP-XX STAFF)." See the "MEMORANDUM FOR THE OPNAV WRITER" on page 82.

Directives

Review your directives often. I made a policy of reviewing all my instructions within nine months of coming aboard, and in one case I was able to cut them down to a fifth *their original size. Once they had been made manageable in this way, I could insist my people knew what was in them.*

—Captain, USN

Figure 2.8 Memorandum-For. This memorandum was prepared for a change of command at SURFLANT.

DEPARTMENT OF THE NAVY

COMMANDER NAVAL SURFACE FORCE
UNITED STATES ATLANTIC FLEET
NORFOLK, VIRGINIA 23511-6292

4 December 1987

MEMORANDUM FOR VICE ADMIRAL _____

Via: N3 ____   O2 ____

Subj: CHANGE OF COMMAND HONORS

Encl: (1) OPNAVINST 1710.7 of JUL 79 (Change of Command Guidance)
        (2) OPNAVINST 1701.7 of JUL 79 (Change of Command Sample
            Program)
        (3) CNSL Change of Command 1982 SOE
        (4) CNSL Change of Command 1984 SOE

1.   The Navy Protocol Manual OPNAVINST 1710.7 indicates that each
principal should receive full arrival honors (gun salute for the
senior official).   Arrival honors for the principals have been
conducted differently for the last two CNSL Changes of Command.
In the 1982 version Admiral _____, VADM _____, and VADM
_____ each received full honors upon his independent arrival
(gun salute for ADM _____ only).   In 1984 VADMs _____ and
_____ received side honors only and awaited ADM _____'s
arrival on the quarterdeck; ADM _____ received full honors
(including gun salute).

2.   Separate full honors are required by Navy Regulations for the
relieved officer and the relieving officer at the hauling down
and breaking of each officer's respective flag.

3.   Enclosures (1) and (2) are highlighted excerpts of the Change
of Command section of the Protocol Manual.   Enclosures (3) and
(4) are the schedules for the previous two CNSL Changes of Command.

4.   Recommend that we proceed as last time: Side honors only
upon arrival of VADM _____ and RADM _____ and full honors
for ADM _____ and for hauling down and breaking of flags.

Very respectfully,

CDR, USN, NOOX

YES ____   NO ____

PLAIN ENGLISH ABOUT INSTRUCTIONS

State rules before exceptions.
Stress important points.
Choose exact words.
Say who does what.
Give examples for difficult ideas.
Divide processes into small steps.
Use headings, subparagraphs, parallel lists.
Answer likely questions.
Test your material.

—"Just Plain English,"
1995 Revision
Written in the Office of the CNO

"If you want to change things for the better of the Navy, put it in an instruction. In part, this is for pass-down-the-line purposes, and in part to make it formal aboard ship (or it will be lost). But also, by putting it in writing you move it up and give it the force of law. You emphasize it and preserve it for the next generation. Make it clear, and make it stand alone. The problem that was around as the genesis of the instruction will be completely forgotten three years hence—but will occur again!"

—Commander

Written directives—instructions and notices in the Navy, orders and bulletins in the Marine Corps—are even more vital in the armed services than in other big organizations because Sailors and Marines transfer from one outfit to another so often. But if directives are too dense, too long, or too complicated, they will not be read, and your people will "fly by the seat of their pants" instead of looking to the directives for guidance.

Unfortunately, a great many naval directives are verbose and very hard to read. One simple example will illustrate the problems with current directive writing. The following passage, the purpose paragraph from a sample instruction, was taken from a guide on how to write instructions and notices. This paragraph should have been an outstanding example of how to start off a directive. Instead, it is an example of how *not* to begin:

Purpose. To produce forth a guide by which originators may formulate instructions and notices following the provisions of references (a) and (b). This instruction covers the procedures that originators will carry out in writing directives in the Navy Directives System.

What's wrong with this paragraph?

- Both sentences say the same thing.
- Extra words abound, even within the sentences:
  — "the provisions of" could be omitted in the first sentence without loss.
  — "in the Navy Directives System" could be omitted in the second.
- Big words obscure simple ideas:
  — "To produce forth a guide" is an awkward way to say "to guide."
  — "formulate" is officialese for "write."
- In sum, all four lines could be condensed to *eight simple words:*

Purpose: To guide originators in writing directives.

In other ways, too, directives are often poorly written. As a result, either they are not read at all or they are not fully understood. Thus they do not govern action as they should. But there are ways to improve.

THE NAVY NOTICE AND THE MARINE CORPS BULLETIN

The Navy notice and the Marine Corps bulletin are distinct among directives in having *short-term authority.* Navy notices, for example, cannot remain in effect for longer than a year, and most last six months or less. Because of their relative impermanence, they are best used for one-time reports, temporary procedures, or short-term information. Otherwise, they have the same force as Navy instructions and Marine Corps orders. Below is a sample Navy notice that discusses how to write clear and usable directives.

"Our worst writing occurs in directive. We go to school to learn to make them hard to understand."

—NAVAL WRITING EXPERT, NAVAL ACADEMY

DEPARTMENT OF THE NAVY
USS EXAMPLE (DDG 14)
FPO AE xxxxx-xxxx

Canc: 8 Feb 95
EXAMPLENOTE 5215
10 Jan 95

USS EXAMPLE NOTICE 5215

From: Commanding Officer, USS EXAMPLE

Subj: HOW TO WRITE DIRECTIVES

Ref: (a) SECNAVINST 5215.1C-Directives Issuance System
         (b) MCO PS215.1—Marine Corps Directives System
         (c) Chap. 10 of OPNAVINST 3120.32B—"Unit Directives System"

1.   <u>Purpose</u>. To guide writers in composing directives (Navy instructions and notices, Marine Corps orders and bulletins) that will be *read and understood.* Writing so they will be *read at all is* the greatest challenge.

2.   <u>Action</u>. Here is brief guidance.

   a.   **Smother "Motherhood."** The reason so many directives are not read, or not read carefully, is that they take so long to get to the point. *Omit* most "Background," "Discussion," and "Policy" paragraphs.

   b.   **Proceed as soon as possible to "Action."** Experienced naval personnel read a directive in pretty much the same way: first they glance at the "Purpose" paragraph, and then they skip to "Action," even if this means skipping several *pages* of the directive. Condense most of your directives so that "Action" follows as soon after "Purpose" as possible.

   c.   **Designate Responsibilities by Individual.** In the "Action" paragraph, itemize exactly what each individual must do. Readers will take notice if they see specific responsibilities assigned to them.

   d.   **Use Inventive Paragraph Headings.** The only two paragraphs required for *all* directives are those for purpose and action. Standard paragraph headings like "Objectives," "Scope," and so on are not necessarily helpful. On the other hand, using more pointed titles (as illustrated here) can sometimes help the reader along.

   e.   **Get Attention by Using Typographic Techniques.** Nothing in references (a), (b), or (c) prohibits you from using modern typographic techniques, especially **bold face**

"Do not write an instruction if higher authority guidance suffices. Write local instructions only to clarify how higher directives impact your unit."

—COMMANDER

"Great discipline is required in writing instructions and notices. People often get hoisted by their own petard. They keep putting the paper out—then failing to do what they have told themselves to do!"

—NAVY CAPTAIN

and <u>underlining</u>, but also perhaps ALL CAPS or *italics*. Used sparingly, these techniques can also help you get the vital points across.

A. T. MAHAN

THE NAVY INSTRUCTION AND THE MARINE CORPS ORDER

Differing from notices and bulletins, instructions and orders are relatively *long-term*. They have continuing reference value or require continuing action. Since these directives are relatively permanent (more often revised than canceled or superseded), they govern most major administrative efforts within naval commands. If we don't write them well, our units, programs, and communities will suffer.

Again, as in the case of notices and bulletins, drafting a good "Action" paragraph is the central skill. "Discussion should be brief; Action is the key; and action must be indicated by *job title* or *billet*," as a commander pointed out. Learn to draft brief and effective instructions or orders; start by reading the sample Navy instruction below.

DEPARTMENT OF THE NAVY
USS EXAMPLE (DDG 14)
FPO AE xxxxx-xxxx

EXAMPLEINST 5215.2
ADMIN: res
10 Jan 96

<u>USS EXAMPLE INSTRUCTION 5215.2B</u>

From: Commanding Officer, USS EXAMPLE

Subj: WRITING THE "ACTION" PARAGRAPH AS A "TASKING" DEVICE

1. <u>Purpose</u>. To guide instruction writers in composing the "Action" sections of directives: the best course is to *allocate each task to a specific billet.*

2. Cancellation. EXAMPLEINST 5215.2A is hereby superseded.

3. <u>Rationale.</u> Specifying detailed assignments to individuals in a directive (as in the "Action" paragraph below) does several things:

   a. **It gets the attention of readers,** who will learn to look for their responsibilities in the "Action" paragraph. A three-page instruction suddenly becomes readable if, in effect, all you have to read is the "Purpose" statement and one "Action" paragraph directed specifically at you.

   b. **It makes drafters do all the vital spade work.** Assigning specific tasking by billet forces a writer to articulate general principles into specific responsibilities. It helps our people to think through and specify in full detail how policies or programs will be made to work.

4. <u>Action</u>. Take action as outlined below:

   a. The **Executive Officer** will ensure that all shipboard directives embody "tasking sections by billet," as appropriate to their content.

   b. **Department Heads** will supervise the training of their junior people in writing directives with good "tasking" paragraphs.

EXCERPTS FROM CLEAR, READABLE BATTLE ORDERS

A special kind of directive is a set of battle orders. Obviously, it is *extremely* important that these be written well (and be well conceived, too). The CO who wrote the battle orders from which the excerpts below are taken not only took care with his writing, but he then discussed his orders with each division on his ship to make sure his points got across.

It is worth noting, by the way, that these battle orders were written (and published in an earlier edition of this book) long before the destructive attack on the USS *Cole,* for which incident 6c below seems almost predictive.

6. COMMANDING OFFICER'S PHILOSOPHIES FOR FIGHTING THE SHIP. The following are a compendium of my battle philosophies.

   a. EXPECT A "COME AS YOU ARE WAR." In spite of the best advance warnings, in spite of the best logistics support, in spite of any preparations we might make, in spite of the promise of high technology, we will never have everything we need when we need it. Our goal, therefore, is simple: BE READY TO FIGHT TODAY. You must take every step to ensure personnel and equipment readiness. Continual quality training, inspecting, sampling, and questioning will ensure we can fight at any time.

   b. BE PREPARED TO FIGHT FROM CONDITION III. The highly structured refresher training evolutions that start from Condition I, a condition to which we've become accustomed, are now history. It is absolutely impossible to maintain a GQ posture for any length of time. We must be prepared to maintain a Condition II or III watch for extended periods. This being the case, you must work with all department heads to ensure that your watch sections are trained, rested, and properly rotated.

   c. BE READY TO COUNTER GUERRILLA WARFARE AT SEA. . . . A relatively new scenario of naval warfare has evolved, one involving guerrilla warfare at sea. This new dimension of naval warfare now includes renegade nations supporting fanatical terrorists. The weapons of these misfits include suicide planes and vessels loaded with high explosives, high-speed launches carrying powerful, armor-piercing munitions, and a bevy of aircraft, conventional warships, and deadly antiship missiles. Many of these craft will not follow expected attack or launch profiles. Rather, they may appear as friendlies or as members of a fishing fleet approaching our ship as "interested observers."

The point is that we must be prepared to fight unconventional naval warfare; we must be prepared to recognize a potentially dangerous situation; and finally WE MUST ACT IN THE INTEREST OF SELF DEFENSE. *If it appears dangerous, it is! If your gut feeling tells you it stinks . . . it does!* We must be ready to counter the modern-day naval guerrillas.

—From Battle Orders of USS CONNOLE, FF 1056.
Used by permission of Commander Kenneth P. Weinberg.

"Checking boxes and giving PowerPoint presentations is not as rewarding as independently planning and executing tasks to support a command's mission. I have never seen another officer get excited when the executive officer assigns a new checklist for action. I have seen officers get excited about figuring out how to best employ their ship in battle."

—FROM LT NATHAN D. LUTHER, USN, "BUREAUCRACY: THE ENEMY WITHIN," U.S. NAVAL INSTITUTE *PROCEEDINGS* (FEBRUARY 2006): 65–68.

"You have to take TYCOM guidance, and lots of message input, and then make it work- able here. *Moreover, you not only have to make sure your ship complies with the instruction, but you have to write it so your E-5s and E-6s understand it."*

—LIEUTENANT COMMANDER, ON WRITING INSTRUCTIONS ON A SURFACE SHIP

c.   The **Training Officer will** prepare lesson plans on directive writing, to feature "tasking" procedures prominently, and will furnish such materials to those conducting training.

d.   All writers of directives will specify in the "Action" paragraphs of their directives specifically *who* (by billet title) is responsible for exactly *what* and, if appropriate, *when, where, why,* and *how.*

D. G. FARRAGUT

Distribution:
List 1, Case A

ON REVISING DIRECTIVES

Most of your work will be *revising* directives; only 25 percent of the time do you actually write new ones. Even if you must draft a completely new directive, you can often find an old one on a similar topic to guide you. As a Marine lieutenant colonel commented, "When you have to put out a new directive, find parallel orders and plagiarize from them, keeping the format." Similarly, a Navy commander suggested that you "plagiarize where you can. Someone else probably already wrote a similar directive. So go find it, change the names, and use it."

While altering an existing document for your purpose—by changing, adding, or deleting details—also *work to revise for readability.* Here's what a DOD Executive Writing Course suggests:

"SORMs and SOPs are usually the most out-of-date *yet* most important *command documents. Keep your portion updated."*

—DIRECTOR, NAVAL OFFICER CANDIDATE SCHOOL

1.   **Shorten the document as much as possible.**
2.   **Write specific subjects.** "Request for Two Parking Spaces" is more helpful than "Parking Spaces."
3.   **Put the action up front.**
4.   **Use the pronoun** *you,* **stated or implied.** As much as possible, talk directly to your audience. As the Correspondence Manual advises, "look for opportunities to talk directly to a user." Instead of: *Personnel who are moving this summer are advised to contact the housing office early,* say If *you are moving this summer, contact the housing office early.*
5.   **Rely on active verbs in the present tense.** Don't rely on the *must be*s, and *will be*s of passive and future verbs. Instead of *All safes must be checked. Each safe dial will be spun by the duty officer,* say *You must check all safes. Spin each safe's dial as part of your inspection.*
6.   **Keep lists parallel.** The rhythm of parallelism sets up expectations that make reading easy. A common violation of parallelism is switching from active instructions to passive ones. The sentences that begin paragraphs 1–6 of this series would lose their parallelism if, for example, *Put the action up front* appeared as a passive: *Action should be placed at the front.*

These steps will help ensure the directive you're laboring on will *begin to govern action* instead of just providing window dressing for an inspection.

3

Staff Writing

General Guidance on Staff Work

Three aspects of staff writing deserve special consideration: the audience, the purpose, and the person writing. Let's take the writer first.

THE STAFF MEMBER NEW TO A STAFF

Many service members reporting to a staff for the first time express frustration with their new duties. Often they come to a staff after one or more operational tours—indeed, many Navy officers first report to staff duty as *commanders* or *captains.* Whatever their ranks, most have had little preparation for the kind of writing they now have to do. And many have a difficult time getting up to speed.

One reason for this "staffer's shock" is the greater formality that may be required, especially on larger staffs. For example, although the Marine Corps has many standard formats for staff documents (in FMFM 3-1 and elsewhere), these formats are sometimes ignored in the field. Informal procedures often take over—a few notes appended to a letter sent forward for signature, or a brief phone call that takes the place of writing. At major staffs, however, you can't succeed with informality.

For example, when a Marine lieutenant colonel first reported to Headquarters, Marine Corps, he found that, hard as he tried, he couldn't get anyone to pay any attention to the *content* of what he wrote until he got the *format* right—the format of a point paper, a position paper, a briefing memo, and so on. Because he had never run into the need for briefing on paper before, he found this situation highly frustrating.

Others have had similar experiences. Navy writers have long operated by finding an old document of the kind they now have to write (a "go-by") and copying that. Yet such an approach is hardly optimal and does nothing to give a person the larger picture of good staff work.

For many new staffers, the greatest difficulty is the writing itself. Indeed, if you're going to get anything accomplished on a staff, you'll have to do it at least in part by the written word. To many, this requirement will seem a major dilemma. One senior Pentagon staffer commented on his sure-fire way of thwarting any upstart staff officer. When someone new on the staff came to him (as new people invariably did) with the standard suggestion on how to completely turn procedures upside down to "improve" them, he would simply mumble, "Sounds good; just put it in writing, and we'll take a look at it." Through long experience, he knew he would usually hear nothing further about the suggestion.

Besides the writing, some new people have been puzzled by the mysterious process of "chopping" or coordinating staff work. Others (especially O-5s and O-6s) are upset when they realize that they will be doing things juniors had done for them in their previous commands. At the Pentagon, such factors as small offices, few yeomen or secretaries, and even small desks irritate many newly assigned officers.

So the situation is frustrating for many a new staffer. Just as frustrating is trying to understand the circumstances of the person for whom the new staffer will be working.

THE SITUATION OF THE BOSS

On a staff there may be many audiences, but most important are the audiences empowered to make decisions. Of course, there are many decision makers, even several layers of them. They are typically highly knowledgeable but also very busy individuals, people capable of absorbing facts and making decisions quickly. Consider the situation of one of the top officials at OPNAV, the Vice Chief of Naval Operations, as described in 1987 by then-CAPT Bill Owens, who was at the time the VCNO's executive assistant. (Owens would eventually become Vice Chair of the Joint Chiefs of Staff.)

As Owens then described it, the Vice Chief had no time to himself—*literally* no time. He attended eight to ten hours of briefings or meetings—or preparations for such meetings, or preparation for speeches, etc.—on each of the five regular days in a week. These meetings left some *four hundred packages of paperwork* requiring action per week, most of them one-inch thick. All of them had to be handled after regular working hours. When could he handle the paper? Well, the Vice Chief began at 0630 on Saturday. . . .

Other top officials have similar schedules. Army General Donn A. Starry once made the same point in a memo to his staff:

> In a week, about 110 staff actions show up in my in-box. 1 could handle this in a week if all I did was work on the in-box. Yet about 70% of my time in the headquarters goes not to the in-box but to briefings. I could handle that dilemma, too—by listening to briefings and thinking about staff papers at the same time. I don't. Most of the information I need is in the field. Much of my time must go there. In February, for example, I was here six days.
>
> Within those six days, add 15–20 office calls, a dozen or so visitors, seven social engagements, two or three ceremonies, and 32 phone calls. These are the realities.
>
> —Cited in Better Naval Writing, OPNAV 09B-P1-84, p. C-2.

With the vast proliferation of email, these time problems have only been exacerbated.

Clearly, any staff writer must work to be brief—but let the former EA for the Vice Chief make the point. Figure 3.1 (page 82) is the memorandum that introduced the short "Guide to OPNAV Writing," put together in May 1987. His memorandum is a good discussion of what the ability of a staff writer should be. We'll discuss techniques a bit later on.

One other subject belongs in this introductory section—a comment on the basic mission of the staffer.

THE BASIC PURPOSE OF STAFF WORK

When discussing purpose, you should remember the dictum "Staffs exist to serve command." But how does that idea relate to writing? It has to do with what should be the end result of the action officer's work. Purely and simply, on most staffs, and especially shore staffs, the major result must be good "staff actions," that is, effective directives, correspondence, plans, and other written documents that are signed out at the top level of the command.

Let's take OPNAV as an example. According to senior action officers there, the ultimate aim of all OPNAV work is legislation and support for the Navy. Consequently, what counts the most there is *what comes out the top,* that is, what documents are signed by the Chief of Naval Operations, or the Vice Chief, or one of the Deputy Chiefs. Almost everything an action officer does (phone calls, staff legwork, briefings prepared or attended, countless emails being read or sent, briefing packages put together, paperwork revised and proofed) should contribute to this primary end, *to what decision makers sign off* or otherwise effect. Otherwise, all your painstaking work has *no real impact.*

The situation on a fleet staff differs somewhat. There the goals are much more oriented toward operational requirements than policy and legislation. Clearly, fleet staff members must often focus much of their time on *liaison,* on helping to keep the ships or aircraft or other equipment in their command operational, and in seeing to it they fulfill their operational missions.

Liaison, of course, is also important on shore staffs—it can be a way of helping the boss even if it does not prepare the way for or help to implement written decisions. For one thing, it keeps lines of communication open; for another, it helps to gain support for the decision maker. In other words, being *right is* not always enough; you must also be *supported.*

Still, liaison effort is almost always secondary to the primary need to support the boss's decision making. This priority becomes more and more evident as you climb the ladder of staffs in the chain of command. The higher you go and the larger the staff, the more the balance shifts away from operations and toward policy, and the more a staffer must concentrate on the research, coordination, and especially the paperwork that can *get that policy effected.*

Clearly, the difference in staff size and staff nature will determine the degree to which a staffer must direct attention to such policy-making documentation. But in most cases, and especially on large shore staffs, wise staffers will focus their attention on *the documents that come out at the end of the paperwork chain.* Whether in electronic form or on paper (usually a staff action will be transferred from email to paper before being presented to the admiral), these packages ideally will be pure or complete staff products, having been so well researched and argued and considered and reviewed—in other words, so well filtered by good minds with wide understanding—that they are *clearly and evidently the very best answers* to the problems at hand. If staffers have done this work well, all that commanders have to do is to sign the documents for their decisions to become realities.

Yes, prior research and paperwork and formal briefings and endless emails and phone calls and often off-the-record negotiation will have prepared the way for decisive

"Young officers aren't taught to think beyond the immediate command. A key element in being a real staff officer is to learn to think bigger: 'How should the boss be using his presence and authority to influence the Navy as a whole?'"

—Captain, CO of a training command

"It was very interesting to see how a paper matured as it went through the staff wickets."

—Former Action Officer, SURFLANT

"On working for a new admiral—and what kinds of questions he'll ask. I play devil's advocate . . . so the answers will be there, and so the staff begins tracking along the same lines. That's when staff work gets good: when all the staff is tracking the way the admiral is."

—Captain, Chief of Staff

Figure 3.1 Guidance on Staff Writing. A memo introduced a helpful pamphlet on staff writing at OPNAV.

MEMORANDUM FOR THE OPNAV WRITER

Subj: A PLEA FOR YOUR PITY

1. This book was written for each of you, whether action officer, secretary, administrator, officer, enlisted, or civilian. No matter how diverse your individual jobs may be, you share with each other, and with me, a common purpose. We are all here to do the staff work that supports those at the top: SECNAV, CNO, VCNO, and, tacitly, the DCNOs and DMSOs.

2. We outnumber them many times over! There are far more people doing the writing than there are doing the reading. That is why each of you must do your part to ensure the product you write, type, or edit for their eventual use is the most concise, decisive, and technically correct package it can possibly be. While it may take you an extra hour in preparation time to trim away the fat, it is an hour far better spent at your level than at theirs.

3. On a typical day, several of these individuals may return to their offices at 1730 from a full day of meetings and briefings. When many of you are already halfway home, they are just beginning the stack of "hot" correspondence requiring immediate attention. With luck, they will finish in time to start the stack of "warm" packages. As they work their way through the stack, they are not impressed with expressive literary style or extensive vocabulary. If you have written the great American novel complete with tabs for their reading pleasure in the hope that it will cause your name to be remembered, you may very well find that you get your wish!

4. I ask that you read this guide carefully and keep it at hand while you write. I hope it will help make your task a little easier and that you, in turn, will make it easier on those at the receiving end.

5. Thanks for your help.

W. A. OWENS
Captain, U.S. Navy
Executive Assistant to the
    Vice Chief of Naval Operations

ADVICE TO STAFFERS AT OPNAV

- Always be honest. When you don't know, say so—and then find out.
- Keep your boss informed. The worst thing possible is not to let your boss know!
- Be thorough, but timely. Two hours is the normal time to answer a tasker. Time here is a resource and commodity.
- Tie yourself to the *resourcing* process—timing is key.
- Your work is critical. We trust your analysis and input; if you lose credibility in this building, you become worthless.
- Recognize you will never empty the in-basket. Learn to manage it.
- Write down acronyms you don't know.
- Watch what you write and how; write succinctly and to the point. Realize that few people read more than two paragraphs.
- Watch *what you say* and *to whom.* In this building, you don't know who's related to whom.
- Take time for yourself and your family. Carve it into your schedule. D.C. is a great place for a family; get out and see it.

—Navy Captain, OPNAV, summer 2006

"The staff should provide 'read-aheads' as it were, for when a flag is coming. About things like what does the admiral want, what information? What decisions is he looking to make?"

—NAVY CAPTAIN ON HIS FIFTH MAJOR STAFF TOUR

documents of this sort. Then, after the fact, the staffer must often put together directives, letters, briefings, and/or countless emails to implement decisions. Both in formulating arguments leading to a decision and in providing means to carry it out, the staff officer has much more to do than just writing the position paper, letter, memorandum-for, or other critical document at the heart of a staff package. Still, such documents as these are the *end results and goals* of all primary staff work.

THE FIVE BASIC PROCESSES OF STAFF WRITING

Good staff writing involves several detailed processes, few of them practiced with anything like the same intensity or detail in the Fleet or Fleet Marine Force as they are on a staff. Mastery of each process is a mark of the effective staff officer, whatever staff you serve on—Navy, Marine Corps, or joint. Described briefly here, the five basic processes are researching, writing the basic document, condensing the writing, assembling action packages, and coordinating one's staff work with other agencies.

1. Do Thorough Research

A letter, email, message, or oral command (usually called a "tasker") typically initiates staff research. Several hours, days, or even months of work may follow, either on your part alone or in a team effort. Clearly, spending this time well is important. Start by carefully *focusing* your research.

First, consider the problem. Analyze it and restate it if necessary so that it is **clear** and its scope is **well defined.** Much of the difficulty in doing focused research is determining *exactly* what the problem is. Sometimes your tasking will be incomplete and vague. Check widely with authorities and good thinkers to make sure you have the larger picture clear before putting out a Herculean effort. And don't hesitate to redefine your original statement of the problem if you find your first description doesn't fit the facts.

Especially make sure you know exactly what your boss wants. As one former OPNAV staffer commented, "How many times have staff officers busted their bums

"As an action officer, you may have to take something home and study it until you are the expert. You'll lose your juice or effectiveness if someone finds you don't know your stuff. You'll be minimalized. "

—ADMIRAL, IN ACTION
OFFICERS BRIEFING
AT OPNAV

on a package only to have the boss say, 'That's not what I asked you to find out'? Ask the boss as many questions as he or she can tolerate when you're given the tasking."

Then limit your scope so you don't spend weeks on a problem you can't affect anyway. And make sure the effort you expend is worthwhile. If your problem is ship stability in the North Atlantic, don't spend much time on the free surface effect in the ship's toilet bowls and coffee pots. Follow this additional advice:

- Develop (and state) *criteria for solutions.* Sometimes the tasking memo or other order that has initiated your staff work will give the criteria for a solution; sometimes they will be obvious. But if you take care to formulate them in writing you will be sure to focus on the particular cruxes of the problem—the meaty, difficult parts.

  For example, when giving directions for convoy route planning, a fleet staffer might formulate the following criteria: "Any acceptable convoy route (1) will allow for land-based air cover throughout, (2) will avoid known transit lanes for enemy submarines, (3) will skirt navigational hazards by X miles, and (4) will require a maximum of Y days and Z hours at standard convoy speed."

- Gather data, and seek additional data, as necessary, following up leads your first research has suggested. Use your own wits as well as the collective experience of your coworkers to define the best sources for data.

- Interpret the data, with an eye to solutions. Work out the implications of the information you've researched. Organize the information into possible solutions to your problems.

- Make whatever assumptions you need to fill in for unattainable facts. Often you won't know all the conditions that might affect the subject of your research in the future. Especially if you're writing contingency plans, but also when doing other research, you'll have to make some assumptions about the future. Find out as much as you can so you can reduce the need for assumptions to the bare minimum. Then base even those few assumptions on inferences from concrete data. In a scenario involving an aggressor state, for instance, base your assumptions on how the enemy has operated in the past, our demonstrated political and economic constraints, firm information as to geographical and political boundaries, the military capabilities of both sides, etc.

- Identify and evaluate the alternatives. Use the criteria you've developed in your evaluation. Remember these three classic tests of any proposed answer to a staff problem:

  — Suitability: *"Will it in fact solve the problem?"* Scores of planners have stumbled because, having designed a weapons platform, discovered a new tactic, or worked out a new system of personnel motivation, they find that *it doesn't solve the problem they faced originally* (and they should have known that shortcoming beforehand).

  — Feasibility: *"Can it actually be done?"* A brilliant concept is one thing; working it out in practice is another. Do all the spadework to see if a great idea is practicable.

  — Acceptability: "In the overall picture, *is it worth the cost?"* Many solutions may meet the first two tests, but the question may become one of cost. Cost can be measured in terms of money, equipment (including ships, tanks, or aircraft), lives, or troop morale and energy; it can be measured in moral, social, or political terms as well.

"Be the person who, in the midst of an especially busy day, can take a tasker and write a response and lay it on the admiral's desk with a note, 'Boss, this might be a possible solution.' If you can give him an 85% solution (maybe you won't be able to add, 'Say hello to Sally and the kids'), you'll be a hero to him."

—REAR ADMIRAL
MASSO, IN OPNAV

(Incidentally, the ancient Greeks developed a series of questions that is very similar to the three tests just mentioned. They suggested the following three questions could be asked of any proposed course of action: *Is it possible? Is it expedient?*—that is, *what good will it do?*—and *Is it just?* Don't forget that last question.)

Many a solution will pass one or two of the tests outlined above, but only a solution that definitely passes all of them is likely to be rock solid.

Realize also that sometimes the answer you come up with will meet all the criteria but won't mesh with the way your boss thinks. At other times, your boss will like it, but his or her superiors won't—it isn't "what they want to hear," as the saying goes. You can't always give superiors answers they will be comfortable with. You should, however, get a feel for the political climate before making recommendations and try to measure the costs of fighting for any particular solution.

- Once you have evaluated the alternatives, decide on your recommendations. Here, you should consider some classic advice on "completed staff work," written by an anonymous university administrator. It suggests the importance of a staffer using resourcefulness and daring to come up with forceful recommendations:

> It is so easy to ask the President what to do, and it appears so easy for him to answer. Resist that impulse. You will succumb to it only if you do not know your job. It is your job to tell the President what he ought to do, not to ask him what you ought to do. HE NEEDS ANSWERS, NOT QUESTIONS. Your job is to study, write, restudy and rewrite until you have evolved a single proposed action—the best one of all you have considered. The President merely approves or disapproves. Alternate courses of action are desirable in many cases and should be presented. But you should say which alternative you think is best.
> —Cited in Better Naval Writing, OPNAV 09B-P1-84, p. C-I.

That's a brief discussion of the basic process of staff research. Listen to colleagues or old hands for good advice beyond that outlined above if you haven't done any staff research before. Figure 3.2 presents a vice admiral's expectations on staffers becoming the "subject matter experts" (SMEs) in their specific areas, among many other things.

2. Write Up the First Draft—And Have It Reviewed for Substance

Having thoroughly researched the problem and determined the best solutions, you should write up a complete draft of a report. Whatever the format and whatever its stipulated length, the best way to start is by writing up the report thoroughly, recording the problem, assumptions, criteria, evaluation of alternatives, and recommendations as mentioned above. Then you can assess your thought processes and look for holes in both data and logic (often called a "logic check") before you put that logic up for review.

When you have your thoughts in a more or less presentable form, have some of your colleagues review what you've put down. This step is especially important for new staffers. But even old hands who are experienced authors of Pentagon staff work, *Proceedings* articles, and speeches for senior officials depend on reviews by knowledgeable colleagues for feedback somewhere in the process. Often such review will prompt you to more reflection and even more research. If that extra work results in a better product, it's usually worth it.

"CINCPACFLT had this standard guidance for action officers: 'Never give higher command a problem unless you also identify a solution.'"

—COMMANDER, XO OF AN NROTC UNIT

"Besides needing to write well on a staff, one must also write quickly. I once had to draft four short reports or recommendations in a single day, each affecting a decision on a multimillion-dollar project."

—COMMANDER, ABOUT HER TOURS IN BUPERS AND CINCUSNAVEUR

Figure 3.2 In 2006, a Vice Admiral in OPNAV explained his expectation of Staff Action Officers with this page.

N1/CNP TOP 10 Expectations

of a Good Action Officer

1) Always return emails and phone calls. If not, you become obsolete.

2) Communicate, coordinate, & collaborate with fellow AOs. You will be asked if your work was coordinated. There is seldom time for a "do-over."

3) The coordination block of any memos should NEVER say "none." Your job is to break down the bulkheads in the Pentagon.

4) You are expected to be the SME in your area. *Be brilliant on the basics.*

5) Learn how to prep emails for your boss based on his/her style.

6) USE MICROSOFT OUTLOOK CALENDAR!! Focus on your boss' calendar and ensure he/she is prepared in your area of expertise.

7) Answer the question in the first sentence. Use sub bullets to support. Do NOT provide megabytes of info and expect your boss to weed through it.

8) If you know the question and understand the answer, you should be able to tell the story in 10 slides or less. If not, you do not understand the question or the answer. *A picture is worth a thousand words if it is the right picture.*

9) Use your original thought. Be creative. Offer solutions to problems.

10) Communicate effectively. *Use plain English.*

It may be useful on an especially long or complex project to have periodic reviews at early stages, so later effort isn't wasted. In any case, on the basis of all reviews, rethink your concept and reformulate it as needed.

3. Now Draft the Good Memo, Paper, or Report

Logical as your thought process and extensive as your research may be, your document must now go through another stage. Once you've done all your research, decided on the best course of action to recommend, and written up the whole process in logical order and thorough detail, you must then write the *brief* memo, letter, or point paper that will get that action put into effect.

In others words, having the perfect solution and even laying it out in perfect clarity and detail isn't enough—you must also convince your busy boss to adopt it. At this point in staff work the editing discussed in chapter 1 comes into heavy play. That is, instead of that ten-page research report that you originally wrote, you need to condense that report into a one-page briefing memo. Why so short? Again, consider the predicament of the boss for whom you write. As General Starry commented, "To work the problems of the central battle within the restrictions of the realities, I need *less information.* But every piece of the less has to be pure. . . . You need to synthesize, condense, strip out, boil down . . . like a good newspaper editor."

How do you boil it down? Condensing your ideas can be difficult, but good editing skills can help greatly. Summarized below are some of the most pertinent editing techniques for staff work.

Craft a Good Subject Line

To get the reader's attention from the start, make the subject line as detailed as possible in a few words (just one line, if possible). Write "Eliminating Restrictions in Camp Lejeune Training Areas" rather than just "Training Areas," or "Seabee Participation in Fiji Aid Program" rather than just "Aid for Fiji."

Start Out with Your Main Point

Except in circumstances in which you want to talk a reader into an idea (as in the point-paper format, below) start out with your main point, as advised throughout this text. As the CO of a recommissioned battleship once commented, "Make your bottom line your top line; put your main point up front. Flag officers don't have time to read anything but the very key points." Then put supporting points in *descending order of importance.*

Use Headings

Headings help the reader skim. The longer and more dense the document, the more important the headings. Note that putting the main point first is not as important on a single page as on longer documents if headings guide the reader quickly to all the key information.

Remember the Advice on Writing Abstracts or Executive Summaries

Found in chapter 9, these classic summarizing techniques can be especially useful in highlighting the key results of experiments, surveys, investigations, or other research projects.

Make Use of Tabs and Annexes

Tabs and annexes organize essential material that won't fit on the one-page briefing memo. Highlight important passages within that extra material.

WRITING STAFF WORK

If you're the writer,

• Talk a project over with your reviewer at the start. Learn the points and emphasis to use.
• Write a draft. Keep in mind your reader's knowledge and interest. Do your homework and head off questions.
• Revise ruthlessly. Have you been clear and accurate? Try to find fault with your work.
• Try to see the reviewer's changes from his or her viewpoint. Be grateful for the times you were saved from blundering.

—The pamphlet "Just Plain English," 1996 Revision

"Sometime you'll be told you can use pen-and-ink to correct a typo or two. The reality is that all documents for a two-star's signature go up picture perfect."

—LIEUTENANT, NAVAL STAFF

Use Concise Sentences and Short Paragraphs

Follow the advice on "Plain English" (briefly summarized in chapter 1 of this book): suspect wordiness in everything you write. Write in active voice, and avoid rambling qualifiers, legalese, doublings, superfluous and pretentious words, and other prose-expanding habits.

Always Proof Your Work

Finally, make sure your document is technically correct in every way—or it is likely to be sent back or delayed. Double check to make sure you're using the right format, for one thing. Of course, this should have been done earlier, but it's surprising how often the long arm of "incorrect format" reaches out to trip people up.

Proof all aspects of your document. As the "Guide to OPNAV Writing" once pointed out, "A so-so paper that is technically correct will frequently get signed off, but a paper that needs to be returned for a typo invites a closer look and additional corrections of every kind." Use your spell-checker and have others proof your work as well. Even if it's a rush project and you're hustling to get it all done overnight, *don't forget to proof.*

4. Put a Correspondence Folder Together

Having written the briefing memo, letter, point paper, or other documents that the particular problem requires, you must assemble the correspondence package. Gather together all the paperwork pertinent to any staff action: the document to be signed or approved, the briefing memo, and all necessary explanatory material.

"My view is, if they're not following the formats, maybe they're not following the other regulations, either."

—NAVY CAPTAIN, EXPERT IN STAFF WORK

Pay special care to putting the folder together well. No matter how well you write, your boss will probably send your package back to you if you haven't included the basic references (or excerpts from them), or if you haven't made the required number of copies, used the right forms, etc. *This package must be technically correct in every detail.*

Figure 3.3 shows guidance on a correspondence folder, guidance once issued by BUPERS. More elaborate than that used by many commands and issued more than twenty years ago, the format shown by figure 3.3 nevertheless reflects the current process. Note that most commands now send their day-to-day staffing by email. However, email briefing packages typically are reduced to hard copy before being submitted for signature.

TOO MANY COOKS

The greatest danger of staff work is the "too many cooks" syndrome. A great idea, a novel recommendation, or a forceful piece of writing gets neutered in the bureaucracy. Thus, some forms of communication to the boss don't lend themselves to staff work very well. Speechwriting is a perfect example. I learned early at SECNAV that you can't write a speech by committee. The PAO had his agenda, the EA had his, CHINFO threw in his two cents, and before long we had a loose, stream-of-consciousness speech that was forty minutes long and didn't say anything.

This is "office politics" in all its glory. The new staff officer should be warned about its sometimes unpleasant realities, and how to survive it. For one thing, get clear on who really needs to see the stuff you put together. Work to *shorten the pipeline.* Get the right person to give you the okay, and then *modify the chop chain so* your stuff is seen only by those very few who absolutely must see it.

—Lieutenant, former speechwriter for SECNAV

"There are three filters on a staff. I'm the first filter; I put a letter in the admiral's style. Then the Chief of Staff and the Flag Writer look at it, checking for format, content, errors, etc. Then the letter goes to the admiral for signature. This process typically takes one or two days."

—Flag Secretary, SURFLANT

5. Coordinate: Learn How to Get Paperwork through the Top

Finally, there is an art to routing and negotiating a package through a major staff. No matter how good the research is, how pointed and cogent the writing has been, and how technically correct your correspondence package is, you will accomplish nothing if you don't send that *package to the right people, in the right order, for the right kind of comments or reviews.*

Realize that at big commands (like OPNAV and HQMC) the boss will look for the coordination signatures or "chops" first, before signing. Without the right chops, the substance will be meaningless; the package will be returned to you, unsigned. On the other hand, if all the chops are done, the package may be signed and sent on immediately.

Here are a few pointers on good coordination, drawn from interviews with various Navy and Marine Corps authorities and from the Correspondence Manual.

Consider Who Should Sign the Briefing Memo

The briefing memo (or "route sheet") accompanies a document through coordination. If the matter is very important, the boss of your office or "shop" had better sign this document.

Decide Who Needs to Coordinate

Some staff members must see your package before you have it signed, and others can be informed afterward. If unsure whose chops to obtain, ask an experienced coworker or consult an organization chart. Many commands have desktop guides that spell out the required coordination. A large staff will often have a "Secretariat" (that's its name at OPNAV) designated to review your chops before your package goes to the boss. Seek out this office and use it regularly to learn all the nuances of "chop chains."

"In Washington, you learn to couch things politically. Often, crucial deliberations are not put down on paper but are carried out over the phone."

—Marine Corps Colonel

Establish Your Own Network

Establish contacts in other offices in your building with whom you can talk about your packages. Find out to whom you can send material, and learn who might shepherd your package through their shop in a hurry, if need be.

Figure 3.3 Correspondence Folder. BUPERS once issued helpful guidance on correspondence folders.

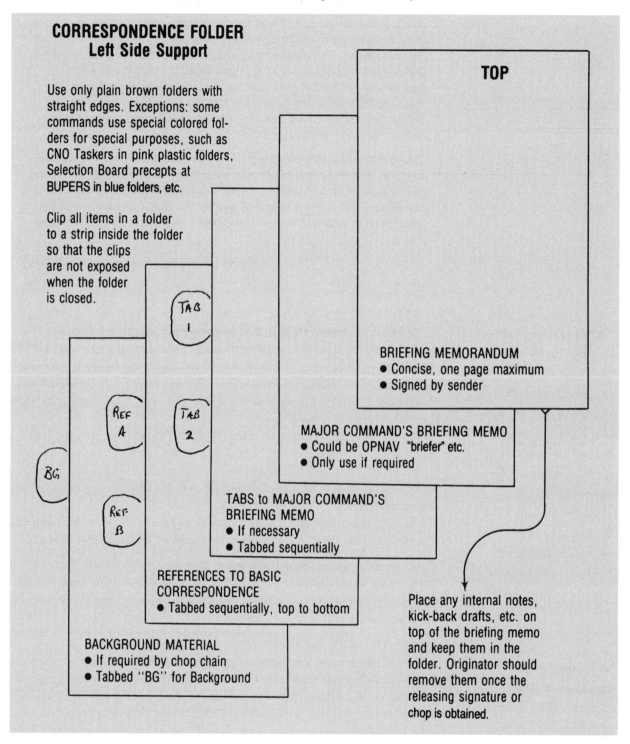

CORRESPONDENCE FOLDER
Left Side Support

Use only plain brown folders with straight edges. Exceptions: some commands use special colored folders for special purposes, such as CNO Taskers in pink plastic folders, Selection Board precepts at BUPERS in blue folders, etc.

Clip all items in a folder to a strip inside the folder so that the clips are not exposed when the folder is closed.

TOP

BRIEFING MEMORANDUM
- Concise, one page maximum
- Signed by sender

MAJOR COMMAND'S BRIEFING MEMO
- Could be OPNAV "briefer" etc.
- Only use if required

TABS to MAJOR COMMAND'S BRIEFING MEMO
- If necessary
- Tabbed sequentially

REFERENCES TO BASIC CORRESPONDENCE
- Tabbed sequentially, top to bottom

BACKGROUND MATERIAL
- If required by chop chain
- Tabbed "BG" for Background

Place any internal notes, kick-back drafts, etc. on top of the briefing memo and keep them in the folder. Originator should remove them once the releasing signature or chop is obtained.

Figure 3.3 (*continued*)

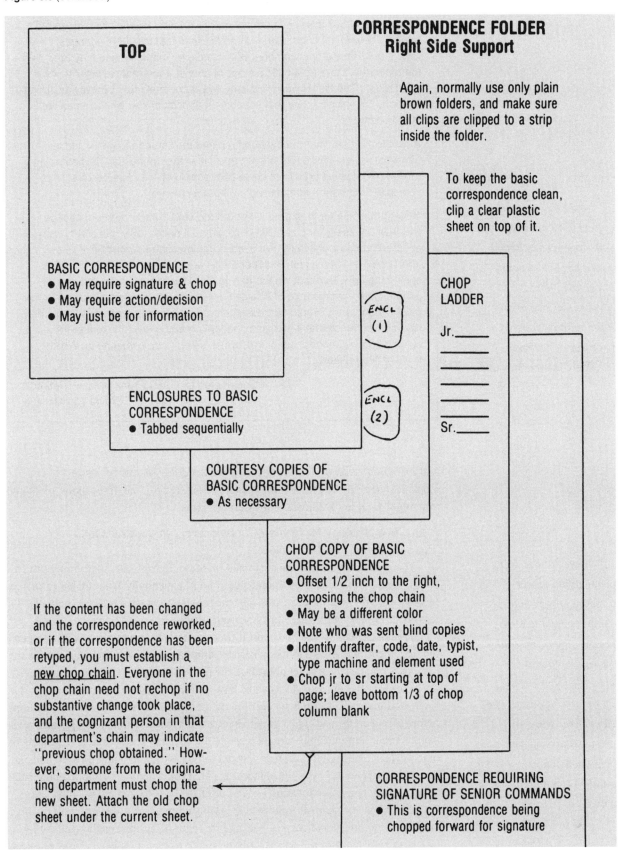

TOP

BASIC CORRESPONDENCE
- May require signature & chop
- May require action/decision
- May just be for information

ENCLOSURES TO BASIC
CORRESPONDENCE
- Tabbed sequentially

COURTESY COPIES OF
BASIC CORRESPONDENCE
- As necessary

**CORRESPONDENCE FOLDER
Right Side Support**

Again, normally use only plain
brown folders, and make sure
all clips are clipped to a strip
inside the folder.

To keep the basic
correspondence clean,
clip a clear plastic
sheet on top of it.

ENCL
(1)

ENCL
(2)

CHOP
LADDER

Jr._____
_____
_____
_____
_____
Sr._____

CHOP COPY OF BASIC
CORRESPONDENCE
- Offset 1/2 inch to the right,
  exposing the chop chain
- May be a different color
- Note who was sent blind copies
- Identify drafter, code, date, typist,
  type machine and element used
- Chop jr to sr starting at top of
  page; leave bottom 1/3 of chop
  column blank

If the content has been changed
and the correspondence reworked,
or if the correspondence has been
retyped, you must establish a
new chop chain. Everyone in the
chop chain need not rechop if no
substantive change took place,
and the cognizant person in that
department's chain may indicate
"previous chop obtained." However, someone from the origina-
ting department must chop the
new sheet. Attach the old chop
sheet under the current sheet.

CORRESPONDENCE REQUIRING
SIGNATURE OF SENIOR COMMANDS
- This is correspondence being
  chopped forward for signature

THE LAW OF THE CHOPS

Back in the 1950s a Navy lieutenant new to OPNAV was advised by an old hand on how to get a staff paper through the gauntlet without changes. "The trick is to fill up the briefing sheet with initials, no matter whose they are," said the old hand. "Develop a critical mass of chops. If four people initial it, it will get through. The higher-ups want to be reassured that the proposal has strong support. The initials prove that support—it doesn't matter whose—use your staff buddies."

A couple of years later the old hand ran into the lieutenant again, and asked him whether his advice had proved true. "It worked perfectly," the lieutenant replied. "I got signatures from all sorts of people on my Blue Blazers. Like you said, things went right through without a change.

"As a matter of fact, one time it worked too well. I worked on a message that was unusually long and complicated, so it necessarily had a very long chop list, and lots of initials. For a while, the message dropped from view. Then one day I had a call. 'Admiral Burke would like to see you.' This was something new. I went down the hall, to CNO's office and was immediately ushered into the presence of Arleigh Burke himself. I saw my message on his desk. 'Young man,' Burke addressed me, 'I've been around here a long time. It's my experience that if this many people agree on anything, either the subject is of no importance, or you are all trying to do someone in. Which is it? I'd like to know.'"

—Contributed by CAPT Frank Snyder (Retired),
Naval War College

Vary Coordination by Reference to the Particular Matter at Issue
Consider chopping by phone if the matter is brief and routine. If revisions are likely, you might want to coordinate in the drafting stage.

Plan Out a Strategy for Getting Chops on Very Important Issues
There are several possible methods.

The *sequential chop* is the customary method. In this case, you simply send an email package or paper correspondence folder sequentially from office to office, indicating on the routing sheet who gets the folder and in what order. Eventually, the last office on the chain will return it to your office.

The *shotgun chop* can be useful if time is short. In this method you "shotgun" the document or package to many offices simultaneously and then summarize the responses on a briefing sheet to preface the package as it goes up for signature.

However, the shotgun chop can be a two-edged sword, creating extra work. In a sequential chop chain, each succeeding office gets to review the preceding chops before acting on the package. Often this review mitigates or tempers suggested revisions. With a shotgun chop, writers respond without any knowledge of the inputs of other offices. The drafter must reconcile all responses before going forward and may have to get a "re-chop" from one or more people. It isn't good staff work to send a batch of conflicting responses forward, leaving it for the boss to iron out the differences.

There is at least one other method of getting chops. If you are *very* short on time, you can sometimes *hand carry* a package through offices personally (indicating to all individuals the material specifically pertinent to them). This way, you can keep

"How do you resolve the conflict with a 'shotgun' email chop when different recipients all take the original in widely divergent directions? You may end up spending more time getting the parties to converge than you saved by using the shotgun method. Understand this risk before using a wide dispersal pattern."

—Navy Captain, Pentagon

superfluous changes to a minimum and often get a document through the process very expeditiously.

Track Your Package, and Keep It Moving

Your job isn't done when you send your package off. Correspondence packages can collect dust for weeks in some offices. Although the best offices have a tickler system that keeps track of when correspondence comes through and when (and if) it moves on—in OPNAV, the "tasker" system will keep things flowing—not all of them do.

As an LDO on a major staff once pointed out, "Sometimes a package will wait too long for somebody's signature and will get to CNO and SECNAV *months* after its origination. Then they'll send it back for a rechop, and it will have to go back through all the very same offices. This *will double* the time before it's signed off."

Know where your package is, and keep it moving along.

COMMENTS ON THE USE OF EMAIL IN STAFF WRITING AND COORDINATION

Since this book was first published, the use of electronic mail (email) has proliferated enormously. Because of its efficiency and speed, many commands have come to depend on email for a great many purposes. Local area networks (LANs), wide area networks (WANs), and other vehicles for electronic desk-to-desk communications are in wide use aboard many naval activities, most staffs, and even between staffs and ships at sea. At some commands email is now being used not only as a substitute for phone conversations but even to "task" (assign tasks to) subordinate commands and to transmit official communications.

Advantages of Email

"You know the admiral got the package that day, and so you sit around and wait for him to call. And you better have your answers ready."

—Experienced naval staffer

The advantages of email are so obvious that they don't need much discussion. Like the telephone, electronic mail is an instantaneous system, but in many ways email is better than the phone. For one thing, an email message shows up at one desk or at many desks simultaneously, ready for a recipient to handle at his or her convenience—no endless "phone tag" here. For another, whole documents can be sent from one computer to many other computers instantaneously.

As a result, it's much easier to get things staffed. You can draft a letter (on the computer) meant ultimately to be sent to CNO or SECNAV and attach it to an email memo, asking a Washington office to "CHOP and send comments." After receiving those comments, you can modify the document as required and quickly route that letter through the local chain (office by office or via a shotgun chop) and then to the chief of staff, the deputy, and the admiral—all on the computer. Today a great deal of a command's coordination or chopping is done via computer.

The computer has begun to enable communications in many other ways. For instance, email writing style is usually bullets and fragments; stiff, standardized formats are often ignored or abbreviated. On the other hand, standard formats of various kinds—for point papers, briefing memos, etc.—can be loaded into a computer and readily used.

But disadvantages almost as great can offset such advantages. See the discussion (and a few accompanying pointers) below.

"With email, we shoot from the hip because we can."

—Navy Lieutenant

Email Problem Areas

- Email is not necessarily quicker. If not used with care, email can make more paperwork, not less. This is especially the case in editing other people's documents.

"Because you apparently so easily can make a document perfect (with a couple of keystrokes)," said one frustrated staffer, "you tweak it again and again." The pamphlet "Just Plain English" argues for discipline in reviewing staff work; this advice applies to email chops above all: "Avoid making changes just to feel you've left your mark. Tinker only to prevent real damage."

- Email breeds informality and carelessness. A former staff officer argued that "with a message or letter, you really thought about what you were going to say. You were careful with the pencil. But email is as informal as a phone call. And as with a phone call, there tends to be lots and lots of chit-chat." One result is that the official can mix with the unofficial. As yet another officer said, "An email memo will show up in a correspondence package (as back-up data), and all that garbage before and after will be there with the policy statement. Because humor can be misunderstood and tone can offend, one command counsels: *Never say anything in an email that you would not say in any written correspondence OR that you would not say to your MOTHER!!*

  Another result is sloppiness with the language. One chief of staff sent an informal email directive pointing out that staff work had too often been careless and that, in the future, documents for the commander's signature should be correct in all respects. Subordinates were not impressed. The two-paragraph email message in which the O-6 counseled correctness contained no fewer than twenty grammatical errors.

- With email there's often no paperwork trail. In staffing correspondence forwarded in the traditional way (by hard-copy folders), everyone in a lineal chop chain sees criticism by other offices and understands why changes have been suggested. Even when revisions are finalized and the folder is sent forward for signature, written concurrences and "nonconcurs" are automatically included in the file.

  But in many cases email critiques of staff documents are not printed out or even kept. As a result, officials reviewing staff work sometimes have little understanding as to why a document appears as it does.

- Tasking by email is fraught with problems. In the past, a commander could double check whether the command was answering all requirements easily. One simply glanced through the message file in radio and the tickler file in ship's office. It's not so simple now. Frequently, a command will be tasked on email (by an office or code in a superior command) *without the commander's even knowing.* One commanding officer found that some of his subordinates were turning down a headquarter's request without his ever hearing of it—and had he known about it (and thought it important enough), he might have been able to change priorities in order to say "Yes." He directed that his people "never say 'No' without my say so."

  In response to problems with email tasking, more than one command has ordered that his people simply refuse to accept tasking other than by letter, message, or word of mouth. However, because insisting on the way senior commands task your outfit is fraught with problems, this advice is probably impractical. As for the issue of offices within senior commands tasking more junior offices at other commands and not notifying the commander, such issues have not as of this writing been solved by formal naval directive. See the next chapter for further discussion.

- Finally, email is a poor substitute for the personal. As one commander lamented, "with email we tend to lose the face-to-face." This comment was echoed through-

**THE STAFF WRITER AND THE ADMIRAL—
SOME DOS AND DON'TS**

DO — Earn the admiral's confidence. Many times your boss will pass on insights that are for your information only.

DON'T — Ever assume that anything the admiral says is for anyone's ears but yours. Sometimes the obvious difference between "I didn't like that" and "Tell him I didn't like that" is not so obvious. Don't take any chances.

DO — Faithfully communicate both the spirit and the letter of those messages you are asked to communicate. Write these things down . . . your memory may betray you.

DON'T — Add or modify anything your admiral says. There is nothing wrong, though, with honestly qualifying what you say with caveats that discriminate between what the admiral said exactly and what one believes the admiral meant.

DO — Delete expletives when quoting or citing the admiral, unless told otherwise.

DON'T — Compromise your admiral's trust by agreeing with some disgruntled staffer that the admiral is in fact a "dummy." There is a fine line between saying, "I think you'd better get the Lieutenant to sign this first. You know how the admiral is about the chain of command," and "I know it is a dumb idiosyncrasy, but the admiral insists on going through the chain."

DO — Realize the admiral's time is always limited and that you should command the smallest portion of it. Learn to communicate with your boss by means of simple "Yes—," "No—" notes. When your boss wants or needs to talk to you, you'll be called.

DON'T — Ever expect any feedback. If you need frequent warm fuzzies, you are in the wrong business. Remember: "No news is good news."

—Selected Advice from *Navy Flag Writers Handbook*

"Good manners precludes using ALL CAPS AS A ROUTINE JUST BECAUSE ONE THINKS EMAIL IS JUST LIKE A NAVAL MESSAGE. No one likes being shouted at."

—PENTAGON STAFFER

out naval staffs. Naval men and women should, of course, be leaders—not computer junkies. *Know when to shut off the computer, walk down the passage, and have a cup of coffee with your shipmate.*

OTHER RESOURCES FOR GETTING UP TO SPEED ON A STAFF

Your predecessor may give you a turnover file. Mastering the information will make you effective weeks earlier than you otherwise would be.

Learn Staff Code Numbering

The larger the staff, the more frequently the offices are referred to by number rather than by the name of the occupant. This numbering is subject to some standardization; for instance, most naval staffs have converted to "JCS Style," which is based upon Army patterns. In the Army (and Marine Corps), when the commander is a general officer, staff organization follows this pattern:

G-1: Personnel
G-2: Intelligence
G-3: Operations and Plans
G-4: Logistics

If the commander is a colonel or below, the codes are S-1, S-2, S-3, and S-4. On joint or unified staffs, the designations are typically J-1, J-2, and so forth.

Many Navy staffs have converted to a similar pattern; here's the OPNAV numbering in effect in 1996:

N-1: Personnel
N-2: Intelligence
N-3: Operations (current)
N-4: Logistics
N-5: Planning (strategic level)
N-6: Communications
N-7: Training
N-8: Requirements and Resources

"Research your own staff code carefully. Be sure you list exactly who you want to see your document—and remember that staff codes change frequently."

—Pentagon staffer

It's useful to know the OPNAV listing even if you're serving on some other staff because in reference to decisions made or tasking required by Washington, you'll hear these codes referred to all the time. However, there is no Navy-wide pattern, and your own staff codes may deviate from this pattern. Master the local codes; moreover, make sure you use the most recent organizational list or diagram when doing so. As in civilian organizations, the only sure thing is change: *reorganizing naval staff functions and renumbering the codes is a constant.*

As for personal codes, the short codes for commander and assistants are still pretty common:

00:    Commander
01:    Deputy, Chief of Staff, or Executive Officer, with other deputies coded 02, 03, 04, and so on
001:   Flag Lieutenant and Aide
002:   Flag Secretary and Aide

Often the number "9" designates a Deputy or Vice Chief, as in the following:

00:    Chief
09:    Vice Chief
051:   Division Director
0519: Deputy Division Director

Some small commands prefer to use initials derived from an office or officer's title. One Marine air base, for example, uses the following system:

M: Manpower
ADJ: Adjutant
O: Operations
PAO: Public Affairs Officer
SJA: Staff Judge Advocate
T: Training and Education

Beyond these general guidelines, the best advice is to become very familiar with your particular staff's coding system as described in its organization chart, beginning with your own immediate office, and then branching out. Then stand by to come about: any staff's particular coding (like its staff organization) is likely to change overnight.

Make a Turnover File

Even if your predecessor hands you a turnover file, you can probably enhance it. Be sure it includes:

- your job description, and those of your immediate associates
- the local organization and regulation manual
- an organization chart of your own command
- organization charts of commands to whom your command reports
- phone books of your own command and of those you must often call, with space for you to add important numbers and email addresses
- examples of point papers, briefing memos, executive summaries, letters, and messages that your command has recently approved and issued
- recent "lessons learned" written at or affecting your command
- any available instructions on how the command does paperwork, to include:
  — a locally written chapter 4 of the Correspondence Manual, if it exists;
  — a local writing guide, if one exists;
  — instructions on the specific briefing-memo format used;
  — guidelines on putting the local briefing folder together;
  — local instructions on other formats, if any;
  — any available guidance on the current commander's preferred style.

Make Sure These Standard References Are at Hand or Nearby

- the Correspondence Manual
- a current edition of this book
- the pamphlet "Just Plain English" (or the similar version found in chapter 1 of this book)
- a good college dictionary (*not* a paperback)
- perhaps a college grammar handbook
- a thesaurus
- the Standard Navy Distribution List (SNDL)
- the Plain Language Address Directory (PLAD)
- the instructions and notices file, to include
  — the Directives Manual
  — evaluation and fitness report instructions
  — other important instructions

Read as Much of the Past Year's Correspondence as You Can

Take some extra time (after working hours, if need be) to get familiar with the activities of your office in the past. Review past correspondence, message traffic, old briefing folders, and other such documents (perhaps kept in a turnover file). They will give you insight into current issues, peak periods of office operation, common contacts outside your office, personalities and opinions of key players, the boss's buzzwords, etc.

   If you prepare this way, you'll take less time to adapt to your new job, and sometimes you'll know more than those already at work. One young Navy lieutenant (jg) was assigned collateral duty as legal officer on joining a ship. His XO counseled him never to show up at the XO's office on a legal matter without the pertinent references

"I was given this advice on coming to OPNAV. 'Pull your boss's read file; learn how he writes his letters.' So I did it, and then I wrote a document just like he wrote. The admiral called me in; 'How did you learn to write so well?' he asked."

—06 IN OPNAV

in hand. Very quickly he found that some officers he dealt with would not know the regulations but would try to bluster their way through an issue as if they did. Having the reference on hand gave him absolutely sure footing in such circumstances.

This experience taught him to get his act together before he went to a senior on any issue; the habit served him well when he was later assigned to a staff.

Typical Staff Documents

"Professionally, you have to read—because the sooner you use the right buzz words, the better."
—SENIOR OFFICER
IN OPNAV

The following section gives descriptions and examples of several kinds of documents used on a typical Navy or Marine Corps staff. Other kinds of staff writing—letters, memos, the memorandum-for, instructions and notices, and so on—have already been discussed in chapter 2. Guidance on email and messages can be found in chapter 4. The next few pages cover:

The Briefing Memo
The Correspondence Folder
The Point Paper
The Talking Paper
The Trip Report
Lessons Learned
The Plan of Action and Milestones

THE BRIEFING MEMO OR ROUTING SHEET

Naval officers are trained not to leave any stone unturned—but that's only half the job. The other half is boiling it down to one page on a briefing memo.
—NAVY CAPTAIN

"At the senior officer level, a good route sheet or briefing memo is invaluable."
—MARINE CORPS
COLONEL

In OPNAV a briefing memo used to be called a "blue blazer"; it is now called an "executive summary memorandum." In HQMC, paperwork usually moves by a "routing sheet." Joint commands use many names, including "decision paper" and "summary sheet." But whatever the name, the ability to write a good one is an essential ability for any staffer, whether officer, senior enlisted, or civilian. Here's some guidance on how to put one together.

SUBJECT

WRITING THE BRIEFING MEMO OR ROUTING SHEET

ISSUE: A briefing memo is an explanation sheet. It's a piece of paper that explains any letter, memorandum, instruction, or other document that needs to be signed by the boss and issued. You can also use it to brief the boss even when there is no outgoing correspondence.

RECOMMENDATION: Use the briefing memo to give a brief history of the package, with supporting and explanatory remarks. Specifically,

— Keep your memo to <u>one page</u>.
— Use headings to guide the reader, like those on this page—vary as needed.
— Make sure one of those headings is "Recommendation," "Summary," or "Action," so the boss can find the bottom line quickly.
— Write in brief, logically ordered bullets.

— Neatly paperclip the briefing memo to the left side of a folder, across from the document to be signed.

BACKGROUND: Wherever used, the briefing memo has the function of

— explaining what you're proposing and why.
— discussing any rejected alternatives.
— addressing why the package is late, if it is.

But don't use it to

— duplicate what is in the proposed correspondence.
— just make the recommendation "Sign the attached correspondence."

COORDINATION: Ensure you obtain all necessary chops (reviews). Mention the important coordination you have obtained, if not clear from elsewhere in the memo or correspondence. For instance: "The proposed response was coordinated with 04B, and it was chopped by PERS-9."

Signature:	Office Code & Phone:	Date:
Action Officer, LCDR, USN	03A/x5-5555	30 NOV 96

Below is an example of the particular kind of briefing sheet used not long ago throughout OPNAV—the "executive summary memorandum." This example is fictional but is based on actual OPNAV documents. Note that some writers prefer numbered paragraphs in the discussion section rather than the "bullet style" used here.

16 April 1997

MEMORANDUM FOR Chief of Naval Operations

FROM: RADM A ———
       Director, Intersubair Operations
       Prepared by: CAPT B ———, Head
                     Subair Warfare, NXXX, 697-xxxx

SUBJECT: PERSONAL FOR Message Response to COMSECONDFLT—
          ACTION MEMORANDUM

PURPOSE: To obtain CNO's release of PERSONAL FOR message in response to COMSECONDFLT message discussing aircraft "Dive-Under" attack maneuvers and fleet training.

DISCUSSION: • COMSECONDFLT (RADM C____) sent PERSONAL FOR message (attachment 1) to inform CNO of benefits of fleet training during mock attack by PELICAN model Dive-Under aircraft. These aircraft are usually armed with sub-cruise tormissiles.
             • Message included detailed comments by CO USS FAMOUS CITY upon the effectiveness of MK-99 lightweight SUPER-DUPERs in encountering intermittent subair threats, but urged extensive real-time training in the use of such countermeasures.
             • There were no controversial issues. CNO asked for simple response.
             • PERSONAL FOR response prepared; at attachment

RECOMMENDATION: CNO sign message release form to right.

ATTACHMENTS:
1. COMSECONDFLT message 141415Z APR 97

"Keep the Reserve component on the radar scope in your projects, and involve us early . . . not as an afterthought late on a Friday afternoon!"

—Captain, Naval Reserve Staff

Retired Naval Officer: "You start to work pretty early, here, don't you."

LDO, in SECNAV: "Oh, about 8:00. But CNO's office has to get here earlier; they work for us."

THE LENGTH OF BRIEFING MEMOS—TWO OPINIONS

A favorite response will be that your topic can't be explained in one page. I know of no issue that can't be laid out in one page, or in a 15–20 minute briefing.

—Navy Captain, EA for VCNO

Branch heads at OPNAV know that the CNO won't read three pages. So by the time a briefing memo gets to CNO, its information value is limited. Some things simply can't be covered at this length. Recently I got a message drafted for me asking SURFLANT for $20,000 for joiner doors, this in an austere budget climate. It simply had to be written with all the background information or it had no chance of getting approved.

—Navy Captain, Commodore of a DESRON

---

2. CNO PERSONAL FOR message response

Chop	VCNO					
DATE						

"I carve out three times a week to run. And you should, too. I do my best thinking then."

—Vice Admiral Crenshaw, to action officers at OPNAV

THE CORRESPONDENCE FOLDER

Correspondence folders are vital tools for doing staff work. While the structure of these folders varies slightly from command to command, all such folders serve to (1) collect all the important documentation regarding any particular staff action in one place and (2) organize all relevant documents and information in a standard, usable order. For example, you normally clip the letter, memorandum-for, message, or other document to be signed on the right side of the folder, and any briefing memo explaining that document on the left. Tabs, appendixes, and other supporting documentation go behind these surface documents.

Again, the folder illustrated in figure 3.3 on pages 90–91 is based on a recent BUPERS correspondence folder; most major naval commands use a similar structure.

THE POINT PAPER

I had to consolidate point papers for ships in a squadron—one of the hardest writing tasks I've had aboard ship. I learned that you need to know lots of extra information about the topic in case the boss asks for it, but all that extra dope doesn't have to be in the point paper.

—Navy Lieutenant

Point papers are good ways to press forward recommendations in a direct and objective way. Instead of writing a letter or other document for signature and then attempting to persuade seniors to buy your approach, you can write a point paper seeking a decision and wait to implement what your boss decides. As one Navy captain remarked,

"With the point paper you create a grenade with the pin out, but without requiring anyone in the chain to sign it. It's an excellent way to direct things."

Point papers are used widely in many contexts. For instance, you can use a point paper to bring up issues in conferences, to help develop policy, to help resolve differences between offices, and to prepare senior officers for appearances before important bodies, such as congressional committees.

In most of these documents you are trying to talk your audience into something, so often (unlike a briefing memo or other staff action papers) you can leave the recommendation till the last. As long as you *keep the point paper to one page* and *use clear headings,* the audience can skim the document and find your "bottom line" very quickly. Here's a model point paper; it follows the format found in the Correspondence Manual (SECNAVINST 521G.5, current edition).

POINT PAPER

Rank and Name
Staff Code, Phone Number
12 Dec 96

Subj: USE OF POINT PAPERS

BACKGROUND (or PROBLEM)

Point papers are a good means of stating background, ideas, and recommendations in a relatively formal way for the consideration of the command. Use a point paper primarily to direct the attention of seniors to an issue or problem and to seek a solution.

DISCUSSION

- Keep to **one page** in most cases; use tabs for additional material.
- Be factual and objective.
- Keep the language simple. Explain all technical terms or unfamiliar acronyms the first time you use them.
- Don't make the point paper so detailed that significant points are lost in minutiae.
- Indicate who concurs or does not concur.
- For classified papers, follow markings found in Correspondence Manual.

RECOMMENDATION(S)

- State recommended actions. Be brief but specific, outlining who, when, where, how much, etc. List options, if desirable, but always make your choice clear among them.

Below is an example of a point paper prepared aboard ship some years ago for use at a conference at an operational staff. It follows the format outlined above, except that it uses numbered paragraphs instead of bullets.

Point Paper for COMCARDIV STAFF

ORIG: USS CARRIER
DRAFTER: LCDR R. ENGINEER
DATE: 2 DEC 87

SEA/SHORE DUTY ROTATION FOR NONNUCLEAR-TRAINED MACHINIST'S MATES

PROBLEM

Sea-duty obligation for E-7 through E-9 machinist's mates has been increased to 60 months.

<u>DISCUSSION</u>

1.   For the second time in less than three years, the sea-tour length for nonnuclear machinist's mates has been increased. The total extension has been 24 months. As a result:

     a.   Shore-tour planning has been superseded because detailers and career counselors do not have an accurate list of options to discuss.

     b.   Family planning in regard to PCS moves, retirement options, and future education plans for children is in jeopardy due to uncertainty about career options.

     c.   Personal career planning—to stay in or get out—is being affected: many senior qualified personnel are choosing to leave the service.

2.   Personnel on board USS CARRIER are confronting a sea tour with not just one or two six-month-plus deployments, but possibly three. For senior enlisted, the options are limited—either retire or deploy. Prior to this extension policy, some had decided to stay in and contribute at a shore facility that could use their technical expertise and knowledge.

<u>RECOMMENDATIONS</u>

1.   On a case-by-case basis, review the sea/shore rotation dates of all senior machinist's mates. Send men whose shore-tour length (two years) has been fulfilled back to sea to relieve those men whose tours have been extended.

2.   Reestablish SRB for machinist's mates at a level that will support the required retention level. Many predicted the current problem when SRB was reduced several years ago.

And the example in figure 3.4 uses the same basic organization. A civilian manager at Military Sealift Command, Pacific had identified a problem, and his naval commander asked him to outline the problem in a point paper that could be used in a conference with CINCPACFLT. Through the discussions on the topic as described in this point paper, MSCPAC obtained its objective.

THE TALKING PAPER

Another staff document similar to a point paper is a talking paper, so named because you usually prepare it for someone to use while "talking," that is, while speaking in informal circumstances. These circumstances might be interviews with visiting officials, informal talks to groups, visits with the media, etc. *Keep the talking paper brief and simple.* Further guidance appears below.

<u>TALKING PAPER</u>

Originator's Name
Code/Phone Number
Date Prepared

Subj: HOW TO WRITE A TALKING PAPER

<u>BACKGROUND</u>

- Specify in the "Background" or "Issue" section:
  — The name of the official for whom this paper has been prepared, the name of the meeting, etc.
  — The event or situation that has brought this issue up now.
  — Any other brief background needed.

Figure 3.4 Point Paper. This point paper gets across its point very well.

Logistics Directorate
MSCPAC N4; (510) 302-6273
April 1995

SUBJECT: Transferring Material Handling Equipment (MHE) to MSC

REFERENCE: (a) COMNAVSURFPACINST 4100.1E
             (b) COMNAVSURFPAC San Diego 211317Z DEC 94

ENCLOSURE: (1) COMNAVSURFPAC San Diego 050517Z APR 95

BACKGROUND: USS FLINT is currently preparing for a "hot transfer" to Military Sealift Command. Previous ship transfers to MSCPAC, including SAN JOSE, MARS, and NIAGARA FALLS, have included their onboard MHE assets. However, FLINT's MHE had been scheduled by COMNAVSURFPAC to be offloaded for ultimate distribution to other ships. Following a formal request for reconsideration by MSCPAC to COMNAVSURFPAC, this process is currently pending further disposition instructions from NAVSUP and SPCC. Encl. (1) applies.

DISCUSSION: Current guidance provided by COMNAVSURFPAC in reference (a) applies only to the deactivation and subsequent retirement or sale of USS ships. Reference (a) briefly mentions MSC ship transfers and states that "removal of equipment and material is generally prohibited except as authorized by the Type Commander *and coordinated with COMSCPAC*" (emphasis added). However, reference (b) directed the offload of MHE from FLINT to FICP San Diego.

Actual ownership of MHE is the primary issue. Reference (b) defers to NAVSUP and SPCC for FLINT's MHE disposition instructions. Seemingly, a more logical choice would be for these instructions to originate from the owners of afloat MHE assets--Fleet Commanders. MHE shortfalls may adversely affect operational readiness and/or financial planning for the CINCs. For example, replacement of FLINT's MHE represents an unplanned shortfall of 1.3 million to MSC and up to 2 years for new MHE units to process through existing contracts at SPCC.

RECOMMENDATION: CINCPACFLT establish a policy for COMNAVSURFPAC, NAVSUP, and SPCC which clearly states that MHE remains onboard for any "hot transfers" or deactivations where eventual transfer to MSC is anticipated.

<u>DISCUSSION</u> (or <u>TALKING POINTS</u>)

- Use this outline as a memory aid in a meeting, or as an informal agenda. Also use it as a tickler to prepare seniors for meetings with important officials, such as senior Navy or Marine officials or Congress members.

- Include the <u>key facts</u>. Change headings as needed.

- Be concise—normally keep paper to <u>one page</u>. Use bullet style. Single space; subordinate points.

- Say what to avoid talking about, as well as what <u>to</u> talk about. Also note, if needed, who has been involved/who concurs/who does not concur.

- Mark classification (and paragraph classification) as required. See SECNAVINST 5216.5D.

<u>RECOMMENDATION(S)</u>

- Include a "Recommendation" section if needed. If there are no recommendations, omit this section. Consider prefacing the talk by saying, "This presentation is for information only."

Here is an example of a talking paper, adapted from a talking paper once used at BUPERS:

<u>TALKING PAPER</u>

CDR S. F. Housing
OP-999H/#5-4321
13 April 1992

Subj: SHORTFALL IN FAMILY HOUSING (MFH) AT BIKINI ATOLL

<u>BACKGROUND</u>

- This paper was prepared at OP-99's request, in response to an inquiry by Assistant Secretary of the Navy (Logistics). This issue may come up in a meeting between OP-99 and the Secretary next Tuesday, April 17.

<u>TALKING POINTS</u>

- MFH assets at Bikini are owned and managed by the Air Force.
- Navy owns no housing there.
- Average waiting time for personnel to get into housing is 8 to 10 months.
- Figures relevant to MFH at Bikini:
  — Total requirement (Air Force and Navy families)—900
  — Total of 392 Air Force & Navy personnel are on the housing waiting list
  — Current assets—182 units
  — Programmed for construction:
  — FY 93———150 units (approved)
  — FY 94———150 units
  — FY 96———100 units

<u>COORDINATION SUMMARY</u>

- USAF point of contact is LtCol D. A. Quarters at 1-2345, who provided some of the above information.

THE TRIP REPORT

Trip reports can have the benefit of keeping the boss informed. Also use them to make your case and to inform the boss of impending action on which you need support—a sort of "preparatory fire."

—MARINE COLONEL

A trip report can be an important and very useful document, not the meaningless paper exercise that it sometimes becomes. As a Navy captain remarked, "It's not worthwhile reading trip reports that list the lectures you heard. Trip reports seem to be used to account for your time—but no one cares about that. Give a sense of what you are discovering." Or, as a Marine lieutenant colonel commented, "Don't just say 'I came, I saw this, I talked to so-and-so'; *make recommendations.*"

Ideally, trip reports will be worked into a long-range command strategy, a strategy that will have had a point in sending you to the meeting in the first place. The commanding officer of a Navy training command, for example, had this strategy:

> I send my people to get things to happen at meetings, not just to listen. If we're not playing, we're not going.
>
> So the trip report isn't a drill—it is the end of the trip, the reason you went. It becomes a management tool that (through its recommendations) has an impact or gets things done, either in the Navy at large or at home in your own command.

As this captain suggests, many staff members who attend meetings are unprepared to contribute significantly to the proceedings. A *pretrip report* that requires staffers to outline their reasons for the trip, the people who will be there, the business they will conduct, and any controversial topics they expect to arise can help staff members learn to regard conferences as *means to an end,* or as opportunities to make things happen. After such formal preparation, a posttrip report (like the example below) can be a way to report recommendations for action and changes in policy, as well as to relay new information.

Whatever your command's strategy, remember to keep a sense of priority as you pen your final report. As with many other staff documents, make a habit of *putting the vital points up front*—at least on the first page—or they simply won't be read. Leave for appendixes such peripheral material as topics covered at the conference and lists of speakers. Follow a format like the one shown below.

---

15 March 2007

From: Senior Officer or Officers Who Made the Trip
To: Commanding Officer—via the Chain of Command

Subj: TRIP REPORT TO MEETING, CONFERENCE, ASSIST VISIT, ETC.

Encl: (1) Agenda or itinerary
            (2) List of attendees
            (3) Minutes or other enclosures as pertinent

1. <u>Trip Purpose</u>: Record the objective of the trip you took. Why was the meeting held, and why did staff members go? What did they expect to get out of it? Whom did they expect to influence, and why?

2. <u>Highlights</u>: Comment in bullet format on such matters as
    *   Whether the organizers achieved their aims.
    *   What major decisions participants made and what new information they issued.
    *   What milestone status on projects, proposals, etc., participants reported.
    *   Whether you achieved your objective in taking the trip.

3. <u>Unresolved Issues</u>: Report here
    *   Newly discovered problem areas.
    *   Unresolved issues, including their current status.

4. <u>Action Items or Recommendations</u>: Note in this section
    *   What items were assigned to your command for action.
    *   Anything else you committed your office or boss to.
    *   What recommendations you have regarding ways of doing business, new developments or projects, etc.

5. <u>Opinions and Impressions</u>: In this closing paragraph, comment on such matters as the overall success of the trip, developments in other areas, ideas about what the future holds, etc.

Very Respectfully,

S. OFFICER
LCDR USN

"Keep a record of the people you work with in coordinating a trip or program. Always send thank you letters; people appreciate recognition and respond positively to it. Remember, you may pass by again, and need help again."

—Navy Flag Writers Handbook

As an example, here is a trip report written by the operations officer at the Fleet Anti-Submarine Training Center, Atlantic, to his commanding officer. The report does very well in giving the CO a sense of what the issues are and where things are headed.

MEMORANDUM   5 December 1987

From: N3
To: CO
Via: XO

Subj: TRIP REPORT FOR 14A6 UPGRADE MEETING, 2 DECEMBER 1987

Encl: (1) Agenda
        (2) List of Attendees

1. <u>Trip Purpose</u>. To review 14A6 upgrade program progress.

2. <u>Highlights</u>.
    — Various areas were briefed per agenda with one exception: no one briefed EW since EWC Britton was not present.
        — Milestones are being met, in general. Hard spots are in paragraph 3.
        — NAVSEA estimates hardware will start arriving mid-January.
        — HP 9020 will be replaced by HP 825 as central computer; more power.

3. <u>Unresolved Issues</u>.
    — Passive acoustic system. Several options are being pursued:
        — SYSCOM training system developed for P-3 operators.

— SONALYSTS system, which is a spin-off of ASWETA (no raw rams). Our position is: we want grams, but if not achievable in prototype, we will settle for processed data with grams to follow later. FLEASWTRACENLANT will not pick a system; we will only give our requirements.

— EW. OP-392C says he has arranged with EW detailer for EWC Britton to be ordered to CARON via CNSL. He would be TAD here during that period to work on the OTX system. If that plan falls through, an industry system that also meets our needs can be ready in time.

4. Action Items. None for Fleet ASW but our active involvement now includes:
    — Working with EDO to get up a prototype work-up. Already started.
    — Reviewing the manual for the SYSCOM gram trainer to see if it meets our needs.
    — Briefing. Joe McCartney attended and briefed CLF science advisor, A1 Densinbacker. Subsequently, Densinbacker briefed CAPT Gionet who asked to be briefed fully on the program. I agreed to do so this Friday at 1530.

5. Opinions and Impressions.
    — I like PADS myself but don't want to dictate which system to use. When asked, we'll give our opinions on which system can do better/ worse.

Very respectfully,

C. F. GORE
CDR USN

LESSONS LEARNED

Lessons learned are naval problem summaries. Widely used on both operational commands and staffs, lessons learned report on difficulties in recent operations, exercises, inspections, and many other evolutions. These papers usually report on problems that *have already been solved,* a solution being recorded along with each particular problem. (For problems that still *need solving,* staffers typically compose point papers and then follow them up with Plans of Action & Milestones [POA&Ms], briefing packages, proposed revisions to directives, etc.)

We record lessons learned both to keep present commanders informed and to guide personnel in the future. Not only can individuals forget from one evolution to the next, but given the rapidity of personnel transfers (or wartime casualties), the next month's or next year's evolution will often see different personnel in key positions. These new people will badly need guidance to rely on and will not want to start from scratch.

One wide use of lessons learned during peacetime is to record problems solved during Fleet or Fleet Marine Force exercises, as in *"Red Flag* Lessons Learned," *"Exercise Provide Promise* Lessons Learned," and so on. But we write lessons learned on many occasions other than exercises—after major inspections or after standard training evolutions, for example. In such cases, their purpose is to guide those who must prepare for the next INSURV OPPE, REFTRA, or whatever.

Further, a ship or unit "chopping" into a new operational area (a destroyer reporting to the Indian Ocean, for instance) will often receive from the ship or unit it is relieving an after-action report itemizing lessons learned. In this instance, the document would fit into the standard naval relieving ceremony as a kind of turnover file.

Very comprehensive lessons learned are often written on major naval events, to discuss strategy, tactics, successful employment of new weapons systems, and the

"Too often, 'Lessons Learned' are not a part of the process of staff planning. We never learn from our mistakes; we reinvent the wheel every time."

—COMMANDER

like. For a good ten-page example of one of these studies, see the "Lessons Learned on The Falklands War," in former Secretary of the Navy John F. Lehman, Jr.'s book *Command of the Seas* (New York: Charles Scribner's Sons, 1988, pp. 279–89). Lehman himself drew on two *book-length* lessons learned studies for his discussion.

Write lessons learned often—whenever specific experience has taught something you (or someone at your ship or station) may need to know in the future. Make sure to incorporate these documents into your turnover file. Whatever the topic, remember not to talk just about what went wrong; also discuss what went right. Sound procedures, reasonable rules not to bend, planning ahead that proved right on target—all this information is as important as "problem-solved" commentary.

The example below is one of many lessons learned drawn up following a Marine Corps Reserve exercise. It follows a widely used format, first describing the background, then presenting a brief discussion, and then making a recommendation.

Lesson Learned

TOPIC: Problems Involving Communications Security

BACKGROUND: Drawing on the exercise plan and additional guidance received during prebriefing, units employed communications-security procedures (mainly shackling) from Day 1 of the exercise.

DISCUSSION: Such employment of communications security is doing more harm than good. During the exercise, grids were coded or decoded incorrectly, important messages were delayed because of coding and decoding requirements, CEOIs were not where they were needed, aircraft were on the wrong frequencies, etc.

RECOMMENDATION: For a short Reserve exercise, we should waive shackling. It is invariably done improperly, wastes time, confuses personnel, and therefore delays other training objectives. In addition, on D-day the enemy is likely to know exactly where you are, and shackling your grid coordinates from a known position allows him to break your code.

Another good example of lessons learned is the SURFLANT document (in memo-for-record format) reproduced as figure 3.5. The author was officer in charge of the 1987 SURFLANT change of command. He recorded his lessons learned and placed them in the local "Change of Command" folder so that future changes of command would also go well.

And then see figure 5.2, an illustration of a "Lessons Learned" message, p. 129.

THE PLAN OF ACTION AND MILESTONES (POA&M)

The Plan of Action and Milestones (POA&M) is a planning document used widely throughout the Navy and Marine Corps. It is exactly what its name suggests. It is a plan of (1) **what steps have to be taken** to complete a project, inspection, or other evolution, and (2) **mileposts for each step.** Virtually any organizational activity can formulate a POA&M, but it is especially appropriate in cases where responsibility for action involves many different departments.

POA&Ms are perhaps most widely used in the surface Navy, both on staffs and on ships. Staffs use POA&Ms for instituting new programs or getting initiatives off the ground. Ships use POA&Ms to guide preparations for a myriad of inspections (NTPIs, OPPEs, Supply Management Inspections, etc.) and to schedule the correction of discrepancies after inspections. You can also use POA&Ms to schedule change-of-command ceremonies and to plan deployments and training exercises.

The POA&M is very simple in concept and appearance. Usually published in an instruction or other official directive, the basic plan consists of a schedule of action to be taken and a designation of the cognizant official for each action. In print the document usually consists of three columns labeled Action Item, Action Individual, and Due Date, these three columns simply designating *what* needs to be done, *who* has to do it, and by *when*.

This simplicity may be misleading. Besides taking care to be accurate, you must be very thoughtful and farsighted to make the plan a workable document, one that makes allowance for other unit evolutions that may affect the plan. Even after you design it, it's not set in concrete. As one officer on a DESRON staff commented, "The POA&M never happens as you schedule it. Crises are always coming up to interfere with it." You need to revise it often. Indeed, good as it is in concept, a POA&M will be absolutely useless in practice unless you check progress frequently, identify and overcome obstacles, and hold people to the stipulated deadlines. Without such rigorous management, the POA&M will simply be ignored.

POA&Ms have special value for commanders, who can gauge the command's progress toward a goal simply by glancing at the chart of goals and accomplishments it comprises. Because a superior will often judge a department's or division's progress by looking at a POA&M, you can put yourself on report by being less than farsighted in working one up. Make sure you have a reasonable chance to complete any tasking before you assign yourself responsibility to do it. Have the same consideration for your subordinates when giving them responsibilities. In short, *formulate this plan with discretion,* and *evaluate it with understanding.*

In summary, when composing the POA&M,

Do:

- Be very detailed with assignments. Separate complex activities into a number of individual steps.
- Assign responsibility for each step by billet or code to *one specific individual.*
- Assign reasonable due dates.
- Update the plan periodically, adjusting the dates and responsibilities according to changes in schedule, available personnel, etc.

Don't:

- Formulate a POA&M for a period longer than one year. The longer the time and the greater the detail, the more unwieldy the plan becomes. It is likely to become meaningless if stretched too far into the future.

Here is a POA&M used aboard a surface ship for scheduling the qualification of Enlisted Surface Warfare Specialists (ESWSs). POA&Ms on staffs are often more complex (sometimes they have many sections), but otherwise are usually very similar.

POA&M for ESWS QUALIFICATION

Milestones. PREBLE has established two weeks before outchop as the deadline for 100 percent ESWS qualification of eligible petty officers. Adhere to the following schedule in accomplishing that objective:

> *"I learned in the Army, if there's no date, there won't ever be a plan."*
> —A character in the novel *The Passage,* by David Poyer

> *"Know what your boss's schedule is. Be prepared for his events. Consider giving him a single-page, classic comic version of what he might be asked about or what issues might arise in the next few days . . . this in addition to your day-to-day job."*
> —Rear Admiral, about staff work

Figure 3.5 Lessons Learned. Here are lessons learned in the form of a memo for record.

DEPARTMENT OF THE NAVY

COMMANDER NAVAL SURFACE FORCE
UNITED STATES ATLANTIC FLEET
NORFOLK. VIRGINIA 23511-6292

5 January 1988

MEMORANDUM FOR THE RECORD

Via: (1) N3
        (2) 002
        (3) 02

Subj: CHANGE OF COMMAND 1987 LESSONS LEARNED

1. This memorandum addresses the planning for and execution of the 1987 COMNAVSURFLANT Change of Command. In general, it was a successful effort; areas that required more than routine effort will be emphasized.

2. As background, a successor to VADM _____ was not known until very late in the game. The same was true of the actual date for the change. As a consequence, specific planning was delayed until about four weeks prior to the event. This time compression had the greatest effect in the expected areas: invitations printing/mailing, program printing, etc. VADM _____ was frocked after the programs were printed, which necessitated printing them again - SHENANDOAH did it in three days.

3. Specific responsibilities were assigned by COMNAVSURFLANTNOTE. Three TEMDU officers were assigned to the project and were able to devote almost full time to it, which blurred some lines of responsibility. This minor disadvantage was outweighed by the clear advantage of full-time help.

4. The "hard" areas included:

    - <u>Communications</u>: Although ultimately resolved, a lack of hand-held comms was an issue. Need to resolve early, identify requirements, and <u>get</u> the radios as soon as possible.

    - Portable comms didn't work well from LP-1.

    - Don't depend solely on NAVSTA to provide hand-held comms. Task one of the Groups early to provide units from ships' assets.

    - <u>Ceremony timing</u>: The "ceremony" was scheduled to start at 1000, which meant that the CNO arrived at 0959. This meant that the principals arrived sometime before that, causing the forward brow to be secured in preparation.

    - Flag officers attending a 1000 event will arrive at 0955. Some did and had to use the after brow.

    - Philosophical question. Does the "ceremony" start with the benediction, or when the principals arrive?

    - The issue should be broached next time.

Figure 3.5 (*continued*)

Subj: CHANGE OF COMMAND 1987 LESSONS LEARNED

    - <u>VIP transportation</u>: N7 handled this perfectly, but it took
a major effort.

    - It's a moving target, but identify VIPs who need transportation,
then add five and order that number of cars.

    - Ask for a list of escort officers from the staff (ACOSs) <u>early</u>.
One per car per run, basically.

    - Drivers were staff CPOs — trained by N7 — worked well.
Lots of practice runs help.

    - Attention to minute detail required in this area. Fertile
ground for OMIGODs.

    - VIPs (aside from principals/principals' families) were out-
of-town flags who flew in for the day.

    - <u>Standard change-of-command items</u>: Don't overlook mundane
items such as UNITREP, releasing signatures, security badges, etc.

    - <u>Reception</u>: Nail down as early as possible. Provide options.
Sensitive issue — personal money involved. No government funds should
be expended on solely reception items. N7 will explain.

    - <u>Uniform Issues</u>: Make the uniform requirements <u>clear</u> for
<u>every</u> event and then get the word out.

5. Expect full cooperation in the overall effort. Navy Regs and
the Protocol Manual provide lots of guidance as questions arise.
<u>Start as early as possible</u>.

                        Very respectfully,

                        Commander, USN, NOOX

Action Item		COG	Due NLT
a.	Promulgate list of Chiefs/POs aboard	XO	01 May
b.	Revise Monthly PQS reports to track ESWS quals and progress toward	XO	01 May
c.	Conduct review of ship's program, and establish reporting requirements	CO	15 May
d.	Promulgate updated ESWS Qualifiers list	XO	15 May
e.	Develop timeline that reflects time remaining vs. number of qualification points completed, in order to qualify no later than 15 October	XO	15 May
f.	Develop bank of 500 questions for use in ESWS qualification exam. Publish question list for crew's review	SMCS	01 Jun
g.	Commence review of ship's program and ship's qualifications	SMCS	15 Jul
h.	Identify individuals who have not made acceptable progress, and report delinquents to XO	CO/XO	01 Aug
i.	Establish after-hours schedule of instruction for delinquent personnel, and promulgate sked to crew	SMCS	01 Aug
j.	Review ship's program and status of crew' qualifications	CO/XO	15 Aug
			31 Aug
			15 Sep
			30 Sep
			15 Oct

4

Naval Email

Everyone knows the great usefulness of email as sent on the Naval and Marine Corps Intranet (NMCI). A letter can be forwarded as an attachment to an email and, instead of being sent via the U.S. mail and the naval mail system (to say nothing of fragile mailbags transported by highline or helo to a ship at sea, a process that sometimes used to take weeks), that letter attachment now can arrive virtually anywhere in the world in seconds. Moreover, that very letter will reach twenty commands or two hundred individuals in the same short time that it takes to reach one of them. Providing that the letter is subsequently discovered on the computer terminals at which it arrives, it may almost immediately result in understanding or appropriate action on the part of its recipients.

However, drawbacks can occur with email as with every other communication process. "Email encourages senior commanders to micromanage," a commander at an inland station complained, "and senior commanders have come to expect immediate gratification." To this one can add that the great volume of email has become a burden for everybody. "I left for seven days, and when I returned, there were 971 emails in my inbox!" commented the chief of staff of a mid-level command, this in 2005. Things have probably gotten worse since then.

At last report, neither the Navy as a whole nor fleet commanders have developed much active management of email, although there are some understood protocols. Meanwhile, technology and software affecting email are continuously being improved. Hence, writing on this subject is something like taking a snapshot of a sprinter in the middle of a 200-meter race: because of the speed involved, not only might the subject be blurred in a developed photo, but that snapshot will not reflect the situation at the finish line. Still, the general direction of things is clear. With the aid of interviews with dozens of knowledgeable professionals, we can point out some major trends and difficulties.

<table>
<tr><td colspan="1">"AFTER EMAIL"?</td></tr>
</table>

"AFTER EMAIL"?

In the Old Navy:

"I'll see you in the morning right after Quarters."

In the New Navy:

"Come by Monday morning, at 9:30, right after Email."

—Overheard at NAS Pensacola

PROBLEMS WITH EMAIL

A quick glance at several problems with email will prove useful.

The Enormous Volume

The huge volume of email can overload not only electronic systems (so that periodically inboxes are purged by the system) but it can overload individuals too. Throughout the service, officers, enlisted people, and civilians must daily expend valuable time attempting to cope with a seemingly ever-increasing load of emails.

It is not by accident that the informal system we all use to sort email messages is often compared to "triage," the process used by emergency medical technicians to differentiate between those patients who can wait for treatment and those who cannot. "The first thing we all go to when we arrive in the morning is emails—to see what we've been tasked with," a naval aviator pointed out: "What are the *hot taskers?*"

In this triage process, important documents can be overlooked because of the great amount of material involved or because of a related problem: inadequately titled subject lines that lead a reader to misinterpret or underestimate the importance of an email's content. A Naval Academy instructor pointed out that no one has directed that *everybody* must read *all* their email, or that *you personally* must read all of yours—which suggests that many things may be lost because of inattention. When interviewed, the XO of a small naval base reported that he and the CO sorted through *a second time* the hundreds of emails received each day, just to make sure they hadn't missed anything.

Once upon a time, someone in the ship's office or in radio (or in the equivalent Marine Corps offices) was always at hand to receive a letter or a message and then to make sure that the responsible officials saw it. However, now an email message—perhaps a reply to a query or a tasking message—may be sent to a particular email address and, without procedures to prevent it, can sit there for days before anyone at the command knows about it.

In the fall of 1995 a young man applied to the Marine Corps Officer Candidate program. His application had been sent weeks before the deadline, but there was a difficulty with an eyesight waiver, and the medical tests and paperwork were forwarded to BUMED for a decision. The date for the selection board to meet came and went, and no word from BUMED had been received. Upon inquiry, senior Marine Corps officers searched and discovered that the approval message from BUMED had been sent well before the deadline to a computer in the relevant office at Headquarters, Marine Corps. No one had thought to look for the message on that official's e-mail. Meanwhile, although that young man's credentials were otherwise excellent, his file was incomplete, and consequently he was not selected.

"Administrative triage is the skill that enables you to separate the inconsequential from the critical and everything in between. . . . The appearance of a message in your box does not mean it merits your immediate attention—in fact, the vast majority of messages do not. Email is not created equally."

—CDR ROBERT P. GIRRIER, "EMAIL IS A TWO-EDGED SWORD," U.S. NAVAL INSTITUTE *PROCEEDINGS* (JULY 2003).

To prevent such problems, the Correspondence Manual directs that activities must spell out how to access and process email that comes to users who are absent for any significant period; such procedures might include automatic forwarding of emails to other users or sending automatic reply messages to email originators informing them that the addressee is not on hand (and indicating how to contact somebody else). Prudent commanders will regularly review and enforce such procedures.

An executive officer pointed out that it is particularly important not to use email to send operational items—lest a ship or unit's whole mission be derailed because somebody missed a key email or because the email sat undiscovered too long on someone's computer.

Problems Posed by Email Tasking

To what extent can email be used for tasking, and if it *is* used for tasking, what problems can this pose? Offices within major commands now routinely task equivalent but subordinate offices in the field by email—rather than tasking the field commanders. Not too many years ago, to understand what their ships or units were required to do, naval commanders followed the message board very closely and paid close attention to the serial file in ship's office or admin to see what their particular ships or stations had been tasked to do. This enabled them to carefully track compliance. Now, however, many fewer messages are being sent, and letters that are written often skirt ship's office entirely—again, usually because they are attached to an email sent to a code within a command rather than sent via snail mail to the ship or command itself (although even today paper letters often follow by regular mail). Hence the skippers of a ship or unit must set protocols of their own to understand what taskings have been assigned, what the related deadlines are, and how their ship or outfit is responding.

The command master chief of a naval base reported that his CO had an excellent policy on email tasking. At department head meetings, the CO had all the department heads report what they had been tasked to do and give Admin a copy of each related document. Often the CO and XO would learn of a tasking for the first time at one of these meetings. As the master chief concluded, "The XO insists, 'When you get a tasking in, forward me a copy *so I have a track record.*' Neither the XO or CO likes being back-doored by overdue suspense dates."

Although operational units are less often tasked by email, a naval aviator in command of a squadron was doubtful whether he could take action based just on an email. "My rule is, if something is directive in nature, *an email is not enough,*" the Captain said. Clearly, senior operational commanders should set policy in this area; in the meantime, the rest of us have to keep alert.

Intemperate Emails

Yet another problem that virtually everybody comments on is the ease with which one can send intemperate emails, documents laden with complaints, satire, or perhaps demeaning remarks. It's so easy to do . . . to write down what one would *like* to say, and then in a fit of pique to actually go ahead and send it! In commenting on this, a chief of staff shook his head and grimaced: "You just hit the send button—and you can't get it back!"

The problem can take several forms. The first is simply to flame out at somebody without forethought—and perhaps thereby make a permanent enemy. But it's just as easy to make a remark that might be interpreted as satirical or pejorative without the writer intending any such thing. "Sixty to seventy percent of communication is in body language," said the CO of an NROTC unit, reflecting about this. The Colonel's point is clear: in person, a joke, exaggeration, or well-meant satire is usually picked up. But email is *not* in person. Along the same line, a Navy commander pointed out that emails are typically very impersonal but often are taken very personally. "And now, if you offend somebody, that person not only is offended, but they also have documentation of the offense!"

Others think the problem is less often in mistaken impression than in the writer's original meaning. "People write things in email they would *never* say to *anybody!*" an XO exclaimed. Once again, this is probably attributable to the ease of immediate email communication—and the absence of the deterring effect of having your listener standing right there in front of you. Hence the importance of "taking a deep breath," as a senior chief YN put it: "Be as dispassionate in emails as you are in regular naval correspondence." A naval writing expert recommended not addressing email drafts while you're working on them (or erasing the address you've already typed in). This way an email can simmer in the draft file until you have time to think twice and you won't inadvertently send it out with the touch of a key.

Injudicious and Uncontrolled Forwarding of Emails

Of course, there's at least one other related pitfall involving unwise speech and email. As a master chief advised, "Watch casual conversation in emails. Once you hit the 'Send' button, you have no control over where your document goes; who sees it; or how it will be interpreted."

The Superintendent of the Air Force Academy found out about this lack of control a couple of years ago when an Air Force Academy doolie (a freshman cadet) somehow discovered the Sup's email address and wrote him to complain about the general's recent relief of a colonel on his staff—the young man had admired the colonel and was speaking in his support.

In his reply, the Superintendent seemed to be offended that any fourth-class cadet would dare write him at all, and he wrote back in a most pejorative and demeaning way to the clueless young student. Although the doolie perhaps should have known better than to write personally to the Sup, the student's original email sounded a lot more professional than the general's intemperate response. This fact must have been rather embarrassing to the general and to his staff, especially because this unpleasant exchange somehow was forwarded from one computer to another and eventually found its way to the Internet (you can find it there to this day).

A navy chief of staff recently advised, "Always know who is on your email's distribution list." He had once been sarcastic in an email. Thinking back on the situation, he still thought the sarcasm was justified, given the circumstances, for the command had suffered much from someone's error. However, after he sent the email he realized that in addition to addressing his primary audiences, because of the structure of the distribution list, he had inadvertently sent the email "for information" to the commander of the individual who had made the original error—something he never would have intended to do.

Similarly, the XO of an NROTC unit insists that people look at what they're *forwarding* before they *forward* it. She points out that the software command to "reply" does not involve sending all the attachments in an email; however, the command to "forward" does. Hence, your comment to someone in an attachment—"Nope. We don't want to tell him that" or "Why is the XO sending us this stuff; it's all worthless!"—could easily embarrass you. "That's like sending one's first draft to all the chop chain," the commander concluded.

The problem is similar with a *chain* of emails, perhaps those involving staff coordination of a particular project. When interviewed, that same NROTC XO (a veteran of tours in the Pentagon) reported she had seen pejorative, thoughtless comments in attachments or email chains *at the highest levels of the Navy.*

Finally, to What Extent Is Email "Official"?

When asked about modern emails, a Navy chief of staff reflected on the breakdown of the traditional protocol that used to govern letters and memos. In the past, a memo was always considered "internal" while a letter was "external"; that is, a letter was always sent from one command to another (or sometimes from a command to a service member, or vice versa), but a memo never was. Emails are a different kind of beast altogether, possessing qualities of memos, messages, and phone calls all mixed together. While they often look like memos, emails are sent externally, and often from an individual within one command to an individual within another. They also can be very informal in language.

The chief of staff reflected on the problems caused by the breakdown of this protocol. He commented that when we used to write a letter, we took care with it, recognizing that even if it was signed "by direction," it still was understood as a representation of the command. In his view, we should regard our emails to be just as representative of the command as our letters are. Along these lines, a commander said that in her judgment the main issue is to what extent emails are "official." Certainly, the more official one's job, the more one is expected to write one's email in official memo format, with the exception that one usually does not number the paragraphs with emails (as one does with memos). She thinks one should always treat emails as official.

A related issue is the ease with which subordinates can end up making command decisions on informal emails. A master chief yeoman argued that it is very important that senior enlisted administrators not make command decisions on email. She reported that YN master chiefs in particular are notorious for speaking for the command without authority, or for answering a query and only afterwards researching an issue—and then having to back down.

And a commander mentioned this difficulty: "One lieutenant at a shore command answers a question of his counterpart lieutenant (or lieutenant commander) at his governing command. He's thereby sent out official correspondence. Often, that lieutenant should check with his chain of command first." In his opinion, with email just as with paper correspondence, there's always a proper "releasing authority." Maybe this is not spelled out officially anywhere, but it is generally understood, the commander added.

This seems pretty extreme, given the free flow of email communication between naval offices (which in many ways reflects the freedom of phone conversations), and the commander thought twice about what he had just said. "Of course," he continued, "it is second nature just to return the answer, especially if it's a simple answer, such as how many personnel are on board your command. But your own chain of command may well want to know that such information is being asked for . . . and *why* that information is being requested."

The point is that often your boss may have a specific interest in what you've been asked and what you're responding. You should keep that in mind and maybe pass some of that information up the line. "Otherwise, you'll learn by experience," that same commander concluded. "That is, you'll learn by screwing something up."

NAVAL EMAILS, PART BY PART

We can now discuss the various parts of ordinary emails as used in naval communication and make a few recommendations based on the experience of a variety of experienced Navy and Marine Corps people.

Consider the Protocol of Email Addresses

One of the first things one sees in an email is the address, which is usually straightforward. The traditional protocol of "action" addressees being identified by the "To" line still obtains as it did with messages (traditionally, of course, if you are an "Info" addressee, the message is for information only; this still seems a protocol with "Cc" in emails). One command issued written guidance directing that when anybody sent out emails with multiple addressees in the "To" line, the originator should spell out who should take the lead among the "To" addressees, should there be any question about that.

If there are several addressees, the order of this list (in each of the fields) is sometimes a concern. With messages it is important that addressees are always listed in rank order. A Marine junior officer recently discovered that certain of his commanders were sticklers that email recipients also be listed in rank order (within each "To" or "Cc" block) while other officials he reported to didn't care what the order was. Of course, the structure of email lists (where addressees are primarily arranged by email address rather than by command name and are presented in paragraph form rather than listed line by line) affects the perspective here, which makes rank order less noticeable on emails than on messages.

"On manner of address in emails—why use 'Sir' or 'Madam'? Why not just use rank?"

—SWO LIEUTENANT

Craft a Very Specific Subject Line

Given the crush of emails everyone endures and the fact that, as of this writing, on many computers all one sees of an email before opening it is the subject line (amidst a barrage of other subject lines), making subject lines genuinely informative is even more important than it once was for naval messages.

Upon reading dozens or even more than a hundred subject lines at a single email screening, people inevitably guess at the meaning of some emails and misinterpret others. Subject lines that do not introduce the subject in enough detail or that identify it poorly mean that readers spend extra seconds opening and reading emails that do not affect them—and miss emails that do. As the seconds mount up, so can the frustration.

Hence, the best advice: *Be very specific.* A commander argued that "if you've managed to get your new ship's required manning [SMD] even further reduced, say in your subject line, 'As of 20 Mar 08 DD-XXX SMD down from 270 to 247.' For those who recognize the significance, that will catch their eye." In fact, he pointed out that sometimes a knowledgeable reader will not need to read the email itself if the subject line is especially well crafted.

One other common error with subject lines was noted by the person editing this text prior to publication. She pointed out that sometimes people use an old email to generate a new email thread but will keep the old subject line. "For example, if I have had email communication with an author about the editing of their manuscript and weeks later the author wants to ask me about indexing, the author will pull up my last email with a subject line like 'review of edits' and will leave the subject line unchanged in an email that questions me instead about the index. As a result, I may have many emails with the subject line 'review of edits,' several of which actually discuss different topics. This makes it difficult to find specific email threads later." We've all seen this. Remember to change the subject line when you change the topic.

The Body—Putting "The Bottom Line" at the Top

Second in importance to crafting the subject line, throughout this text we advise *getting to the point quickly.* That's even more important with emails than it is with messages, letters, and memos.

There are two reasons for this. First, whenever a harassed officer, enlisted person, or naval civilian actually opens your email while reviewing a long stack of them, he or she is still looking to do "triage" to find out quickly what the point of the email is and whether it must be attended to quickly. For this reason, help that person: *get the key information into the first paragraph.*

A lieutenant teaching at the Naval Academy pointed out that this can be important even when sending emails *to your own boss.* "Your XO may have asked you at morning quarters for your report but that afternoon may have forgotten what he asked you for! And he won't know what your report is unless you remind him at the beginning." To be sure, while sometimes you'll be submitting your report in person, just as often these days you'll send it by email so the XO can then easily use or manipulate the information it contains. Or perhaps (if you've ghosted a document for the XO) he or she will then quickly edit it and just as quickly send it on. In either case, a quick summary in the very first lines (in addition to a good subject line) informs the reader of the report's point or contents.

Officer to Chief: "Did you see my email?"

Chief to Officer: "Well, I saw it for a second, sir."

A second reason to put important information up front in an email has to do with enhanced software. On computers with newer software, subject lines are now enhanced by "preview panes." That is, as one maneuvers the mouse down the long stack of subject lines, the first lines or paragraphs of each email appear in a "windowpane" alongside that email's subject line without a reader having to take the time to open anything. Because this highly useful feature will no doubt become more and more common as time goes on (and remember: even if your computer does not have this feature, others computers will), you should consider some old journalistic advice. Journalists have always advised their students to attempt to get their stories "above the fold." That advice refers to the fact that traditional newspapers are folded in half, and a story (or at least a headline) above the fold means readers are much more likely to see and read it. In addition, for news releases journalists have always been instructed to put the most important information, the who, what, when, where, why, and how, at the very beginning of the story (in what is called a "news lead"), thereby enticing readers to read down and ultimately to turn to the back pages of the paper to complete reading the story.

Similarly, the advent of preview panes makes it all the more important to "make one's bottom line one's top line," or to get a quick summary of the most important information in the first few lines of the email. Doing this will ideally give the reader enough information to decide whether to open the email and read on—or, upon opening it, whether to scroll down the page to glance at material not immediately visible.

Several email experts advise using frequent headings to help the reader skim material faster; they also advise that you should never pen long paragraphs in email communication. And remember this startling comment from a highly experienced Navy captain in OPNAV, who is quoted elsewhere in this book. She commented that, because of the press of business, *"few people read more than two paragraphs"* from any particular document!

Briefly Summarize Attachments

Opening attachments also requires time; hence the importance for summaries of the attachments as well. A submariner teaching at the Naval Academy argued, "Mids have to be taught to make clear what's in the attachments they include. It can save somebody thirty seconds to know what's in the attachment (and whether and/or when to open it)."

The CO of a training command pointed out that such summaries are not just "nice to have" features but are now more and more expected. An example of such a summary would be, "Attached you will find our proposed ship requirements for the XXX-Class Ship." You might need a short paragraph to summarize a complicated document, not just a sentence.

Remember Protocol with Closings

Some people forget standard protocol for the naval complimentary close of documents sent to seniors or juniors; that is, "Very Respectfully" used to seniors, and "Respectfully" used by seniors to juniors. In email, these are typically rendered

v/r or VR (juniors to seniors)   and   r or R (seniors to juniors)

Occasionally one also sees w/r, which means "with respect," by which one speaks "nicely" to peers. (Someone commented in an interview that Marines do not usually make use of such penned salutes; instead, they typically end their emails with "Semper Fi.")

Informality is so rampant with email, however, that these standard salutes are frequently forgotten or have never been learned in the first place. "Use the same rules of military courtesy as you would in naval correspondence," a professional writing instructor advised.

That same instructor also counseled to "make sure you are happy with what goes out in the email signature block." For example, she pointed out that in the signature format that regularly includes a place for a personal message or famous saying,

Name   Title
Office   Phone Number
"Don't Sweat the Small Stuff"

the last line might not be appropriate.

Decide on Whether to Keep an Email Chain

When interviewed, officials pointed out reasons to keep—and reasons to expunge—an email chain (earlier emails that have led to the current one). A Navy captain reported his regular frustration at spending ten minutes with a string of emails, each with its own attachment—only to find that the key information was in the very last attachment! Given such difficulties, one might consider summarizing the negotiations from all those emails and deleting the chain, especially if one's document is to be sent to multiple addressees or if it is setting policy based on a long chain of such email conversations.

When coordinating staff work, such email chains do serve the purpose of letting everybody know how the negotiations have gone on a particular issue, that is, which

GHOSTING AN EMAIL

Sometimes you have to ghost an email for your boss to send, with a prefatory comment like this: 'Sir: Below is a ghost email responding to CNO's question.' Your boss has to learn to delete this prefatory comment, or to cut and paste what you say into his email so that the prefatory comment is not there. He has to clean it up, in other words.

Your boss might have to be coached as to what final version will come out when he or she pushes 'Send.' Otherwise, if that prefatory comment remains in the document, CNO will realize that your boss's response was really authored by a commander. It can make a big difference in how the boss's response is received. It definitely shapes the perception.

—Commander coming from an OPNAV tour

"Many people use email to circumnavigate work. When you ask if they've dealt with an issue, they say 'Yes' . . . when all they've done is to forward the email to somebody else! 'Did you take care of that?' 'Sure. I forwarded it.'"

—NAVY CAPTAIN

offices have pointed out specific problems (or specific solutions) and their reasons. Yet just as often people keep email chains not because they are particularly important but just because keeping them is easier than deleting them.

Looking at the issue from another point of view, a commander advised that a writer should "read down the email chain to see if something is politically sensitive and ought to be deleted. Some people don't like you forwarding their emails." This would be particularly important if the conversation in those emails had gotten heated in some way. (See the section on intemperate emails, earlier.) That commander also noted another problem: "a Captain sends you an email with obvious grammatical errors. Do you correct those before forwarding?"

In a written directive, a navy command warned against any such correction: "*Never* modify the text of another's email without their permission." Getting such permission, though, would mean "noticing" their grammatical problems, and you might not want to do that either (you could possibly mention the error discreetly by phone). If it is important to include this information anyway, you might want to summarize it rather than include the problematic email itself.

Filing Emails?

Once the coordination is done, the coordination chain usually has served its purpose. A chief warrant officer at NETC said that once the policy statement or formal decision is issued, he deletes the paper trail on correspondence or staffing, both the email chains and paper documents. Those who kept such documentation—and many did—he called "packrats."

Others, however, noted that email was very handy for recordkeeping. A commander pointed out that one could log one's phone calls—but one seldom did. With email, though, one automatically had a logged copy of past discussions. Why keep such conversations? To protect oneself, in some cases, or for "historical" use. Or maybe for post-mortems, as with naval exercises.

Of course, sometimes you *don't* want to keep sensitive material. In her current NROTC billet, the commander mentioned in the paragraph above sometimes had to speak to a doctor several times about a student's medical condition. She usually avoided talking about such issues in email and used the phone instead. A YNCS listening in to the commander's remarks said that in a particular office at OPNAV, his office had regularly shredded all prior working papers dealing with a sensitive issue once a decision was made, to avoid possible legal inquiries.

"Don't automatically hit 'reply to all.' If you're responding to an announcement about paying your mess bill and hit 'reply to all,' that means that fifty people will be getting your message!"

—NAVAL AVIATOR

CHANGING AN EMAIL?

In this NROTC unit, we frequently correspond with parents. Occasionally somebody responds in nasty ways.

One parent challenged me; he was a former Marine. I began to answer him by email . . . but then I realized that my email could be modified so as to differ from what I originally said, and could be published that way. (It's too bad that we sometimes have to think like lawyers—but we sometimes have to.)

In such a case, I learned to use hard copy instead of email.

—Marine Corps Colonel

"WE need to adapt the electronic system to our requirements."
—CHIEF OF STAFF

Clearly, the issues of whether to include email chains and whether to retain them can be complicated. See in relation to this topic the discussion of keeping message references (found in chapter 5) and the section on staff coordination (in chapter 3).

A FEW LAST WORDS

Learn the System

It is important to learn something of electronic "office management" systems. Take the email distribution system, for instance. There are lots of groupings possible on email—emails to be sent to "All COs on base," "All Master Chiefs," and so on—and within a command, emails also have many possible distributions—to the whole command, to each code, to all officers, and so on. Knowing this, you can cut your workload by *adjusting your profile.* A chief of staff at Naval Reserve headquarters found that until he got the distribution list changed, for some unfathomable reason he was getting dozens of "Explosive Impact" reports. And frequently after you have moved to a new position email still comes from your old job until you let people know you've moved on.

"Courses on Microsoft Word and Excel are usually offered on base. They're good, they're fun, and they're during working hours!"
—NAVY CHIEF

Email systems allow for many useful alternatives. You can usually set up a file grouping the emails you should read first—perhaps "everything from your CO" to start with. Then a CO can set up the system so everything he sees also goes to the XO, or whatever comes to the XO can also be sent to the command master chief. Such determinations are of particular use when someone is on leave or Temporary Additional Duty (TAD) so the command will not miss crucial information, or will not fail to meet deadlines.

You can profit by many computer tools if you learn how to use them. A captain pointed out you can usually set up your email to be automatically spell-checked. He always did this, for who knows what spelling errors one might commit on a quick email response, and who knows where that quick response will end up. However, he also discovered that material written in ALL CAPS was *not* spell-checked—something that is also important to recognize because of the wide use of all caps in naval writing. Another important tool has to do with archiving material so it is not lost when the Navy's system regularly purges email.

"Some people send a two-page email instead of holding a meeting . . . usually it's better face to face."
—MARINE FIRST
LIEUTENANT

To sum up this issue, as a Navy commander counseled Navy people in Naval Institute *Proceedings,* we should all learn to *"use the applications.* Microsoft Outlook is the tool we use for managing email and you should understand all of its capabilities" (then-CDR Robert P. Girrier, "E-Mail Is a Two-Edged Sword," July

"At AIRPAC (now AIR FORCES) in San Diego, people would sit at their word processor and send an email to somebody instead of walking four doors down and talking to him!"

—SENIOR NAVAL
AVIATOR

2003 issue). And a Navy IT specialist at OPNAV advised that, from the standpoint of efficiency and correctness and much more, you should "learn NMCI so you can exploit it to your best advantage. It's a complicated beast."

Get Away from the Computer

Finally, it should go almost without saying that although electronic communication is a part of a job, it's not all of it. Yes, leadership is always embodied in words, and although email can be used to harass, written messages can also do much to get across a good leadership climate, to pat people on the back, to keep one's bosses informed, and to urge one's people to initiate action. However, as then-Commander Girrier pointed out in his excellent *Proceedings* article, "*Leadership is a contact sport, especially on board ship*" (italics added). Get out into the work spaces, among your people. Don't succumb to the temptation to try to lead from your desk.

Message traffic retains an important place—because it is unquestionably official.

—Navy Chief

5

Naval Messages

Because of geographic separation, naval commands write and receive many naval messages. For many reasons, those messages are very important. Ships could not receive or respond to orders without them—quick reaction to emergencies throughout the world depends almost entirely on telegraphic messages. Staffs must often communicate with underway units on administrative as well as operational matters. Efficient coordination of ships' repairs and the ordering of supplies, ordnance, or spare parts for vessels, embarked aviation squadrons, and embarked or deployed Marine units also must often go by messages, though in recent years emails have taken over some of that coordination and administrative load.

On the other hand, messages that take time to comprehend, that omit crucial information, or that violate protocol or procedure will sour the image of your command— probably much more so than messages in the nonnaval services.

Writing messages well, of course, means much more than just the technical matters of getting all the characters in the right blocks. Although such matters carry weight, more weighty still are such subjects as what gets said, to whom, from whom, and why. In other words, the content is much more important than the form, and, as always, the basic communication situation is the first thing to be understood.

The Naval Message—Section by Section

While a synopsis of guidance can be found in figure 5.1, this chapter proceeds by discussing each major section of a nonformatted or "GENADMIN" naval message. Appropriately, the first section of a naval message brings up that key element we have discussed several times before—the audience. The first section of a message is the message address.

THE ADDRESS: GET IT RIGHT, AND GET IT *POLITIC*

Send It to the Right People

Obviously, writing a top-notch and timely message does no good if you don't send it to the right people. Get a strong grasp of command relationships and address all who really need to know.

Who really does need to know? You'll quickly discover that there is much more than just technical accuracy to addressing messages—there are also "political" aspects to this skill. You need to have a good grasp of how significant messages differ from letters in their routing and in who reads them.

Realize Who Will Read Your Message and Why

To begin with, aboard ship *perhaps 90 percent of incoming messages are read by commanding officers.* Moreover, on a ship or operational staff, all officers and many chiefs will also read most incoming messages. (Sometimes these will be seen on a message board aboard ship as in the past; sometimes they will appear on NMCI.)

Beyond the attention of commanding officers in the fleet or field, *flag officers* read messages avidly. If you accidentally add COMNAVAIRLANT to your message as an INFO addressee, NAVAIRLANT himself (the admiral) will probably read your message. So when addressing your message, not only do you want to make sure that everyone who is supposed to see the message gets it, and that you have listed all the required ACTION or INFO addressees, you must also be sensitive about who (from your CO's point of view) should *not* see it. Young command duty officers have probably been called on the carpet more often because of who they addressed a message to than for what they actually said in it.

One Navy ship nearing port in the Northern Pacific began conducting a helo operation to get the mail off the ship expeditiously. In the process a fifteen-pound bag was accidentally blown over the side and sank. The official responsible for the mail—the chief petty officer who was mail clerk—drafted the required message about the loss of the mail sack and included, as INFO addressees, CINCPACFLT, COMNAVAIRPAC, and the embarked flag. Soon the captain summoned the mail clerk. "Who's required to get this message?" the captain asked. "The mail office," responded the chief. "How about these other addressees? Why are they here?" "Well, the flag had some mail in that bag," replied the chief. "How about the others?" "Just general information," said the chief. "*Then don't send it to them,*" replied the captain.

The captain knew the admirals whose commands were listed as INFO addressees in that message would probably read each message personally, and he made a policy of not reporting mishaps to anyone except those with a specific need to know. Obviously, we all have a moral and legal obligation to inform our seniors and those affected of significant mishaps. However, this captain knew that "what people know of your command is what they read," and neither he nor any other alert commanding officer wants every detail of the command's activities spread out unselectively in front of seniors.

Sometimes a CO will *use* the fact that the admiral reads every message. Occasionally a commander will send a message to one organization (the ACTION addressee) to get a heavy-hitter at another organization (an INFO addressee) involved. Sending a message INFO to an admiral is a common way to try to get action taken, especially if the addressee responsible for action hasn't responded to the originator's problem.

On a former skipper's advice: "He told me, 'There is a tone that can be used in a message, a quality of junior talking to a senior, up the chain. Remember, we're the littlest frigate in the Navy, so don't forget to say please and thank you.' The difference was immediately evident in the way people responded to the ship."

—LIEUTENANT
COMMANDER

"Realize that part of the decision as to whether to send things by email, mail, message, or otherwise (hand-carried, flashing light, etc.) is because of timeliness, part is because of bulk, and part of it is to get the elephants involved."

—LDO, ADMIN OFFICER
ON A CARRIER

Figure 5.1 Message Guidance. This message outlines key guidance for all naval messages.

```
R 151001Z JAN 97

FM   TEXT AUTHOR//N1//
TO   NAVAL PERSONNEL//JJJ//
     MARINE CORPS PERSONNEL//JJJ//

INFO CIVILIAN DON PERSONNEL//JJJ//

UNCLAS //N01000//

MSGID/GENADMIN/TEXTAUTHOR  N1//

SUBJ/PREPARATION OF STANDARD NAVAL MESSAGE//

RMKS/1.   MSG CIRCUITS ARE OFTEN TIED UP, ESP DURING
CRISES.   IN HIGH TEMPO OPS OR DURING COMBAT,  EVERY
PRECEDENCE IS AT LEAST IMMEDIATE, AND FLASH MSGS CAN TAKE
OVER AN HOUR TO TRANSMIT. MSGS ARE ALSO EXPENSIVE. LIMIT
NAVAL MSGS TO URGENT COMMS THAT CANNOT REPEAT CANNOT BE
HANDLED BY OTHER MEANS.

2.   MAKE USE OF EMAIL, FAX, PHONE, AND MAIL TO EXTENT
POSSIBLE, ESP WHEN COORDINATING W/STAFFS.  EVEN AT SEA,
EVEN OVERSEAS YOU CAN OFTEN SEND/RCV EMAIL (VIA SALTS,
ETC).

3.   ALSO LIMIT MSG SIZE.   CUT OUT UNNEEDED WORDS, AND
FREELY USE ABBREVS.   PRETEND EACH WORD COSTS A DOLLAR,
AND HONE TEXT. CUT PAGES, PARAS, SENTENCES, WORDS, EVEN
LTRS.

4.   DON'T BURY ACTION.   FIVE PAGE MSGS WITH ACTION AT
END, THOUGH COMMON, ARE COUNTERPRODUCTIVE. PUT ACTION UP
FRONT, AND USE SUBJ LINE AS TITLE, NOT JUST ROUTING
DEVICE.

5.   PRACTICE ART OF MSG WRITING. WATCH HOW CO, XO, CSO
WRITE MSGS, HOW THEY EDIT YOURS.   NOTICE POLITICS OF
MSGS, IMAGE PUT ACROSS, TONE, PROTOCOL, EFFECTIVENESS
ABOVE ALL. LEARN TO GET THE MSG THRU.

BT
```

"In messages we are SAMUEL GOMPERS; not SAM, FAT SAM, GOMPERS, the ship, the platform, or anything else. Other ships are also addressed by their full names."

—Guidance issued aboard USS SAMUEL GOMPERS (AD 37)

Know the consequences of addressing messages. As an LDO on a carrier commented, "Don't get the elephants involved *by chance.*"

Remember Protocol

Besides misaddressals, originators can also displease by forgetting simple rules of naval courtesy. Separate action from information addressees first, but then within either group, list addressees by proper protocol: highest echelons before lower, then by alphabetical order within echelons. Again, remember that all correspondence out of a command is a direct reflection on that command—and this principle is especially true of messages, which have such potentially wide and senior audiences.

Of course, observe protocol not only in the address element but also throughout the message. Remember the assumptions that go with certain usages. One familiar piece of naval advice is that "seniors *direct* attention while juniors *request* or *invite* attention to an issue or problem."

PROTOCOL RATHER OVERDONE?

U.S.S. WASP, 4th Rate

At Sea: Lat:—30–09'N.,
Long:—88–41'W.
June 29, 1904.

Sir:—

1. *I have the honor to report* that on the 27th instant, at about 6:30 P.M., while the "Wasp" was proceeding through the thirty-two mile long narrow dredged channel . . . she sheered out of the channel and ran on to the soft mud flats to the Eastward of the Cut.

. . . .

3. The vessel was not injured in the slightest degree. . . .

—Contributed by Richard Collin, Professor of History,
University of New Orleans

Be Consistent with Plain Language Addresses

As NTP-3 points out, the use of automated message-processing systems has made consistency in format and spelling of Plain Language Addresses (PLAs) critical. If you want the message to get to its destination on time, don't rely on memory. Instead, look up all military-wide standard addresses in the *Message Address Directory;* USN PLAD 1 is the naval section of that publication. Here is further specific guidance:

Spell out numbers in Plain Language Addresses:
- 1–19 as one word: EIGHT or ELEVEN or THIRTEEN, etc.
- 20 and up as: COMDESRON FIVE ZERO or TASK FORCE NINE FIVE PT THREE, etc.

Spell out letter designations phonetically:
- FAIRECONRON ONE DET ALFA

Use no punctuation within each Plain Language Address:
- Use PT for period, DASH for hyphen, etc.

Specify Office Codes in the Addresses of Naval Shore Activities

Navy shore commands are often much bigger than ships, and their decision-making processes are much less centralized. So NTP-3 requires that we spell out office codes in the Plain Language Addresses (PLAs) of all Navy shore activities. If you list more than one code at the end of any PLA, the first one listed should designate the one responsible for action.

Of course, familiarity with the ordinary responsibilities of such shipboard departments as CIC, OPS, ENG, and WEPS does not necessarily help us understand what offices make decisions at a shore command. If you do not know the office responsible for the subject of your message, use the letters JJJ (following the PLA and enclosed by double slants) in place of the unknown code. Having used //JJJ// for any addressee once, however, take note of the code of the shore command that responds to your message, and address that code in subsequent messages or other correspondence.

"Make sure you use the right code *when sending a message to a staff. If an office code in the addressees of a message is wrong, the message will go to the wrong guy, he'll ignore it, and all the work you put into crafting the RMKS will go for naught."*

—NAVY CAPTAIN,
OPNAV

THE SUBJECT LINE: MAKE IT A TITLE, NOT JUST A ROUTING DEVICE

The subject line as title helps key the reader to the main issue in the message, gets the reader's attention, and aids a reader in skimming messages for what is pertinent to the reader's own area of concern. Composing a good subject line takes some care.

Remember the Correspondence Manual's excellent advice: use the subject line to *avoid mystery stories*. Announcing the topic in the subject line prepares the reader for what is to come and helps to get the right people to read the message.

Note that the main purpose of a subject line is not to aid in message routing, although it may help. The subject line is only one of many parts of a message that communications personnel key in on to decide where to route the message aboard ship or within a particular command. Because the subject line is primarily a title, use it as a title and, as with emails and memos, *make it as pertinent and descriptive as possible.*

Write

RECOMMENDED CHANGES IN SQUADRON MESSAGE
HANDLING
instead of
MESSAGE HANDLING

Write

DECISION ON BAQ ENTITLEMENT FOR MEMBER MARRIED
TO MEMBER
instead of
BAQ ENTITLEMENT

If a message were titled just DAMAGE CONTROL rather than LESSONS LEARNED FROM FIGHTING FIRE ABOARD THE USS COLE, it would clearly have fewer readers, and maybe not the most important ones.

Descriptive titles will also help anyone who is searching through files to find the right message quickly—and, of course, such titles will help those service members who have to route a message within a large command. Naturally, there are some subjects that don't require more than perfunctory titles. Also, in most cases a subject line longer than a line or two will just slow the reader down.

The message represented by figure 5.2 was titled "Man Overboard Lessons Learned." This was a suitably brief subject line because everyone in the Submarine Force to whom the message was directed would have already known to what this referred (a widely reported "man overboard" episode had recently cost the lives of two Navy men). The complete message first outlined the circumstances of the event and then proceeded to cite lessons that would have to be taken to heart so such a tragedy would not recur.

THE REFERENCES: AS MUCH AS POSSIBLE, *MAKE THE MESSAGE STAND ALONE*

With tightened security rules, sharply limited distribution, and requirements to destroy files earlier, depending on references is neither efficient nor dependable. Unless the action officer can lay hands on that original copy in the correspondence file, the reference simply may not be available. Under these circumstances, drafting messages that depend on information in prior message traffic is a sure recipe for

Figure 5.2 Lessons Learned Messages. This "Lessons Learned" message was issued by Commander, Submarine Force concerning a man overboard tragedy on the SSN MINNEAPOLIS ST. PAUL. (Parts of the original message have been deleted.)

```
RATUZYUW RUCBKMC7435 0462143-UUBB--RUCBKMC RUCBKME.
ZNR UUUBB ZUI RUCOMCB5917 0462213
RUCBKME T CTF 84
R 152143Z FEB 07 PSN 655980I33
FM COMSUBFOR NORFOLK VA//JJJ//
TO ALSUBFOR
BT
UNCLAS FOUO //N05102//

***THIS IS A 2 SECTION MESSAGE COLLATED BY DMDS***

MSGID/GENADMIN/COMSUBFOR NORFOLK VA/-/FEB// SUBJ/MAN OVERBOARD LESSONS LEARNED//
REF/A/OPNAVINST 3500.39B/CNO/YMD:20040530// AMPN/OPERATIONAL RISK MANAGEMENT (ORM)//
POC/MICHAEL W. BROWN/CAPT/COMSUBLANT/LOC:NORFOLK, VA /TEL:(757)836-1225// RMKS/1.
THE FOLLOWING ARE LESSONS LEARNED (LL) FOR A RECENT MAN OVERBOARD INCIDENT....



..,INCIDENT DESCRIPTION: DURING A RECENT UNDERWAY FROM PLYMOUTH, THREE SAILORS WERE
SWEPT OVERBOARD AS THE SHIP EXITED PROTECTED WATERS BEHIND THE LEE OF THE PLYMOUTH
BREAKWATER WITH PERSONNEL TOPSIDE AND THE FORWARD ESCAPE TRUNK (FET) HATCH OPEN.
TWO ADDITIONAL SAILORS WENT OVERBOARD WHILE ATTEMPTING TO PROVIDE ASSISTANCE. FOUR
WERE EVENTUALLY RECOVERED BY SMALL BOATS OPERATING WITH THE SHIP. ONE WAS ABLE TO
REENTER THE FET. A CONTRIBUTING FACTOR IN THE TWO FATALITIES WAS PERSONNEL REMAINING
TETHERED TO THE SHIP'S DECK WHEN WASHED OVERBOARD IN HEAVY SEAS....



C. LESSONS LEARNED:
1) SEAMANSHIP:
A) ANALYSIS OF A PORT REQUIRES AN IN DEPTH LOOK AT NOT ONLY THE NAVAIDS AND
NAVIGATION HAZARDS BUT ALL OTHER SIGNIFICANT HAZARDS INCLUDING EXPECTED SEA STATE.
IN THIS CASE, THERE WAS EXTENSIVE DISCUSSION ABOUT THE NAVIGATION IN AND OUT OF THE
HARBOR BUT VERY LITTLE DELIBERATE DISCUSSION ABOUT THE EFFECTS OF WEATHER AND
SPECIFICALLY WHERE THOSE EFFECTS WOULD BEGIN TO BE FELT.
B) PROPER INTERPRETATION OF WEATHER REPORTS IS KEY TO A SUCCESSFUL PLAN. IF THE
NAVIGATION PARTY IS UNCLEAR ON THE SIGNIFICANCE OF WHAT PAGE 06 RUCBKMC7435 UNCLAS
FOUO IS REPORTED, THEN DEMAND THAT EXPERTS FULLY EXPLAIN THE SITUATION.
IN THIS CASE, THE WEATHER REPORTS WERE ACCURATE; HOWEVER THE SHIP DID NOT INTERPRET
THEM CORRECTLY.
C) WAVE HEIGHT IS DIFFICULT TO DETERMINE FROM A SUBMARINE BRIDGE.
BOWDITCH CHAPTERS 32 AND 36 PROVIDE GOOD DISCUSSION ON WAVES AND THE EFFECTS OF WIND
AND SHOULD BE REVIEWED AS PART OF THIS TRAINING.
D) STATIONARY FEATURES SUCH AS SHORELINES, BREAKWATERS AND LIGHTHOUSES ARE USEFUL TO
JUDGE THE SEA STATE AND THE SEVERITY OF THE WEATHER. FOR INSTANCE, WAVES BREAKING ON
AN OBJECT OF KNOWN HEIGHT CAN AID IN THE ASSESSMENT OF THE SEA STATE.
2) OPERATIONAL RISK MANAGEMENT (ORM):
A) USE OF DELIBERATE ORM AS DISCUSSED IN REF (A) MUST INCLUDE AN ASSESSMENT OF ALL
SIGNIFICANT HAZARDS.
B) THE USE OF DECISION POINTS FOR WORST CASE SCENARIOS MUST BE UTILIZED DURING THE
PLANNING PROCESS FOR MOST NAVIGATION EVENTS.
TYPICALLY THESE ARE EXPRESSED AS GO-NO-GO POINTS ON THE CHART USED.
C) TRIPWIRES SHOULD BE ESTABLISHED TO INDICATE THAT ASSUMPTIONS USED IN THE PLANNING
PROCESS ARE NO LONGER VALID....

BT
```

delay, retransmittal requests, and misunderstandings. The lesson? *Make your message stand alone* as much as possible.

Referencing and Summarizing Prior Messages and Other Documents—The Pros

Should we try to avoid referring to prior messages and other references *at all?* Yes and no. Referencing past messages or directives and summarizing their import in an AMPN line or short NARR paragraph (standard GENADMIN procedures) can sometimes serve important purposes.

To start with, if a message coming into a staff requires action from higher than the ordinary action officer, then in addition to preparing the recommended response to that message, the action officer on the staff usually has to prepare a briefing memo for the admiral. A message that summarizes pertinent references cuts the action officer's time spent preparing the briefing memo.

Besides saving the action officer on the other end the potentially big headache of searching for the references (that search can sometimes take half a day—as an LDO remarked, "I can't guarantee the guy on the other end will be able to find the crucial reference—even if it's *from him*"), another reason for summarizing the background for the addressee's action officer or commander is that such a summary helps readers get a good feel for the context. It helps them to see what you are asking or arguing and encourages them to proceed to an immediate decision. If you don't handily bring all relevant information to bear right there in the message itself but instead depend on the addressee to look up the references, the decision maker may want to look up all the past message traffic on the subject, read it all carefully, and think about it a while before proceeding to a decision.

Using this same line of reasoning, you can occasionally use a summary of the relevant past emails, messages, and directives to "prompt the witness." If your addressees have to go back and read several detailed references on a subject, they may come up with a different conclusion than you have (especially on a complex subject). But if you summarize the past references, you can make sure that nothing essential (from your point of view) is overlooked. Thus, your summaries can make it much more likely for the addressees to agree with you. For them to disagree formally, they have to go to the extra effort of looking up and reading all the references themselves.

Referencing Past Documents—The Cons

There's another side to this issue, however. For one thing, a commander giving an order seldom needs to cite all the references—often the commander simply says "Do it" and, except for making clear exactly what is wanted and why, has no need to refer to the past at all. The commander is establishing a new procedure, thereby cleaning the slate.

For another thing, both listing past references and summarizing them have often gone much too far. A summary has become for many message and email drafters a habit or crutch, clogging up message traffic with unnecessary volume and encouraging skimming. There has to be a specific usefulness to the summary and a real need for the past references; using references is not just a drill to go through.

Clearly, much past referencing has not been helpful. Because of the requirement to refer to each reference somewhere in the message (originally an attempt to cut down on unnecessary references) we often find paragraphs like this one:

REF A WAS RESPONDED TO BY REF B DELINEATING THE PROBLEMS WITH EXPANSION OF THE SUB-COST CENTER ORGANI-

ZATION WITHIN THE G-3'S COST CENTER UNDER CURRENT DATA PROCESSING CONSTRAINTS. SUBSEQUENTLY, REF C WAS RECEIVED REQUESTING EXPANSION OF TRAINING AS A SEPA-RATE SUB-COST CENTER UNDER THE G-3. REF D RAISED THE SAME ISSUES AS REF A WHICH HAD BEEN ANSWERED BY REF B AND REF E WAS FOLLOW-UP TO REF D.

Before writing such a paragraph, ask yourself this question: *Do the addressees really need to know how negotiations have proceeded on this topic?* If not, is there any other major reason for going into such detail? Often, the answer to both these questions is no.

Yes, summarizing all the relevant correspondence on an issue may be important for a senior command—each document may direct action on a certain aspect of the problem, and if so, all commands affected should have a complete file. Months may pass before the appropriate superior puts all those messages together into a comprehensive instruction.

But for many messages, just giving the general background is enough without extensive reference to past correspondence.

A Solution

Three conclusions seem reasonable, a three-step decision chain, as it were.

First, because the general background is often enough by itself, see if "CNO HAS REQUESTED . . ." or "PREVIOUS COMMUNICATION HAS SPELLED OUT REQUIREMENTS FOR . . ." can effectively replace "REF A WAS RESPONDED TO BY REF B WHICH CANCELED REF C," etc.

Second, if you believe a summary is either necessary or helpful, do your best to reference as few messages as possible and to make any summary as brief as you can. Strive above all to keep in mind the needs of the action officer you're writing to.

Third, in almost all cases, be sure to put the main point up front, in the very first paragraph. The change to GENADMIN format has made that possible in almost all cases.

THE TEXT: GET TO THE MAIN POINT QUICKLY

Chief among concerns having to do with the text is the need to get started right—if you do, the rest of the message tends to fall together nicely.

Jump Right in with the Action

How do you get to the main point quickly? Sometimes your addressees just need to know the action required or requested, with specifics in later paragraphs after a general announcement in the first. In this case, an effective opening paragraph is simple and to the point. For example:

RMKS/I. EFFECTIVE IMMEDIATELY DO NOT PROCESS PARTIAL PAYMENTS ON PREPAID RESUBMISSION INVOICES. PROCESS THE EXACT AMOUNT LISTED ON THE PITR.

This message opening informs the reader immediately of the basic action required; the reader may at leisure review the specific details found in subsequent paragraphs.

On other occasions, an effective opening makes a simple, direct reference to a prior message that made a tasking or a request:

"With messages . . . senior officers are not looking for the way you write but for the MEAT."
—Navy Commander, submariner

IAW REF A, FEEDBACK ON RELIABILITY OF ORDNANCE TEST EQUIPMENT FOLLOWS.

—or—

THE USNTPS PREPARATORY CURRICULUM REQUESTED BY REF A IS APPROVED.

These openings are effective because they are clear and immediately grasped. The reader knows exactly what is to follow.

Use the CAP Formula for Opening Summaries

Sometimes giving the reader a brief context for what follows is important. For this purpose, use a paragraph modeled after the CAP formula:

Context—specific Aspect focused on—message's Point

As an example, the following opening paragraph gives brief context and focus and then gets to the main point quickly, leaving details to follow in subsequent paragraphs:

Context:	1. PLANS FOR CHANGE OF COMMAND ON 30 DECEMBER INCLUDE A RECEPTION FOR APPROX 700 IN HANGAR BAY OF USS IWO JIMA.
Aspect:	AUGMENT OF IWO JIMA FOOD SERVICE PERSONNEL IS NECESSARY TO ASSIST IN FOOD PREPARATION/ SERVICE.
Point:	UNITS WILL RESPOND AS OUTLINED BELOW.

Such an opening prepares those with action obligations for the details that follow and gives a brief executive summary to others who can either stop there or read further for information. Whatever their needs, all readers have gotten the gist of the message and have not had to wait several paragraphs to discover what on earth the writer is getting at.

Remember: except on long, detailed messages, you'll usually have no standard paragraph headings such as "Purpose," "Background," and "Action" that help the reader to skim. Clearly, then, briefing the whole matter in the first lines is at least as important in messages as it is in other kinds of naval writing.

A "PERSONAL FOR" NAVADMIN That Quickly Gets to the Point

In a "PERSONAL FOR" message, commanders speak personally to specific individuals or groups and back off from telegraphic style a bit to do so. The following NAVADMIN quickly gets to the point, both in its subject line and in the very first sentences. It then provides telling details to get its point across.

R 252128Z JUL 94

FM CNO WASHINGTON DC//N 1//

TO NAVADMIN

UNCLAS PERSONAL FOR COMMANDERS, COMMANDING OFFICERS AND OFFICERS IN CHARGE//N00000//

NAVADMIN 134/94

MSGID/GENADMIN/PERS323//

SUBJ/TIMELY SUBMISSION OF PERFORMANCE EVALUATIONS AND FITNESS REPORTS//

RMKS/1. THE PURPOSE OF THIS NAVADMIN IS TO SOLICIT YOUR HELP ON AN ISSUE THAT HAS A VERY REAL IMPACT ON OUR MOST IMPORTANT RESOURCE, PEOPLE. THE TIMELINESS AND ACCURACY OF OFFICER FITNESS REPORTS AND ENLISTED EVALS ARE WAY TOO IMPORTANT FOR YOU, THE LEADERS OF OUR NAVY, TO LET SLIDE. THE SINGLE MOST IMPORTANT FACTOR IN BOARD DECISIONS IS PERFORMANCE AS DOCUMENTED IN EVALUATIONS AND FITREPS. AN INCOMPLETE PERFORMANCE RECORD IS POTENTIALLY DETRIMENTAL TO A CANDIDATE'S CAREER. LAST YEAR, OVER 140,000 EVALUATIONS WERE RECEIVED LATE, AND IN THE LAST THREE MONTHS ALONE, 6643 FITREPS WERE RECEIVED LATE. IN ADDITION, ALMOST 4000 MESSAGES REQUESTING MISSING EVALUATIONS JUST FOR E7/E8/E9 SELECTION BOARDS WERE REQUIRED. SIMILAR REPORTING DEFICIENCIES ARE NOTED BY EVERY OFFICER AND ENLISTED BOARD.

2. EVALUATION OF PERFORMANCE IS A FUNDAMENTAL RESPONSIBILITY OF COMMAND. FAILURE TO DO SO IN A TIMELY MANNER IS AN ABDICATION OF AN IMPORTANT RESPONSIBILITY.

3. REPORTING SENIORS MUST ENSURE THAT THE RECORDS OF ASSIGNED PERSONNEL ARE COMPLETE. THE ONLY WAY THE NAVY CAN BE SURE OUR PEOPLE'S ADVANCEMENT, ASSIGNMENT, AND TRAINING ARE HANDLED FAIRLY IS TO BE SURE THEIR FITREPS AND EVALS ARE CORRECTLY COMPLETED THE FIRST TIME AND ARE FORWARDED ON TIME. WE NEED YOUR HELP ON THIS.

4. RELEASED BY FRANK L. BOWMAN, VADM, USN.//

BT

THE TEXT: OTHER GUIDANCE

Of Course, Use Telegraphic Style . . .

"Keep your messages short; you lose if you write more than a page."
—CO OF A COMM CENTER

- Do not waste words. Except in PERSONAL FOR messages, normally leave out unnecessary adjectives, adverbs, prepositions, and most articles (a, an, the).
- Use the imperative voice liberally. Instead of WE REQUEST THAT, say REQUEST; instead of YOU SHOULD CONTACT MR. HERBERT, say CONTACT MR. HERBERT.
- Use small words instead of big ones where the sense is the same. Leave out words used only for the rhythm or aesthetic quality of a sentence.

Revised by use of standard rules for message brevity, the following paragraph from a Military Sealift Command letter can be put into brief and clear message style. The letter, with wordy expressions italicized, reads:

In order to eliminate *any* delay in *the* ammunition loading *operations, we* request *that, if possible, you* correct all deficiencies prior *to your ship's* arrival *at* Naval Weapons Station, Concord. *In the event* you do not have sufficient crew *members* on board *to accomplish this work, you are hereby authorized to* employ *the services of a* commercial contractor to correct *these* deficiencies.

"Be most concerned with communication, not length. Make it free-standing, so that someone who knows nothing of the subject can get the point."

—CAPTAIN

The message reads:

> TO AVOID DELAY IN LOADING AMMO, RQST YOU CORRECT ALL DEFICIENCIES PRIOR ARRIVAL NWS CONCORD. IF TOO FEW CREW ON BOARD, YOU MAY HIRE COMMERCIAL CONTRACTOR TO CORRECT DEFICIENCIES.

. . . But Beware of False Economy

- Never sacrifice clarity for brevity. Word a message so that it clearly expresses the meaning that the drafter desires to convey.
- Be sparing with punctuation, but use it where necessary for clarity or emphasis.
- Don't customarily omit little verbs (is, are, was, etc.). They don't cost much in transmission time, and often their omission leads to confusion.
- Abbreviate where useful with standard, well-understood abbreviations, but don't overdo it. Sometimes words have to be spelled out or the transmission time saved will be much less than the time readers spend trying to decode or correctly construe unfamiliar abbreviations.

Try Using One Governing Statement

Consider reworking longer messages so that, as in "bullet" format, a series of statements or questions falls under one governing statement. By using this method and by making a few other astute changes, a Marine colonel shortened the text of the following message (in pre-GENADMIN format) by one half. The message originally read:

> FROM: USNA ANNAPOLIS MD
> TO: CG FIRST MARBGDE HAWAII
> BT
> UNCLAS //1531//
> SUBJ: MARINE SUMMER OPTION CRUISE
> A. PHONCON USNA MAX WHITE/FIRST MARBGDE CAPT PALANCIA OF 10 FEB 83
> 1. REF (A) REQ THAT ALL REQUESTS FOR INFORMATION CONCERNING THE MARINE OPTION CRUISE BE SUB BY MSG.
> 2. IAW REF A, THE FOLLOWING INFO REQ.
> A. IT IS DESIRED THAT THE MIDSHIPMEN BE ALLOWED TO EAT IN THE ENLISTED DINING FACILITY: WHAT PAPERWORK IS NECESSARY?
> B. WHAT IS THE TOTAL NUMBER OF MIDSHIPMEN THAT THE BRIGADE CAN HANDLE? IS ADEQUATE BOQ SPACE AVAILABLE FOR THIS NUMBER?
> C. DURING THE SUMMER OF 1982, A SCUBA TRAINING PROGRAM WAS OFFERED, IN THE LATE AFTERNOON. CAN THE PROGRAM BE OFFERED IN 1983?
> D. IT IS NOT DESIRED (FOR FINANCIAL REASONS) THAT THE MIDSHIPMEN MISS ANY MEALS. CAN "C" RATIONS BE PURCHASED THROUGH THE BRIGADE TO PREVENT MISSED MEALS?
> E. IS IT POSSIBLE TO PROVIDE A STANDARD WELCOME ABOARD PACKAGE FOR EACH MIDSHIPMAN WHO PARTICIPATES IN THE PROGRAM?

F. CAN THE MIDSHIPMEN GET THEIR AVIATION PHYSIOL-OGY TESTING COMPLETED IN HAWAII?

G. SEVERAL OF THE MIDSHIPMEN ARE AIRBORNE QUALI-FIED. WILL THERE BE AN OPPORTUNITY FOR THEM TO JUMP WHILE THEY ARE WITH THE BRIGADE?

3. MAJ WHITE IS CURRENTLY SCHEDULED TO ARRIVE IN HAWAII ON 4. MARCH. HE WILL BE AVAILABLE UNTIL 11 MARCH TO ACCOMPLISH ANY COORDINATION NECESSARY FOR THIS PRO-GRAM. CAN HE MEET WITH THE BRIGADE LIAISON OFFICER DURING THIS TIME?

The revised message reads:

FM USNA ANNAPOLIS MD	
TO CG FIRST MARBGDE HAWAII	
BT	
UNCLAS //N01531//	
SUBJ: MARINE SUMMER OPTION CRUISE	
1. MAJ WHITE, USNA LIAISON OFCR FOR MARINE SUMMER OPTION CRUISE, WILL BE IN HAWAII 4-11 MAR TO COORDI-NATE WITH 1ST BDE REGARDING THIS PROGRAM. REQUEST HE MEET WITH BDE LIAISON OFCR AT THIS TIME TO DETERMINE IF MIDSHIPMEN CAN:	← Eliminated unneeded "Reference A" and all subsequent references to it
A. BE BILLETED IN BOQ? HOW MANY?	← Combined separate questions in lines A–G into one question with seven parts
B. EAT IN ENLISTED MESS?	
C. BE FED ALL MEALS? (C-RATIONS ACCEPTABLE WHEN ENLISTED MESS NAVL; USNA WILL PURCHASE IF REQUIRED)	← Omitted reasons and background wherever obvious or unnecessary
D. PARTICIPATE IN SCUBA TRAINING?	
E. BE PROVIDED STANDARD WELCOME ABOARD PACKAGE?	← Inventively reduced wording through-out; used parallel structure for all verbs to fit with overall question "If mid-shipmen can . . ."
F. GET AVIATION PHYSIOLOGY TESTING COMPLETED?	
G. PARTICIPATE IN AIRBORNE JUMPS? (QUALIFIED MIDSHIPMEN ONLY)	← Condensed 3 paragraphs into 1
BT	

—contributed by Colonel C. E. McDaniel, USMC, Retired

Specify the Format for the Reply in Tasking Messages

Tasking people to do work for you is an art. A DESRON staff officer outlined a technique for tasking ships to send information to the squadron. He said that to get good input, you should be sure to specify the following:

- The titles of applicable references—and sometimes you have to actually send the references too.
- A date to respond by, the date selected so you can collate all information and draft a response to your superior by your due date.
- A format that helps you work with the data, that is, a format specifying both what data you want *and* in what order.
- Specific units of measurement required, for if you don't specify, they'll send you a general answer and then you'll have to go back again to ask for more.
- A point of contact at your location, including a phone number and email address.

Here's part of a message that shows an effective tasking, along with a typical response to that tasking. Note that the tasking message specifies both the *order* and the *kind* of information required.

3. TO DETERMINE SCOPE OF SUPPORT REPLACEMENT/REPAIR INITIATIVES RQRD ON ABOVE CRITICAL TEST EQUIPMENT, REQ YOU PROVIDE SPECIFIC COMMENTS/FEEDBACK AS FOL NLT 30 OCT 87:
  A. TYPE OF ORDNANCE TEST EQUIPMENT (TS-147 OR MK 368)
    (1) EQUIPMENT RELIABILITY
    (2) EQUIPMENT MAINTAINABILITY (AVG TIME RQRD FOR REPAIR OR CALIBRATION AND CAL RQMTS)
    (3) DOCUMENTATION AVAILABILITY (TECH MANUALS, APL SUPPORT)
    (4) RECOMMENDATIONS FOR IMPROVEMENT

The following would be a good response:

1. IRT REF A, FOL FEEDBACK PROVIDED:
  A. ORDNANCE TEST EQUIPMENT TS-147
    (1) TS-147 OPERATIONAL APPROX HALF THE TIME.
    (2) INPORT CONUS, CAL/RPR TAKES UP TO 120 DAYS. ANNUAL CAL/RPR CAN BE DONE CONUS ONLY.
    (3) TW-147 NOT COSAL OR APL SUPPORTED AND AVAIL OF RPR PARTS LIMITED. TECH MANUAL OUTDATED AND GIVES LITTLE TROUBLESHOOTING GUIDANCE.
    (4) RCMD REPLACE TS-147 WITH TS-145.
  B. ORDNANCE TEST EQUIPMENT MK 363 MOD 3/4 MEST SET
    (1) MEST SET ONBD VERY RELIABLE WITH ALMOST ZERO DOWN TIME.
    (2) MK 363 RQRS ANNUAL CAL WITH AVG TIME APPROX ONE WEEK. RPRS DONE CONUS.
    (3) ONBD TECHMAN OUTDATED, DOES NOT REFLECT EQPT CHANGES, OFFERS LITTLE USEFUL TROUBLESHOOTING GUIDANCE, NOT COSAL SUPPORTED.
    (4) RCMD INSTITUTE COSAL SUPPORT AND UPDATE TECHMAN.

THE USEFULNESS OF AMBIGUITY

In the early '60s a Captain (D) led his Mediterranean Destroyer Flotilla into the Black Sea, where he soon sighted a squadron of Russian Cruisers closing his flotilla at high speed.

From leading Russian Cruiser (by light)

WHAT ARE YOU DOING IN THE BLACK SEA.

Turmoil ensued amongst the Staff on the flotilla-leader's bridge while signal logs were sent for and Diplomatic Clearance discussed. At last Captain (D) raised an elegant hand for silence, and said quietly to the Signalman,

Reply:
    TWENTY-ONE KNOTS.

—From Captain Jack Broome, *Make Another Signal*
(London: William Kimber, 1973), p. 248.

A LAST WORD

Of course, besides learning prose-cutting techniques, abbreviations, and so on, there is at least one other method of keeping costs down and the circuits clear. Limit all electrical transmissions to urgent official business that other means cannot satisfactorily handle. Use email, fax, mail, or telephone whenever possible *in place of* naval messages.

CHECKLIST FOR COMPOSING STANDARD NAVAL MESSAGES

Radiomen and Communication Centers have checklists to help you double check the technical details of message writing and message handling. This checklist has a different intent: it is formulated to help you get the right points across.

"Yes, there are lots of formatted messages. But 80 percent of messages written on a staff are still GENADMIN."

—Navy Lieutenant

- Have you included all necessary ACTION addressees? INFO addressees?
- Should you omit any addressees?
- Within respective categories, are addressees listed according to protocol?
- Have you included office codes for any Navy shore activity PLAs?
- Have you included the pertinent references?
- Can you do without any references?
- Is there any correspondence needed for understanding this message that addressees do not hold? If so, have you summarized it or sent it along?
- Will the subject line adequately identify the subject to all readers?
- Have you assigned the appropriate precedence?
- Is the classification proper, and have you followed all proper procedures for classification?
- Does the main point appear in the first paragraph of the message text?
- Consider the commands and officials receiving this message—will they all understand it? Do you need to add or clarify any statements?
- Can you eliminate explanations nobody needs?
- Consider the words carefully; if each one cost you a dollar, would you include all those you have written?

- Could you condense the message substantially by changing the format?
- On the other hand, have you stressed brevity over clarity? Is the message understandable? Are all abbreviations standard and clear?
- Is the paragraphing logical?
- Can you use indentation or headings to good effect?
- Will anything in this particular message or the way it is written give the command a bad image?
- Have you included all of the essential—but only the essential—information?
- Has everyone seen this message who should see it before it goes out?
- Does this information really have to go by message?
- Will the CO release this message?

On Formatted Messages: The CASREP

When writing a CASREP, put yourself in the place of the person who reads it. Ask, "What would I want to know if I were getting this report?"

—Chief Electronics Technician

Besides standard naval messages in GENADMIN or other specified formats, naval communicators use a variety of fully "formatted" messages designed to ensure that all of specific kinds of crucial information—such as ship's movement, logistic requirements, etc.—gets from a ship to multiple audiences regularly and efficiently.

By filing a MOVREP, a communicator won't have to reinvent the wheel when announcing the ship is getting under way—something each ship does dozens of times during a year. The addressees are standardized so the communicator won't forget anyone who ought to know this information. Typically, the formatted message must go to a great many addressees.

You might think that writing formatted messages would just be filling in the blanks. But mere bits of information can never communicate everything we mean, so throughout formatted messages we find "Amplification" (AMPN) lines and "Narrative" (NARR) and "Remarks" (RMKS) sections, which call for good, brief naval prose. Take, for example, one of the most critical of all naval messages in the surface Navy, a form also important to submarines and aviation units: the CASREP.

WRITING CASREP REMARKS

You need a remarks section in a CASREP because no amount of formatted information can convey the exact technical information required to fix the casualty. Especially on surface ships, the exact impact of a specific casualty on a ship's operations and the difficulty of fixing the problem will vary widely from vessel to vessel, even among identical ship types.

Leading petty officers, chiefs, and officers at all levels may have to write or revise CASREPs. On some ships, division officers write the whole CASREP even though they often don't have specific technical expertise on the particular equipment involved. No matter who does the basic draft, COs and XOs give intense scrutiny to the remarks section (checking for pertinence, completeness, and brevity too) before a CASREP leaves the ship. For many reasons, writing a CASREP is a *high-priority item* at most commands.

"We have to compose the REMARKS and AMPLIFICATION sections with great care because our admiral reads every one of them. Politics plays a part: we have to work it so as not to slap the tender in the face, because we need their assistance, nor can we make ourselves look bad."

—Lieutenant on a DD

Write Your CASREP Remarks for a Multiple Audience

Who will read your CASREP? A great number of people at many commands. Some of them will be experts in the particular technical area involved, but most of them probably will not be. Your "RMKS" section must serve both expert and nonexpert audiences. Solve this dilemma by following three procedures. First, use headings and indentations in the RMKS section to help the reader. Second, pen an executive summary at the beginning of the section for your operational commanders and other "generalists." Third, follow the summary with a technical description composed for the technical expert.

Use Headings and Indentations

Just as they help the reader find a way through any notice, instruction, or technical report, typographical features can help the reader find crucial information in a glance at a CASREP. NTP-3 allows indentation in naval messages when it will increase readability or clarity. The free-form nature of RMKS and AMPN sections also allows for the use of headings.

Write an Executive Summary for Commanders and Nonexperts

Suppose you serve as an officer aboard a combatant. Your commodore and other superiors will want to know the ship or submarine's exact condition so they will know how to employ her and whether her full war-fighting capability is available. The commodore and fleet commanders will need to know when she'll be completely ready again, if and where she'll have to go for repairs, what they might do to expedite the process, and so on.

Experience suggests a ship's operational commander will immediately look at the following areas of the CASREP, skimming the rest:

- the name of the ship
- the specific equipment CASREPed—all in the formatted portion
- the C-rating
- the summary portion of the remarks

Obviously, your summary is very important. A tested procedure must begin by carefully describing *the exact nature and extent of the casualty.* Write this description for a general Navy reader, not a technical expert. After this description, discuss the casualty's *impact* on the ship's immediate and near-future operational, exercise, or inspection schedule. Then speak to the *mission degradation,* that is, the effect of the casualty on the ship's ability to carry out primary and secondary missions.

Operational and administrative commanders may have issued specific requirements (C-ratings, etc.) for what you must cover in these areas. If not, by your remembering to write for the informational needs of commanders, and by your keeping your remarks general enough that all of them can get the gist, both captain and chief will be able to grasp the big picture immediately.

Follow the Summary with a Technical Description for the Experts

The technical description must supply the technical staff on the beach with enough detailed information that they can start the repair process in motion, sometimes well before the ship returns to port.

The ultimate readers will be personnel with technical expertise on the specific equipment CASREPed. These experts will usually work at a repair facility and will arrange for parts, organize technical assistance, and act as the control point for

"It's traditional: in the first sentences of the first paragraph of a CASREP, place the sentence to be read to the admiral."

—Chief Engineer
on a destroyer

"Make sure you comment on the impact of the casualty on the command schedule—what you won't be able to do next week, what problems the casualty will present in the ship's sked. The admiral himself won't pick up the impact necessarily just by being told the specific casualty; the staff might not either; but the ship will certainly know. And the admiral goes up the wall if not told."

—Commander,
XO of a DD

"In the Navy, it's important to be as self-sufficient as possible. So in point papers, emails, messages, or CASREPs, always include what *you've done* about the problem. Don't raise any new issue without answering this. Your boss or a shore command is much more likely to help if *you've already started on the problem."*

—LIEUTENANT
COMMANDER ON A
DESRON STAFF

"It's always better if you can do the research, rather than the repair facility. It's not as important to them as it is to you; and it will speed up the process if the chief on the other end doesn't have to punch the pubs for every detail."

—FORMER CHIEF,
LDO LIEUTENANT
(JUNIOR GRADE)

all services. They will need detailed and specific technical information with which to begin.

Do not, however, be obscure in this description. A duty officer or chief on the squadron or group staff must often get the repair process started, and neither of these people will necessarily be an expert in the specific area of the casualty. For example, the chief who reads the CASREP may be a chief electronics technician, and the casualty may be to a piece of engineering equipment he or she has never seen. Nevertheless, this reader may have to interpret the message and initiate action in response to the CASREP without expert assistance, especially if the message comes in on a holiday or a weekend.

So although the technical description should detail all the vital specifics, it should include as little jargon and technical obscurity as possible.

Be Very Careful about the Details

A chief on a naval supply ship learned just how vital specific details could be. Deciding he was obliged to do a CASREP, he looked at the specific piece of equipment in front of him, called it a "motor generator" on the CASREP form (the name everyone aboard ship customarily gave the equipment), and reported the number he found in front of him.

The Navy Supply System, however, called only the *bottom* part of the equipment a "motor generator"; the equipment that fitted on the top had another name and different stock number. It would be like requiring a *lamp* to be called, for repair purposes, a *lamp* and a *lamp shade.* As a result, the contractor assigned to the repair said, "We can't go further with the repair; we haven't been contracted to work on the top part." The confusion cost the Navy an extra $2,000 and several days to straighten out.

Give the Repair Facility Enough Information

If a ship is in its home port, completeness may not be crucial; a phone call can clear up questions pretty quickly. But if the ship is under way or at another port, the facility vitally needs *complete* information. Any need to query you because you didn't put in enough detail could result in a substantial delay in the repair—perhaps two to four days, according to a median estimate. A senior chief at a SIMA estimated that *50 percent of the time,* there are not enough data in the CASREP.

The Navy's general need to reduce fleet message traffic sometimes conflicts with the needs of the shore-based technical staff to get detailed answers for fixing vital equipment. Only experience will tell you how much is too much information.

One lieutenant wondered why the shore facility was advising him by message how to troubleshoot a type of equipment having a different voltage than the CASREPed equipment aboard his ship. Only later did he find out that the executive officer had cut out the specific voltage he had listed in the CASREP before it left the ship to shorten the message's length.

Think twice before cutting out details.

POOR CASREP REMARKS

Here's the REMARKS section of a CASREP from a ship away from her home port. The duty officer on the staff who received the CASREP says that as soon as he read it he knew SURFLANT would call. Sure enough, they did. But before that, the chief staff officer had already hit the roof. Why? See the duty officer's comments annotated below (the underlines have been added for clarify).

"Accuracy in the APLs is especially critical. We have six different ships of this type; the same valve for each ship might have been made by six different companies. Some engineers will put 88 and their SSN in the blank—but the wrong company's valve simply won't work! And a bad APL is a really big problem for an RSG, because we begin researching long before the ship pulls in!"

—COMMANDER OF A READINESS SUPPORT GROUP

RMKS/MK 42 MOD 9 5″ 54 ELECTRICAL SYSTEM NOT FUNCTIONING. NO IMPACT ON CURRENT OPERATIONS. REDUCES SHIP'S AAW AND ASUW CAPABILITIES. CASUALTY TO ELECTRICALLY DAMAGED SOLENOIDS THAT CONTROL CARRIER AND LOADER DRUM VALVE BLOCK ASSEMBLIES. SOLENOIDS ON ORDER PRIOR TO CASREP CONDITION. SHIP'S SKED: ENRT NEWPORT RI 23 JAN; IPT NEWPORT 25 JAN-26 JAN; IPT PHILADELPHIA 29 JAN–15 FEB.//

Too generic—is it completely down?

Far too nonspecific: how?

So why did they CASREP now?

We don't know from this what happened or how it happened. Did the technician break it? Was it bad PMS? We can assume some things, but he doesn't tell us or SURFLANT enough for operational purposes or for repair.

GOOD CASREP REMARKS

Below is the REMARKS section of a different CASREP, this one cited by the same duty officer as an excellent message. It affords a clear and concise summary, vital operational information, and a fully detailed technical description of the problem. See the duty officer's comments noted below (again, the underlines have been added and would not be in the actual message).

"Messages are hard to read—they're like sets of orders. To this day I can't find the applicable information in a set of orders easily. Similarly with messages. And if you write a formatted message and in the midst of all the hieroglyphics, leave out a comma, it gets sent back to you!"

—NAVAL AVIATOR

RMKS/CASUALTY: MK 53 ATTACK CONSOLE WILL NOT POSITION KEEP THEREFORE WILL NOT UPDATE-PREDICT TARGET COURSE AND SPEED. MK 53 AC WILL ACCEPT NDT FROM ALL SONAR UNITS. MANUAL INPUT OF TARGET COURSE AND SPEED CAN BE USED FOR ASROC-TORP FIRINGS. IMPACT: MAJOR IMPACT ON INSURV TO BE CONDUCTED WEEK OF 29 FEBRUARY. MISSION DEGRADATION: MINOR IMPACT ON ASW MISSION AREA. TECHNICAL DESCRIPTION: 12A1A4A15 MG2 (MOTOR-GENERATOR) HAS SAT INPUT BUT HAS INSUFFICIENT TORQUE TO TURN CLUTCH CM3 WHEN CLUTCH IS ENERGIZED. STRAY

Identifies both the specific casualty and the ship's continuing capability, thus clarifying the exact scope of the casualty.

The Opn'l Cdr will probably realize this on his own, but the ship makes sure of it.

Tells Opn'l Cdr the ship can live with the casualty; she can do an ASW operation if needed.

VOLTAGES HAVE BEEN
INTERMITTENT AND BELIEVED
TO BE RELATED TO CAUSE OF
CASUALTY. WHEN "GOING INTO
CONTACT" OR WHEN NDT FROM
SONAR THE CLUTCH ENGAGES
MOTOR BUT IMMEDIATELY SEIZES
DUE TO INSUFFICIENT TORQUE
STATED ABOVE, THEN BY
PULLING RELAY K1 OR "COMING
OUT OF CONTACT" THE CLUTCH
DISENGAGES AND SYSTEM WILL
PK UNTIL NEXT NDT OR WHEN
GOING BACK INTO CONTACT.
SIMA NEWPORT R-5 ASSISTED IN
TROUBLESHOOTING. CASUALTY
DISCOVERED WHILE
TROUBLESHOOTING TIMING
CIRCUITRY FOR CONSTANT 7
SECOND FLASH. REQ TECH ASSIST
TO DETERMINE WHERE STRAY
VOLTAGES ARE COMING FROM.
SHIP'S SCHEDULE: 25 FEB ISE (PRE-
INSURV); 25 FEB–7 MAR INPORT.

Identifying particular components as it does, this technical description describes the problem in detail. As a result, the repair agency may be able to troubleshoot the problem by message.

This tells the staff that the problem is beyond SIMA's scope. It also shows that the ship is doing its best to be on top of things, already getting what help it can.

Additional detail that may help the repair agency identify the problem.

CASREP REMARKS WITH INDENTATIONS FOR READABILITY

NTP-3 authorizes indentation (up to twenty spaces) in messages where it will aid graphic clarity. It does so here, breaking up long two-blocked material into readable (and skimmable) chunks. Consider using indentation in all long RMKS or AMPN sections of formatted messages.

RMKS/CASUALTY: MK 53 ATTACK.
  CONSOLE WILL NOT POSITION
  KEEP THEREFORE WILL NOT
  UPDATE—PREDICT TARGET
  COURSE AND SPEED. MK 53 AC
  WILL ACCEPT NDT FROM ALL
  SONAR UNITS. MANUAL INPUT
  OF TARGET COURSE AND SPEED
  CAN BE USED FOR ASROC-TORP
  FIRINGS.
IMPACT: MAJOR IMPACT ON
  INSURV TO BE CONDUCTED
  WEEK OF 29 FEBRUARY.
MISSION DEGRADATION: MINOR
  IMPACT ON ASW MISSION AREA.
TECHNICAL DESCRIPTION:
  12A1A4A15 MG2 (MOTOR-
  GENERATOR) HAS SAT INPUT
  BUT HAS INSUFFICIENT

Executive Summary

TORQUE TO TURN CLUTCH
CM3 WHEN CLUTCH IS
ENERGIZED. STRAY VOLTAGES
HAVE BEEN INTERMITTENT
AND BELIEVED TO BE RELATED
TO CAUSE OF CASUALTY. WHEN
"GOING INTO CONTACT" OR
WHEN NDT FROM SONAR THE
CLUTCH ENGAGES MOTOR BUT
IMMEDIATELY SEIZES DUE TO
INSUFFICIENT TORQUE STATED
ABOVE, THEN BY PULLING   Technical Description
RELAY K1 OR "COMING OUT
OF CONTACT" THE CLUTCH
DISENGAGES AND SYSTEM WILL
PK UNTIL NEXT NDT OR WHEN
GOING BACK INTO CONTACT.
SIMA NEWPORT R-5 ASSISTED
IN TROUBLESHOOTING.
CASUALTY DISCOVERED WHILE
TROUBLESHOOTING TIMING
CIRCUITRY FOR CONSTANT 7
SECOND FLASH. REQ TECH
ASSIST TO DETERMINE WHERE
STRAY VOLTAGES ARE COMING
FROM.
SHIP'S SCHEDULE: 25 FEB ISE (PRE-
INSURV); 25 FEB–7 MAR INPORT.

6

Performance Evaluations

Few documents are read so avidly as enlisted evaluations and fitness reports. The following pages focus on Navy performance evaluations.

The Navy Evaluation System—A Quick Glance

In the late 1990s, the Navy instituted a completely new fitness report and enlisted evaluation system, the first wholesale change in decades. Patterned on the best of modern personnel systems, the new system aids Navy people in

• telling the truth;
• counseling their people; and
• selecting the best possible people to be promoted.

The system is fully spelled out in BUPERSINST 1610.10 (current edition). What follows here is guidance based on interviews done throughout the naval service; the many examples provided in this chapter are based on actual Navy evals and fitreps. (Note that although counseling is a major part of the evaluation system, this chapter deals only with the writing of evaluations, not with the counseling. See the memorandum on pp. 68–69 in chapter 2 for a good example of a counseling memo.)

We begin by presenting five key points.

"HIT HARD AND HIT FAST": PRESENT ONLY THE MOST IMPORTANT INFORMATION

Even though there are many numerical rankings or percentages on evaluations, most of these markings do little to get across a sense of the person's real accomplishments or potential. Written comments are still very much needed. By painting a word picture of a particular individual's strengths, a writer can help readers distinguish one person from another. For one thing, comments can specify important personal qualities of an individual. For another, they help to substantiate the promotion recommendation (pointing out the reasons the commander made a particular recommendation in the first place). In such ways they can greatly aid a selection board diligently attempting to ferret out slight distinctions between dozens or even hundreds of highly touted individuals. A person whose write-up does not include convincing substantiation (in the form of specifics) will often suffer in comparison to someone whose write-up does—whatever the overall recommendations may be.

However, with only a relatively small space available for write-ups, the ability to *synthesize and summarize* is vital. In particular, one must learn to

- present only the *vital facts and key qualities,*
- present them *succinctly,* and
- phrase them clearly—in plain English, not jargon.

Let's look at a couple of examples.

A Draft of a Modern Fitrep in 12 Point/Pitch

Here is a Navy officer fitness report that focuses on a few achievements and on some special qualities of the person being evaluated. It presents only the *key information*—summarizing the rest. Note that there is no underlining or boldface, for these are prohibited by instructions. The numbers in parentheses—#33, #37—refer to specific performance traits that the phrases in the write-up illustrate. For all such trait areas in which the individual is ranked 5.0 or 1.0, justifying comments are required.

STANDARD FITREP (12 POINT/PITCH)

> **41. COMMENTS ON PERFORMANCE.** * All 5.0 and 1.0 marks must be specifically substantiated in comments. No numerical ranking permitted. Comments must be verifiable. Bold, underlined, italic, or other highlighted type is prohibited. Font must be 10 or 12 pitch (10 to 12 point) only. Use upper and lower case.
>
> An extremely determined officer—my top officer recruiter—LT Johnston has:
> - Attained a 140% productivity increase in the 1st Quarter of FY 81 over the entirety of FY 80 recruiting efforts for her programs. (#37)
> - Contributed greatly to the 115% increase in 1980 command productivity.
> - Earned awards of two gold wreaths for recruiting excellence.
> - Volunteered to develop a major new managerial concept for the command that promises to contribute greatly to the officer recruiting effort.
> - Succeeded in nation's largest recruiting district—a formidable challenge.
> - Presented all her collateral duty assignments on time and well prepared. (#33)
> - Won nomination as the FY 90 "Recruiter of the Year" for Navy Recruiting Area X, and nomination for CNRA-X Officer Recruiter of the Quarter, 1st Quarter, FY 91.
> The "cornerstone" of the officer recruiting team because of her support of all officer programs, she is most strongly recommended for promotion.

The first and last bullet are particularly noteworthy, but all of them are pertinent and strong, while the opening and closing comments (particularly "my top officer recruiter" and the very strong closing recommendation for early promotion) are key.

Note that specific recommendations for future duty assignments have been left for other blocks on the form.

The Same Fitrep, with Smaller Typeface

The version above uses 12-point type height and 12-pitch spacing. The version below uses 10 point/pitch; these are the only two sizes authorized.

STANDARD FITREP (10 POINT/PITCH)

---

41. COMMENTS ON PERFORMANCE. * All 5.0 and 1.0 marks must be specifically substantiated in comments. No numerical ranking permitted. Comments must be verifiable. Bold, underlined, italic, or other highlighted type is prohibited. Font must be 10 or 12 pitch (10 to 12 point) only. Use upper and lower case.

An extremely professional and determined officer—my very top officer recruiter—LT Johnston has:
· Attained a 140% productivity increase in the 1st Qtr of FY 81 over the entirety of FY 80 recruiting efforts for her programs; contributed greatly to the 115% increase in 1980 command productivity; and earned awards of two gold wreaths for recruiting excellence (#37). Her success results from her superlative rapport with people, her complete understanding of Navy opportunities (#33), and her meticulous follow-up.
· Developed astute advertisements, initiated excellent mail campaigns, and visited numerous college campuses to promote her programs. She has succeeded in the largest geographical recruiting district in the nation—a formidable challenge.
· Presented all her collateral duty assignments on time and well prepared.
· Volunteered to develop a major new managerial concept for the command, which promises to contribute greatly to the officer recruiting effort.
· Kept excellent physical fitness and showed keen civic awareness in a local nursing home program.
· Won nomination as the FY 80 "Recruiter of the Year" for Navy Recruiting Area X, and nomination for CNRA-X Officer Recruiter of the Quarter, 1st Quarter, FY 81.
The "cornerstone" of the officer recruiting team because of her direct support of all officer candidate programs, she is most strongly recommended not only for early promotion but also for XO of a recruiting district or OINC of a major recruiting district "A" station.

As you can see, the second evaluation (the one with smaller typeface) allows more space for comments (and for recommendations about future duty assignments), but it is also harder to read, almost guaranteeing the selection board member will skim the information, not read all of it. Some of the additional information presented (such as this officer's meticulous work and "superlative rapport with people") does portray this officer's special qualities. However, the drafter might consider omitting other information so as to open some white space. That would make the fitrep a bit easier to read.

GET TO THE POINT QUICKLY WITH A SHARP OPENING.

A short and sharp opening sentence (not a long generalized paragraph) can set the tone of a report and be crafted so as to catch the eye of a reader. It's the place for an important numerical comparison, a vital comparative statement, or an incisive summary judgment.

The openings or reports listed below (each of which would be followed by specifics in the form of bullets or short paragraphs) all get to the point quickly and are crafted so as to be noticed.

Each of these openings is composed of a verbal statement:
- Exceptionally creative and innovative officer—a real problem solver.
- My best division chief—already performing at E-8 level.
- Most emphatically recommended for VS command selection now!
- A typically effective first-class engineman. (Note that "typically effective" might be interpreted as faint praise—nothing special. Perhaps that's what the author intends.)
- A top-notch S-3 sensor operator.
- A very junior chief who has propelled herself toward the top of her peer group through sheer hustle and enthusiasm.
- Newly arrived! Off to a successful start on his first sea tour.
- An O-5 unmistakably displaying the early signs of flag potential.

"THE BIG X"—OR THE NEED FOR A CHANGE

Navy people have become expert in making a person think he or she got a good eval, because the eval was marked 4.0. But the secret buzz words were missing.

On the board for LDO, it would seem that I was being approved strongly because all the Xs were in the highest blocks. But I didn't know the hidden detail: those with highest approval *had their boxes marked to the left.*

One evaluation				The higher evaluation		
4.0	3.0	2.0		4.0	3.0	2.0
X	☐	☐		X	☐	☐

—Chief Warrant Officer

The openings below include overt numerical comparisons:
- The number three performer among the six E-5 RMs at this command.
- (From a recruit training command): A superior company commander who easily ranks in the top 10 percent of 225 handpicked, competitive E-6s.
- A superior petty officer and yeoman: #20 of 72 E-6s on CRUISER.
- Chief Quickstart is number 4 of 143 chiefs on VESSEL.

These openings denote where an individual fits within a promotion category:
- LCDR Smithman, though very junior, ranks #1 of 5 "Promotables."
- A rapidly improving leader and petty officer, #2 of 4 "Must Promotes."
- Ranked *#2* of 6 "Early Promotes"—simply an outstanding chief.

USE SPECIFICS TO ILLUSTRATE OR VERIFY ACHIEVEMENTS

Those who invented the eval and fitrep system urged that *specific details of the performance of an individual* be foremost. The specifics of the performance should appear immediately in an evaluation and comprise by far the greater part of it.

Performance that can be quantified should be, for numbers often speak volumes. "His department scored 97% on the latest REFTRA" speaks for itself about job performance.

Qualities (like "courageous," "dedicated," "diligent," "self-starter," etc.) also should be mentioned because not everything can be given a numerical score, and we all know that the personality and virtues of individuals differ remarkably. Such qualities are extremely important in painting a word picture of the service member.

But the problem in the past was that personal qualities were expressed by the carload—often without evidence of any kind, or with only weak evidence. It's better to mention *a few noteworthy* qualities or personality traits of an individual and cite enough evidence to illustrate and exemplify the qualities claimed. (Of course, the evidence should also support the numerical grades assigned.)

Again, "verifiable performance"—which can be illustrated by *facts, numbers, and specific achievements*—is the key to effective write-ups.

Here is a very poor write-up on a supposedly top performer. The write-up has virtually no substantiation for its tiresome adjectives, no specifics connected to the many qualities mentioned. It is also highly repetitive.

---

43. COMMENTS ON PERFORMANCE. * All 5.0 and 1.0 marks must be specifically substantiated in comments. No numerical ranking permitted. Comments must be verifiable. Bold, underlined, italic, or other highlighted type is prohibited. Font must be 10 or 12 pitch (10 to 12 point) only. Use upper and lower case.

```
Petty Officer Smith is an outstanding petty officer and developing techni-
cian. He is self-motivated, resourceful, and persistent, projecting a con-
cerned personal involvement in his work duties. An experienced supervisor,
he can be relied upon to complete whatever task lies before him or his
workcenter and get top-notch results. EM1 Smith in a short time has estab-
lished himself as intelligent, mature, and experienced, with a strong
sense of personal responsibility for the quality of work produced regard-
less of the job. Manifesting a creative mind and sound judgment, he has
demonstrated his capacity for effectively and efficiently directing and
controlling the activities of others and for assuring successful results.
He has earned
this top evaluation.
```

Of course, one can *intend* to write weakly; a weak evaluation is usually meant to mirror weak performance. But besides using "top-notch" adjectives, the eval on Petty Officer Smith was written for a Sailor with very high marks. Selection board members often discount high promotion recommendations and trait marks if *they are unsubstantiated in the comments*—as in the case here.

Good evidence of superior performance is found in the bullets in the following evaluation on "an original thinker," written according to the requirements of the current system.

NOTE: In addition to the standard eval write-up in block 43, enlisted evaluations also include important information in block 44. This space is meant to include such things as awards received (not just recommended); honors received; courses or qualifications completed (but not courses in progress); college credits received; and special certificates awarded.

---

43. COMMENTS ON PERFORMANCE. * All 5.0 and 1.0 marks must be specifically substantiated in comments. No numerical ranking permitted. Comments must be verifiable. Bold, underlined, italic, or other highlighted type is prohibited. Font must be 10 or 12 pitch (10 to 12 point) only. Use upper and lower case.

An original thinker and a totally resourceful leader—#5 of 38 E-6s aboard ship.
* (37, 39) — As LPO of EMO1, consistently maintained the engineroom in an "OPPE Ready" status, ensuring all Main Propulsion equipment was "ready to answer all bells." Also consistently maintains tag out, lube oil, and EOSS programs at the highest level of administrative readiness. Regularly receives laudatory comments from inspectors about his program readiness.
— As Division Career Counselor carried a first-term retention rate of 85, career 100, and responsible for two first-term BOOSTs, one first-term to sub duty, and one career to EEAP.
— Upon reassignment to "B" Division, completely revamped workcenter EAO 1 by using personnel resources more effectively and initiating a trouble-call system, enabling division to maintain all equipment in commission and "SM 1 Ready." Also took charge of ship's MHE program and established an effective fork truck service program, orchestrating workcenter preparations for upcoming MHE inspection.
— Top quality EOOW. Instructs new EOOW's on proper propulsion plant operation, casualty control, and administration.
The epitome of his profession, Petty Officer Brown is poised and mature, has a thirst for knowledge and a desire for challenge. His achievements suggest his great potential.

INCLUDE WRITTEN RECOMMENDATIONS AND COMPARISONS

A written recommendation serves to restate numbers and marks in other areas of the evaluation form and also can add additional information. In addition, "soft" comparisons (not marked elsewhere on the evaluation form) may serve to "break out" a person from among his or her peers.

Here are several examples of such summaries; each of the following statements would either begin or end the comments section:

Summary restating recommendations already marked on the form:
ICC White is an outstanding leader and technician, a genuine "Must Promote" to senior chief. Send her to the Senior Enlisted Academy too.

Summary noting comparative ranking and specific duty recommendations:
RM1 Black is #4 of 7 "Must Promotes"—highly recommended for LPO in a communications facility or other challenging communications duty.

Summary that makes recommendations beyond those already marked:
Possessing tact far beyond his years, IT Green would also excel in foreign liaison or would make a superb admiral's aide. Promote now to LCDR!
[Early Promote, XO, and PG School already marked elsewhere on the form.]

Summary explaining a low promotion recommendation:
OS1 White reported aboard after four years of working ashore with the Air Force. He shows great industry, has completed 70 percent of ESWS PQS, and is rapidly getting the underway CIC time needed to get back up to speed.

Summary adding one more reason to support the promotion recommendation:
Chief Brown's inspirational leadership is the main reason AIMD New Orleans has the second-highest RFI rate for jet engines in CNATRA. Promote him now!
[Chief Brown is directly linked to the command's recent achievement.]

SPOTLIGHT KEY POINTS

It had become standard in the past to use underlining, **bold print,** *italics or script lettering,* * * centering * *, ALL CAPS (for emphasis, not just for abbreviations), and even stars and "happy faces" (!) in fitness reports to draw attention to the most important details of an evaluation and otherwise impress a reader. Although some variation in typography for emphasis has its legitimate use in naval writing (indeed, the BUPERS instruction on evaluations itself uses its share of boldface and underlining), its enormous overuse in Navy personnel evaluations made the writer's clever use of typography, rather than excellent performance or potential on the part of the service member, the focus of past evaluations or fitreps. Hence any use of what one might call the "tricks of typography"—print highlighting—is no longer allowed.

However, one must still be careful to see that

- comments are readable,
- vital information is not buried in the midst of dense blocks of type, and
- key information is in key places.

One should avoid long paragraphs in all evaluation writing, either breaking them up by the use of bulleted lists or otherwise changing them into short, pithy paragraphs. "Bullets" (or hyphens or asterisks) and the white space surrounding bulleted lists help draw the eye to key items. Bullets also facilitate skimming (and in organizational writing of all kinds, skimming is necessary and expected).

An Evaluation That Buries Key Information

Here is an evaluation that uses only the space available for comments and that, through lack of bullets or paragraphing and through long adjectival description, buries the key information about a petty officer's performance. It also begins with a long "preamble," which could easily be cut to a short sentence. The question to ask: if you were a harried selection board member with only twenty seconds to read any particular report, could you find the key accomplishments here?

---

43. COMMENTS ON PERFORMANCE. * All 5.0 and 1.0 marks must be specifically substantiated in comments. No numerical ranking permitted. Comments must be verifiable. Bold, underlined, italic, or other highlighted type is prohibited. Font must be 10 or 12 pitch (10 to 12 point) only. Use upper and lower case.

Petty Officer McCarthy is an extremely exceptional second class Boatswain's Mate who always manifests initiative and creativity. His positive and mature approach to any situation have continually impressed this command by the outstanding standards of performance he achieves. He has been the driving force behind the major improvements in the material condition of the after boatswain's mate locker, the ship's two boats, davits and boat decks, and the DC damage control equipment throughout the division. His inspirational leadership has been instrumental in the development of 1st Division's personnel. His outstanding sense of work ethic, personal example, and his demanding supervision have brought the best out of all the men assigned to him. His accomplishments this period include: as petty officer in charge of after UNREP and refueling station, his rig team has achieved the highest rates of cargo transfer, rigging, and derigging in the Seventh Fleet, has maintained his spaces in the highest standards of material conditions which continually earn the highest marks in zone inspections. As damage control petty officer, he actively has the highest degree of readiness of damage control equipment; as acting leading petty officer, he managed the daily division matters and provided a vital continuity during a hectic and intensive IMAV period. BM2 McCarthy has demonstrated a performance that far surpasses the contribution of a second class petty officer. His deep pride in the Boatswain's Mate rate and the naval service are vividly reflected in his work and the manner in which he molds his men. He is a topnotch petty officer.

An Improved Evaluation

On the same individual, this write-up cuts the dead weight and foregrounds the most impressive achievements.

---

43. COMMENTS ON PERFORMANCE. * All 5.0 and 1.0 marks must be specifically substantiated in comments. No numerical ranking permitted. Comments must be verifiable. Bold, underlined, italic, or other highlighted type is prohibited. Font must be 10 or 12 pitch (10 to 12 point) only. Use upper and lower case.

Petty Officer McCarthy's inspirational leadership has been the driving force behind major improvements in division material and operational readiness. (#39)
· As petty officer in charge of after UNREP and refueling station, he has enabled his rig team to achieve the highest rates of cargo transfer, rigging, and derigging in the Seventh Fleet. (#34)
· He has made major improvements in the conditions of the boatswain's mate locker, the ship's two boats, the boat davits and boat decks, and the DC equipment throughout his division.
· His spaces continually earn the highest marks in zone inspections.
· As damage control petty officer, he maintains the highest degree of readiness of damage control equipment.
· As acting leading petty officer, he provided a vital continuity during a hectic and intensive IMAV period.

BM2 McCarthy's outstanding work ethic, personal example, and deep pride both in his rate and in the Navy are vividly reflected in his work and in the manner in which he molds his division. He is a top-notch petty officer; most strongly recommended for early promotion.

In this eval, in addition to condensing the information and formatting it effectively, the high rates of cargo transfer, rigging, and derigging have been given greatest prominence by making them the subject of the very first bullet. However, a selection board member would want to know *who validated* those "highest rates in the Seventh Fleet." Was there a competition? Did these ratings come from an inspection? The writer should specify the *source* of such assessments or a reader may wonder if this comment just reflects somebody's pride in his own unit and not an overt, objective judgment.

Having taken a first look at our subject, let's proceed by discussing the major audiences for performance documents—especially Navy selection boards—and what those audiences are always looking for.

The Critical Audiences for Navy Performance Evaluations

While their focus of attention may have changed somewhat, the nature of the various audiences for Navy performance evaluations remains pretty much the same as before.

THE NAVY SELECTION BOARD AS AUDIENCE

Several audiences for Navy enlisted evaluations and fitness reports can be identified, but you should only write for the most important of them. That's the formal Navy selection board.

A Promotion Board's Predicament

An E-8/E-9 board whose president was interviewed a while back met for six weeks; fifty people served on the board. They reviewed twenty-five thousand records, and each of those records was reviewed by at least two "briefers," sometimes three. So each board member read at least one thousand records over those six weeks—an average of some thirty records per day—besides spending time briefing, being briefed by others, and voting. With maybe ten to twelve minutes to spend on any one record, a board member simply had no time to dwell on any one report.

Officer boards are similarly beset. However, where enlisted boards typically review only the five or so most recent evals in a service record, officer briefers will typically review all the fitness reports in a jacket. Take the record of a commander going up for captain as an example. Such a record will include perhaps thirty fitreps. On any count that's simply an enormous amount of reading for any particular board member.

Besides these time constraints—which warn against burying vital details in the middle of a report when a briefer expects them to be at the beginning or the end—you should keep in mind another feature of a selection board. That feature is the breadth of its makeup.

Who's on the Board?

Although boards vary in composition depending on the level (mainly E-8s and E-9s on an E-7 board, Navy captains on a commander's board, etc.), the important point is that a line selection board is typically a mixed group. A line officer's selection board, for instance, is composed of all line communities (aviation, surface, subs, etc.). Similarly with a chief's board: many different rates are represented. Even though a chief's board may separate into smaller panels of similar ratings for some deliberations, still, any one of those panels may not contain two members of the same rate.

"The President of each board tells the members what they are to look for. Leading petty officer? Leading petty officer at sea? College courses? Lots of deployments? This specific guidance varies from board to board."

—CHIEF
WARRANT OFFICER

"I was surprised to see how many times someone on the board would know the situation on a staff, and the likely reason for the promotion rankings, e.g., that a Flag Secretary always gets the nod."

—FORMER SELECTION
BOARD MEMBER

Even in a restricted-line board, you can't expect each member to know the finer points of any particular job. All the board members will understand warfare-fighting capabilities, leadership, directing, individual effort, and so on, but they certainly won't care whether it was "Number 5" or "Number 7 BQA-8 Hydrophone" that the petty officer you are writing about repaired. By using *generic* terms—"directed the replacement of a self-noise hydrophone"—you can make an evaluation easier to read *and* easier to evaluate. In all cases, you must learn to write for a mixed audience.

What Are They Looking For?

Board members are looking for several different kinds of comments in a write-up. They must pick up a great deal of specific information, including what a person has accomplished, what qualifications another person has achieved, who has profited from his or her performance, and so on.

Then board members must determine whether the write-up manifests *qualities* important in a chief or officer. Besides demanding leadership and supervisory abilities, a chief's board will also diligently look for such qualities as initiative, perseverance, grace under pressure, and so on. Specific accomplishments can suggest the candidate has some of these qualities, but you should also speak explicitly to the qualities themselves.

The point is that in an evaluation a selection board is looking for many different topics: detailed evidence of strong accomplishment; outline of special difficulties overcome; discussion of various personal qualities; and a good general *feel* for the person being evaluated.

THE "MURDER BOARD" AT YOUR OWN COMMAND

The official Navy selection board is only one decision-making audience for an evaluation or fitness report. There is usually another less formal but sometimes even more critical selection board much closer to home, a board that determines what officer gets the "must promote" designation, or which chief will be marked in the "early promote" block in the first place. These decisions are typically not made by the XO or CO acting individually but instead by the collected members of an informal "murder board" held aboard your ship or station.

There are no rules about this—each command operates differently, and some commanders keep their specific methods of going about it closely guarded. But all commands must make such decisions, and most of them convene a group of chiefs or officers to help them do so. On one destroyer, the practice was for all the department heads to get together with the executive officer on a certain day to rate the chief petty officers and on another day to rate the junior officers. The officers handed around and read all the write-ups. "Oh, I see why you ranked Chief Garcia so highly," the operations officer would say after reading the evaluation of the supply chief. Together, under the direction of the executive officer, this group would come up with a list of suggested promotion rankings for the commanding officer.

Of course, the commanding officer could approve or modify that ranking. But the point here is that informal, unsigned write-ups can affect the assignment of promotion recommendations (and perhaps even the trait markings) themselves. The size of the command, of course, can play a part in this.

As a commander commented, "On a large shore staff, the write-ups can make a *huge* difference. There may be 100 chiefs, and the officer who signs the document may never have seen the individual he's writing about. Or maybe he's seen him play on the command softball team, but that's about it. The write-up may be the only thumb-

---

DIFFERENCES BETWEEN ENLISTED AND OFFICER REPORTS

Two major differences in their uses distinguish fitreps on officers from evals/fitreps on enlisted men and women.

1. Reports on enlisted personnel are kept in the service record aboard ship or station (although information from these reports is forwarded to BUPERS); therefore, an enlisted person's superiors can review the most recent reports on the spot. In contrast, once signed, an officer's fitness report is filed in the officer's service record at BUPERS (and a newly reported CO is not to read prior fitness reports on the vessel's or unit's officers).

2. Chiefs' selection boards (for E-7 and E-8/E-9) use a complex rating sheet and numbering system that requires board members to rate each person's performance numerically in several particular areas, based on information gathered partly from the write-ups (and partly from other parts of the service record).

As a result of the numerical scoring system outlined in paragraph 2, enlisted evaluations and chiefs' fitness reports must differ somewhat from officers' fitness reports and should be a bit more specifics-oriented. If you don't list specific accomplishments in volunteer work, initiative, educational achievements, and community involvement in addition to the standard and vital leadership, managerial ability, technical expertise, and so on, you may be hurting the enlisted person you're evaluating.

Of course, specific qualifications/achievements actually obtained during a reporting period (not just recommended or pending) should be recorded in Block 44 of the enlisted evaluation. There is no comparable block on the fitness report, so for E-7s, E-8s, and E-9s, such achievements should be recorded in the Comments on the fitrep form, Block 41.

"In a squadron, department heads got together, and recommended what junior people were #1 and #2 in the command. Yes, the CO could change the rankings—but I never saw it happen."

—LIEUTENANT, AVIATOR

On calibration: "If one ship gets none of its chiefs selected to E-8 and E-9, the XO often touches base with other XOs to see what went wrong—how they wrote up their chiefs. Outside of service on selection boards, that's the standard way calibration occurs beyond the ship."

—LIEUTENANT COMMANDER ABOARD A DESTROYER

nail sketch of the chief he has at hand to inform him about the individual." Obviously, in these circumstances, the write-up becomes critical to the local decision.

The smaller the command, the more informal the murder board tends to get. Some people on destroyers said their determinations were all oral; no one brought the evaluation drafts with them. Nevertheless, even here the write-ups might affect the local process. All evals or fitreps must be signed by seniors, who, upon seeing how much weaker one write-up is than another, may have the evaluations rewritten or may even revisit the recommendations.

It should go without saying that when the final decisions have been made on relative markings, someone, maybe the XO, must take a final look to make sure that the "verifiable details" in the comments justify the strength of the promotion and trait marks. Otherwise, when the official Navy board reads those evals or fitreps, board members may decide—as some did in the first boards that saw the new evaluation forms in the mid-1990s—not to believe the numerical rankings.

OTHER LOCAL USES OF ENLISTED EVALS AND FITREPS

Enlisted evaluations and fitness reports written on chief petty officers have other local audiences. Your own command will use such evaluations widely, as will any new command to which an enlisted service member reports.

WHAT SELECTION BOARDS TYPICALLY WANT TO SEE

It only makes sense to write evals and fitreps partly *in light of what selection boards are looking for.* Selection boards periodically share their experiences with service members. Here are what members of four 1995 boards regarded as especially important and reported to their respective communities:

A chief's board looked for

- Sustained superior performance,
- Challenging assignments in and out of rate,
- High peer ranking,
- Collateral duties, and
- Meeting prescribed sea/shore rotation.

An LDO/CWO board considered these things important:

- Arduous duty assignments, especially two or more in a row;
- Instructor duty, or attainment of Master Training Specialist designation;
- Higher education (although not a must for selection, this helped in the crunch; they specifically looked for mention of this in evals); and
- Sustained superior performance, especially
  — improving work spaces,
  — motivating troops, and
  — taking the initiative to excel.

A department head screening board was impressed by

- Assignment to more than one department during a tour;
- Second division officer tours on a different platform;
- Bonus qualifications like EOOW, CDO, and TAO;
- Awards, especially mid-tour awards; and
- A positive trend between fitness reports.

A CO/XO screening board (fleet support) suggested that one should

- Take the hard jobs;
- Take the job with the larger scope of responsibility in terms of
  — people,
  — money, and
  — equipment;
- Get a master's degree in your core area;
- Excel in assignments in arduous locations; and
- Be the best at your job.

Such comments are typical of selection board reports.

When a new division officer, department head, or leading chief reports aboard a ship or station, one of the first things he or she may do is to read key enlisted service records. Similarly, when enlisted men or women report aboard a new duty station with records in hand, their department heads, division officers, and chiefs are all likely to read the evals in those records to find out the qualities of the people they're receiving. That will help them assign the new people where they will be the most productive.

A MINI-SELECTION BOARD

A major shore staff holds a mini-selection board to make its decisions on promotion recommendations. For example, in considering the evals of the twenty-seven command chiefs (E-7s), the leading chiefs of each department (all E-8 or above) and department heads assemble with the XO. They place each draft evaluation on the overhead projector. Everyone reads the eval, and the responsible department head (or leading chief) answers questions.

Each chief is discussed in relation to all the others, and the board sorts the evals into categories (promotable, must promote, early promote, etc.).The board adjusts inflation in the marks and looks at the more competitive evals a second time. Comments that don't fit the recommendation are sent back for revision; the command master chief keeps a master record.

According to the admin chief, such a system works far better than preceding ones in which records were passed around the room from person to person. In the new system, the focus is on one eval at a time, and everyone on the board gets a full picture.

And then a petty officer may lay down the copy of the evaluation you gave her in her workplace, and soon her whole work center may know how you rated her—as well as anything you may have said about *them* in her report.

Officers, too, may see the remarks sections of locally prepared fitness reports other than their own. For example, two junior aviators may compare notes to try to understand the nuances of what their senior is saying about each of them. Beyond such incidental viewing, however, officer reports have no official audience at the local command, for Navy officer fitness reports are not kept for any local use (only the reporting officer keeps a copy).

Finally, detailers at BUPERS will read through evals and fitreps before making assignments. They will see recommendations for specific billets made there, as well as the other recommendations and comments. Actually, detailers may read these comments very thoroughly because they are not under the same kinds of pressure as selection boards.

THE SERVICE MEMBER AS AUDIENCE

"Being frank in counseling is hard; we're not used to it. Even the Chief of Naval Operations and the Vice Chief don't do it well."

—MASTER CHIEF PETTY OFFICER OF THE NAVY

Finally, you are almost always writing the report for at least one more audience—the person being evaluated. In the Navy fitrep/eval system initiated in the mid-1990s and fully in force a decade since, the reports play a big part in counseling the service member. Between submission of formal reports, the eval forms are to be used orally in counseling, and the formal reports necessarily become part of the counseling process too.

It should go without saying that the counseling and written report should be closely aligned so service members know exactly where they stand and how to better their performance. But there has always been one special problem with writing evaluations: the necessarily close relationship between the person evaluating and counseling and the person being evaluated and counseled. In these circumstances, the evaluation inevitably tends to become, as one officer put it, a "psychic paycheck" for all the effort the person has done for the command. So there is a strong tendency when composing the remarks to write to the subordinate rather than to the selection board, or to try somehow to write to both.

This dual audience is in part responsible for the inflated grades and also for the inflated language that have been so prevalent on past performance evaluations. Even if a subordinate's performance has been mediocre or worse, a superior is often reluctant to alienate the person being evaluated with verbal criticism or mediocre written remarks. Even with a good performer, the fact that he or she will see the report you draft may sway you in the wrong direction. That is, because a Sailor is still working for you, and because you will be confronting the Sailor personally with this piece of paper, you often may want to put *too much information* or *the wrong kind of information* into the report.

As one officer put it, "The member needs to know how he or she's doing in order to improve and to get that needed pat on the back for good performance. So the writer needs to acknowledge jobs and include detail that selection boards may not score or score highly." Overall, however, probably the best advice is to find other ways than the write-up to give an extra pat on the back, that "psychic paycheck." One should write all evaluations and fitness reports *primarily with the selection board in mind.*

Writing Navy Performance Evaluations— A Detailed Discussion

Following are detailed guidelines for writing Navy evaluations, based upon interviews, research, and experience with past reports. To a considerable extent, this guidance applies to non-Navy evaluations as well.

1. CITE SPECIFIC ACCOMPLISHMENTS

Supreme among the assets of a report writer's skills has to be, now as ever, an able use of *specifics*. In every service, and for officer or enlisted, all the literature on performance evaluations cites specific evidence as crucial to a report's success. The Navy forms underline this principle, calling for "verifiable facts" or "examples of performance and results" and otherwise insisting that the performance "speak for itself." Partly from the past overuse of typography, the "fluff" of meaningless adjectives, and even "code words" recognizable only by a few, instructions insist that writers focus directly on exactly what this person actually did that suggests potential and promotability. There are several ways in which to do this.

Use Quantitative Terms

Quantitative measurements are often particularly clear-cut. How many personnel did the officer in question supervise? How many dollars did she manage? Did she save a substantial amount? What was the grade on the latest administrative inspection? What were the scores on the recent REFTRA?

Similarly for enlisted: How many enlisted shipped over in this leading petty officer's department? What RFI rate did he attain for the cruise? How many spaces were repaired and repainted under his direction? And so on. Figures, numbers, percentages, dollars, ratios, grades—whatever you can quantify—might conceivably be meaningful to a selection board sweating hard to judge one person against another fairly. Figures are graphic and hard to dispute and sometimes seem to be more objective than descriptive statements. Seek them and make use of them, within reason, and with good knowledge of their likely effect.

Fill the Comments Block with Detailed Accomplishments

Details regarding nonquantifiable achievements are equally useful and usually more plentiful. Did this officer qualify as OOD and CDO all on the same deployment? Say so. Did that enlisted attain his ESWS overnight? Say that. Accomplishments affecting the primary mission are perhaps most significant, and the variations of actual achievements beggar description. Combat experience, participation in major fleet exercises, and hazardous duty illustrating leadership talents obviously comprise major subjects for a report, as do important qualifications attained.

But don't omit mentioning awards, voluntary additional duty, and selections to special assignments or service schools, even if some of these achievements will show up elsewhere in the service record. If you also put them in an evaluation, they'll be highlighted in both places, and you'll be doubly sure a selection board will notice them. Moreover, the accumulation of several such accomplishments in the space of a year or six months can sometimes take a reader's breath away.

Written or oral commendations from outside the command should also find a place. If someone highly praised the person you're evaluating, tell the readers who did the praising and for what. Also, rather than stating "This program received high praise from senior officers," specify *which* senior officers, either by billet or by name or sometimes by both. On the other hand, random praise from members of an inspection team could translate to "Fleet Training Group, San Diego, commented . . . ," or "This is the cleanest galley in the fleet, according to Environmental Preventive Maintenance Unit, Norfolk," and so on.

Quotations from flag officers, squadron commanders, or other authorities can be most effective. In the eyes of board members numb with reading volumes of extravagant praise, quotations not only constitute additional evidence of excellence but, because they come from outside observers, they also add objectivity to laudatory comments.

Back Up Superlatives with Evidence

Adjectives without supporting details are weak, so support the accolades with facts. There's a world of difference between saying "This junior officer is an excellent writer" and pointing out "He's such a good writer that I had him draft all the award nominations, budget justifications, and fitness reports we had to do this last quarter aboard ship."

On the other hand, bullets recording facts without accolades can be equally uninformative. A reader often wants to know not only *what* but also *how* the member did. A comment on an officer assigned to BUPERS such as "She supervised the writing of five precepts for the convening of selection boards" leaves up in the air whether the precepts were any good. But to say of an officer "He prepared extensive correspondence for SECNAV's signature, all of which was signed without change" suggests the quality was very high.

Master the Use of Adjectives and Other Qualifiers

As long as supporting details back up overall judgments, carefully chosen adjectives and adverbs—terms known by everyone, not just by a tiny group of lexicographers—can greatly strengthen the overall judgment. Most people are aware of the criticality of adjectives and adverbs in recommendations for promotion: the difference between "he is recommended for promotion" and "he is most strongly recommended for early promotion" is often decisive.

Modifiers can be used throughout the comments, and used to diminish as well as build up. Consider the case of an officer who was made personnel officer so that

"Give us your opinions, but then give us the data to back it up. Don't just generalize. If a chief prepared the division for a super inspection, what were the inspection results? And if you tell us percentages, tell us percentages of what. To improve retention is fine, but that doesn't mean much if you improved retention from one to two in a department of one hundred."

—Former selection
board member

"We're looking for the whole YN. We like to see a person's work on the DC party, or work on PQS. And be specific, *not generic:* not *'She compiled 20 hours of community service,'* but instead *'She put in 20 hours with Habitat for Humanity.'"*

—Master Chief YN

THE WORDS YOU WRITE CAN MAKE A DIFFERENCE

The following bullets are selected quotations (they are called "Pearls" on the distribution list) from E-7 and E-8 evaluations read during the FY00 selection board for Senior and Master Chiefs. Some are complimentary; others are not.

- Walks on water, leaves no wake.
- Received accolades from the crew for coordinating "the best parties in recent years."
- Dedicated to the successful employment of women in his division.
- This CPO hits home runs—pitch him additional responsibility and authority.
- Chiseled from a polished block of professionalism.
- Continually improves old ideas.
- A master at translating complex theory and concepts to the simplest of terms. He is especially adept at training junior officers.
- Routinely chooses the hard right vice the easy wrong.
- One of my franchise players.
- His yard was selected as NAS Barbers Point "Yard of the Month."
- Lives and breathes "Can do."
- Satisfied the palates of over 40 discriminating CPOs.
- My right and left arm.
- A Master Chief in waiting.
- Established finest coffee mess in the HS community.
- Every time he walks in, he makes my blood pressure go down.
- Hurdles or bulldozes over obstacles.
- Quickly grasped the importance of providing safe, high-quality aviation water survival training.
- He runs the air station.

"his daily efforts could be supervised and evaluated." After six months this officer received another evaluation, a report that contained the following bright words of praise:

> In this assignment he has been able to handle most routine office work satisfactorily.

"Most"—not all. "Routine"—nothing out of the ordinary. "Office work"—neither management nor leadership nor even physical labor, apparently. As for "satisfactorily," that word itself in an evaluation will often be interpreted as a warning signal. Clearly, when carefully chosen, adjectives and adverbs can have great effect, for better or for worse.

Examples of Bullets Itemizing Specific Accomplishments

Here we illustrate a variety of bullets or phrases itemizing specific accomplishments and comment on their effectiveness.

Problematic Bullets/Phrases—Possibly Signaling a Problematic Sailor?

- Supervised numerous unconventional foreign refuelings with NATO forces in Northern Europe. *[But <u>how did he do</u> in the supervision?]*

- Member of Engineering Casualty Control Team. *[just a job description.]*
- Reviews all AC&R logs and effects corrective action. *[Another job description—no help.]*
- Her training program was singled out in a successful command inspection as one of the two best training programs audited. *[Top two—out of how many? And who singled it out?]*
- Was officer in charge of the ship's firing squad during a most impressive burial at sea. *[But no credit is given specifically to him—apparently he was just there. It's stronger to say—as long as it's true—"Was responsible for an impressive performance by the firing squad during a burial at sea."]*
- Scored 92.6 at Vieques in October. *[The briefer may not know Vieques, nor the kind of test or exercise conducted there.]*
- Supervised the writing of five precepts for the convening of selection boards. *[Yes, but were they any good?]*
- Thoughtful author. Submitted article to *Approach* on "The LSO's Role in Safety." *[OK—but apparently it wasn't published.]*
- LT Oscar substantially enhanced office morale by orchestrating and acquiring approval for a plan to obtain new office furniture in order to better utilize available space. *[Wordy and unimpressive. Getting new office furniture for a single office isn't high-level achievement for a lieutenant.]*
- CDR Whiskey is a strict disciplinarian whose emphasis on the military aspects of the naval service has struck a responsive note with the most self-disciplined and most valuable elements of the crew. *[A peculiar statement—how does he succeed with ordinary Sailors?]*

More Definite, Noteworthy Bullets

- BTC (SW) Victor's detailed preparations earned high praise from board inspectors during the INSURV and resulted in a superb engineering performance, including full-power turns and emergency crash-back achievements on the first try. *[Good specifics.]*
- Repeatedly failed to ensure proper endurance of stores. Inability to properly order basic foodstuffs resulted in gross overages of perishable foodstuffs, including enough oranges for six months. *[Specifics help substantiate weak performance, too.]*
- During REFTRA at Flag Officer Sea Training at Portland, UK, consistently impressed Royal Navy observers with his vitality, skill, and uncommon ability to control the situation, regardless of its complexity. *[Impressing the Royal Navy is strong. A quotation would be stronger yet.]*
- As Vault Yeoman, instituted major improvements in the handling of classified material, with the result that four other major commands have adopted her specific procedures in their handling of classified material. *[Results stretching beyond one's own command are especially impressive.]*
- Stands outstanding submerged OOD watches, an exceptional accomplishment as an ensign. *[Rank is obviously very important here. But was the ship or the ensign submerged?]*
- Resourceful, efficient: Recovered and restored the crew's galley and mess deck from severe smoke and fire damage after a mass conflagration onboard. Food service management team said it would be "impossible." *[Quotation helps makes this a telling accomplishment.]*

"You certainly need to use a thesaurus—I highly advise it. But you have to have a vocabulary to use one in the first place!"
—MASTER CHIEF PETTY OFFICER OF THE NAVY

"It can hurt you if you fib on the statistics or don't have them right. Someone at a senior level will say, 'What?' A Master Chief will know that some things aren't possible."
—COMMAND MASTER CHIEF

- The driving force behind VS-28's embarked ready room rehab. The squadron was cited by CO, CV-59 (Capt.) for having the "Showcase of FORRESTAL." *[Good use of memorable quote in what would otherwise be a forgettable line.]*
- The only lieutenant of 70 on board who is qualified as an Assistant Command Duty Officer. Routinely stands an impressive watch. *[The only one out of 70 is tops anywhere]*

2. WRITE FOR THE GENERALIST READER

"I think you need to re-emphasize using plain English—avoid the big words, limit the acronyms, and shun the jargon-speak."

—FITNESS REPORT
EXPERT

Board members come from all communities. For chiefs' boards, some members are officers, but most are E-8s and E-9s from a great variety of rates and every major community (aviation, surface, and subs). The one or two board members who brief a particular record will usually have good general knowledge of the area of a selection member's expertise but are not necessarily of the same designator or rate.

Avoid Jargon and Unknown Abbreviations

Write in a way that a generally well-rounded and knowledgeable board member can understand what you're saying. Don't use jargon; avoid abbreviations that are not known Navy-wide. Don't depend on the reader's knowing all the ordinary measures of success on your platform or in your workplace.

For example, don't write bullets like the following from some enlisted evals, which were obviously written by a specialist and for a specialist—but not necessarily for members of a selection board:

"We need not get compulsive with defining acronyms in all situations. It is not useful to use half a line to spell out what LPO means to selection or awards board members who wouldn't be there in the first place if they didn't know what LPO stands for."

—NAVY CAPTAIN,
OPNAV

- Helped to replace the AN/BQN-2 and AN/BRN-3 during ERP.
- Assisted in rewriting of NASNIINST 8025.1 OTTO Fuel instruction and AUW Organization Manual.
- Provided primary RSC Operator Support and SPY-1D maintenance during DDG 51 DT/OT-11D1 13–19 March 2003.
- Provided primary RSC Operator and SPY-1D Maintenance Support for DDG 51 independent steaming exercise (ISE #1) 12 January–September 1993, (ISE #2) 04 February 1993, and (ISE #3) 18 February–October 2003.

These long-winded titles and figures must be interpreted to someone not knowledgeable in a specialty. The specific dates in the last bullets hold no interest for a selection board member and further clutter the narrative. That aside, note in addition that most of these bullets once again are mainly job descriptions: they outline *what* was done, but not *how well*.

Altogether, this is the kind of documentation that might belong in a *technical* report—not in an enlisted evaluation. Experts say that technical jargon remains a persistent problem. So translate technicalese into ordinary English, remembering the needs of your readers.

Describe Unfamiliar Aspects of the Job

While the eval or fitrep should not be a mere job description, you may have to describe out-of-the-way billets and accomplishments a bit so that readers can justly appreciate job performance. For instance, the Navy publication *Perspective* once argued of shore billets, "It is more meaningful to read about a division officer with 30 troops, a $200,000 budget, and four buildings to maintain than to see only the words 'Division Officer.'"

Ideally, this information will be presented in the "duties" block on the form (Block 29 on both evals and fitreps). But such details tend to get "buried"—being

"'Command employment' and 'Duties' blocks really are important for describing unique duties. For instance, everyone knows what a communications officer does, but not many would know what a WAN facilitator's duties are. These blocks have to explain the 'whats' of the job while the comments do the 'how wells' and the job's significance."

—FITNESS REPORT
EXPERT

"If the XO can't produce a signable fitrep—you should find another XO."

—NAVY COMMANDER

"Once an enlisted man says he's not going to re-enlist, he's ranked toward the bottom. But what happens if he changes his mind and re-enlists?"

—NAVAL AVIATOR

very hard to read—in Block 29 by all those standard listings *of every* single primary and collateral duty and months spent in each—and the board member pressed by time may not look carefully at that block anyway. Beyond that, the eval/fitrep instruction suggests that the "Job Scope Statement" can be continued in the comments block as necessary. So it's certainly okay to put some job description there. You can also usually work critical facts about the job right into the write-up, often preceding a specific comment, like this: "Responsible for 450 personnel and a $35K consumable OPTAR, she. . . ." Even though it takes more space, you'll be sure readers will see the description in the comments block.

And if your ship or unit took part in some highly unusual activity or faced special difficulty, spell that out in the remarks. The command employment description (Block 28) may help here. But the relation of command employment to the service member's performance may not be immediately understood—and many drafters don't have control on what's said in that block, anyway. Italicized below are aspects of several bullets from past fitreps and evals that helpfully describe the context of a particular job performance. (Of course, you cannot use italics on the actual form.)

Bullets Showing the Context

- Initiated extensive cross-training. As a result, *a five-day work stoppage by foreign nationals* had absolutely no adverse effect on communications services for the fleet, *despite* his site's extreme isolation.
- Was hot-work coordinator for CVN 69 (*approximately 200 jobs daily*) without an incident.
- Instrumental in stores offload of reefers and storerooms resulting in less than $1,000 in surveyed items, *despite continued operation of the galley four weeks prior to decommissioning.*
- Outstanding seamanship and high morale marked the 55 safe, successful UNREPS that he supervised. *Most of these UNREPS occurred at night during an Indian Ocean cruise that included a stretch of 111 days at sea.*

Give Comparisons in the Bullets Whenever Possible

Board members must know the norm for quantities or percentages to mean something. If they don't, the figures themselves will leave readers wondering. In many cases a nonspecialist will need some comparison. So, if you can, spell out the ordinary standard, and then show how this person's work has been specifically above or below that standard.

Occasionally, the comparison will be the ship's schedule—for example, if a chief engineer so managed an overhaul that it was accomplished three weeks ahead of time. Sometimes one compares performance with what people did in the past—as when a DCTT trainer's unit got 97 percent in Medical Readiness during REFTRA, which officials said was "the highest ship's score in that area in over two years." Perhaps you could say a person increased her unit's Personnel Qualification Standard percentage from 65 to 97 percent, or that in a technical area she "achieved a 98 percent test-bench availability against a Navy average of 87 percent."

By all such comparisons, one gives readers a standard by which to judge the accomplishment.

3. PLACE THE KEY STATEMENTS IN THE KEY PLACES

The placement and relative density of information have become even more important than in the past because bold type, different sizes of type, and other highlighting have been prohibited. By placing information in familiar, expected locations and being careful not to overload the form, one will ensure that readers will see the key comments. Here are several pointers.

Include Both an Opening Line and a Summary Statement

Drafters sometimes wonder about the usefulness of opening and closing "summary" statements. Won't the details speak by themselves?

They sometimes do—particularly for the very best and very worst performers, whose accomplishments (or failures) are stunning, or when numerical ranking is either very high or very low. But for those evals and fitreps in the middle range—on those who have neither won medals of honor nor grounded the ship or been guilty of serious misconduct—they don't necessarily. Some impressive accomplishments carry obvious promotional implications. Others don't—especially to a board member sick of superlatives.

That is, as we have seen, selection board members are confronted on report after report with glowing accomplishments, typically filling the form. Over a couple of weeks, they must make judgments on each one of literally hundreds of evals. It simply makes sense for a drafter to help them assess the *meaning* of what they see.

Moreover, Navy people are long accustomed to looking to the summary of an eval or fitness report to find the conclusive judgment of the commander. The beginning of a report and the end—these are the crucial locations, and anyone skimming or rereading will be sure to look *here.*

More Good Summary Statements

An officer who has earned the CO's trust:
LCDR Uniform knows everything about aircraft maintenance, shipboard procedures, and management—I depend totally on his judgment. He's a "Promotable" the Navy simply has to promote!

An E-6 who has had difficulties in the past:
Petty Officer Victor has overcome a slow start and is performing all his duties very well; he has strong potential as an LPO and technician.

An individual with special qualities:
HM1 Whiskey is inquisitive, creative, and prudent—she makes a difference. Mature and forceful, she has my strongest endorsement for immediate advancement and for only the most challenging billets.

A nuclear engineer—opening says "#3 lieutenant on NIMITZ":
LT Xray has achieved more in this shipboard tour than most officers complete in two. An obvious "Early Promote," he is most strongly recommended for department head on a major surface combatant.

"You look at the first lines and the last couple. The first will indicate where this person was in the breakout, #3 of 20, etc.; the last will indicate overall assessment, as in 'rarely exceeds expectations,' 'never failed to underachieve,' etc."

—NAVY CAPTAIN

"Verbiage will play a part at a local ranking board. In a squadron, you often have twenty lieutenants, so the next higher rank gets together to rank them. A lieutenant commander will often use the draft fitrep in order to present an organized argument, selecting from the fitrep draft he sees in front of him, and outlining the actual achievements of the officer."

—NAVY CAPTAIN

> ### THE FIRST AND THE LAST
>
> In general, the *first line,* the *opening bullet,* and the *closing summary* are the crucial parts in evaluation writing.
>
> Think of how we read messages. I read the subject line, the first line, and the last line (the action—for what the boss wants me to do). In general, with most documents, we read the beginning and the end, *the first line,* and *the last line.*
>
> We don't drop the habit when we drop off the brow.
>
> —Captain, Navy supply ship

An extremely good OS—why just "Promotable"?:
OS1 Yankee ranks behind three other OS1s, two of whom have been selected for chief; the third was the leading OS on an admiral's staff. At virtually any other command, OS1 Yankee would rank first.

"Number 1 of 18 squadron lieutenants":
LT Zulu's career goal is fighter squadron command, and I have no doubt he'll get there—he's got what it takes. Promote this outstanding officer—now!

"You have to get through to a guy at 1800 who has been reading all day, is tired of it, but is still doggedly trying to form a picture."
—Navy Captain, just returned from a selection board

One final reason to include such beginning and closing summaries is because after holding a murder board the XO will usually adjust the summaries to ensure that (1) they match the promotion recommendations and (2) they are suitably varied from the top to bottom of the group of evals or fitreps the board has been looking at. The tones of the beginning and the ending, then, are likely to have been specially modulated or nuanced.

Modulation of the comments (ideally, adjusted not only in the summary but in the whole evaluation) is an important responsibility of command. Following is an example of how a frigate captain crafted closing comments about some of his department heads and junior officers. These summaries were written under the system in place prior to 1995, and they'd have to be shortened now. Also, they originally included promotion recommendations, which would make their intent clearer still. Nevertheless, they give one a feel for the possible variation of summary comments on a group of officers from the same ship.

Closing Comments on Five Officers from the Same Ship in the Old System
LT Alpha is an absolutely super officer who has repeatedly demonstrated his ability to execute every aspect of a Supply Officer's duties in an exemplary fashion. He is, without question, the finest and most efficient Supply Officer with whom I've ever worked.
The captain's favorite department head.

LT Bravo has rapidly developed into a solid, capable department head. He has aggressively taken charge of his department and made significant improvements department-wide. Already a proficient OOD and TAO, he is rapidly expanding his knowledge in all areas of Surface Warfare.
A solid officer somewhere in mid-tour.

LT Charlie is a solid department head and superior leader. Eager to excel, he has built an extremely competent cadre of professionals who have given him undivided loyalty. I anticipate his rapid qualification as EOOW and TAO once the current yard period is over.

Perhaps the best officer in potential—especially in leadership—but not yet fully qualified.

Ensign Delta is a young man of sharp wit, effervescent personality, and unmatched energy. He has the right stuff for a successful career. He must, however, work somewhat more diligently to conform to Navy weight standards.

The captain obviously likes the ensign but makes it clear he'll have to shape up physically.

LTJG Echo has been a diligent and steady performer who has given his job 100 percent effort. However, he has not completed his SWO PQS and is simply not cut out for the SWO community or for department head.

No damning by faint praise here.

Note that this closing statement on LTJG Echo and the one regarding Ensign Delta, just above it, fall into the category of "adverse" comments—which must be used with care, and about which the eval instruction has special guidance (the evaluated officer has to be offered the chance to make a comment, for instance). The summary on LTJG Echo is a decidedly "adverse" summary—on a lieutenant report it would be a career-ender—and must be used with special care and adherence to all the requirements of the fitness report instruction.

That's not to say one should never write such a comment; if we're to be honest with our people and with the Navy, we'll tell it like it is. However, under the evaluation system, substantial formal counseling should take place prior to taking this step. Even the much milder comment on Ensign Delta may be of significance, given the fact that boards up to lieutenant commander look for reasons *not* to promote, and obesity (especially habitual obesity) is one of these.

Place the Most Impressive Accomplishment First

In a narrative block that must stress content, the most impressive achievement should come immediately, not after a long build-up. Readers always skim information. Although they sometimes may read every comment, even when they go back through a report to check their work or to find highlights they will always look back at the start.

Whatever is said in the introductory statement, the reader's attention will be riveted upon the opening bullet, and he or she will naturally expect such things as the "Combined Federal Campaign" bullet (usually a minor accomplishment) to come near the last. It will be an unusual report writer who can keep the close attention of the reader all the way to the end. You have the reader's attention *now:* make use of it.

Here are some relatively impressive opening bullets for senior petty officer evals:

- Qualified throttleman and engineering POOW—the only SELRES ever to qualify as throttleman, oiler, and POOW aboard this ship.
- Praised for exceptional performance as an instructor by three different commanding officers: COs of USS HAYLER (DD 997), USS SCOTT (DDG 995), and USS HAWES (FFG 53).
- Primarily responsible for maintaining 97 percent availability of bow catapults, resulting in 2,350 mishap-free aircraft launches during MED deployment.

"My chief would give me the dates, times, and technical terminology. Then I'd make it look pretty, and pass it on to the XO."

—SWO LIEUTENANT

And here are some opening bullets that are not especially impressive.

- Reviewed and revised old recordkeeping system to eliminate redundancy and paperwork.
- Volunteered to set up and demonstrate a damage-control display to promote the Navy for "Career Day" at the ship's adopted secondary school.
- Built storage shelves at a local recreation center for better organization, accessibility, and inventory of rental gear.

To begin the comments block by narrating such relatively ordinary, unstriking achievements is a way to suggest mediocrity. Don't begin with the remarks in the second group above without intending to.

Don't Necessarily Fill the Entire Space

Drafters often feel obliged to fill the comments block top to bottom. Another reason drafters are drawn to fill the space is because a subordinate may submit a two-page brag sheet and expect you somehow to mention everything. But again, one must remember to *write primarily to the selection board,* not to the individual.

As for that selection board, even with a relatively short form, briefers can feel overloaded with information. Real accomplishments are easily lost in the snowstorm of a dozen bullets. Yes, some thirty-three of thirty-six lieutenant reports noted at SURFLANT filled up the entire space available—but selection board members reading those forms thought some of the best evals and fitreps they saw were shorter ones.

Consider the story told by a ship's captain whom we'll call Dick O'Flynn. He described a fitness report he received years ago on the old page-long forms, when comments typically ran at least three-quarters of a page. He had been working for a three-star, and the three-star wrote only one line on the whole page:

Give Dick O'Flynn a ship.

Everyone who saw that fitness report remembered it. And—he got his ship.

Clearly, one shouldn't write every report in such an abbreviated manner, and obviously there were special circumstances here—the credibility of a three star, for one thing, which can often substitute for the "verifiable."

Still, the fitrep described above was enormously refreshing to its intended audience. Even in the new system, board members must plow through page after page of evaluations crammed with very dense blocks of 10-point type. When, in the midst of this grueling process, a reader comes across a fitrep in 12-point type that fills only two-thirds of the form (which is also studded with frequent indentations and ample white space), that board member will tend to pay greater attention to the lesser amount of information presented, if for no other reason than because of the relief the short eval affords the eye.

"Hit hard, and hit fast. Then get out. If there's nothing more to say, don't waste a paragraph on all the 'hard' stuff you put in."

—NAVY CAPTAIN, ON
WRITING EVALS

4. PUTTING IT ALL TOGETHER—THREE BASIC STYLES

Despite the limitations on typography, there are better and poorer ways to format the information and opinions in the comments block. A full-block paragraph, for instance, is possible on the new form, though inadvisable. Also possible are shorter paragraphs or bullets of various sorts. Let's discuss some popular styles or formats used on evals and show examples of each.

Résumé Style

Of course, "bullet style" is common to naval documents. One standard use of bullets is to follow a "résumé" format in which *a strong verb begins each of many individual bulleted accomplishments*. This method is familiar to naval writers who have often used such bullets on evals, fitreps, and award justifications. Here's an example—an adaptation of a lieutenant commander's report from years ago (a very strong report, incidentally).

```
41. COMMENTS ON PERFORMANCE: All 5.0 and 1.0 marks must be specifically substantiated in comments. No numerical ranking permitted. Comments must be verifiable. Bold, under-
lined, italic, or other highlighted type is prohibited. Font must be 10 or 12 pitch (10 to 12 point) only. Use upper and lower case.
LCDR Gallery has been nothing short of brilliant. The best of three top cruiser department
heads, specifically, he:
* Saw to it, by his management of the 1200-psi Steam Plant, that the ship met all its
    commitments safely and on time—including three major exercises and four months of an
    Indian Ocean/Persian Gulf deployment. (#37)
- Managed the ___'s INSURV inspection so well (as shipwide coordinator) that ___ had few
    major discrepancies, none at all in engineering.
* Managed three highly successful availabilities—two in the US, one overseas, obtaining all
    major work requested on time. All of it! (#33)
- Guided one of his DC work centers to a confidence factor of 100% in the annual 3-M
    inspection, a rare occurrence in fleet units.
- Was praised for his work as ship's coordinator for the visit of the Vice Premier of the
    People's Republic of China. The Premier said his visit to ___ was "the high point of
    his trip to San Diego."
* Served expertly as "Alpha Whiskey" for the RANGER Battle Group and for combatant forces
    within the Persian Gulf. Also made significant contributions to the Vector Logic
    approach to tactical employment of CAP. (#39)
- Qualified both as EOOW and as TAO. As conning officer showed magnificent "seaman's eye."
- Clearly deserves full credit for the ___'s second consecutive Engineering "E" and Damage
    Control "DC."
Dan Gallery has my very strongest recommendation for early promotion, and for command of a
surface combatant.
```

As mentioned above, evaluations in 10-point invite skimming because they can be difficult to read. But it would be impossible to fit all of the above accomplishments in 12-point type. One has to decide whether some of the bullets listed above can be omitted or combined so the shorter fitrep as a whole (changed to 12 point) will be easier to read and more likely to be read through. Given the impressive accomplishments listed above, it's a hard case to make.

Here's an enlisted evaluation written in the same style, but in 12 point.

```
43. COMMENTS ON PERFORMANCE. * All 5.0 and 1.0 marks must be specifically substantiated in comments. No numerical ranking permitted. Comments must be verifiable. Bold, un-
derlined, italic, or other highlighted type is prohibited. Font must be 10 or 12 pitch (10 to 12 point) only. Use upper and lower case.

Petty Officer Jones is a hard-charging, completely reliable leader:

    * Superbly managed an 11-man CIC watch team. Ranked number one in the
      Harpoon engagement planner (SMG-1A) course. (#39)
    - Was singled out for praise by the DESRON Commander for his performance
      as CIC watch supervisor during NATO Exercise Recon Charlie 94.
    * Oversaw superb improvement in mess deck cleanliness and food service
      attendant performance while Mess Deck MAA. (#35)
    - Managed the S-3 Division Storeroom as MAA, keeping accurate inventories
      of dozens of fast-moving food items. Worked with senior MS's ordering
      and receiving provisions.
    - Is one of the primary reasons CARTER was chosen as a finalist for the
      Francis Ney Food Service Awards.

Industrious and extremely knowledgeable, Petty Officer Jones was assigned as
the enlisted dining facility MAA because he was the junior OS1 onboard.
Clearly eager to make his mark, he quickly earned the respect and trust of
every member of the division.
```

The closing comment in this evaluation is very helpful to board members. For one thing, it helps them understand why Jones was assigned as an MAA rather than in a supervisory capacity within his division; for another, it might help explain why this petty officer may not have gotten an "early" or "must promote" (if he didn't). He's the junior man on board; those senior to him will normally get the nod first. Yes, board members may figure that out on their own—but by explicit statement, the drafter inhibits any doubt from forming.

Descriptive Phrase Style

One other "bulleted" style begins each bullet with a descriptive phrase. Here, the phrases serve as titles of a kind and catch the eye. Below is an eval on a first class fire controlman written this way.

---

43. COMMENTS ON PERFORMANCE. * All 5.0 and 1.0 marks must be specifically substantiated in comments. No numerical ranking permitted. Comments must be verifiable. Bold, underlined, italic, or other highlighted type is prohibited. Font must be 10 or 12 pitch (10 to 12 point) only. Use upper and lower case.

```
An excellent petty officer and our finest Mk 56 technician. Details:
* Accomplished troubleshooter. Corrected many casualties during gunnery
   exercises. Fixed MK4 TDS system that had not worked well in years. (#37)
* An outstanding fire controlman—brought about dramatic turnaround in
   material condition of gun plot and MK 56 fire-control system. (#34)
- Excellent administrator—designed and implemented the annual budget for
   work center while temporarily assigned as Mess Decks MAA.
- Versatile—a great duty MAA; an excellent (temporary) divisional chief; a
   diligent watchstander: performed exceptionally on gunnery exercise.
- Good at attention to detail—greatly responsible for division's 100
   percent in 3-M inspection.
PO1 Golf has an excellent working relation with his subordinates.
Personally of great integrity—he sets the example for his division.
```

As you can see, just skimming the "key phrases" above by themselves can give a reader a word-picture of the individual, and each phrase is supported by a follow-on statement. As for content, note that this eval, though strong, is not exceptional. While Golf apparently is an excellent technician, in another area he sets an example and has "excellent working relations"—but he does not evidently *lead*.

Below is a fitness report on a CEC lieutenant commander written in a similar way:

---

41. COMMENTS ON PERFORMANCE: All 5.0 and 1.0 marks must be specifically substantiated in comments. No numerical ranking permitted. Comments must be verifiable. Bold, underlined, italic, or other highlighted type is prohibited. Font must be 10 or 12 pitch (10 to 12 point) only. Use upper and lower case.

LCDR Sierra is a superior CEC officer—already performing at the 0-5 level. Specifics follow:
* 33 (Prof exp) Thoroughly knowledgeable engineer: formulated and executed award of $3 million window replacement project. His superbly articulated justification/briefings earned end-year and mid-year $ to complete the project.
- Junior member of an 0-5 level working group: A star in senior role! Managed start up of design on $20 million MILCON project for a new wargaming center. Coordinated command input for facilities requirements.
- Great leader: takes the misfits and makes them productive. Developed tremendous teamwork between his military and civilian personnel.
- Incredible talent: Saved command $25K by preparing ductbank and conduits and by using in-house labor for installation of fiberoptic cable.
* 35 (Mil Bear/Char) Personally responsible for energizing physical fitness program with varied yet vigorous training. Number of outstandings rose from 18 to 28%; failures dropped 19%! Scored outstanding.
- Extraordinary foresight: developed long-range plans for quality of life improvements that yielded FY98 $ where previous attempts netted nothing.
- Supervised end-stage design and construction start-up of new $200K gym and fitness facility.
- Smooth manager: executed over 200 transportation and furniture move requests and 500 maintenance and minor work requests.

LEARNING TO BRAG

It took a while to learn to write brag sheets for my department head:

- The first time, I just wrote bullets about my activities.
- The second time, I wrote them as they had appeared in my last fitrep.
- The third time, I drafted them *as I wanted* them to *read.*

—Lieutenant (junior grade) aboard a destroyer

"Every naval officer should sit in on a selection board. They're always looking for recorders. When you're talking to your detailer, tell him you want to sit on a board."

—Navy Captain

The person who drafted this report said he foregrounded the engineering (rather than leadership) because he thought the technical work more important for a technical designator. Anyway, once again, the impressive phrases are immediately exemplified —and given credibility—by a wide variety of remarkable statistics. The performance here does tend to speak for itself—which is the ideal of the eval system. Nevertheless, the omission of a summary statement remains problematic. A couple of the less important bullets toward the end might be deleted or combined to afford space for a conclusion.

Note also the effectiveness of the indentation above. Here the lines following each bullet are indented to make the first words of each bullet—"Junior member," "Great leader," "Incredible talent"—stand out. Compare this report, say, to the example on page XX about Petty Officer McCarthy, in which each line is two-blocked to the left. It is clear that the "hanging paragraphs" used above enhance this report's readability.

"Marine-style"

One often hears about "Marine-style" evals. Even the Marines don't necessarily write this way anymore, but what has been styled "Marine-style" is effective in its own way.

This style typically uses one or more paragraphs with a series of several fragments or short sentences linked within each paragraph, one following the other and occasionally interspersing brief adjectives.

Navy reports of this kind typically use two or three short paragraphs, grouping like subjects with like. Here are a few paragraphs from a fitrep upon an officer attached to an NROTC unit, written in this way.

---

41. COMMENTS ON PERFORMANCE: All 5.0 and 1.0 marks must be specifically substantiated in comments. No numerical ranking permitted. Comments must be verifiable. Bold, underlined, italic, or other highlighted type is prohibited. Font must be 10 or 12 pitch (10 to 12 point) only. Use upper and lower case.

```
Our top-rated lieutenant. An outstanding leader in a large and successful NROTC unit.
* (Professional Expertise - 33): My finest instructor. A recognized expert in his field.
Frequently utilized for difficult, challenging assignments. Extensive understanding of
NROTC program administration and operational functions. Maintains a 3.8 GPA in a
Master's curriculum in Mechanical Engineering. Applied for registration as a Nuclear
Engineer and awaiting results from Principles and Practices Exam taken Oct. 96.
* (Military Bearing and Character - 36): Outstanding role model for future naval
officers. Exemplifies Navy Core Values. Honor and integrity unquestionable. Extraordinary
commitment to excellence. Moral and physical courage are admired and respected.
* (Mission Accomplishment - 37): Summer Cruise Coordinator for the nation's fifth largest
NROTC unit. Aggressively coordinated and executed summer training for 80 midshipmen
dispersed throughout the world. Top notch Nuclear Field advisor. Designed and supervised
extensive, demanding Naval Reactors interview preparations, resulting in selection of
seven midshipmen for the naval Nuclear Power Program. . . .
```

NAGGING QUESTIONS

Will a report be viewed as weak if it does not include a specific promotion recommendation *in the narrative* as well as in the "Promotion Recommendation" block? Will it be weak if the narrative also lacks explicitly stated recommendations? Will the enormous exaggerations in comments and recommendations that occurred in the past resurface?

Only time will tell, but two things can be said for sure. First, knowing the *actual practice* of eval/fitrep writing is vital. Second, that practice will certainly change. What people have their fingers on the pulse of that practice? Those who sign evals and fitreps and those who serve on selection boards. So *keep track of eval writing* on your ship or at your station, and *listen to selection board members on their return from the boards.*

—Writing Guide author

"After you've written your eval, leave it alone, let it rest. Then come back to it. And let someone else read it."
—LIEUTENANT COMMANDER AT THE NAVAL ACADEMY

Finally, below is one more illustration, an excellent example of an evaluation on a yeoman second class. Despite having only one 5.0 mark, this YN was one of some six individuals (out of thirty) rated "Early Promote" (in other words, this command's grading was tough). Note: This eval was written before comparisons and recommendations were reauthorized for the comments section; if written now, no doubt both an opening and a summary would be added.

---

43. COMMENTS ON PERFORMANCE. * All 5.0 and 1.0 marks must be specifically substantiated in comments. No numerical ranking permitted. Comments must be verifiable. Bold, underlined, italic, or other highlighted type is prohibited. Font must be 10 or 12 pitch (10 to 12 point) only. Use upper and lower case.

```
* 37 (Initiative).  On her own initiative, downloaded and installed new evaluation
program on 25 computers throughout the command. Assumes responsibility. Enterprising.
Can reliably fill any position in the Admin Department and the Chief of Staff office.
Self taught ADP expert-earned apprenticeship based on 2,000 documented hours of data
processing.

 Monitored awards program/administered LOM/MSM Board - processed 1,000+ awards with less
than 60 day turnaround and streamlined board procedures from 60 to 7 days. Self reliant.
Recognized by field and staff commands as the ultimate awards expert.

 Education achievements: Word Perfect Office, Watchdog Security, Superbase, Advanced
Word Perfect.
```

44. QUALIFICATIONS/ACHIEVEMENTS—Education, awards, community involvement, etc., during this period.

```
 Awarded Navy and Marine Corps Achievement Medal (2nd award). Achieved Dept of Labor,
Data Processing Technician Apprenticeship.
```

Although the above report doesn't even fill up the page, it doesn't need to, for one is convinced by the impressive achievements listed with respect to the striking one-sentence statements "Enterprising" and "Self-reliant" and the extremely strong assessment—"can reliably fill any position in the Admin Department and the Chief of Staff office." The latter statement seems to indicate this Sailor could immediately take on first class and chief's jobs—which is probably what the writer intended. And the comment that this YN is "recognized by field and staff commands as the ultimate awards expert," which speaks to the great degree of confidence placed by lots of people in this particular YN2's work, in effect strongly summarizes the evaluation.

Other Formats and Combinations of Formats

The styles and formats described above do not exhaust the possibilities. Some evals use short paragraphs with full sentences, and others use the performance trait titles themselves for organization, as in the NROTC example just above. Many other drafters combine bullets with paragraphs or have no dominant style.

Most important are the opinions and evidence, not the format; the format ideally just makes the opinions and evidence come alive. But one must remember the audience as well as the evidence, which is one reason for considering varieties of formats. The main audience—future selection boards—will eventually become accustomed to subtle changes in format, which means that the audience itself will subtly change. They will begin to look here or there for this or that kind of comment or hint or brief discussion. Omitting the expected comment in the expected place will inhibit one's best people from getting promoted. Clearly, keeping track of the ways Navy people write and use evaluations is perennially an essential task.

Last Words

Three final comments. First, *let the drafts of your evals and fitreps sit a while,* and then come back to them. You'll be surprised how different they seem—and how much better you can make them. Second, *proof the comments.* These drafts are among the most important documents you'll write, and putting mistakes in someone's official file can be both harmful and embarrassing to your people. Neither you nor they need that problem. And finally—get *the reports in on time.* Timeliness is a perennial problem with fitreps and evals.

"On proofing, my favorite falls into the 'one letter does make a difference' category. Actual quote from a report: 'Tasted 800 urine samples. . . .'"
—FITNESS REPORT EXPERT

I learned that when I was struggling with the writing of the award, usually the award was not really merited.

—MASTER CHIEF

7

Awards and Commendations

"The citation is comparatively easy. The hard part is the justification—selling to the reviewing authority that the award really is merited."

—NAVY LIEUTENANT

Awards and letters of commendation help build morale on a ship or in a unit. They can hurt morale too if the paperwork snarls and people who should get commendations don't get them, or if the paperwork becomes too burdensome on those who have to write up the awards. Of course, whoever proposes the award must follow the guidance in the Navy and Marine Corps Awards Manual (SECNAVINST 1650.1 series) and in amplifying local instructions. Beyond that, what's most important is to master the two kinds of writing and the informal briefing involved in award nominations.

An award package beyond the level of letters of commendation or appreciation normally consists of two documents: a write-up or summary of action (also known as the justification) and the citation. You might ask, why two documents? Both describe the actions of an individual and also commend that person. Couldn't one piece of paper do the work of two?

Despite the similarity of the two documents, they have one crucial difference: they serve two very different audiences. The summary of action sheet is written for those who must approve the award while the citation is aimed at the service member, shipmates, family, and friends. These two audiences have much different needs and levels of understanding. To write one document for both groups usually serves neither group well.

Complicating the subject of award writing further is the enhanced need for verbal justifications at local awards boards. In such circumstance there often is no requirement to write a formal justification. However, good *informal* oral justifications (often based on informal notes) can make the difference in one of your people getting a merited award or not. Here both writing and speaking can play a part.

Let's first look at this issue of local award boards, and the informal briefings they usually require.

"The department representative usually takes a page of bullets per nominee to the local awards board. They're basically a summary of action, but very informal."
—COMMAND MASTER CHIEF, NETC

AWARDS BOARDS AND "INFORMAL" JUSTIFICATIONS

In the early 2000s, the Navy abolished the requirement for writing formal justifications or "summaries of action" for all awards that the local command is authorized to approve leading up to and including the Navy and Marine Corps Commendation. A formal written justification is still required for "Navy Comms" that must be approved beyond the local command level, but not for those—or for Naval Achievement Medals—that are authorized to be approved locally.

However, justifications have not really gone away; the process simply requires less formality. All naval commands, large and small, hold "awards boards." One or more awards boards will convene at your command, perhaps as often as every two weeks, to consider what enlisted people and officers merit awards—and *which* awards.

For example, the XO and all department heads aboard a ship might meet to determine which junior officers merit awards for their achievements during a recent deployment. Meanwhile, the junior officers will meet to talk about their chiefs while the chiefs will get together to decide to recommend which E-4s, E-5s, or E-6s get medals.

In such local circumstances you are attempting to compare achievements by officers and Sailors in quite different specialties, and many of those recommended will be people you don't know well. While perhaps you've stood watch with some of these people and worked with others on a specific project, seldom will any officer or chief know all the hard chargers well.

In such circumstances, you often find yourself arguing for your own men and women while attempting to understand the comparative accomplishment of others. Specific details are vital, here. You'll essentially be "the briefing officer" for those you supervise, and some informal notes can make the difference. Also, the more time you put in thinking about your petty officer or chief's specific accomplishments, the better you can draft your notes and think of pertinent things to say.

"Here we hold the awards board electronically. Each member of the board votes on write-ups alone, on the computer— there is no discussion."
—AWARDS EXPERT, EAST COAST COMMAND

At local boards, then, the oral recommendation must play the part that the written justification once did. Ideally, as a briefer you will find the notes in your hands playing the same part as the bullets that once were provided by the summary of action. If you don't submit a strong input orally—in terms of what your petty officer or chief actually did during that recent deployment—he or she may not get the award that is really deserved. Most people depend on notes in briefing their people.

To summarize, then, once written skill could enhance a justification and help you win your case; now oral briefing skills (as informed by thoughtful consideration of your recommendee's achievements, and incisive notes on which to depend) can be crucial.

One officer, when interviewed, said that aboard her destroyer she knew what the chiefs were doing. She didn't need to bring any notes. A master chief demurred, arguing that "even *our own bosses* don't know what we're doing on a day-to-day, hourly basis." In his judgment, you had to go out of your way to get input on your people's performance, to weigh and craft it verbally, to really assess their achievements. Another master chief customarily brought the drafter of a recommended citation along with her to provide any needed clarification. At such meetings, she often found out much she did not know about individuals and their accomplishments.

In boards that are held electronically (as is sometimes done), written input is obviously even more important than in informal meetings—and depending on a draft citation alone is unlikely to be sufficient.

Because award justifications can be useful in both formal and informal circumstances, we proceed by discussing formal justifications. Although some of the justifications treated here were written for earlier editions of this book, before the Navy dropped requirements for written justifications for most Navy and Marine Corps Commendation Medals, they still make the whole process clear.

THE FORMAL JUSTIFICATION

Recommendations of higher-level awards beginning with the Meritorious Service Medal require formal justifications, as do recommendations for Naval and Marine Corps Commendation Medals that must leave the command.

Remember the Audience: The Awards Board

A justification will first go to a board of officers at one's own command. If this board approves the nomination, and if the captain of a ship or squadron or a Marine Corps battalion commander does not have authorization to sign the proposed award personally, the package will be forwarded further up the chain of command to whoever does. Thus, the award must often go through more than one committee of approval—a local board first, then to the commodore or higher. Obviously few members of the higher board will know the nominee. Even if the nomination goes just to a local board for approval, board members will look to the justification comments to *prove* that the service member merits recognition.

In addition, when board members are provided formal justifications, they will customarily read the whole document, not just skim it. Unlike a Navy or Marine Corps selection board, this group will have a comparatively limited number of nominees to consider, and only one evaluative write-up per person. They will not, like selection boards, have to read from five to thirty evaluation comments on every single individual (a quantity that guarantees skimming). So awards board members will have time to read the *whole* summary of action.

This difference is profound. Looking for patterns under severe time pressure, selection board briefers focus on numerical ratings and the opening bullets and closing comments in evaluations before them, and then, if they need to, will scan the accomplishments. In contrast, an awards board will normally *turn immediately to the accomplishments* to see if this person's actions or services merit the recommended award.

Pay Special Attention to the *Middle* of the Justification

The space on the summary of action form (the back of SECNAV Form 1650/3) is most of an 8.5″ by 11″ sheet. One is wise to begin this summary with a tone-setting opening statement and to conclude with a summary or convincing close. Again, however, the board member usually focuses on the details found in the middle portion to discover *just what this person did* that might be worthy of special recognition.

Normally, bullet format is appropriate for the write-up, as it is with evaluations. Indeed, in beginning your draft you may want to borrow some of the bullet descriptions from the individual's fitrep or eval (if on hand). Some of them will serve as good starting points, at least; you don't need to reinvent the wheel with every new piece of paper. However, besides differences in the period covered or the exact events discussed, the aims of the two kinds of documents differ subtly. The performance evaluation focuses on *potential for the future;* the award nomination on *how exceptional the past service has been.*

Rather than having to decide whether this particular first class should take on a chief's responsibilities or this O-5 should be made an O-6, the awards board will be deciding whether past accomplishments merit public recognition. Also, because too many awards cheapen any single award, an awards board always has standards to

"I back up the awards that my department heads tell me they want, when we meet at the local awards boards."

—Navy XO

uphold. As a result, the board will be deciding both whether *any* award is merited, and if so, *what level.* In the latter case, they'll usually be asking whether to lower it from what you've recommended—very few award nominations are bumped up.

So besides describing the accomplishments very clearly and quantifying or objectifying them in some way, in the write-up you should repeatedly imply comparisons with the norm and show how this particular service has been *consistently above it.*

Follow This Advice Too

When writing for the awards board, you may assume knowledge of standard abbreviations, common terms, and even specialized terminology because the members will usually be seniors in the same chain of command and generally familiar with the kind of work their subordinates do. If the nominee had very unusual duties, you should explain those duties briefly to make clear the nominee's special impact. The higher up the line the award package has to go for approval, the greater the need to explain unfamiliar achievements.

Length? Normally, except for very high awards or awards for valor (about which the Awards Manual has special rules), the write-up should fit on the form, with no continuations. On the other hand, several squadron and ship commanders suggest you write at least eight to ten short bullets per write-up, or the achievements may not come across as very strong.

How to go about the writing? Here are a few pointers.

Avoid
- generalities
- a "job description" approach
- excess superlatives (they tend to obscure the basis for the award)

Pursue
- an objective summary
- specific examples
- explicit comparisons with the standard or norm

Stated in other terms, you should *recount specific details or achievements,* as in the following examples:

- Personally authored three TACFACTS including "S-3A Radar Offset Mining," "Acoustic Tripwire," and "Viking Chainsaw," articles lauded by seniors in the chain of command.

or

- Repaired a function generator, part of the CAT IIID test station vital to the bench operation, saving the Navy $3,800 in replacement parts and avoiding long test-bench downtime.

or

- Established effective management programs to monitor the processing of over 14,000 demands per month and the reconciliation of over 18,000 outstanding system requisitions.

And then make sure you use quotes or other laudatory citations, if available.

- Was cited by COMCARDIV ONE for "extremely sound judgment and tact."

or

- The equipment was characterized by inspectors as "the best Basic Point Defense Missile System we've ever seen."

Finally, specify comparisons or improvements that the individual has made:

- Made major reductions in the error rate on fitness reports, from the traditional 35–40 percent error rate to 15–20 percent.

or

- Reduced the average time per service call from 4.6 hours to 3.5 hours in FY 87, reducing costs by 25 percent.

or

- Developed new techniques for torpedo overhaul, techniques that resulted in a 60 percent increase in torpedo production, significantly expanding the total number of available weapons for the Atlantic Fleet.

Figure 7.1 is an example of a good summary of action justifying a proposed Navy and Marine Corps Commendation Medal (penned before the requirement for a justification at this level was waived). This medal is meant to be an "end-of-tour" award for a Navy lieutenant after service aboard an FFG.

And following is a brief summary of advice on writing award justifications. In writing these documents, the best writers will:

- Always remember to say *how well* the member performed, not just what he or she did (avoiding mere job descriptions);
- Specify figures, dollars, or percentages when these numbers clarify the special magnitude of the service member's achievement;
- Make explicit comparisons with the standard or norm, showing how the performance has conspicuously surpassed that normally expected of the individual's rank/rate and time in service;
- Delineate specific improvements the service member has brought about by comparing the results of the service member's work with what went before;
- Cite praise from commanders and other authorities whenever possible, quoting the actual words used where those words shed light on the individual's performance;
- Take special care to highlight personal initiative, voluntary work, and service beyond the call of duty;
- Remember to cite several specific examples of the individual's performance (including names, dates, and places), giving the readers a good general feel for this individual's unique accomplishments;
- Overall, always ensure the level of award is appropriate for service rendered and that the justification supports the recommended level of the award.

A Case Study: The Guantánamo Bay Training Group Case

To further exemplify the process of justification writing and to show something of its typical context, here is a case study involving an actual award nomination from a few years back. We've changed the name of the officer involved but not the basic circumstances. The case study's subject is how to enhance a write-up just by remembering what made the achievement so special.

The Situation

A commander at the Fleet Training Group in Guantánamo Bay told one of the lieutenants to write himself up for a Navy Commendation Medal. (This was before the renaming of the Navy Achievement and Commendation Medals to the Navy *and Marine Corps* Achievement and Commendation Medals.)

For many reasons, having your subordinate write his or her own award nomination is not a good idea. Not only can it encourage self-justification and therefore prove

Figure 7.1 A Summary of Action for an Award Nomination. Taken together, the bullets in this write-up document impressive performance.

SUMMARY OF ACTION ICO LT ANDREW MICHAEL MATTHEWS XXX-XX-XXXX

LT Matthews' performance as Disbursing and Sales Officer during his tour of duty was nothing short of remarkable. Proficient, knowledgeable, and dedicated, LT Matthews instilled a spirit of pride and teamwork in his subordinates, and his untiring efforts led to outstanding results during all of his inspections. There was no job too difficult or tasking too large for him to attack. His accomplishments include:

- Became the first Supply Officer onboard USS NICHOLAS (FFG 47) to qualify as both OOD Underway and as a Surface Warfare Officer.

- Passed two major surprise disbursing audits by Defense Accounting Office with outstanding results.

- Was an excellent Helo Control Officer. An expert on FFG/SH-60B helo operations, ensured the safe execution of many flight evolutions during a six-month deployment and several major exercises.

- Was an exceptional DC Trainer, key member of DCTT as Repair Locker Evaluator. His contributions were critical in excellent DC assessments during LOE, REFTRA, and OPPE.

- Ran a superb Ship's Store. It received a grade of Excellent during the Logistic Management Assessment Inspection and was noted as one of the best Ship's Stores on the waterfront.

- Showed outstanding organizational ability. As the point-man in homeport shift, he provided quality presentations and information to families and crew on the full spectrum of personal and financial requirements and options relating to the Norfolk move.

- Assumed additional duties as Administrative Officer and quickly instituted new procedures to improve effectiveness and efficiency of the Ship's Office.

- Coordinated Combined Federal Campaign in which the command exceeded the annual goal by 35%.

- Ranked as my top Division Officer for two years and one of my top underway OODs.

- Received Navy Achievement Medal from Commanding Officer USS NICHOLAS for his outstanding performance during six-month deployment to Adriatic/Med/Red Sea.

LT Matthews' relentless pursuit of excellence proved invaluable to NICHOLAS during his tour of duty. His aggressive, "can do" attitude helped motivate his entire division to a higher level of accomplishment. His performance strongly merits presentation of the Navy and Marine Corps Commendation Medal.

ON WRITING YOUR OWN AWARD—AN OPINION

I have some strong opinions on "writing up your own award." Absolutely, positively, never, never! Every award should be a surprise; the intended recipient should be completely blind to the whole process.

Consider it this way. "Hey, Joe, you're a good guy, how about writing yourself up for the Medal of Honor? I don't really know all of what you've been doing 'cause I'm too busy flapping about other stuff or playing golf [to pay attention to you], but you deserve a medal. Don't worry; I'll make sure you get taken care of."

Later: "Gee, Joe, I guess you're really disappointed about that letter of commendation you got from the admiral after we had discussed getting you a nice medal. Well, maybe they just didn't read between the lines enough. We sent in your write-up pretty much unchanged because we figured you had the best view on what you did. Well, don't worry; it's fitreps and not medals that count, anyway."

Now how does the guy feel? If he had never known what he was being considered for, he wouldn't have been disappointed. Awards are often downgraded, so if you don't tell him he's being put in for a Navy Comm, he won't be upset that he got only a Navy Achievement Medal.

Evaluations are different. The guy will see those in the final form. Here too I never ask my people to write their own, for many of the same reasons outlined above, but I do ask them for inputs, preferably in the form of bullets I can use directly. If the guy wants to write the whole thing, great; but since I sign it, I will edit it—it's never a straight shot from him to signature, even if I just change the "happys" to "glads."

—Navy Commander

awkward for a fittingly humble service member but it also suggests that the superior really doesn't know enough (or care enough) to do the recommendation personally. Moreover, it can ultimately prove disappointing to the person you're recommending, as many award nominations are disapproved or downgraded after being submitted. Not least in importance, having a subordinate write up his or her own flies directly in the face of official policy as outlined in the Awards Manual, which says not to disclose recommendations for awards either to the recommended individual or to the next of kin.

This particular story, however, concerns the lieutenant who was asked, not the commander doing the asking. Faced with this request, and believing his service had indeed merited the award (though feeling a good deal of awkwardness about it all), he went ahead and typed up the cover sheet, and then composed a summary of action and citation. The summary of action he turned in appears as figure 7.2.

Believing himself worthy, and having written up his achievements in such a way, Lieutenant North was greatly surprised when he heard later that he would receive a Navy Achievement Medal while another lieutenant, who in his opinion had not done nearly as much, would receive a Navy Comm. His command's administrative officer later informed him that his write-up simply had not been strong enough. "But I just told them what I did," was his reply, "and they know many of these jobs themselves, how important they are. Besides that, the other fellow hyped his collateral duty, and

I purposely played down mine—I didn't want it to overshadow the gas turbine engineering work." Despite Lieutenant North's feelings, judging only by the justification, the board might have been right. Many aspects of the lieutenant's accomplishments, factors that explained the quality or magnitude of his performance, had failed to come out in the write-up. (This deficiency turned out to have been especially important because on the day the awards board met, no one from his own department could attend the board—and sometimes that happens!)

Later, Lieutenant North recalled that the commander had put it together at home, at night, and hadn't revised it after that; he was in the midst of a heavy ship-riding schedule at work. Had he had time to work on it again—and he would have *found* the time, had it been for someone other than himself—the board's vote might have been different.

With some assistance from an expert writer, Lieutenant North sat down much later and considered ways in which he might have clarified the special quality of his work. Below is a detailed commentary as to how, by explaining his varied achievements, he could have substantially improved the write-up.

Discussion of Lieutenant North's Award Write-Up

Introduction

The introduction in the write-up does little to set the tone for the whole report, includes some unhelpful standard navalese—"pursued a set of initiatives enhancing the utilization of"—and is too long. Readers of justifications tend to be impatient with long paragraphs of introduction, and the subject does not justify the length of the introduction since every item it brings up also appears later in the bullets.

Accomplishments

The set of accomplishments is the key section of the justification comments. Lieutenant North's effort is not especially well formatted, and it could use some <u>underlining</u> or **bold-facing** for emphasis. But it does use bullet format, puts the bullets in proper parallel grammatical structure, and makes no errors. The key issue is what is said. Let's go through it line by line.

- "Supervised the engineering training of 32 LANTFLT gas-turbine ships." This phrase is simply a "job description," and a very skimpy one at that. Yes, the board members probably have a general idea of what these duties involve. But most of them will have no idea of all the specifics and, more importantly, will not appreciate *how well* he performed the job. In a sense, Lieutenant North lost out from the beginning by failing to describe in any detail at all *how well* he performed his primary duty.
- "Qualified as Senior Engineering Instructor for DD 963/DDG 993/CG 47-class ships." The interview revealed that this qualification was not a requirement but a voluntary achievement on Lieutenant North's part. Again, the vital aim of award write-ups is to show unusual, "head and shoulders" behavior, so you must take full advantage of opportunities like this one. The following revision is both truthful and persuasive:

  At his own initiative, and even though his billet did not require it, he qualified as Senior Engineering Instructor for DD 963/DDG 993/CG 47-class ships. Moreover, he qualified in only four months, rather than the usual eight.

Figure 7.2 Summary of Action for an Award That Got Downgraded. Not all of Lieutenant North's achievements got into this summary.

OPNAV 1650/3 (Rev. 3-76) BACK
S/N 0107-LF-016-5015

INSTRUCTIONS

1. Before completing this form see SECNAVIST 1650.1E.
   a. Para 121 and 122 explain the preparation and submission of a recommendation.
   b. Chapter 2 contains the criteria for each award.

2. Insure all blanks are filled in and the form is dated.

3. The Summary of Action *(Item 25)* is required in all cases in addition to an attached proposed citation. *(double space)*

4. This form should be forwarded directly to the authority authorized to approve the award recommended or to the appropriate Fleet/Force CINC *(whichever is lower in the chain of command).*

25. SUMMARY OF ACTION

During the period from 30 July 1985 to 31 July 1987 Lieutenant North consistently performed his demanding duties as Gas Turbine Branch Head in an exceptional and outstanding manner. As the senior gas turbine engineer at Fleet Training Group, he was responsible for the Propulsion Systems training on all LANTFLT gas turbine units conducting refresher or shakedown training. Volunteering for the additional responsibilities of command Reserve Training Coordinator, he aggressively pursued a set of initiatives enhancing the utilization of assigned reservists. Lieutenant North's success in this area was evidenced by numerous laudatory remarks and comments by members of the reserve force as well as representatives of COMNAV-SURFRESFOR and COMTRALANT. Specific accomplishments during this tour include:

--Supervised the engineering training of 32 LANTFLT gas-turbine ships

--Qualified as Senior Engineering Instructor for DD 963/DDG 993/CG 47-class ships

--Performed duties as Training Liaison Officer on seven LANTFLT ships, receiving numerous letters of appreciation from commanding officers

--Designated Master Training Specialist

--Oversaw the development of Instructor Professional Qualification Standards (PQS) for the Gas Turbine Branch that then became the model for the development of Instructor PQS for all other branches of FLETRAGRU

--Represented Fleet Training Group at the 1986 and 1987 CINCLANTFLT PEB conferences

--Managed the training program for 246 selected reservists performing ACDUTRA at FLETRAGRU

--Researched, organized, and updated mobilization plans and requirements

--Planned, organized, and conducted two successful Reserve Training Conferences for FLETRAGRU reserve detachment commanding officers

RANK HATH ITS PRIVILEGES

There are several unwritten rules about award writing—that you have to have a certain rank to get a specific medal, for instance. A major command recommended its Command Master Chief for the Legion of Merit upon his retirement. The man was an institution—the "Old Salt" of the Navy. He had spent some 42 years in the service, well over two-thirds of his life. Two of his sons were even chiefs. But the authorities resisted. The politics were enormous. It took *4-star intervention* to get him a Legion of Merit.

—Commander

- "Performed duties as Training Liaison Officer on seven LANTFLT ships, receiving numerous letters of appreciation from commanding officers." We are left in the dark as to what those duties were, how difficult, and, again, how well performed. The write-up does tell us he was commended for them. How much to elaborate on these duties is a judgment call, but *at the very least* he might have named the ships whose COs wrote letters of appreciation. If he could name three or four specific vessels and even cite key lines from those letters, this phrase wouldn't be a throwaway line (as it almost is now) but a strong justification.
- "Designated Master Training Specialist." Lieutenant North assumed that the board knew what this entailed. After all, the same board that approved awards also approved designations, and several months earlier it had approved his. But he forgot that the specific accomplishments that caused them to approve this designation *then* were not spelled out in writing *now* before the board. Moreover, by not elaborating on what this designation meant, he lost the opportunity to keep the wagon train moving—to show *in every accomplishment* how superior his performance has been. He could have added significant details, summing up with something like this statement:

  For these achievements he was singled out as an expert in training and earned the designation "Master Training Specialist."

- "Oversaw the development of Instructor Professional Qualification Standards (PQS) for the Gas Turbine Branch that then became the model for the development of Instructor PQS for all other branches of FLETRAGRU." Lieutenant North reports that he had worked some time on this particular sentence to see that the value of this achievement came through. And certainly, this is the best sentence in all the summary of action. It indicates that here, at least, Lieutenant North forges ahead and sets the standards for the whole group. Still, the interview with Lieutenant North revealed that the circumstances were even more impressive, as suggested in the changes below:

  which the group commander personally judged so superior as to make them models for the development of Instructor PQS for all other branches of FLETRAGRU.

- "Represented Fleet Training Group at the 1986 and 1987 CINCLANTFLT PEB conferences." Again, remember to say how, or you've just penned another job description. Additional detail, gleaned from the interview, clarifies the accomplishment here:

Represented the Fleet Training Group superbly at the 1986 and 1987 CINCLANTFLT PEB conferences, <u>despite being the only O-3 among O-4s, O-5s, and O-6s</u>.

- "Served as Officer in Charge of Training Readiness Team sent to the Dominican Republic." Lieutenant North completely left out this bullet at the last moment, perhaps noticing that it is merely a job description, as is. This statement needs more specifics—why he was sent, to begin with. The details added below (discovered in the interview) showcase senior officers' confidence in this officer's soundness of judgment:

  > Sent to the Dominican Republic to evaluate the condition of one of the Republic's patrol boats and its readiness to go through FLETRAGRU training. His assessment that the boat was "unsafe to steam" and his list of recommended improvements were accepted in full by the Dominican Navy and immediately implemented by FLETRAGRU.

- "Managed the training program for 246 selected reservists performing ACDU-TRA at FLETRAGRU," etc., to the end. The lieutenant thought, on reflection, that he could have expanded the reserve program management by itself into many more bullets. As originally written, it simply does not support strong medal recognition. That he managed a training program for reservists, did some research, and "successfully" ran two conferences doesn't say an awful lot. The reported laudatory comments mentioned in the introduction (which the readers have probably forgotten by the time they read this far) are much too vague to impress. He could have done a great deal here; let a revision to the final sentence suffice:

  > <u>Single-handedly</u> planned, organized, and conducted two <u>highly successful</u> Reserve Training Conferences for 50 reserve unit commanding officers and training officers, O-3 to O-6. <u>In total charge</u> of every aspect of the conferences, LT North earned highly laudatory comments not only from the reservists themselves but also from representatives of COM-NAVSURFRESFOR and COMTRALANT.

Conclusion

Although summary comments are not as important in award nominations as they are in fitreps and evals, a strong conclusion can help board members decide what to think about what they have just read. A board may interpret the omission of that conclusion as the command's "sending a signal" because it is so seldom done. Here's a possible concluding statement:

> In summary, LT North's service to FLETRAGRU has been highlighted by superb technical knowledge, the utmost of professionalism, and tireless effort. His achievements have always been so far above the norm as to be characteristic of officers far more senior than he. His truly exceptional service would be most fittingly recognized by award of the Navy Commendation Medal.

Of course, not all of the above would fit in a page-long justification statement, but having developed the subject in such a thorough way, you would have more than enough to put together a most impressive justification. With such improvements further cut and crafted to fit the write-up sheet, figure 7.3 presents a fully descriptive version of the write-up.

One Final Comment

Couldn't this rewriting be seen as promoting slick verbal skills when we ought to be getting rid of inflated language, not promoting it?

Ideally, as suggested above, *the facts themselves* will impress readers and listeners. The words, when well used, serve primarily as windows through which the readers can glimpse the real achievement. Fortunately, because it puts the accomplishments center stage, bullet format has decreased the importance of mere verbal skills.

Of course, inflation can still be a problem. Command initiative is vital here, both in toning down comments when necessary and in deciding who deserves awards in the first place. In any case, the proof of good award nominations and of the writing of nominations is in their moral *effects.*

If the process succeeds, and by means of the writing it singles out *actual merit,* the best performers are then receiving support and recognition. Their morale improves because they see that you reward the good work they do. Others around them, acknowledging the justice of the awards, tend to emulate the behavior that you've so highly commended.

On the other hand, if the recipient does *not* really merit the award, if the truth has taken a backseat to politics or cronyism or just self-centered campaigning (including inflating your own or another's achievements beyond their real worth)—then morale disintegrates. The commanding officer of a destroyer, on returning from a deployment, complained to his commodore that he hadn't received an award, yet the skipper of a ship that had gone aground during that same deployment had gotten one. So the commodore gave him an award. But all the destroyer's officers knew the circumstances, and also knew that the skipper had honored few of the crew. As a result, the occasion of the ship's award ceremony—held strictly to hand out that one medal to the Captain—was not a positive one.

THE CITATION

Write the Citation for a Non-Navy Audience

The citation's audience is very different from the justification's. While the nominee and shipmates will listen to the citation at an awards ceremony, other listeners may include children, spouses, other relatives, and friends, many of whom will have little or no naval background. So use very few abbreviations and no acronyms; leave out technical jargon; make the citation so clear that it can *stand alone,* without requiring an expert to explain the details. As you draft the citation, imagine a civilian relative or friend listening as you commend the awardee and try to speak to *that* person.

Because it has to be short, the best idea is to focus on two or three major accomplishments. Normally the exact wording of the beginning and end is specified. The creativity comes in the middle of this document, in giving the readers a sense of the *real accomplishment.*

Keep the attention of this lay audience by citing a few impressive details. As best you can, write so almost anyone can appreciate some major aspects, at least, of what the Marine or Sailor has done.

Don't Try to Impress with Language

One of the chief mistakes citation writers make is to try to impress with language, by using lots of pretentious adjectives and bureaucratese. The write-up should be

Figure 7.3 A Revised Summary of Action. This summary revises and upgrades figure 7.2 by adding key information and structuring it so as to catch the eye.

OPNAV 1650/3 (Rev. 3-76) BACK
S/N 0107-LF-016-5015

INSTRUCTIONS

1. Before completing this form see SECNAVIST 1650.1E.
   a. Para 121 and 122 explain the preparation and submission of a recommendation.
   b. Chapter 2 contains the criteria for each award.

2. Insure all blanks are filled in and the form is dated.

3. The Summary of Action *(Item 25)* is required in all cases in addition to an attached proposed citation. *(double space)*

4. This form should be forwarded directly to the authority authorized to approve the award recommended or to the appropriate Fleet/Force CINC *(whichever is lower in the chain of command).*

25. SUMMARY OF ACTION

During the period 30 July 1985 to 31 July 1987, Lieutenant North consistently distinguished himself in his primary duty as Gas Turbine Branch Head, and also performed exceptionally in a wide variety of collateral and voluntary duties. In this work he:

• Supervised superbly all the engineering training of 32 LANTFLT gas-turbine ships, from each ship's Day #1 Safety Check to its final OPPE Certification.

• Qualified as Senior Engineering Instructor for DD 963/DDG 993/CG 47 class ships although not required by his billet, qualifying in just 4 months rather than the usual 8.

• Performed duties as Training Liaison Officer on seven LANTFLT ships, receiving LOAs from the COs of the COMTE DE GRASSE (DD 974), STUMP (DD 978), and PREBLE (DDG 46).

• Oversaw the development of Instructor PQS for the Gas Turbine Branch. The group commander made this training package the model for all other branches of FLETRAGRU.

• Represented FLETRAGRU superbly at the 1986 and 1987 CINCLANTFLT PEB conferences.

• Served as OINC of the Training Readiness Team sent to the Dominican Republic to evaluate the readiness of a patrol boat to undergo FLETRAGRU training. His assessment that the boat was "unsafe to steam" and his list of recommended improvements were accepted in full by the Dominican Navy and immediately implemented by FLETRAGRU.

• Single-handedly planned, organized, and conducted two highly successful Reserve Training Conferences for 50 reserve unit officers, 0-3 to 0-6. For this voluntary duty, LT North earned highly laudatory comments not only from the reservists themselves, but from representatives of both COMNAVSURFRESFOR and COMTRALANT.

• Was designated "Master Training Specialist" by board action for excellence in training.

In summary, LT North's service to FLETRAGRU has been highlighted by superb technical knowledge, the utmost of professionalism, and tireless effort. His truly exceptional service would be most fittingly recognized by award of the Navy Commendation Medal.

"NEVER use an acronym in a formal citation—always use the 'long form.' Remember the audience (i.e., mom and pop)!"

—Navy Captain,
SUBMARINER

relatively formal, yes—but *formal* doesn't mean *deadly.* Do we really want to put family members to sleep by telling them how their loved one "initiated and implemented" something? Or "developed, coordinated, and executed" something else, even if he or she did it in "an exemplary and professional manner?" Doublings (and triplings!) are the special sins of citation writers. Be on the lookout for tiresome, long-winded, and pretentious ("boilerplated") phrases such as:

- paragon of success
- pinnacle of recruiting quality and proficiency
- highlighted the culmination of
- in a timely manner
- coordinated the planning to upgrade
- was instrumental in the preparation and revision of
- the driving force in the implementation of
- to maximize utilization of available assets
- initiating and implementing an efficient, effective, and accountable organization to gain the necessary visibility and control during . . .
- contributed materially to the success
- had a profound influence on the efficiency and effectiveness of

This list is literally endless.

By using fresh and natural language, make your statement crisp, to the point, and hard-hitting. Keep to the facts, and as much as possible let the facts impress by themselves rather than depending on the crutch of adjectives and adverbs.

Follow These Dos and Don'ts

Don't use jargon, be overly technical, or use abbreviations that will be unfamiliar to a civilian. Don't write statements like:

- Performed timely recalibration of the MK 113 MOD 9 FCS.
- Corrected several difficult problems in the MK 3 MOD 7 Ships Inertial Navigation System (SINS) and the AN/URN-20 TACAN, and completely overhauled and tested all 40 SINS aircraft alignment output terminals.
- Performed superbly through a Middle East Deployment, SRA, Operational Propulsion Plant Examinations, NTPI, DNSI, Command Inspection, and INSURV (Instead, write "Performed superbly during a six-month deployment to the Middle East and several major ship inspections.")

And don't specify items only of interest to those at your duty station. They won't care that you repaired "NR 1 High-Pressure Air Dehydrator, Numbers 1 and 2 High-Pressure Air Compressor, NR 2 Distilling Plant Heater Condenser, NR 2 Sewage Plant Incinerator," and so on.

"At a ceremony giving lots of awards, don't read the required openings and closings of each one. After the audience gets the idea, just give the highlights for each service member."

—Navy Lieutenant

Do follow the guidelines in the following checklist:

- Be specific enough to get across some sense of what the individual has actually achieved.
- Make all details interesting and intelligible for a civilian audience.
- Write the first sentence exactly as specified in the Awards Manual for the particular type or level of award.
- Vary sentence style—don't always begin with the subject.
- Write the entire citation in the simple past tense ("improved," not "has improved"; "was responsible," not "has been responsible").

- Always use the third person, i.e., "he" or "she" rather than "you" (this rule differs from the standard style of some letters of commendation/appreciation).
- Use the individual's name only in the heading, the second sentence, and the last sentence of the citation.
- Make certain the spelling of the full name is correct, including "Jr.," "III," etc., as needed. And use middle initials only—not full middle names.
- Spell out the rank or rate. (See Awards Manual and local instructions for further guidance on "Petty Officer Smith" rather than "Petty Officer Second Class Smith," etc.)
- Capitalize the entirety of any ship's name, and use a ship's designation in parentheses the first time (no hyphen between ship and number), i.e., USS MISSOURI (BB 63).
- Make sure all ship and command names and numbers are exactly right.
- Read the basic instruction, the Navy and Marine Corps Awards Manual (SEC-NAVINST 1650.1), and follow the format found there.
- Find and follow the guidance of the local command, the type commander, or any other relevant authority.

Finally, Remember All Those You're Talking To—And
For How Long

The citation, beyond almost any other kind of Navy writing, is an eminently public document. In addition to friends and family members, you are also speaking in the citation both to the service member you're honoring—who will appreciate accuracy—and to shipmates of that service member. The latter will also appreciate their shipmate's genuine accomplishments but will notice when you're stretching the facts.

Moreover, the citation will have a very long life. Think of it framed, and gracing the wall of the service member's office or home for years. Then write it so it's worthy of such a place.

For Example: Various Citations

The most common naval awards are the Navy and Marine Corps Commendation and Achievement Medals. In October 1995 the requirement for a separate citation to be submitted along with a certificate *and* a justification was waived. The proposed citation is submitted *as printed on the respective certificate.*

Not only is this a paperwork reduction but it also reduces the size of the actual citation slightly—to no more than twelve lines of ordinary type. On the certificate itself, there is at most room for a citation of some three sentences between the opening and closing. It is consequently all the more difficult to make the citation convey something of the actual accomplishments involved. Figure 7.4 shows a citation gracing a certificate for a Naval and Marine Corps Achievement Medal that was awarded aboard the USS LOS ANGELES. And below is another citation for an N&MC Achievement medal, this one awarded to a Builder Second Class (in this example the description is set off from the standardized opening and close by bold italics, to make clear what is standardized, and what is not). Note that citations on the certificates are typically printed in all caps, to skirt difficulties with capitalization.

[FOR] PROFESSIONAL ACHIEVEMENT AS MATERIAL LIAISON OFFICE EXPEDITOR, U.S. NAVAL MOBILE CONSTRUCTION BATTALION XRAY FROM DECEMBER 1999 TO JULY 2000. PETTY OFFICER YANKEE PERFORMED HIS DEMANDING DUTIES IN AN

Figure 7.4 Certificate. This "end of tour" award for a petty officer on an SSN cites several impressive accomplishments.

DEPARTMENT OF THE NAVY

THIS IS TO CERTIFY THAT
THE SECRETARY OF THE NAVY HAS AWARDED THE

NAVY AND MARINE CORPS ACHIEVEMENT MEDAL

(GOLD STAR IN LIEU OF THE SECOND)

TO

ELECTRICIAN'S MATE FIRST CLASS (SS) HENRY DEAN SHENK, UNITED STATES NAVY

FOR

PROFESSIONAL ACHIEVEMENT IN THE SUPERIOR PERFORMANCE OF HIS DUTIES WHILE SERVING AS A MEMBER OF ELECTRICAL DIVISION IN USS LOS ANGELES (SSN 688), FROM MAY 1998 TO AUGUST 2002. PETTY OFFICER SHENK CONSISTENTLY PERFORMED HIS DEMANDING DUTIES IN AN EXEMPLARY AND HIGHLY PROFESSIONAL MANNER. DEMONSTRATING EXCEPTIONAL TECHNICAL ACUMEN, HE FLAWLESSLY PERFORMED UNDERWAY REPAIRS TO A 400 HERTZ MOTOR GENERATOR AND PROPULSION LUBE OIL PUMP MOTOR ALLOWING THE SHIP TO MEET ALL OPERATIONAL COMMITMENTS DURING THE WESTERN PACIFIC DEPLOYMENT. HE LED THE REFURBISHMENT OF BOTH SHIP'S SERVICE MOTOR GENERATORS, A DEPOT LEVEL REPAIR, DURING A DEPLOYED UPKEEP. HAND-PICKED TO BE ON THE WORK CONTROLS TEAM, HIS EXTENSIVE SYSTEM KNOWLEDGE AND WORK ETHIC WERE CRITICAL TO THE SUCCESSFUL FAST START OF A SELECTED RESTRICTED AVAILABILITY. PETTY OFFICER SHENK'S MANAGERIAL ABILITY, PERSONAL INITIATIVE, AND UNSWERVING DEVOTION TO DUTY REFLECTED GREAT CREDIT UPON HIMSELF AND WERE IN KEEPING WITH THE HIGHEST TRADITIONS OF THE UNITED STATES NAVAL SERVICE.

GIVEN THIS   20TH   DAY OF   JUNE   2002

C. B. Thomas

SECRETARY OF THE NAVY

FOR THE
C. B. THOMAS
COMMANDING OFFICER
USS LOS ANGELES (SSN 688)

NAVSO 1650/12 (REV. 7-99)
S/N 0104-LF-982-3000

EXEMPLARY AND HIGHLY PROFESSIONAL MANNER. *SUPERBLY MAINTAINING AN EFFICIENT LOGISTICAL PIPELINE FOR FIVE ACTIVE PROJECTS, HE PERSONALLY REQUISITIONED OVER 1,250 LINE ITEMS VALUED IN EXCESS OF $500,000. HE ALSO ENSURED THE TIMELY DELIVERY OF ALL REQUIRED MATE-RIALS AND, IN THE PROCESS, EARNED GREAT RESPECT FOR FIGHTING FORTY BY BUILDING GREAT RAPPORT WITH OVER 25 LOCAL BUSINESSES. FINALLY, DESPITE CONSISTENTLY LATE RECEIPT OF FUNDING, HE AGGRESSIVELY PURCHASED OVER $10,000 WORTH OF MATERIALS FOR IMMEDIATE "START-UP" PROJECTS, THUS SETTING UP NMCB XRAY FOR SUCCESS DURING ITS DEPLOYMENT.* PETTY OFFICER YANKEE'S PRO-FESSIONALISM AND DEVOTION TO DUTY REFLECTED GREAT CREDIT UPON HIMSELF AND WERE IN KEEPING WITH THE HIGH-EST TRADITIONS OF THE UNITED STATES NAVAL SERVICE.

Citations for awards other than Achievement and Commendation medals typi-cally run between eighteen and twenty-two lines and must be submitted separately from the certificate. Of course, in comparison to citations for lower awards, citations for Meritorious Service Medals and more senior awards will typically spell out achieve-ments having exceptionally high value or broad impact to major organizations or large geographical areas. The awards manual outlines (in general terms) the relative level of achievements corresponding to each award.

Below is a well-written citation for an air medal for heroic achievement during combat (taken from an unclassified COMFIFTHFLT operation order). Typically pre-senting details in chronological order, such a citation should read so that a layperson can get a good sense of the action involved.

For heroic achievement in aerial flight as a Naval Flight Officer on an F-14A Aircraft assigned to Fighter Squadron FOURTEEN onboard USS ENTER-PRISE (CVN 65) deployed with Commander, United States FIFTH fleet on 10 October 2001 in support of Operation ENDURING FREEDOM. In the early hours, Lieutenant Doe launched as an Attack Element Lead in the lead section of strikers on highly defended Bar Lock and SPOONREST radar facilities at a vital Taliban airfield. While maneuvering at high speed and high altitude to avoid multiple observed surface-to-air missile launches, guided anti-aircraft artillery and continuous radar tracking, he expertly positioned the F-14A LANTIRN precisely on the target and on time. Under severe opposition, he guided two GBU-12 precision-guided munitions to direct hits, dealing a devastating blow to the Taliban air defenses. Lieutenant Doe also guided two GBU-12 precision-guided munitions from his wing-man's aircraft; in all these ways he was a key player in the eventual capture of the airfield, which dealt a severe blow to the Taliban regime. His expert night high-altitude airmanship then ensured a safe high-speed egress from the target area through additional surface-to-air missile envelopes. By his skillful airmanship, steadfast aggressiveness, and exemplary devotion to duty in the face of hazardous flying conditions, Lieutenant Doe reflected great credit upon himself and upheld the highest traditions of the United States Naval Service.

THE LETTER AND THE CERTIFICATE OF COMMENDATION

Navy letters of commendation (LOCs) and Marine Corps certificates of commendation, although not personal decorations, often do carry with them material benefits. They can add to the multiple for selection through E-6, and enlisted selection boards often take them into account, especially if flag officers sign them. So they carry weight in advancement proceedings in addition to simply being valued as expressions of approval.

Two Different Formats and Styles

The format and, to a degree, the style of letters of commendations vary. Sometimes they are on official parchment complete with seal, command's heading, and other graphics. At other times they are in standard-letter format. When formalized, they usually resemble award citations: you write them in the third person and past tense, and use specified openings and conclusions. Below is an example of a formal citation from a flag officer:

LETTER OF COMMENDATION

The Commander, Naval Surface Force, U.S. Atlantic Fleet
takes pleasure in commending

MACHINIST'S MATE FIRST CLASS (EOD)
JAMES J. MEAGHER
UNITED STATES NAVY

for service as set forth in the following
CITATION:

FOR PROFESSIONAL ACHIEVEMENT IN THE SUPERIOR PERFORMANCE OF HIS DUTIES AS AN EXPLOSIVE ORDNANCE DISPOSAL (EOD) TECHNICIAN WHILE ASSIGNED TO EXPLOSIVE ORDNANCE DISPOSAL MOBILE UNIT SIX, DETACHMENT SIX FROM 8 THROUGH 11 FEBRUARY 1995. PETTY OFFICER MEAGHER PERFORMED HIS DUTIES IN AN EXEMPLARY AND HIGHLY PROFESSIONAL MANNER. WITH VIRTUALLY NO NOTICE, HE DEPLOYED WITHIN THREE HOURS BY AIR TO COUNTER A POTENTIAL TERRORIST LIMPET MINING AT SEA OF THE U.S. FLAGGED MERCHANT VESSEL "LIBERTY WAVE." FOR THE NEXT 40 HOURS AND WITHOUT REST, PETTY OFFICER MEAGHER ASSISTED IN PREPARING HIS DETACHMENT TO DEPLOY AND CONDUCT AN UNDERWATER SEARCH OF THE VESSEL. DESPITE EXTREMELY HAZARDOUS WEATHER CONDITIONS FOR DIVING AND SEARCH OPERATIONS, HE ENSURED ALL EQUIPMENT WAS ON STATION AND READY WHEN NEEDED. ADDITIONALLY, HE CONDUCTED NUMEROUS PERSONNEL TRANSFERS TO "LIBERTY WAVE" BY SMALL BOAT THROUGHOUT THE OPERATION, AND WAS A MOST INTEGRAL PART OF THE OPERATION'S OVERALL SUCCESS. PETTY OFFICER MEAGHER'S EXCEPTIONAL PROFESSIONALISM AND SELFLESS DEVOTION TO DUTY REFLECTED CREDIT UPON HIMSELF AND THE NAVAL SURFACE FORCE, U.S. ATLANTIC FLEET.

D. J. KATZ
Vice Admiral, U.S. Navy
Commander, Naval Surface Force
U.S. Atlantic Fleet

This document (when signed and printed on parchment with seal, Force Insignia, etc.) is appropriate for formal presentation. The write-up presents Petty Officer Meagher's part in the operation clearly and impressively.

Write the Formal Letter of Commendation Just Like an Award Citation

When writing these formal documents, follow the same guidance given earlier about award citations: write to a lay audience; avoid hackneyed phrases; describe clearly a few specific, impressive accomplishments; and forgo all jargon and acronyms. Your command may decide to present this letter at meritorious mast or on another formal occasion with friends and family present. Do your best to get across a sense of *the actual achievement.*

Here is the citation for an end-of-tour letter of commendation for an Aviation Machinist's Mate Third Class (AW), presented in VAW 117 not long ago. It gets across the achievement pretty well (again, a standardized beginning and ending enclose the key descriptions):

> For outstanding performance as Power Plants Technician in Aircraft Early Warning Squadron One One Seven from December 2002 to May 2006. Petty Officer Whiskey consistently performed his demanding duties in an exemplary and highly professional manner. Demonstrating intense initiative and in-depth technical knowledge, he played a key role in the repair of over 2,000 engine and fuel system discrepancies while successfully completing 12 major aircraft inspections. Displaying superb attention to detail, he ensured the meticulous performance of corrosion preventive maintenance, resulting in an overall grade of "Outstanding" during a Commander, Airborne Command Control and Logistics wing post-deployment material condition inspection. His outstanding efforts directly contributed to the squadron earning the Commander, Naval Air Force, U.S. Pacific Fleet Battle "E" Efficiency award for Y2005.
>
> Petty Officer Whiskey's professionalism and devotion to duty reflected credit upon himself and were in keeping with the highest traditions of the United States naval service.

Be More Personable in Informal Letters of Commendation

To be somewhat more personal and expressive, commanders will often loosen formality just a bit in such letters by using the second person, "you," and by varying from strict past tense.

The officer who wrote the letter in figure 7.5 commends the Sailor on his selection as Sailor of the Quarter. The details she cites are subtle ones, harder to "objectify" than many other achievements, yet they can be very important to a "customer-oriented" military unit. The activities commended here are not all in the past; the use of past perfect and some present tense suggest the Sailor's good works are still going on.

THE LETTER OF APPRECIATION

Writing a letter of appreciation (LOA) is a way to express thanks and sometimes to call another commander's attention to the good job his or her people have done for you. The letter carries with it no points, multipliers, or other helps to advancement, nothing but simple thanks and good will.

The Correspondence Manual gives some good advice on how to write such a letter. It begins by quoting this line from an LOA: "AD1 John Smith did a superb job during our recent engine change." Then the Correspondence Manual goes on to comment: "This is the first sentence of a thank-you letter to Smith's supervisor. Notice

Figure 7.5 An Informal Letter of Commendation. An officer in charge commends a Sailor freshly and naturally.

DEPARTMENT OF THE NAVY
U.S. NAVY PERSONNEL SUPPORT ACTIVITY DETACHMENT
MISAWA, JAPAN
APO SAN FRANCISCO 96519-0006

1650
Ser 00/841
30 Sep 87

From: Officer in Charge, U.S. Navy Personnel Support Activity
Detachment, Misawa
To: PN1 _____ _. _____, USN

Subj: LETTER OF COMMENDATION

1. With great pleasure I commend you on your selection as U.S.
Navy Personnel Support Activity Detachment, Misawa's Sailor of
the Quarter from 1 July to 30 September 1987.

2. The professional and personal traits that have led to your
distinction are numerous. Above all, you have managed busy,
pressure-filled days with maturity and grace, and used quieter
times to find innovative ways to improve efficiency. As the man
"on the front line," you often provide the first impression
customers develop about PERSUPPDET Misawa. Customers consistently
comment on their appreciation for your outstanding courtesy and
patience, and their respect for your professional advice, information, and quick actions on their behalf. Your attention to
detail is daily evident in the reports and messages you prepare
without discrepancies. You have shown great initiative in designing new ways to improve reporting procedures and keep communication flowing well within the detachment.

3. Your unflagging professionalism has been an inspiration to
us all. Well done!

that it avoids a slow buildup. The second paragraph described Smith's long hours, careful trouble-shooting, and determined search for parts. The last paragraph read, 'Please thank AD1 Smith for all his extra effort.' This three-paragraph formula will keep your thank-you letters short, detailed, and focused on the person being praised."

We'll show two examples that vary only slightly from this pattern. Each is effective in its own way. Figure 7.6, to the commanding officer of a Marine Corps corporal and his men, probably didn't take much time to write, but it does its job smartly—as smartly as the performance of the battery that it commends.

The letter below tells an airman—an AMEAN is an aviation structural mechanic equipment airman—that the commanding officer himself took notice of the airman's good work. Written to a junior enlisted man at a very impressionable period of his naval career, the letter is likely to spur him on to more work of the same and even higher quality. Although the letter is very formal, the commander's sincerity still comes through.

Figure 7.6 A Letter of Appreciation. This brief letter does well at praising a team of Marines.

DEPARTMENT OF THE NAVY

COMMANDER NAVAL SURFACE FORCE
UNITED STATES ATLANTIC FLEET
NORFOLK, VIRGINIA 23511-6292

1650
Ser 00W/00193
11 Jan 88

From: Commander, Naval Surface Force, U.S. Atlantic Fleet
To: Commanding Officer, Marine Corps Security Force Battalion
Via: Commander, Naval Base Norfolk

Subj: LETTER OF APPRECIATION

1. The performance of the saluting battery during the COMNAVSURFLANT Change of Command ceremony on 30 December 1987 was marked by cooperation and professionalism. The battery's performance and crisp military bearing made this group perfect representatives of the Marine Corps during this important ceremony. Many remarks were made on their impressive performance.

2. Please convey to Corporal _____ and the battery a job well done.

1650
00/150
24 NOV 87

From: Commanding Officer, Attack Squadron THREE ZERO FOUR
To: AMEAN Jeffery Grant, USNR, xxx-xx-xxxx

Subj: LETTER OF APPRECIATION

1. On 6 October 1987, while performing a routine turnaround inspection, you discovered a three-inch structural crack in the starboard wheel well of aircraft 407. You promptly reported it to maintenance control, which grounded the aircraft for an in-depth inspection.
2. While the crack was not considered a safety-of-flight structural defect, you exercised sound professional judgment in reporting it. Had this discrepancy been more severe, your sharp eyes and attention to detail might have prevented a mishap.
3. Maintenance men of your caliber are crucial to the safety of naval aviation. Your very commendable action was in keeping with the best of Firebird spirit and the highest standards of maintenance professionals. Thank you for a job well done.

D. R. KESTLY

As with other letters of thanks (see the section on thank-you letters in chapter 2), you should strive to be genuine in an LOA and avoid the appearance of writing just because you feel you ought to. For the very reason that a naval letter of appreciation usually carries no institutional reward, it will mean little unless the recipient perceives it as conveying sincere thanks. See also the letter of appreciation from an admiral to a civilian in figure 2.6, earlier in this book.

By the way, good software can aid award writing, as it does evaluation writing. Software for awards is typically much simpler than eval software because there is no need for all the personal data and grades.

CIVILIAN AWARDS

A great many civilians work directly for the Navy and Marine Corps, and others contribute significantly to both services. Let's briefly discuss here awards that may be given to civilians—and the writing that is involved.

By far the most common civilian awards given out by Navy and Marine Corps officials are those given to Department of the Navy employees. They are called Civilian Service Awards, and they are governed by OCPMINST 12451.1 series. Here are their names and the respective awarding authorities:

Navy Distinguished Civilian Service Award—SECNAV
Navy Superior Civilian Service Award—Type Commander
Navy Meritorious Civilian Service Award—Commanding Officer

Although there is no official correlation between these awards and those given to service members, some experts regard the Navy Superior Civilian Service Award to be the rough counterpart of a Meritorious Service Medal, the others respectively higher and lower in level. A look at the write-ups verifies this very rough correlation.

Note that three parallel awards are set aside for *nonnaval* civilians; they are called "Public Service Awards." They are also titled Distinguished, Superior, and Meritorious, but the award authorities differ from those for the Civilian Service Awards mentioned above. See SECNAVINST 5061.12 series.

The procedure for writing up all these civilian awards resembles that for other awards discussed in this chapter. Justifications must be submitted along with citations; there are awards for specific service and for end-of-tour, etc. The only major differences in the process are that (1) a civilian résumé typically accompanies the civilian award package and (2) commanders sometimes endorse these award recommendations (via standard letter endorsement) as they forward them up the chain. If written well, such endorsements can help support the written justification. On the other hand, an endorser can also recommend a change in the level or kind of the award.

Let's look briefly at the civilian justification and citation.

The Civilian Justification

Justifications resemble standard Navy award justifications. Typically written in bullet format, well-crafted justifications will outline many specifics, discuss both quality and quantity, and manifest how this person's service has been consistently above the norm. Within a typical opening and closing a writer will include bullets like those that follow. This award was written for a port engineer (a civilian) who managed two extensive maintenance periods on the USS YELLOWSTONE. This Summary of Action ran a bit over a page (it has been condensed a bit below).

From August 1993 through November 1995, Mr. John H. Daniels, the Maintenance Repair Officer for USS YELLOWSTONE, has provided superb support to the ship . . . Specifically, he:

- Crafted the entire work package for a $10 million DPMA for FY 93. The DPMA was instrumental through several SHIPALTS in enhancing the reliability and safety of the engineering plant and Fleet support.

- Coordinated the addition of AFFT stations, Halon and sprinkler system installations in numbers l, 2, and 3 pump rooms, emergency diesel, flight deck, fireroom, and the engineroom. These SHIPALTS modernized the engineering spaces and improved the fire-fighting capabilities in each space.

- Coordinated the replacement of 15 hot water heaters, a critical alteration for the crew's quality of life, done without formal drawings. As a result of Mr. Daniels's untiring efforts, the crew enjoys hot water at all hours of the day, including peak usage times. The hot water installation was subsequently praised by the INSURV board as safe and reliable with no discrepancies. A FIRST!

- Expertly drafted and orchestrated a work package for a $1.2 million PRAV in 1994. Although it was only 4 months in duration, he ensured necessary engineering repairs were made to guarantee a successful Mediterranean deployment. These repairs included the overhaul of the main circulating pump, the trip throttle valves on all 4 SSTGs, the MS-4 limit torque, and the evaporator feed heater condensers. He also saw to the chemical cleaning of both boilers. As a result of this work YELLOWSTONE is able to maintain both feed and potable water above 90 percent with only one evaporator on line.

- Continuously communicated with the Chief Engineer to provide assistance where and when requested. Mr. Daniels continues to stress material improvements in YELLOWSTONE. He truly thinks of himself as a member of the crew . . . and as far as the crew is concerned, he is a crewmember.

Mr. Daniels has distinguished himself through his diligence, vision, character, and unyielding dedication to the Navy. I have placed my utmost trust in him. My ship's dramatic turnaround and the reputation YELLOWSTONE enjoys today are direct results of his efforts. He is worthy of the Navy Meritorious Public Service Award.

The endorsement to this summary of action (by the YELLOWSTONE's Commanding Officer) commented on how Mr. Daniels "fought tough battles" to get the maintenance through despite a climate of fiscal austerity, and how he gained the respect and trust of the crew and also became "an honorary member of my wardroom," having provided superb counsel to the captain about maintenance and repair work.

Civilian Citations

Civilian citations also resemble standard naval award citations. The openings and closings are stipulated, and the middle sentences should get across a sense of the real accomplishment. At the same time, the writer should remember the audience and avoid both impenetrable bureaucratese and acronyms. The citation proposed below (for the same individual whose summary of action is shown above) does pretty well at speaking meaningfully to its wide audience. Again, a Public Service Award citation like that below is a citation for a non-Navy employee. Citations for the Civilian Service Awards would be similar; the wording in the opening and closing will differ slightly.

The Commander in Chief, U.S. Atlantic Fleet takes pleasure in presenting the MERITO-RIOUS PUBLIC SERVICE AWARD to

MR. JOHN H. DANIELS

For service as set forth in the following
CITATION:

"FOR OUTSTANDING SERVICE WHILE SERVING FROM AUGUST 1993 TO NO-VEMBER 1995 AS MAINTENANCE REPAIR OFFICER FOR USS YELLOWSTONE (AD 38). MR. DANIELS DISTINGUISHED HIMSELF THROUGH HIS DILIGENCE, VISION, AND DEDICATION TO THE SHIP AND TO THE NAVY. HIS EFFORTS IN ORCHESTRATING THE $10 MILLION DOCKING PHASE AVAILABILITY AND THE $1.2 MILLION PLANNED RESTRICTED AVAILABILITY WERE EXCEPTIONAL AND RESULTED IN A SAFER WORK ENVIRONMENT AND A DRAMATIC IMPROVEMENT IN THE QUALITY OF LIFE OF ALL USS YELLOWSTONE SAILORS. HIS EFFORTS ALSO CONTRIBUTED SIGNIFICANTLY TO USS YELLOWSTONE'S MATERIAL READINESS. MR. DANIELS'S DISTINCTIVE ACCOM-PLISHMENTS AND SUPERIOR PERFORMANCE REFLECTED GREAT CREDIT UPON HIMSELF AND THE UNITED STATES NAVY AND WERE SINCERELY APPRECIATED BY THE MILITARY COMMUNITY."

[signed]

4 January 1996

ADMIRAL, U.S. NAVY

NAVAL CONTESTS

To end this chapter, let's look for a moment at a related area—special awards that the naval services have established, both for individuals and units. While we have no space here to discuss unit awards, we can look at a good example of a nomination for an individual award.

The kind of writing recommended above for standard naval awards—*clear writing* pointed by *strong evidence*—works here too. The nomination presented below is especially well written. The accomplishments are clearly described and most impressive, so impressive that the officer recommended won the Vice Admiral Batchelder Award for that year (in the "small ship" competitive category). Winning the award was due both to the lieutenant's performance and to that of the outstanding writer who drafted the nomination.

The nomination's author commented that he purposely touched on several different areas of accomplishment, to show the nominee's wellroundedness. This approach also helped him to avoid technical jargon that would have slowed the reader down. While impressive details stud the recommendation, the author leaves the most stunning accomplishment for the very end.

LT R——'s performance of duty, leadership, and overall support of this command <u>have been extraordinary</u>. His individual contribution to the supply and operational readiness of this fast attack nuclear submarine <u>has been superlative</u>. Significant specific items highlighting his performance are below:

• Completed an extensive 15-month Integrated Logistics Overhaul (ILO), including significant combat system and nuclear propulsion plant configuration changes. He backloaded the ship's repair parts <u>in only three weeks with a 99+ percent validity</u>.

- Took personal charge of identifying and correcting potential supply support problems as the ship neared the end of overhaul, particularly ensuring COSAL support of several significant ship's systems. In conjunction with this effort, he personally ensured that the entire ship was stowed exactly per plan—an accomplishment unmatched in the Pacific Fleet.
- Prepared, opened, and operated the ship's galley at an extraordinarily high level of efficiency, despite frequent short-fuse demands of shiftwork to support major overhaul events and a severe shortage of mess management specialists.
- Completed Supply Corps Officer Submarine qualifications, an intensive, demanding, and rigorous professional milestone.
- Established a highly effective training program for both MS and SK Divisions and the ship's RPPOs. Additionally, he provided quality supply input to officer training.
- As the ship's most proficient and professional Diving Officer of the Watch, was assigned to conduct the first dive after overhaul and the first dive to test depth. His performance during these most significant postoverhaul tests was superb.
- Worked diligently to achieve the NAVSEA 08 requirement of 100 percent nuclear (Q) COSAL on board to support the extensive nuclear reactor critical test program. In particular, he achieved this goal without any need to transfer material from any other activities.

LT R ———— is clearly a most effective and professional Supply Officer. His exceptional work is best measured by the results of the ship's most recent COMSUBPAC Supply Management Inspection: a perfect score of EIGHT OUTSTANDING GRADES, an achievement unmatched in many years. He clearly merits selection for the Vice Admiral Batchelder Award.

The best ideas in the world are worthless if you can't communicate them.

—SPEECHWRITER FOR SECNAV

8

Speaking and Briefing

Few professions need effective speakers as vitally as the military. The reason is partly the military's emphasis on leadership. In so many naval forums—a leading petty officer speaking to the people at quarters, a young officer addressing his or her division, a commander briefing a combat mission—the ability to speak effectively is vital both to mission and morale.

Superiors must speak to their troops in greatly varied circumstances, from such informal settings as speaking to the crew on the public address system to formal occasions like awards presentations, promotion ceremonies, and changes of commands. In all these cases a commander can make a pronounced effect simply by good verbal presentation. Disraeli said, "Men govern with words." A service member makes a good start at the talent of leadership simply by learning to speak effectively.

Somewhat less obvious is the need for good speakers on staffs. Some senior staff people are highly visible—those who must make the case for military appropriations before Congress, for example. Clearly, their presentations can have wide-reaching effects, both in getting support for specific programs and in giving the naval services a good or bad image. As a former Marine Corps commandant, Gen. Robert H. Barrow, once commented,

> If you are testifying before Congress on Capitol Hill, if you speak to the senators or the congressmen effectively . . . they conclude that the Marine Corps has good leadership at the top because of the way you come across to them. They think, "This guy must be a good leader because I asked him tough questions and he was forceful and straightforward and forthrightly gave me those answers." On the other hand, if you go out and mumble around, they may never say it, but somehow deep in them they think, "Is that guy a Marine? Is that what Marines are like?"
>
> —*Naval Leadership: Voices of Experience,* Annapolis: Naval Institute Press, 1987, p. 60.

But besides such public spokesmen, there are untold myriads on staffs who must brief their superiors daily. They must prepare informational briefings, decision briefings, reports on deployments, and briefs on the state of a command, to name just a few important occasions. If they don't do all these jobs well, the Navy and Marine Corps suffer, either from not having crucial programs approved or simply from not functioning well as armed services.

Service members (especially commanders) must also learn how to speak to the public, including local community leaders and the news media, to name just two likely public audiences.

Clearly, in all of these areas, verbal facility can be crucial.

Yet, important as it is, we pay far too little attention to the ability to speak well. College educations usually ignore it, for example, and officer accession programs often give it little more than lip service. If you're prudent, you'll recognize the omission and take steps to enhance your speaking ability. Here are some principles to help you begin.

Speaking in the Navy and Marine Corps

GENERAL GUIDANCE

When you speak as a naval representative, the first matters you should attend to are physical—your personal appearance, general assurance, stance, gestures, and eye contact. All of these factors can affect the delivery of your talk, its effectiveness, and your own feelings about speaking.

Be Smart in Personal Appearance

Make sure your uniform and overall appearance are top-notch. The standard sprucing up is even more important than usual. You'll be the center of attention of a whole group for several minutes, not, as in a personnel inspection, for just a few seconds in front of one inspecting officer. A cleaned and pressed uniform, fresh haircut, shined shoes, straight name tag, and bright rather than faded ribbons—we naturally expect any military representative to look sharp in all these ways.

Knowing you look sharp can help you think sharply too, or at least keep you from getting sidetracked. Worrying that you really need a new pair of shoes can drain your confidence. You don't need any more distractions than are already present in any speech situation.

Be Confident—And *Never Apologize*

Almost everyone is nervous before giving a speech, even when long accustomed to speaking in public. But remember, no matter how nervous you feel, often none of your listeners can tell that you're nervous just by looking at you. Even if your voice quavers a bit, people in the audience will often simply ignore it, thinking you speak that way normally. Whatever you do, *never apologize* for being nervous or in any other way draw overt attention to your heightened emotions. Doing so will make the audience aware of your feelings and perhaps begin to make them feel uncomfortable, and their uneasiness in turn will upset your own confidence.

Your nervousness will usually die down as you get into your talk, so adopt a pose of confidence even if you don't feel very confident at the moment. Speak in a strong voice, and enunciate clearly—a little extra enunciation will make all the words clear

---

SPEAKING WITH CONFIDENCE

We think we got what we thought we were required to come up with . . .

—From the remarks of a student leader in a recent Navy course

---

and will add decisiveness to your tone. Make sure the back row can hear you. Even ask if the audience can hear you there.

There's another reason for not apologizing for your nervousness or for what you have to say: an apology can make your audience lose faith in you or lose interest. As a former speechwriter for the Secretary of the Navy commented, "No speech should ever be self-editorialized. Comments such as 'I really don't know what to say,' 'This is dry stuff so I'll keep it brief,' and 'Thanks for bearing with me' *drastically undermine your effectiveness as a speaker.* Do your best, and let the audience be the judge of the quality of your remarks."

In this officer's experience, even senior naval officials were, unfortunately, prone to begin speaking by shedding doubt on the importance of what they were about to say. "I know it's late and you're cold, and so I won't be long . . . ," began one speaker at a ceremony held outdoors. After that kind of a beginning, a listener starts trying to remember where the car is in the parking lot.

Stand Straight

Your physical presence—beginning with your stance—can affect both the way you think of yourself and the way the audience receives you. We have all become annoyed with speakers who shift from one foot to the other, or look down at the floor, or play with the keys in their pockets throughout a talk. We feel embarrassed for them because we know they must be feeling embarrassed themselves—or why not stand straight and talk to us?

That's a good question. Again, why not at least *act* as if you're confident? Even just pretending to be at ease will help the confidence come. Confidence, direction, and leadership are central virtues of naval service—so try those habits on. For a starter, stand square on both feet, facing the audience—not rigidly, but with two feet on the floor. Stand erect, and don't lean on the lectern. And stand still. Don't cross your legs or shift back and forth on them.

Make Natural Gestures

Don't fuss with your hands, but use them instead to gesture with. Unless you're trained as an actor, don't plan out the gestures you use, but just let your hands float up naturally to enhance your talk. Gesture a bit more broadly if your audience is large.

If you don't feel natural gesturing, leave your hands at your sides or lay them on the lectern, if you're speaking from one (don't grip it tightly, however). Don't constantly smooth your hair, grip your opposite arm awkwardly, or make other nervous gestures. Normally, place your notes on the lectern rather than hold them (it's too easy to play with papers in your hands). If you have to hold the notes, use one or more 5″ × 7″ note cards rather than pages, which can rattle in nervous hands.

Make Eye Contact

Look up from notes or a manuscript frequently, first looking at one part of the audience, then another. Don't stare, of course, and don't look out the window, at the

"The ability to speak well, like the ability to write well, will get a junior officer noticed faster than almost anything else."

—Navy Lieutenant, speechwriter for SECNAV

ceiling, or down at the floor either. Meet the eyes of the people in front of you. If you don't (if you bury your head in your notes, for example), your audience will tend to lose interest.

Looking at your audience will also help you pick up how they are taking the speech. Often you'll find one or two people especially well disposed to you, laughing at your jokes, agreeing with your comments, or simply paying very close attention. These people will do lots for your confidence, and you can key on them as you glance around at the audience.

Besides the eyes, let your face play a part. There may be natural times in your talk to grin, to look skeptical, to frown, and so on. As a rule, simply smiling as you go about your speech will help you express confidence and tend to ingratiate you with the audience.

Be Expressive
Don't forget your voice, but put some natural expression in your talk. Otherwise, if you sound wooden or bored, your audience may get bored too. Try varying both the pitch and the volume of your voice, and make sure you speak strongly enough. Act interested and concerned—be *enthusiastic,* and your attitude will communicate to your audience.

Furthermore, don't talk too quickly. Most inexperienced speakers speak too fast, partly from wanting to get through the talk as soon as possible. Remember that the audience needs time to assimilate your argument. Take your time, and don't be afraid to pause occasionally. (Yes, stay within the time allotted—but when you first outline your talk, plan for pauses and asides.) Don't let any pauses come from fumbling with ideas. The "uhs" and "nows" and other terms that you might tend to throw in from not really knowing a speech well (usually from lack of practice) will get on the audience's nerves.

Decide on the Degree of Formality
Realize that the degree of formality you adopt in your appearance or style of presentation can affect the whole atmosphere. Formality is an especially important consideration in our business. If you're the boss, dressing up and having your unit remain standing while you speak to them can be effective at times—certainly when giving out an award, for example, and (like Patton before the flag) perhaps at other times as well. On the other hand, rank sometimes interferes with communication. A very senior officer's presence, for example, can be particularly inhibiting. By leaving off his uniform jacket, a commander might be able to foster an informal atmosphere with a unit and have more interaction with the group.

Remember to modify your approach when speaking to a civilian audience. At the Naval Academy, about half the faculty is civilian. Once, when addressing the whole faculty at the first of the year, a superintendent decided to forgo flags, the opening ceremony, the salutes, the standing at attention—in short, all the formalities, including lectern and notes. Instead, he simply stepped through the stage curtains (with a mike) and began speaking. The civilian faculty perceived him as speaking *with* the audience, rather than down to them. At an institution where rank inevitably plays a great part, this gesture on behalf of the military superintendent to the civilian faculty was a much-noticed and welcome change of pace. It enhanced rather than inhibited communication—and at no real cost to the dignity of the institution.

"A series of briefings in OPNAV that I attended almost amounted to a catalog of what not to do while speaking.

"One officer talked to the screen instead of to us (using the screen as a kind of crutch), and his voice trailed off at the end of a sentence. Another spoke mainly to the people at the front of the small room. In this room, the projector was on the table, and a rather senior briefer repeatedly walked back and forth through the projection, which was also disconcerting.

"Yet another officer droned on for almost an hour, without ever moving away from the podium on which he leaned, and seldom varied his voice. He had some slides, but for ten minutes at a time he would explain his subject drearily without the help of visual aids of any kind.

"It seemed obvious that the majority of these naval officers had never been critiqued about how not to brief."

—Naval writing expert

"Not every speech will or can be videotaped. However, one other way that you can make technology work for you is to make an audio recording of your speech. You can train yourself by listening to the audio recording."

—COMMANDER, USN

Learn Other Ways to Warm the Audience to You

On many occasions, lightening up your tone can be useful. Find some way to "break down that invisible wall between you and the audience," as one speech expert put it. Humor is one method: telling a joke or two can be very effective in making the audience more receptive, or putting them on your side. A joke is usually most effective toward the beginning of your talk—to establish rapport early. Remember to use good taste, be kind (watch sarcasm or ridicule), and learn to laugh at yourself.

You can overuse humor, of course, and it may not fit all occasions. Another excellent approach (again, usually for the beginning of a speech) is to recognize one or more members of the audience or, in formal settings, to acknowledge those on the dais with you. Try saying a word or two about an audience member in a supportive way. By mentioning that person's views or deeds in your own speech context, you figuratively put the both of you on the same side of an issue. The idea is to try to convince the audience in a subtle way that you are all really soul mates, thus making them more receptive to the points you'll make later on.

Practice!

The way to build confidence and learn is to practice, and to do so *repeatedly* and *out loud*. Don't just give your speech in your head, or you may skip over the hardest parts and then have difficulty expressing them in the actual talk. Whether you plan to speak from a manuscript or from notes, run through the speech out loud a few times in private, perhaps in front of a mirror or into a tape recorder, or both.

If you can find a friend or colleagues to listen to you, practice in front of a live audience. This way you'll be able to practice looking at someone and speaking so you'll be heard. If your colleague can offer pointers—if you choose someone who is knowledgeable in speaking and helpfully critical—that practice will help even more. Often naval staffs will "murder board" a critical briefing before the toughest local audience they can assemble. They figure that the tougher the questions they have to face *now,* the better prepared they'll be *later* in front of a target audience of major officials. Such a critique, in which briefers and staffers try to anticipate and practice answering likely questions, can be an outstanding learning experience in its own right.

"Surface warfare officers in particular get a lot of training in briefing. On my ship, if you were assigned to take the ship out as conning officer the next morning, you had to brief the CO, XO, and department heads in the wardroom the night before."

—SWO LIEUTENANT

If you ever have the chance to have yourself videotaped while speaking, take advantage of it. You'll probably feel embarrassed the first time you see yourself giving a speech, but this experience can be absolutely invaluable for your development as a speaker.

Best of all, you can take a college course in speech, or you can practice by joining a group that practices public speaking. There are Toastmasters' Clubs at most major bases and sometimes aboard major combatants. There may be a club in the community near where you live. Such a group usually meets once a week or so, and there you'll give short speeches, receive critiques, and also get some good material to read. There's nothing like speaking regularly to a live audience to improve your skills, and organizations such as Toastmasters' offer a very supportive audience. The confidence you build in this informal way can come in handy later, on official occasions.

In short, speaking in public and in the military are both part of the job. They merit sound preparation and skillful execution *just like everything else we do.* Speaking is a skill that you can perfect by knowing its principles and by practicing. Work at it until you can do it well, and quit worrying about whether you're up to it or not.

A carrier once returned from a deployment, and the captain had to brief his operational commander about the cruise. According to an LDO aboard, the briefing was essentially a test: how well the captain performed in front of the admiral might deter-

---

SPEECH CHECKLIST—FOR FLAG STAFFERS

1. Get the background of the event. What are the occasion's date, time, place, uniform, and schedule? What do you know of the audience's size, background, interests, and sensitivities? Will other dignitaries be there, and what are their backgrounds? Who have been recent speakers to the group?

2. Has the topic and time length for the speech been set? If the topic is open, provide the host organization coordinator with the topic the admiral will speak on. Also provide a copy of the admiral's biography.

3. Determine what office is responsible for preparing the draft of the speech. Set due dates for speech outline and first draft.

4. See to it that the speech is cleared by PAO, legal, and/or subject-matter experts, as needed.

5. Find out who will meet the admiral: that person's name, title, position.

6. Has the precise time of the admiral's arrival and meeting place been coordinated with the person who will do the greeting?

7. Should there be any photographers? Ours to arrange or theirs?

8. Consider the admiral's participation in the meeting. Will it be limited to the address? Will there be a meal or meeting before or after? Will the admiral need to leave right after speaking? Know the logistics for getting into and out of the room.

9. Do you know what to do if the media covers the event? (Consult the PAO before you go.)

10. Find out from the host coordinator what audiovisual equipment will be available. Make known your requirements, and follow up, follow up, follow up.

11. Personally check out all microphones and projection systems the admiral will use.

12. Ensure that your admiral and event POC have a copy of the speech the admiral is to give . . . and bring another one with you to the event, just in case.

—Naval Flag Writers Guide

---

mine his future assignments or promotions. The skipper reportedly cloistered himself in his cabin, personally selecting slides, practicing his talk, checking clock time, etc. As the LDO remarked, the captain had probably never had to prepare such a briefing before. Had he trained to give briefs earlier in his career, with lots of practice and critiques—"and especially if he had seen himself on tape," the LDO pointed out—he would have been much better prepared for this critical performance.

This advice applies to all those who have to go into flag offices at OPNAV, CINCPACFLT, FMFLANT, or in any of hundreds of other offices where the future of a service member's program, unit, or personal career might depend on how well he or she performs in a few minutes of formal speaking. Simply stated, in the naval service you can distinguish yourself more from others through communicative skills than almost anything else.

HOW TO SPEAK: OFF THE CUFF, FROM NOTES, OR FROM A MANUSCRIPT?

Sometimes you'll have to speak on the spur of the moment, without preparation; another time you may be on a formal program in which your audience expects a prepared text. Usually, however, you'll have at least some choice about how fully to write out what you're about to say.

Speaking Impromptu—Off the Cuff

Often, at a conference or morning briefing, the commander will ask you to "give us a rundown" of your program, or your latest staff trip, or your plans for the preinspection procedures. The commander might brief you ten minutes ahead of time on what to cover, or ask you on impulse when noticing you across the table. This unprepared or impromptu situation has advantages. No one expects you to be polished in such circumstances, and you'll have no time to get jitters. Obviously you can't prepare much, but you might be able to consider whom you're talking to and what they need, and to think out a brief outline.

Practicing quick reaction is worthwhile. In a lull at a meeting, recollect one of the tough questions you're currently dealing with and practice putting together a quick mental outline to answer a superior's sudden inquiry. This exercise will help pass the time, and it will pay dividends when someone suddenly puts you on the spot.

Speaking from Notes

Using notes is the most common and usually the preferred speech situation. Compared with impromptu speaking, speaking from notes provides more security. On the other hand, using notes allows much more spontaneity than reading from a text. Notes also enable you to contract or expand a talk much more easily than a manuscript does, if you need to.

How to go about it? Write brief notes to yourself on each area of your talk. Jot down a phrase or clause, rather than a full sentence. Then you can fill in the rest of the sentence verbally, in this way adding to your talk's spontaneity. Leave gaps in your notes for filling in details that you know well and can describe easily. You might want to pen in the beginning and ending a bit more fully—these parts of a speech are especially important and deserve more care. Of course you'll want to make more complete notes for less familiar subjects than for topics you know well.

Don't write out notes for every sentence. Know whatever subject you're speaking on well enough that you feel comfortable adding entertaining details between the lines of your notes.

Use note cards—probably 5″ × 7″ cards—rather than paper (paper rustles). Whether you use cards or pages, print in large letters so you can read more easily. Better yet, type your notes and print them in as large a font as possible. Make sure to use one side of a page only, and number your notes so you can get them back in order quickly if you drop them.

Reading from a Prepared Manuscript

Of course, reading a manuscript is in some ways the most secure kind of speaking, for every word is spelled out in print, and you can make sure while writing it that you cover all the key points clearly and precisely. However, prepared speeches often lose spontaneity. Read from a manuscript only on very formal occasions, and even then work hard to keep the conversational tone, freshness, and audience contact that naturally enliven a talk from notes or an impromptu performance.

"One of the biggest mistakes is to speed up while reading something to an audience. Perhaps you're reading an award in front of a department. Take the minute to slow down so they'll understand it, rather than just 20 seconds to rattle through."

—LCDR Andre Laborde, USNR

How can you keep it lively? Prepare the speech so your sentences are relatively short and simple, for one thing. Look up often, for another. Keep the text short enough so that you can add some spontaneous examples if they occur to you, or so you can add some unrehearsed remarks to explain the points you have made in the text. Such ad-libbing will help keep the audience with you and will add variety to the talk. Finally, don't read too fast; keep the pace slow, sure, and confident. See the OPNAV guidance on briefing later in this chapter for the use of prepared scripts in formal staff briefs.

WHAT TO SAY—THE SUBSTANCE OF YOUR TALK

What you say will depend on your specific subject. However, you can look into some standard sources for information on general topics. Take the universal military subject of leadership, for example. Whether the occasion is a change of command, an address to a local civic group, or a talk to your own command or division, you need not start from scratch.

You might consult *history* and *tradition*, *literature* and *philosophy*, or *famous sayings*, for instance. All these sources have perennially served military speakers and speechwriters well, as they have politicians. The same can be said for *current events* or *recent military* issues—such topics might well find pertinent reference in a leadership speech. Another great source of effective remarks on leadership is, of course, the treasury of *war stories*, *anecdotes*, and *memorable expressions* that you have encountered personally through your military service. Of course, apt examples to illustrate your points are always important.

Below are a just few instances where topics like those discussed above have filled an important place in a naval or military address.

Arguing from Historical Precedent

The fourth goal of American seapower is to be supreme on the sea in order to be supreme on the land. You might recall the historic race for Tunis in World War II, where the Germans moved a quarter of a million troops from France, principally by airlift, into North Africa, but were unable to control the sea in order to supply and re-equip them. The end result was disastrous. On the strategic level, the Germans lost twice: we captured more than 200,000 of their best soldiers when we took Tunis, and we did not have to fight those soldiers when we invaded Normandy two years later. In building our own strategy for the defense of Europe in today's world, we have not forgotten that control of the sea impacts much more than the war at sea.

—Secretary of the Navy James H. Webb, Jr., at the Ninth International Seapower Symposium, Newport, Rhode Island, 28 October 1987, as printed in "Role of American Seapower," *Defense Issues* 2, no. 58: 2.

Citing an Acknowledged Authority

Naval strength is, I believe, essential to America's national security. To keep peace and deter our enemies, we must be able to defeat them if deterrence fails. As Winston Churchill said of his country in another time, "Nothing in the world, nothing you may think of, or anyone may tell you; no arguments, however specious; no appeals, however seductive, must lead you to abandon that naval superiority on which the life of our country depends."

—Secretary of Defense Caspar W. Weinberger, before the Dallas Council Navy League of the United States, 7 October 1981, as reproduced in NL 102 course booklet, U.S. Naval Academy, 1986, p. 4.

"In my case, I'm a horrible speaker, but I do pretty well in question-and-answer sessions. Often those answers find their way into future speeches or formal documents."

—COMMANDER, USN

Finding Significance in Recent History

Concerning survivability, just look at this ship [*Nimitz*] which surrounds us with its more than 2,000 watertight compartments, designed and constructed to permit this ship to go in harm's way, to accept battle damage, and to continue to fight. It wasn't designed carelessly or recklessly, nor with bigness for bigness' sake in mind. It was designed with survivability in mind.

Let me remind you that in 1969, the USS *Enterprise* had nine 500-pound bombs explode on its flight deck, the equivalent of being hit by six Soviet guided missiles. Not only did *Enterprise* survive, but within several hours—not days or weeks, but several hours—was capable of conducting flight operations.

It is not unimportant to take another lesson from recent history, remembering that in Vietnam we had over 400 aircraft destroyed and 4,000 additional aircraft damaged—on the ground—on land bases—while not one single aircraft aboard a carrier was destroyed or damaged by enemy action throughout that conflict. Nor should we soon forget that every airfield constructed in Vietnam was lost in its entirety. Even more dramatically, at least one of them has been turned against us, as the Soviet Union today operates with impunity from the field we built there.

So much for vulnerability.

> —ADM Thomas B. Hayward, CNO, at the change of command of USS
> NIMITZ (CVN 68) on 26 February 1982, as printed in "CNO Speaks
> Out: Why the *Nimitz* Aircraft Carrier," *Surface Warfare,* May 1982, p. 11.

Linking Tradition to Recent Events

Gustavus Conyngham, the namesake of this fine ship which is affectionately called "Gus Boat," was captured and placed in a mill prison on his first cruise as skipper of a privateer. An individual who did things with pizzazz and a never-say-die attitude, he quickly escaped and was reassigned to a new command. That same spirit is alive today in Gus Boat, in people like MM3 Finan who volunteered to be lowered into a flooded compartment of the STARK with an electric submersible pump which could not be lowered past battle damage by itself. After the line severed on jagged steel, he remained in the compartment, holding down the pump. This heroic action began the dewatering process that stopped the list and probably prevented the ship from sinking.

> —CAPT C. K. Kicker, then Commander, Destroyer Squadron Two,
> at the 14 November 1987 change of command of
> USS CONYNGHAM (DDG 17). CDR David Rose
> was relieving CAPT Don Pollard on this occasion.

Using an Anecdote (from a Film) to Make a Point

I recall a wonderful sequence from the film *Lawrence of Arabia.* T. E. Lawrence has just encountered the culture of Arabia, a world of very different ideas. During a desert trek, one of the Arabs is separated from the group. His companions are resigned to this act of God: "Allah wills it—it is written." Lawrence risks his own life and saves the straggler. Upon returning to the camp he confronts his companions: "See? Nothing is written! *We write!"* As we confront the future, we must remember that nothing is written. Are we doomed to a clash of civilizations? Will military force lose its utility to the nation state? We do not know. But it's a good bet that conflict will continue to be a competition of ideas. Those ideas will compete through logic and violence. Most importantly: nothing is written—we *write*. Through cooperation and careful study we can shape the future, achieving, we hope, a world where logic is more common than violence.

> —ADM Charles R. Larson, USN, Commander in Chief,
> Pacific Command, at the conclusion of an address to the
> Naval War College, 15 June 1994. Reprinted in
> *Naval War College Review,* Spring 1995, pp. 83–90.

Bringing a Sea Story to Bear

Several years ago I was Executive Officer in the diesel submarine TANG, which was the oldest commissioned U.S. submarine at that time. Keeping the boat going was quite a challenge and only a dedicated crew made it possible. In the entire crew, the most energetic and dedicated person was the Captain, Carmine Tortora. One night about 3 AM, at the end of one of those grueling days at sea, the boat was surfaced charging batteries and the Captain and I were the only two sitting in the wardroom. I asked him point-blank why he worked so hard. What was he after? What was his goal in all this labor? I tell this tale now because I want to borrow his response. I expected he would talk of a life-long goal to reach flag rank, or of a desire for a medal or other recognition of his command tour. That's not what he said, though. I asked him what his goal was and he replied with a simple three-word phrase that sums up to me the best there is in the officer corps. His goal, he said, was "Service with Honor."

I need to borrow Carmine's response to describe Jim Parks' Navy time.

> —CAPT John Byron in a speech on an LDO's retirement.

Illustrating with Telling Details

We need to revise our thinking on ordnance requirements and their associated weapons systems. I turned down some war-winning targets because we lacked a penetrating weapon such as the Air Force's I-2000. Further, the Navy was short of laser-guided bomb kits. In the Red Sea, for example, we started the war with only 112 Mk-82 500-pound-bomb kits, 124 Mk-83 1,000-pound kits, and 258 Mk-84 2,000-pound kits—and that was all we were going to get. The day the war ended I had 7 Mk-82 kits and 30 Mk-83 kits left. The Navy needs additional laser-guided bomb capability for the foreseeable future and laser spot automatic track designators in all strike aircraft.

> —RADM Riley D. Mixson, USN, remarks upon his service as
> commander of Carrier Group Two during the Gulf War. He made his
> remarks at a symposium in Pensacola on 9 May 1991; they were published in the August 1991 U.S. Naval Institute *Proceedings,* pp. 38–39.

BASIC RESOURCE MATERIALS FOR NAVY SPEAKERS

Besides the classic speech resources mentioned earlier—history, tradition, literature, famous sayings, and so on—there are excellent *naval* speech resources—many of them readily available via electronic media. You can easily find official Navy and Marine Corps sources (including recent speeches) via a standard search engine. Otherwise, become familiar with the pertinent sources listed below, as well as with the others mentioned in chapter 11, "Writing for the News Media." Many of these sources are now available on the Internet in one way or another (sometimes for a fee); others can be found at libraries.

- *The Almanac of Seapower.* Published annually in April by the Navy League of the United States.
- *Vital Speeches.* A civilian periodical publishing a wealth of speeches and other information, which many naval speechwriters consult for ideas, examples, and ways of writing speeches. Available at libraries.
- Annual Naval Review issue (usually May), U.S. Naval Institute *Proceedings.* Contains summary articles on many Navy and Marine topics. Includes recent events and much general information, as well as an index to the previous year's *Proceedings* articles.
- Reference texts like *The Naval Institute Guide to Combat Fleets of the World,* or *Jane's Fighting Ships.*
- Quotation Sources:
  — John Bartlett, *Bartlett's Familiar Quotations,* current edition
  — *Dictionary of Military and Naval Quotations,* ed. Robert Debs Heinl, Jr., current edition.
  — George Seldes, *The Great Thoughts* (New York: Ballantine Books, 1985).

SPEAKING TO THE PUBLIC—A CHECKLIST

Speaking as a representative of the military to the public can be an outstanding opportunity to help get our Navy and Marine Corps messages across. Such talks can promote excellent public relations and serve many other purposes. Whatever the motive, you should prepare well. Here are some tips about how to prepare, tips drawn from a checklist in "Navy Excellence: A Story to Tell," a booklet once put out for a conference held at CINCLANTFLT Headquarters. (For advice on speaking to the media, see a PAO.)

Accept the Right Speaking Engagement
- Make sure the audience is right. For example, an active-duty service member should not address a partisan political group or any extremist organization; doing so might potentially embarrass them and the service. Do not accept an invitation unless you are going to be proud of your association—in uniform—with the group.
- Make sure, also, that you want to talk to the audience. (If not, don't!) Some factors might influence your decision. For example, have they invited the media? Will there be another speaker in addition to you? If so, what topic will that speaker address? Be sure you understand exactly why the group invited you and the circumstances of your talking before you accept.
- The local area PAO can often provide good advice and put you in touch with local contacts who can tell you more.

Research Your Audience
- Know your audience so you can tailor your message appropriately. (Local contacts are again the key.) Is this group well defined? What do these people stand for? What interests them? Will any topics or remarks offend them? Will they be a friendly audience? What is their level of knowledge? You should also find out what officials will be there so that you can recognize notable civic leaders in the audience during your introductory remarks.

- Make sure you know whether any Navy/Marine Corps topic will be of interest, or if they want you to speak on a specific subject. Also find out what their military interests are. For example, does a local plant produce a weapons system or parts for it? Are local military facilities important to the economy? Discovering such facts might help you tailor your remarks to your audience's interests.

Choose Your Topic Carefully, and Research Your Message

- Tie the topic and message to your direct area of responsibility, past experience, or expertise.
- Flesh out general themes with real-life facts and/or sea stories.
- Get a security policy review, if you need one (see SECNAVINST 5720.44). Check all security questions through your PAO.
- Consider whether you can announce something new, some information your audience won't know but might be interested or excited to find out about. If so, work this news into your talk.

Speech Preparation

- As mentioned earlier, outlines are usually easier to speak from and promote better eye contact than manuscripts. However, some speakers prefer a double- or triple-spaced text, which can be effective if rehearsed and written for oral delivery, in other words, with short sentences.
- With most groups, twenty minutes is the best speech length. If you read from typescript, time yourself reading a page to get a good estimate of how much you can get through. Don't try to read too much or too fast, but read slowly, with emphasis.
- Avoid using visual aids in most public speech opportunities. The larger the audience and room, the less effective visual aids can be, and the greater the opportunity for equipment inadequacy. Moreover, your audience's greatest interest will usually be in hearing from you *personally.*
- Make sure you avoid naval jargon whenever speaking to the public.

Speech Delivery

- Strive hard for
  — Poise
  — Eye Contact
  — Humor
  — Pointedness
  — Brevity (tell them what you're going to say—say it—then sit down)
- Consider whether you should open to questions at the end

Other Tips

- Arrive early enough to mingle with the hosts and audience (this time is a good chance to get names to drop, hear anecdotes, etc.).
- Visit the speaking location ahead of time, or have someone do so for you. Check out the podium, the microphone, the water glass, the cord that you don't want to trip over, and so on.
- Don't drink before your speech.
- Don't make public promises or extend invitations to the audience to visit your unit unless you mean it.
- Do thank your hosts.
- Do enjoy yourself—keep smiling.

"Military briefers are notorious for abusing visual aids. My rule is 'If the picture is worth a thousand words, then use it. If not, keep it off the screen.'"

—Navy Lieutenant

ON NOT INFLICTING "DEATH BY POWERPOINT"

We've all endured it, even cursed about it: a speech or brief in which the technique became so overbearing that boredom or confusion were the overwhelming result.

In a series of routine briefs at OPNAV in 2006, all sorts of mistakes were made. Some briefers had as many as thirty lines (maybe twelve to fifteen bullets!) on *each* of their PowerPoint slides. That's far too much to be comprehended readily. Fonts used on some slides were too small to be read from just twenty feet away. Even on "wiring diagrams" (organizational charts that were very important for that particular set of briefs), print was often tiny.

Poor color choice also hurt: Light-colored letters on a light background were hard to read, and red letters on a dark background were particularly obscure. The use of yellow words on white was another common failure. (If you must use yellow, put it on dark blue.)

As for graphs, the main reason to use a graph is to enhance comprehension, but some graphs used in these OPNAV talks were far too complicated to be understood at a glance—which of course is the goal. For example, one officer presented line graphs which were really two graphs superimposed, with one set of values running up the left-hand scale and another set put up on the right, and several lines on the graph in the middle. It would have taken ten minutes to puzzle it all out. Another problematic visual was a set of bullets presented right alongside a detailed graph— far too much information for a single slide.

PowerPoint can make a presentation visually attractive, informative, and unique. Moreover, frequent visuals do enhance a talk, making both for variety and added comprehension. No one doubts that interesting designs, colors, and background can help to set one's speech or brief apart. But PowerPoint is often misused. So remember the following points.

Don't Put Too Many Words on a Slide

Three to six bullets are probably enough for any single slide. Sure, you can get much more on a slide, but it will not always be understood—or even read. Audience members will find it tiresome to be forced to read large blocks of verbiage "on command," as it were.

You won't go wrong if you always remember to have plenty of white space on your slides.

Use Legible, Large Fonts—And Colors That Contrast

For most talks, the most readable fonts range around 28 to 36 point in size, with larger fonts (maybe 40 point) best used for headings. Of course, some fonts are more legible than others. Arial (especially Arial bold) is a favorite.

The best colors for *legibility* are black on white. If you prefer color, seek a very sharp contrast. Check out the slides personally and with a colleague or two to critique them. But don't just look at the computer screen. Find a briefing room with a projector (ideally the one being used for the actual brief), and view the presentation from the back of the room. Text on a computer screen looks quite different when projected on a screen and read from a distance.

Other Cautions

As a briefer, be very careful to comment *about* the slides, not to read them word for word. One of the biggest complaints about slides is that speakers read them verbatim,

COMPETING WITH THE ROAR OF THE JETS . . . .

Professor Herb Gilliland of the Naval Academy and I once gave a talk at Bolling Air Force Base about a book we had coauthored (a biography of Admiral Dan Gallery, the fellow who had captured a German submarine on the high seas during World War II).

A lecture space in a small building at Bolling had been reserved for the talk on an evening in late fall, but unaccountably, when we arrived there, that room was being used by another group. We were forced to give our thirty-minute talk outside in the dark in fifty-degree weather, competing with loud engine revs from all the landings and take-offs right across the water at Reagan National Airport.

But we persevered, and the liveliness of the question-and-answer period indicated that the talk had been a success despite all these difficulties.

Clearly, speech conditions are not everything.

—Robert Shenk

"Briefs are used in two ways. There's the brief itself, but before that, there's the 'read-ahead.' The office you're briefing will expect the Power-Point brief on paper a certain period ahead of time.

"Actually, sometimes once you've given them the read-ahead, you won't actually have to go ahead and present the brief! The read-ahead is enough."

—COMMANDING
OFFICER, TRAINING
COMMAND

insulting an audience's intelligence. Point out the *key* information, or make ancillary points—but let the audience pick up many things for themselves.

Don't have too many slides. As a captain in OPNAV commented, "A successful briefer will have five or six slides or viewgraphs, will have thought each one out, and will have written a note to himself about the bottom line he wants the audience to take from it. And if you can't summarize that bottom line, *cut out* the slide."

Pay special attention to spelling, grammar, punctuation, and numbers on slides. Spelling or numerical errors, especially, are usually apparent to *somebody* in the audience—and can be quite embarrassing.

And, by the way, check the operation of the projection equipment *before* your presentation. It hurts your credibility if the first thing the audience hears you say is, "How do I back up with this equipment?"

Finally, Always Remember—*Content is Key*

You'll avoid the temptation to overuse PowerPoint's many bells and whistles if you keep reminding yourself that *content is always central.*

Not only is this true in the actual brief but also copies of a brief's slides are commonly used in OPNAV as read-aheads, and afterward officials will make up a missed brief by paging through that same paper brief afterward. For such reasons, the brief should be coherent, informative, and complete *in print.* Still, during the brief itself, the presenter provides much more of the cogency and interest than do the slides. The slides enhance the brief—not the other way about.

In an OPNAV action officer briefing recently, of twenty presentations (some by admirals), the best was by a chief yeoman. The chief spoke easily from behind a podium as if she had been born to the manner, with a natural stance and voice. Her PowerPoint slides had about three to six bullets, all understandable at a glance. The slides were attractive visually, but the bullets themselves were all black on white background with an average 36 point font (Arial). Her slides were the most readable slides of some fifteen or twenty briefers, nor were they too simplistic, either. Finally, the chief neither depended on the slides to keep the talk moving (a common fault) nor kept looking at the screen (instead, she looked at *us*). Her slides perfectly complemented her to-the-point, informative, highly professional brief.

One should point out, however, that despite current technical preferences (PowerPoint briefs are the overwhelming favorite right now in OPNAV, as they are throughout the organizational world), nevertheless, a particular *mode* of presentation is not necessarily all-important.

For instance, in the same three days of briefs mentioned here, not all speakers brought PowerPoint slides along with them. Instead, a three-star brought in a flip chart and used it quite effectively. His method was to ask what questions audience members had, and then to list those questions on the flip chart. He proceeded to orient his brief about those same questions. This method allowed for spontaneity, and the admiral certainly had the knowledge to respond to all the questions posed. (Such a method does require the audience to have some good questions to ask in the first place.)

Another admiral (a one-star) was giving the talk normally presented by his boss (another three-star). He used only a single PowerPoint slide, really an outline, for his thirty minute brief—something one does not normally advise. (For variety's sake alone, more slides are preferable.) Yet the admiral made the talk completely his own, illustrating his boss's points with wide and apt reference to OPNAV procedures and personal experience.

Both these admirals, incidentally, walked around the room and shook hands with everyone at the conference table to begin their talks. Other effective speakers also went out of their way to establish personal contact with some members of their audience, sometimes by referencing concerns of particular OPNAV codes to which officers in the audience were assigned.

A female Navy captain who spoke with a very high-pitched, nervous voice commented in passing that this was simply the way her voice worked. That odd voice was certainly not what one expected to hear in the masculine corridors of the Pentagon, but her brief turned out to be one of the very best of those presented because her talk was filled with excellent advice about how OPNAV worked and how one could succeed in such a difficult environment.

The point is that method of presentation is always trumped by important content, along with interesting and cogent examples and liveliness of presentation. Dynamic speakers who know their stuff typically succeed despite the particular way in which they work.

Naval Briefings

While the principles and techniques of effective speaking apply to military and naval briefings just as to any other type of speech, military briefings are distinctive in several ways. Typically, they are relatively brief and to the point. Because the audience is a "command audience," briefers don't usually need to use attention-getting devices or to ingratiate themselves with the audience. You seldom need to explain terms and concepts. When briefings are directive in nature, you have less need to persuade than you would otherwise.

Still, be on your guard. Argument is possible in many more situations than you would expect. In all briefing situations where important differences of opinion might exist, you should habitually *expect opposition.* Usually, you will be briefing an issue or recommendation because you're the expert on the subject. So *prove your expertise* when someone challenges you in a brief.

"It is turning into an understood protocol that you should provide a read-ahead copy 24 hours ahead (at the latest) to the official you are to brief. It doesn't have to stand alone, but will provide the subject and food for thought."
—Navy Commander, just off a Pentagon staff

"If you give me something to read ahead, I will read it. *Then at the brief itself, we can spend much of our time in dialogue."*
—Rear Admiral Sonny Musso

Know your subject backward and forward. Murder board your presentation with as tough an audience as you can get. Occasionally you won't win your case despite all your good preparations because of sudden new developments that completely change the situation you are briefing. But don't let your presentation fall into disarray because you don't know the material well enough, haven't looked into all the consequences, have not prepared for the specific concern of those you are briefing, or are astonished that someone dared to disagree with you.

INFORMATIVE BRIEFINGS

Many briefings exist to keep the commander and the staff informed. Besides ensuring an exchange of information among staff members, they offer opportunities to announce decisions, issue directives, share information, and give out general guidance. These purposes serve a command's larger goals of unity and coordination.

Many variations of informative briefings exist. One officer may brief the entire staff, or several staff officers might speak in succession. The method and the formality of such a briefing will depend on the size of the staff, the nature of the command, and custom. The executive officer or chief of staff will usually preside and set the agenda, and the commander will normally conclude the briefing. Both officers may take an active part throughout the presentation.

Informative briefings are very similar to staff briefings although they may be more formal and deal with only one rather than many issues. All informative briefings deal mainly with facts rather than recommendations. A simple, standard speech organization—

- an introduction that announces the topic and orients the listener;
- a body that presents facts in an orderly, objective, clear, and concise way; and
- a conclusion that reiterates the main points

—will usually work well. Try to anticipate questions that might arise and treat most of them in the briefing itself, before the audience asks. Bring along any background information that might help you respond to questions, but know your subject so well that you can respond directly to any reasonable inquiry.

Of course, some commanders will use staff briefings to help them make decisions; in that case, the presentation is really a decision briefing.

DECISION BRIEFINGS

You will have many occasions to advocate one course of action or another. You'll often be making your case before a superior who has the responsibility for decision. This presentation might be in informal circumstances, perhaps while standing before your boss's desk, or on a very formal occasion, while giving a decision briefing before an officer of flag rank and several members of that officer's staff.

Whatever the circumstances, keep in mind that several factors other than what you actually say will influence the outcome of your briefing:

- The audience's knowledge and acceptance of you. Have you, or has anyone, explained to those you're briefing what your background is or why they should listen to you, if those reasons are not obvious? (Also, do you have the *right rank* to give this briefing?) Might some in the audience be antagonistic to you, to your office, or to your topic for any reason? If so, how should you deal with your opponents? On the other hand, will anyone in the audience help you? How can you best "use" such supporters?

- Where you give the briefing. Speaking in your own offices, on your own turf, might be a subtle psychological advantage. Any of several other physical factors might also affect the outcome of your talk, such as whether you brief in a large room or a small one; to a large group or a very small, private meeting; with the audience sitting around a table or all facing you in theater-type seats; etc. Check with senior staffers on their experience with each choice.
- The timing of the brief. Have you given yourself enough time? Will another evolution interrupt? Remember that the time of day (early morning, just before lunch, mid-afternoon, etc.) may influence the mood, attentiveness, or even the wakefulness of your audience.

Of course there are many other such considerations.

EXAMPLES OF GOOD STAFF BRIEFINGS

Rather than continue in such general terms, we turn here to two excellent examples of briefings. The first is a comprehensive outline of an information briefing on how to give OPNAV briefings. This brief was once regularly given in Navy offices at the Pentagon. The second is a sample "decision brief" (with briefing guidance) developed for Marine students at Quantico.

Bruce Powers, a civilian employee at OPNAV, regularly presented one version or another of the briefing summarized below to naval officers newly arrived in the Pentagon, this in the late 1990s. One of Mr. Powers's points is that every brief should be *complete in the slides themselves.*

Why should the slides tell the whole story? Because (as mentioned earlier) some of the audience will want to read the slides ahead of the briefing (having been provided a "read-ahead" copy), and because other action officers will be unable to attend the oral presentation, and hence will know the brief only from a printed set of slides. In fact, often the people who will know the briefing through the printed slides will outnumber those who have attended the actual presentation! And these attendees-via-slides won't just be using the slides casually but will often have to use the information on those printed slides in their own staff work.

Mr. Powers's brief is presented here via a selected set of his own slides:

The OPNAV Brief on Briefings

I. *Preparing the Brief*
- Focus on what you are trying to do
    — information only?
    — seek a decision?
- Focus on the *fundamental concept* you are trying to convey
    — e.g., "Ship maintenance underfunded . . . need $xxM to fix."
    — keep focused on the basic theme throughout
    — stay out of the weeds
- Remember the intended audience
    — how much do they know of the subject already?
    — how much detail do they require to get the point?
- Proceed logically
    — start with an outline, the basic building block
        ▫ consider using a storyboard (a list of needed slides) as an outline
    — keep to a logical sequence

"If you find yourself developing PowerPoint slides totally from scratch, you're probably not doing your job. There's almost always a slide somewhere that's close to what you need. It's authorized to plagiarize, and it can save you lots of time.

"I learned this while watching a brief on a new topic, and suddenly seeing my own slide up on the screen!"

—NAVY CAPTAIN, OPNAV

"There are great graphics in PowerPoint. But the key question is how much of the graphics should be used?"

—LIEUTENANT FRESH FROM DUTY ON A SUB, NAVAL ACADEMY

— keep to 1–5 *main* points (no more)
— keep to about 30 minutes (for most OPNAV briefings)

II. *Preparing the Slides*
- Remember that a picture is worth a thousand words
  — it's much easier to grasp graphic information than text
  — try to facilitate the viewers' comprehension
    - e.g., align pros and cons
  — if it's worth remembering, *put it on a slide*
- Be clear and concise
  — don't put too much on one slide
    - 3–5 bullets is the most anyone can absorb
  — don't overuse acronyms
  — yet don't sacrifice completeness
- Ensure consistency in appearance
    - beware lest input from several sources makes the pitch disjointed
  — slides should have the same look, style, and feel
  — text should be the same size and font
  — slides should use the same units, periods of time, etc.
  — bullets should begin with all nouns or all verbs
- Make slides stand alone
  — titles, subtitles, axis labels, and units should say it all
  — remember: not everyone will see the brief
- Display figures logically
  — ensure all decimals line up
  — show "as of" date
  — for $, indicate year, constant dollars, etc.
- Use graphs whenever possible
  — easier to grasp than text/figures
  — choose display carefully
    - bar chart, lines, areas, etc.
- On graphs, avoid
  — 3-D (no value added)
  — different left and right axes
  — more than two or three lines
  — anything that detracts from the messages: fancy fonts, borders, grid lines, etc.
  — "too much at once" pictures
    - use overlays to add additional information as the story unfolds
- Prepare backup slides
  — try to foresee questions
  — keep the slides that you omitted from the final version (you made them for a reason!)
  — make backups of the same quality as up-front slides
  — make a numbered backup index
  — don't show a backup that doesn't answer or avoids the question

III. *Writing a Script*
- Sometimes use a *prepared script:* a formal briefing demands it
  — rare in OPNAV, but for presentation to a 4-star
  — ensures you say what you mean
  — clarifies and enhances slides
  — keeps you from getting nervous and failing to make key points
- Ensure that slides and script work in harmony to tell the story
  — don't reread what's already on a slide
  — bring out the important points on a slide

— use text to discuss alternatives, identify pros and cons
— avoid slide/script mismatch
- Write the final script yourself
  — use inputs from others as your basis
  — write in a conversational tone using plain English
  — don't use words you might stumble over later
- Know the script well
  — becomes a guide, not a crutch
  — enhances credibility if you "know" the material, aren't just reading out loud
  — allows you to maintain eye contact with your audience
  — lets you "walk and talk" (move away from the podium to help relax the audience)

IV. *Mastering Mechanics*
- Know when and where the briefing will occur
  — be prepared for schedule/room changes
  — rear projection? dual projectors?
  — large or small room?
  — can people in the back easily read the slides?
  — ensure they have the slides numbered, in order, facing the right way
- During development, try your pitch on someone unfamiliar with the material
  — if they understand it, you're on the right track
  — don't wait until the last minute to "shine it on the wall"
- Keep control of the hard copy
  — don't spread drafts around
    - but don't work in a vacuum; coordinate as necessary
  — number the pages of the final version
  — for better reference during the brief
  — remember classification stamps/markings
  — distribute the hard copy early enough for other action officers to brief their bosses
- Develop a "time-is-short" version of the brief
- *Practice beforehand:* there is no substitute

V. *Presenting the Brief*
- Pay attention to your appearance
  — look your best (credibility factor)
  — point with a pen or pointer or laser light (not your fingers)
  — avoid hand-waving
  — keep your hands out of your pockets and away from coins
  — don't lean on the podium
  — if not walking and talking . . . STAND STILL
- Pay attention to the way you speak
  — speak in a conversational tone
  — speak clearly and at a normal pace
  — *avoid monotone:* use your voice to emphasize the key points
- Do:
  — view the problem as the decision maker does
  — respect his or her time
  — be aware of the wider issues
  — make the alternatives clear
  — be indifferent about the answer
- Don't:
  — describe analyses chronologically
    - the audience cares about *results,* not the research phase
  — present results poorly

"Count on the principal being ten minutes late and leaving ten minutes early—and wanting ten minutes for discussion. So the thirty slides you have prepared to talk about now have to be pared down to fifteen."
—Experienced officer on OPNAV staff

— be unable to answer questions

— push for a particular answer

- And don't:

— become argumentative when challenged

▪ support your position

▪ move on if you're getting nowhere

VI. *In Your Conclusion*

- Summarize the main points

— hammer home your central theme

- Say exactly what you mean

— what positions do you recommend?

— what decision do you want made?

— what should the audience remember?

—Adapted from Brief to OPNAV Action Officers given by
Mr. Bruce Powers, summer 1995.

"Don't give more than a brief introduction. On 9 topics out of 10, they don't need details back to Genesis."

—GUIDE TO
OPNAV WRITING

Below is a proven format for a formal decision brief, with guidance. It is based on the classic staff-study format, as adapted to oral briefing requirements. Alter it as you wish, based on your particular subject matter, the occasion of the brief, and your knowledge of the decision maker.

One Format for a Decision Brief

FORMAT	*EXAMPLE*
Greeting. Use military courtesy. Address the decision maker and other key persons in the audience. Identify yourself and your organization, if necessary.	Good afternoon, General J ———. I'm Colonel M ———, the Staff Operations Officer.
Type of Briefing, Classification, Purpose.	This is an unclassified decision briefing.
Subject and Problem. State very briefly the background and present context of the problem at hand.	As you know, one Marine per year is killed in the mine field at Guantanamo Bay, Cuba, and incidents are occurring more frequently. Lately, this problem has attracted congressional attention.
Basic Recommendation. Put your bottom line up front—this is perhaps the most important advice of all. Don't leave your listeners in any doubt as to your basic recommendation. Tell them early, and speak forcefully.	To solve this problem, I recommend that we replace the conventional munitions in the mine fields at the U.S. Naval Base in Guantanamo with FASCAM Munitions.
Detailed Statement of the Problem. If necessary, outline more fully the problem this briefing intends to solve.	Defense of the U.S. Naval Base at Guantanamo Bay has been a significant issue since 1959. Much of the existing barrier relies on antitank and antipersonnel mines. We must emplace and replace these conventional munitions by hand.

"Don't tell me what I want to hear . . . but tell me what the facts are, and let me make a decision."

—VICE ADMIRAL
CRENSHAW AT OPNAV,
DURING A BRIEF TO
ACTION OFFICERS

This process is time consuming and dangerous . . . .

Any Necessary Assumptions. State any assumptions needed to bridge gaps in the data. Make sure they are reasonable, and be prepared to support them if challenged.

We can assume that the political situation will remain the same for the foreseeable future and that the mine barrier must continue to remain in place. Thus, an improved process to emplace the mines would seem a long-term need.

Facts Bearing on the Problem. State pertinent facts objectively. Present both sides of the issue, even if recommending just one. Research indicates that a high percentage of audience members will lean toward your argument when you present both sides, but just a few will when you present only your side. Be sure to cite authorities and relevant supporting opinions.

1. FASCAM munitions now available offer some antipersonnel, antitank capabilities with distinct improvements over conventional land mines. . . .
2. FASCAM munitions can be emplaced by artillery and so offer a significant safety improvement. . . .
3. FASCAM munitions allow for a more flexible response because they can be fired in reaction to enemy action. . . .

4, 5, 6, etc.

Possible Courses of Action. State major feasible options. Explain the advantages and drawbacks of each, and any potential dangers involved.

1. The major alternative to using FASCAM munitions is the current method, which is to bury mines below ground level by hand, a tedious and dangerous process. With this method we must painstakingly record mine locations and replace each mine before its shelf-life expiration date. . . .
2. The major advantage of the present system of mine emplacement is cost. Equivalent mine munitions are considerably less costly than FASCAM rounds, and FASCAM will require augmenting the Security Battalion with a 155mm howitzer battery. . . .

3, 4, 5, etc.

Analysis. Present your conclusions briefly. Mention any concurrences and nonconcurrences.

1. The admittedly significant increases in cost, personnel, and equipment are worthwhile when weighed against the recurrent loss of life presently incurred in handling conventional mines. The employment of FASCAM will totally eliminate this loss of life.
2. Besides being safer, FASCAM mine fields are more effective and more flexible.
3. CMC received a brief during a visit to GITMO and liked the idea of FASCAM.

"You see people at meetings working Blackberries nonstop while they're supposed to be listening."
—XO, Naval Station

Restated Recommendation. Restate your recommendation, wording it so it requires only approval or disapproval.

We recommend that FASCAM munitions replace the current mines emplaced at Guantanamo Bay.

Opening for Questions. Try to anticipate questions; conduct murder boards if you can. Do your best to have thorough knowledge of the whole issue so you can respond intelligently to questions or arguments.

Are there any questions?

—Example based on instructional material used at Marine Corps Development and Education Command, Quantico, VA

"One thing that a j.o. on a sub might have to help produce is a 'Patrol Debrief for the Admiral.' Here it would be useful to know about how to create slides, how much verbiage to use on the slides, where to stand with reference to them, etc. The j.o. makes the slides; the Captain tells him how to edit them; then the j.o. polishes them.

"But the speaker *is always key,* not *the brief dynamics."*

—Lieutenant, USN

In some settings, you can expect a decision on the spot. In fact, the flag or flag's staff may have asked for the decision brief for the very purpose of deciding the issue quickly. In that case, you might end your brief by saying, "General, I have completed my presentation, and I am prepared for your decision," or words to that effect. This is standard procedure on some Marine staffs.

But be careful, as a briefer, not to try to force a public decision. If the senior renders no decision immediately, leave the issue at the "recommend" level, and pursue the decision later through staff channels. Note that Navy briefers seldom ask the admiral for a decision as directly as in the statement above. Be guided by staffers experienced with your command's way of operating.

MISSION BRIEFINGS

Service members deliver mission briefings to Marines, ship drivers, and naval aviators alike as they are about to embark on operational missions either for training or for actual combat. Although such briefings will vary widely in technique, subject, and location, they each have one central aim: to instill the best possible understanding of an impending operation in all participants.

For example, a Marine patrol going out will normally learn of its specific mission through oral orders. Then a mission briefing may provide further specific instructions such as the route of march, what to look for, identification procedures, and so on. The briefing may also afford the Marines a brief explanation of why the patrol is necessary and what it will contribute to the overall mission of the command.

Ships have similar procedures. Key officers and senior enlisted personnel on a destroyer, for instance, might go over to the flagship by high-line or helo for a mission briefing on an impending operation, perhaps an operation involving naval gunfire support, air operations, search and rescue, or a missile shoot. The briefing would include all manner of specifics, from call signs, radio frequencies, and emergency procedures to formations, tactics, and weapons employment. Here too, besides rendering specific plans and details, the briefing officer would usually touch on how the operation fits into larger operational or training objectives.

Naval aviators pay great attention to effective delivery of mission briefings, partly from having to give them so often. One naval school that has developed a strong program of operational briefings and debriefings is the Naval Fighter Weapons School (TOPGUN). Below are excerpts adapted from a version of that school's guidance on mission briefing. Although originally designed to guide those who must brief Navy and Marine Corps fighter squadrons about to fly a tactical exercise, this advice is adaptable to many other situations.

Briefing and Debriefing at TOPGUN

A. Introduction. Tactical flight time will continue to be at a premium in the months and years ahead because of funding constraints and aircraft availability. We must take advantage of every opportunity to refine our aviation skills. Your squadron has made a large investment in OPTAR, TAD funding, and maintenance support to provide for your attendance. It expects a return on the investment. One way you can pay off is by giving professional briefs and debriefs. Comprehensive briefs and debriefs are the cornerstones of an effective squadron training program. While you may not use all these pointers on every sortie, they apply to almost any tactical fighter mission.

B. Preparation. If the first time the briefer has considered the mission is thirty minutes prior to the flight brief, then the briefer has done a disservice to the squadron by not taking full advantage of a valuable training opportunity. Mission planning varies widely, but certain elements are applicable to all missions.

1. As flight leader, have a clear idea of what the mission and/or training objectives are. If the flight leader doesn't have it clear, certainly no one else in the flight will.

2. Start mission planning early—at least the day prior.

3. Involve other members of the flight. This will be no problem if the mission is an air superiority sweep in the Gulf of Sidra but some arm twisting may be required for night max-conserve 2v2s off the coast of Diego Garcia. Make sure all members of the flight arrive at the brief having familiarized themselves with the SOP, mission objectives, operating area, and any other information required to maximize the performance of the aircraft. Anything less is unprofessional.

4. Develop a scenario that will be challenging but within the capabilities of all members of the flight. Don't give a lengthy dissertation on a country's political-military situation, but rather make the situation a detailed framework from which the fighters can make intelligent tactical decisions.

5. Review written material for guidance on tactics, maneuvers, and the threat. Refer to Tactical Manuals, TOPGUN Manuals/Journals, VX-4 Newsletters, etc., for information. Dust off the contingency plans from the last cruise or deployment for reference.

6. Allow for contingencies such as maintenance problems and weather aborts. Plan an alternate mission.

7. *Write it down.* Putting the brief on paper—either in outline or paragraph form—will help briefers organize their thoughts and make them more familiar with the material. The result will be a smooth brief that is not repetitive and disjointed. If the brief is large and complex, a practice run-through is worth the effort.

C. The Brief. Below are some specific pointers on the brief itself.

1. WHERE. During shore-based operations, it's not too difficult to set aside a briefing/debriefing room—complete with whiteboard, models, and VTR/monitor—that allows for a quiet atmosphere without interruptions. Unfortunately, the reality of shipboard life is such that Navy and Marine Corps squadrons must often conduct their briefs amid the confusion of the all-purpose ready room. The squadron duty officer must ensure minimal interference with a flight that is briefing or debriefing. Try posting a sign on the ready room door that alerts everyone that a brief or debrief is in progress.

2. WHO. The flight leader traditionally conducts the brief. However, briefing can provide valuable training to a less-experienced member of the flight. Naturally, any briefer should have been intimately involved in the planning.

"It's always important in a brief to put your bottom line up front. Leave out the fluff."
—Navy Commanding Officer

3. WHEN. Most squadrons brief 1–11/2 hours prior to man-up, depending on the mission and size of the flight. You'll have enough time to cover all the necessary items— *if you're prepared.* When the squadron is operating in a new locale, you may have to lengthen the brief to cover local course rules and operating areas. *DO NOT SACRIFICE THE TACTICAL PORTION OF THE BRIEF FOR ADMIN ITEMS.*

4. SETTING UP. Here are a few general pointers:

   - Be at the squadron early to take care of any last-minute items such as aircraft availability, weather, scheduling changes, etc.
   - Set up the briefing room so that everyone has a full view of the briefer, whiteboard, and other briefing aids. Clean the whiteboard of all items not pertaining to the mission. Check that models and colored markers are available. If time constraints prevent whiteboard preparation, have the briefing items photocopied and passed out.
   - Start on time! A flight that briefs late will walk late, take off late, etc. It only takes one instance of losing a hop for tardy players to change their ways.
   - As briefer, remain standing throughout the brief. This posture makes for better delivery and reinforces the briefer's leadership.
   - If you have players who were not involved in the planning, start with a brief overview of the mission.

   [The TOPGUN instruction continues with details of the "ADMIN Brief" on take-off times, comm plan, weather and divert procedures, mission and training objectives, etc.; and with details of the "TACTICAL Brief"—the heart of the mission and the set-up of each engagement. Then the instruction goes on to . . .]

5. BRIEFING TECHNIQUES. All of us have our own briefing styles. Note others' effective techniques, and use what works well for you. Here are some suggestions:

   - Keep an eye on the clock and pace yourself during the brief. Allow ten minutes at the end for questions, crew coordination, and a pit stop prior to man-up.
   - Maintain eye contact with the flight members. It will keep them attentive and provide feedback as to whether your points are getting across.
   - Ask questions from time to time to keep everyone involved in the brief. They can be rhetorical or specific. However, be careful not to bilge your wingman by playing NATOPS Trivial Pursuit in front of the CO.
   - Recap the mission in general terms as a conclusion to the brief, with a review of the training objectives.
   - If you complete the brief with time to spare, cover any tactical contingencies/issues that are relevant. As Navy and Marine Corps officers, we accept the paperwork burden as an unavoidable price to pay to fly high performance fighters. Don't sacrifice a scheduled opportunity to talk tactics just to read the message board, make a phone call, or push papers between the brief and strapping on the jet.

   [A section on "Remembering the Flight" comes here, then . . .]

D. The Debrief. The most important consideration about the debrief is to have one! We neglect or gloss over many debriefs because of follow-on missions, lack of space availability, crew rest, or a hundred other reasons. Too often, we lose valuable training/learning because we're not interested enough in conducting a meaningful analysis of the mission. If the mission was so mundane or routine that it doesn't merit a debrief, then the flight lead was negligent in identifying training objectives.

The debrief should not be simply a chronological regurgitation of the mission: It should emphasize analysis and should identify lessons learned for subsequent missions.

The debrief begins as soon as the brief is over. Jot down any point worthy of discussion. After the mission, review your notes and VTR/microcassette to organize your debrief comments. Ask yourself some pertinent questions: Were the mission objectives achieved? How about the training objectives? What mistakes were made? Were the mistakes due to poor planning, briefing, or execution? A few minutes taken to organize your thoughts will dramatically improve the quality, expeditiousness, and professionalism of the debrief.

Follow these additional guidelines:

1. Have the debriefing room set up—whiteboard, colored pens, models, VTR/monitor. Draw notable geographic features of the operating area on the board, with north oriented to the top, and include the position of the sun. In one corner of the board list all the players next to the color of the arrow that will represent them, and list the training objectives as well.

2. Make sure all players attend the debrief, including the controller and the adversaries.

3. The overall debriefer—generally the flight lead—is responsible for maintaining control of the debrief. Emphasize that everyone will have a chance to talk, but only after the debriefer has first addressed the important points.

4. Spend the first few minutes of the debrief covering any ADMIN problems (clearance, line procedures, rendezvous, recovery, etc.). Get these matters out of the way quickly to clear the air for the important TACTICAL debrief.

5. As the debriefer, actively promote an atmosphere that encourages frank discussions without recriminations. See that all participants set aside personal feelings, friendships, and rank as they walk in the door. At TOPGUN we strive to "take the who out of ACM" by recounting engagements in the third person. Instead of, "Here's where I gunned you, Dirt, when you were obviously out of knots and tried a nose-high guns defense," say, "At this point the A-4 achieved a valid gunshot when the F-14 attempted a nose-high guns defense at a low airspeed." Both examples address the ACM mistake but the players will accept the lesson more readily in the second case.

6. Solicit input from the crowd to keep everyone interested in the analysis. Admit mistakes to maintain credibility, and acknowledge good performance to reinforce the positive. Keep the discussion oriented to the mission objectives and relevant points.

7. Structure the TACTICAL debrief to cover the important points thoroughly. You can address relatively minor points that didn't affect the success of the mission at the end of the debrief, or perhaps not at all.

   [The TOPGUN instruction goes on to cover methods of boardwork in drawing fighter engagements and details of the TACTICAL debrief. Finally, . . .]

8. After the TACTICAL debrief, summarize the flight with reference to the training objectives identified in the brief. At TOPGUN we use a "Goods and Others" format. This discussion provides the basis for determining training objectives for subsequent flights.

E. Summary. The trademark of the TOPGUN graduate is being the best briefer and debriefer in the squadron. In the next five weeks, carefully observe the techniques of all the instructors. Select what works the best for your own personal style, and perfect your briefing and debriefing skills. Lessons learned in peacetime training must equip us for the challenging scenarios we can expect in modern aerial warfare. In the final analysis, the aircrew's flying skills will determine success or failure of the mission, no matter how well equipped they might be with weapons, intelligence information, and policy guidance. These aviation skills are a direct function of how well you've briefed, led, and debriefed your aircrews.

—Adapted from NFWS TM B&D 5-88.

9

Technical Reports, Executive Summaries, and Abstracts

Naval personnel must often work with industry, or with reports and other documents prepared by industry. Those doing research at naval labs, naval test centers, or naval schools must help generate technical reports while others will just have to use them.

Specifically, naval personnel will often encounter technical reports when they work on staffs that monitor military contracts, perhaps while working for an O-5 or O-6 project officer or program manager. That officer may have requested an analysis, a proposal, or a progress report of some kind. Perhaps the Navy wants to build a helicopter engine that will operate effectively in deserts. The program manager might have contracted for a report that details what such a design would look like, how reliable the engine would be, and how much it would cost.

In the latter case, the company with the contract would respond with a feasibility report, which Navy officials would use to guide them. The report would first help them decide whether to build the engine. Then, having decided to build it, they would use the report to persuade senior officers and other government officials to award them the funds.

If the company with the contract were to do its work well, it would organize the report so everyone could use it intelligently. Who would likely readers be? First, the *technical experts* on the program manager's staff. These engineers, technicians, accountants, weapons experts, tacticians, and so forth (some of them military, some civil servants) would be tasked by their boss to examine the design, the engine's capability, and the costs in great detail. Possessing the technical background to understand all kinds of charts, tables, diagrams, and descriptions, they would expect detailed technical explanations.

However, many others who might read this document would not be experts, among them the most important audience—*decision makers*. These readers would probably not understand all the technical parts of the report, nor would they need the detail that experts require. The project manager, for example, might be generally knowledgeable in tactics and weapons systems but would not necessarily be an engineer. This person would need a semi-technical explanation, one emphasizing conclusions and recommendations.

Senior military officials would also need a semi-technical discussion of key, summary information (rather than a highly technical discussion of all the details). So would elected government officials and their staffs. Still, at any point an official up the line might need to examine—usually by assigning staff members to examine—the specific technical features of the project.

So both highly technical and semi-technical discussion must be present in the same report. Moreover, usually *one document* must satisfy both experts and decision makers. Similarly with the many other kinds of documents needed if the government were to go ahead with the project. Each report would have to address readers with very different backgrounds and needs. Whether a later document were

- a formal proposal by a firm to build the engine;
- a progress report submitted by the contracted firm;
- a research report used in the technical design;
- an instruction manual designed for operators; or
- a final report submitted upon the project's completion,

it would still have to address multiple audiences.

We can't go into each kind of report mentioned above; refer to one or more of the references on technical writing mentioned at the end of this chapter for thorough discussions of various technical writing genres. What we *can do*, however, is to discuss the organizing and summarizing techniques industry has used for decades to satisfy such diverse audiences. In the process, we will mention some of the other naval uses these methods have come to serve.

ORGANIZATION OF TECHNICAL REPORTS

Following are several proven methods of designing technical reports so they reach their multiple audiences (1) with the right kind of information, (2) at the necessary reading level, and (3) with the appropriate detail. (Actually, you can apply these methods to a variety of complex naval documents, not just technical reports.)

Present Conclusions before Rationales

Of course, when investigators have a problem to solve, they typically begin by assessing the problem, then they conduct the investigation or research, and eventually they come to conclusions. Sometimes investigators write up their reports following this same order—with conclusions last.

However, as we've seen before in other contexts, the chronological order of the investigation may be backward to the reader's needs. Just as naval readers habitually glance at the action paragraph of a document before reading the whole document through (sometimes *instead* of reading it through), decision makers typically look for the conclusions and recommendations first. Often they only skim the rest of the report—they don't need to read it all.

So help these readers out. As the author of "Just Plain English" points out, "Avoid Mystery Stories . . . Put requests <u>before</u> justifications, answers <u>before</u> explanations, conclusions <u>before</u> discussions, summaries <u>before</u> details, and the general

"Technical reports are meant to be skimmed! *Hence the frequent occurrence of executive summaries, abstracts, section summaries, appendixes, frequent headings, even summaries* of *summaries."*

—TECHNICAL WRITING EXPERT

<u>before</u> the specific." Here's an example of what this guidance might mean for a standard investigative or research report:

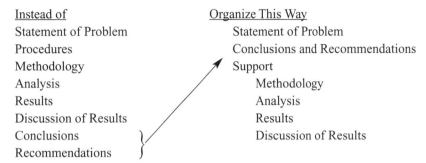

Instead of	Organize This Way
Statement of Problem	Statement of Problem
Procedures	Conclusions and Recommendations
Methodology	Support
Analysis	Methodology
Results	Analysis
Discussion of Results	Results
Conclusions	Discussion of Results
Recommendations	

Sometimes you might have to write your report in a rigidly specified format, and that format may resemble the one in the left column (though even this report will usually begin with an executive summary to include conclusions and recommendations in a brief form; see the following section). If not, put the conclusions and recommendations at the beginning to give readers a head start on the vital information. That's just plain English.

Use Appendixes

Relegate to appendixes material only specialists need. Don't let numbers, designs, and other data overburden the text of the report. Full-length reports, like operation orders, often have many appendixes.

Subdivide into Short Sections with Many Headings and Tabs

You can help the reader immensely by organizing your reports into sections. Use care in carving sections out—design your sections and headings with the *readers' needs* in mind.

On hard-copy documents, add paper or plastic tabs to make sections readily visible. On very long documents, consider adding indexes too. With online documents, provide links for the longer report sections.

Use Reviews, Surveys, and Summaries throughout the Report

Summaries aid everyone. Remember that even those few reviewers who read a report straight through will seldom be able to avoid all interruptions from meetings, office visits, and phone calls while they read. Actually, in the Navy and Marine Corps, you are almost always writing for the distracted reader. Hence, at strategic locations in your text (such as the beginnings or ends of major sections), review topics that you've presented before, and summarize the information that follows after. Above all, after you've written the whole report from introduction to the conclusions and recommendations. . . .

Carefully Compose an "Executive Summary"

The executive summary is a summary of vital information, described in the following section.

THE EXECUTIVE SUMMARY

Design the executive summary so that by reading it—perhaps along with a couple of other key sections of the report, but not much more—an executive will have enough information to proceed to a decision. Actually, whoever picks up a report with a good executive summary can use it to get a quick feel for the report's contents, and almost all readers begin with the executive summary if one is provided. Still, the main purpose of an executive summary is to *provide executives with what they need to make decisions.*

The length of an executive summary varies—it may run twenty pages for a book-length document but only a page or two for a twenty-page report. Here is a common rule of thumb: Keep the executive summary no more than *one-tenth the size* of the report it summarizes. Sometimes summaries are a great deal shorter than that.

Place an executive summary at the beginning of a report, soon after the title page. Some Navy labs make sure a reader can immediately locate the summary by printing it on blue or green paper. A tab, of course, would serve the same purpose. The point is to set off the summary from the rest of the document because everyone is likely to read this section. The summary identifies the gist of the report, its overall import.

You've probably seen many an executive summary before, even if you didn't recognize it at the time. An email that introduces a lengthy attachment can be an executive summary—telling you the gist of the document so you'll know whether to open it and read further. A briefing memo for a correspondence package on a staff is a kind of executive summary because the briefing memo also enables a superior to understand the matter at hand quickly without having to page through the whole package. Submarine patrol reports typically begin with executive summaries because here, as well, not everyone needs all the details. When a personnel board convenes in Millington, Tennessee—the Retired Personnel Board, for example—an executive summary begins the board's report.

Often, when a naval command issues a change to a major instruction, authorities will draw attention to the essence of that change by sending an executive summary in message format. Figure 9.1 is the message that introduced the 1983 change to the Correspondence Manual, noting in particular its stress on Naval Writing Standards or "Just Plain English." As you can see, the message is extremely brief but it very effectively (by example) gets across its central summary. Figure 10.1 (in the next chapter) is a condensed version of yet another message that summarized the change to a major naval manual; in effect, it too is an executive summary.

"You have one chance to get to the decision makers —emphasize the key ideas, the key findings."
—NAVAL WAR
COLLEGE PROFESSOR

You can construct the executive summary in various ways. What usually sets this document off from other summaries is its emphasis on *results, conclusions,* and *recommendations.* Executive summaries differ in how much they discuss background, procedures, and methodology (some treat each of these items briefly while others don't discuss them at all). But the best of them focus mostly on *what all the factors lead to,* that is,

- what results show,
- what conclusions you can draw, and
- what action your audience should take.

Don't try to cover everything in an executive summary, but include only the most essential information. Also, remember not to write the executive summary until you have written the whole report in its final form, or it may not do justice to the actual report.

Here's an example of a formal executive summary. Released in 1993 by the Center for Naval Analyses, it summarizes a report that had two phases and ran to fifty-six pages of very tight, small type. This summary appeared in a four-page glossy that

Figure 9.1 An Executive Summary in Message Format. It introduced the 1983 revision to the Navy Correspondence Manual.

```
FROM:  SECRETARY OF THE NAVY
TO:    THE NAVY AND MARINE CORPS

SUBJ:  REVISED NAVY CORRESPONDENCE MANUAL, SECNAVINST 5216.5C

1. SECNAVINST 5216.5C, NOW IN DISTRIBUTION, IS MORE THAN JUST
ANOTHER EDITION OF THE OLD CORRESPONDENCE MANUAL; THIS EDITION
REVISES THE MANUAL THROUGHOUT.  THE BIGGEST IMPROVEMENT IS THE
NEW FIRST CHAPTER, WHICH SETS NAVAL WRITING STANDARDS.  WHETHER
YOUR DUTIES REQUIRE YOU TO WRITE OR REVIEW THE WRITING OF
OTHERS, READ THIS CHAPTER AND APPLY IT.  SOME OF THE CHAPTER'S
MAIN POINTS ARE:

    A.  START YOUR WRITING WITH THE MOST IMPORTANT INFORMATION,
AS NEWSPAPERS DO.  AVOID MERE CHRONOLOGY.

    B.  USE SPOKEN ENGLISH, I.E., EVERYDAY WORDS, SHORT
SENTENCES, AND PERSONAL PRONOUNS.

    C.  PRUNE YOUR WRITING.

    D.  PREFER THE ACTIVE VOICE, "WEAR APPROPRIATE CLOTHING" FOR
"APPROPRIATE CLOTHING SHALL BE WORN" AND "WE REQUEST" FOR "IT IS
REQUESTED THAT."

2. WITH EFFORT BY WRITERS AND ENCOURAGEMENT FROM REVIEWERS,
THESE TECHNIQUES WILL IMPROVE OUR CORRESPONDENCE.  THE RESULT
WILL BE GREATER PRODUCTIVITY FOR US ALL.


                          --062047Z APR 84 (ALNAV 048/84)
```

was distributed to select naval and other governmental audiences. Interested readers could order the whole report or simply become better informed by reading the summary itself.

The Future Russian Navy—Final Report
Summary

Background and approach

CNA undertook the Future Russian Navy study at the request of the Director of Naval Intelligence. We were to evaluate the historical, current, and future interests and constraints that will help shape any future Russian Navy, and to derive a range of potential naval force postures and their implications for the United States Navy.

The study had two phases. Phase I examined current and near-term constraints on existing Commonwealth of Independent States naval forces and potential future foreign policy, economic, and security interests of the Russian state that would support a need for naval forces. Phase II evaluated competing interests and constraints and derived a range of possible Russian naval postures and their likelihood. Capsule descriptions of phase I findings follow.

Key findings

Historically, the Russian and Soviet navies were linked to the political leadership's assessment of the threat from the sea. They depended on Western technology, designs, and personnel. Internal political changes affected the navy more than the other services. And through most of Russian history, the United States was seen as a natural ally.

Sociopolitical factors have resulted in draft-dodging and lost prestige of military service. Life in the military has deteriorated through shortages of consumables and a breakdown in supply lines. The military have thus had to allocate more resources to personnel welfare, to engage in commercial activity in an effort to become self-sustaining, and to increase their activism at the local level on which they have become economically dependent.

Economic constraints at the national level have caused the military and defense industry to compete with the civil sector for resources. The shift from autocracy to democracy has strengthened the position of those favoring the civil sector. Economic upheaval has severed the links between central government, local industry, and military installations. Recovery will likely spring from the local sectors, further isolating the central government and diminishing its authority.

At the fleet level, commanders focus their resources on the newest platforms with highest priority missions. They have been disposing of "surplus" equipment to get funds for housing and other necessities. Even newer units have been deteriorating rapidly. There's hard evidence that only ships with high-priority missions are fully operational.

Military interests . . .

Economic interests . . .

Foreign policy interests . . .

Conclusions

These phase I results provided us with the context for the phase II synthesis. This synthesis led to the following conclusions:

- Through the 1990s, the Russian Navy will decline in both numbers and capabilities.

- Economics will force it to focus on the seas contiguous to Russia.

- The Ministries of Defense and Foreign Affairs will use the navy to integrate Russia into the Western Security system.

- Cooperation and deterrence will compete for scarce operating funds; cooperation may win some of those competitions.

The Russian Navy of the next century will wind up in one of four different configurations (or a mixture of two or more):

- Niche navy—high technology, regional focus, globally deployable specialty, assessed at a .15 probability

- High-tech deterrent navy—globally deployable but regionally oriented navy with a strategic nuclear deterrent responsibility, assessed at a .3 probability

- High-tech warfighting navy—globally oriented, conventional and nuclear-capable navy designed to contest the seas with any other navy, assessed at a .05 probability

- Obsolescent, residual navy—survivors of the late 1980s Soviet Navy plus a few newer coastal patrol ships, assessed at a .5 probability

Implications for the Navy

For the United States Navy, defusing the adversarial relationship that exists between U.S. and Russian naval forces and influencing the future Russian Navy are the most important opportunities that this new situation has created. Naval cooperation is the most effective means of seizing this opportunity.

References

Documentation of this work appears in CNA Research Memorandum 93-115, *The Future Russian Navy Final Report,* by Floyd D. Kennedy, Jr. et al., September 1993, and its supporting research memoranda.

TWO KINDS OF ABSTRACTS

Another kind of summary device for technical reports is the "abstract," which may preface a report whether or not the report also has an executive summary. The abstract differs from an executive summary primarily in function and audience. That is, where an executive summary is a synopsis of a report's conclusions/recommendations and is meant for decision makers, an abstract is a *screening tool* that is usually intended for researchers. Also, where the executive summary is designed so the decision maker can read it *instead of* reading the whole report, the abstract helps a researcher decide *whether to read the report at all.*

Writers compose abstracts for professional articles as well as technical reports. But whatever documents they summarize, abstracts have certain standard features:

- They often include much technical detail in a very condensed and highly technical discussion that a layperson will have trouble following.
- They are typically short—from a couple of sentences to about three hundred words (but they still use full sentences, not fragments or bullets).
- They usually are written as one paragraph.
- They don't focus on conclusions or recommendations but either give equal value to every part of a report or concentrate on a project's results, quickly letting the expert reader see the scientific or *technical significance* of the research.

Write each abstract so it makes sense as a separate document. You have two different styles to choose from.

The Informative Abstract

The informative abstract is meant to *reproduce the report in small,* mirroring all its essential features. In fact, some texts recommend that to write such an abstract you should first identify the topic sentence from every major section in the report, and then simply string all these key sentences together, just smoothing out the wording. Others suggest you work from an outline. However you proceed, include in the informative abstract a brief discussion of the background of the research project, its intent, the way you set it up, the procedure you used to carry it out, and the results.

Reading such a summary will tell the researcher whether to order the whole report or not. Here's an example of an informative abstract put out at the Naval Academy in 2003 titled "Fracture Toughness Characterization of HSLA-100 Steels for Carrier Crack Arrestor Applications."

HSLA-100 steel is being considered as a replacement for HY-100 in aircraft carrier crack arrestor applications. The various compositions of HSLA-100 were evaluated and compared to 1.25 in. thick HY-100. Tests were conducted to measure tensile properties, Charpy impact energy, dynamic tear energy, fracture toughness and the reference temperature. The two alloys compared favorably on all tests except the fracture toughness tests at −40°F. HSLA-100 in the T-L orientation exhibited fracture by cleavage after ductile crack growth, whereas the HY-100 remained ductile. This result was unexpected since it is commonly believed that fracture behavior can be correlated with impact tests and the reference temperature. At −20°, fracture remained ductile in the HSLA-100. Consequently, it is recommended that HSLA-100 in the T-L orientation only be used where the minimum service temperature is above −20°F.

—Graham, Stephen M., Assistant Professor, Mercier, G. P., L'Heureux, B. P., and Waskey, J. P. NSWCCD-TR-2003/11 August 2003.

Clearly, the emphasis here is not on conclusions/recommendations but rather on faithfully representing the whole report. By using this abstract, researchers looking for information on HSLA-100 steel, on fracture toughness tests, or on steel performance at low temperatures might find information enough to decide whether to read the whole report.

The description of a safety intervention that had been carried out at a navy mail center (found in a 2006 Naval Safety Center's online listing of "1,001 Safety Success Stories") is another good example of an informative abstract—although the Naval Safety Center terms it an "executive summary" (note the fungibility of naval titles for technical summaries).

"Ergonomics Intervention at COMNAVREG SW San Diego Mail Center Prevents Injuries"—A routine industrial hygiene survey identified several physical risk factors at the Commander Navy Region Southwest (COMNAVREG SW) San Diego Dockside Mail Center. Heavy lifting and working in awkward postures while processing the large volume of mail handled at NAVSTA San Diego Dockside Mail used to put its mail handlers at risk for work-related musculoskeletal disorders (WMSDs). Funding was provided through the Navy's Hazard Abatement and Mishap Prevention Program (HAMPP) to revamp the mail room service area and purchase ergonomically designed equipment. The estimated savings to the Navy are $41,433.00 every year for a return on investment in 519 days, or approximately one year and five months.

The Descriptive Abstract

A descriptive abstract simply describes from *an outside point of view* what the report contains. The descriptive abstract is a kind of prose table of contents. It serves the same general purpose as the informative abstract, but rather than reproducing the original report in small (like an informative abstract), the descriptive abstract *describes what the report contains.*

Here's an example of a descriptive abstract for an interim report that the Naval Postgraduate School at Monterey issued in 1987. The report is titled "Opportunities for Tropical Cyclone Motion Research in the Northwest Pacific Region" (author Scott A. Sandgathe).

Tropical cyclone track prediction problems in the Northwest Pacific region that need to be researched are reviewed from the perspective of the operational forecaster. This information is provided as background for the upcoming Office of Naval Research field experiment on tropical cyclone motion. A short-term climatology of the frequency and spatial distribution of tropical cyclones is provided. Seven classes of operationally interesting track forecast situations are described. Each cyclone from 1982 through 1985 is tabulated in terms of these classes.

Government and industry widely use both descriptive and informative abstracts. The informative abstract is generally more helpful, for it gives a reader more information. However, some kinds of research do not lend themselves easily to informative abstracts. Whichever kind you write, wait to compose the abstract (as you wait to draft your executive summary) until you have completed the final draft of your report. That way, you'll be sure you summarize only what is *actually in* the report.

Abstracts for Articles

Many technical journals require that authors submit abstracts along with the articles they submit for publication. These abstracts are used in abstract databases but also often preface the articles themselves. Following is an example of an abstract published in the PubMed online database, an abstract that prefaced an article published in 2004 in the journal *Military Medicine*. The article was titled "Viral gastroenteritis: The USS THEODORE ROOSEVELT experience."

Although the spread of disease on board Navy ships is not a novel concept, the medical department of the USS THEODORE ROOSEVELT recently experienced a significant outbreak of viral gastroenteritis while at sea. The impact on the crew and medical department is reviewed in this case report. The use of the Navy Disease Non–Battle Injury tracking system was validated. Furthermore, we proposed the placement of waterless, isopropyl alcohol-based hand-cleaning systems in strategic locations throughout the ship to help prevent and minimize the spread of future disease. Finally, more stringent recommendations regarding sick-in-quarters status and careful utilization of consumable resources are necessary components of an effective outbreak management strategy.

—Whittaker, D. R., Campbell, J. T., McCarten, M. N. D.,
Medical Department, USS THEODORE ROOSEVELT; report
published in *Military Medicine* 169 no. 9 (September 2004): 747–50.

This abstract focuses on the medical department's conclusions about the experience they went through. Half descriptive abstract and half executive summary, it typifies abstracts that preface articles in military journals.

"Key Words": Abstracts and Computers

Where will an investigator see an abstract? Now that libraries and researchers are making great use of computers, a researcher will typically turn to a computer abstracting service for online researching. The articles themselves may or may not also be available online.

If a researcher types in a key word or phrase in one of these computerized indexes, perhaps the term "missile detector radar," then the titles of all the recent articles on such radars will appear on the screen. The researcher can select some of these articles to investigate further, and the computer will put their abstracts on the screen as directed. By reading each abstract, the researcher decides whether to order the articles represented. By using computer links, researchers now have access to technical information from throughout the world.

On the Department of Defense "Report Documentation Page" (Standard Form 298), you'll not only supply an abstract, but you will also fill out a section called "Key Words." List there the terms that best indicate the substance of your report, both the subjects that it addresses directly and others that it touches on significantly. Take some care in selecting terms; don't make them too complex. In some cases, you'll have to conform to a printed list of standard terms.

For example, the documentation page for the article on tropical cyclone motion research (whose abstract appears above) listed "tropical cyclone motion," "tropical meteorology," "tropical cyclone path prediction," and "typhoon motion" as its key words.

PASSIVE VOICE AND NOUN STRINGS IN TECHNICAL WRITING

One other matter is noteworthy in the abstract on tropical cyclone motion reproduced above: It is written in the *passive voice.* Indeed, in that abstract *every sentence* is passive, the main verbs being "are reviewed," "is provided," "is provided," "are described," and "is tabulated." Because principles of plain English insist that you avoid the passive voice as a general rule, such heavy dependence on the passive calls for comment.

Passive voice is widespread in technical writing. Why? Mainly because scientists have purposely used passive voice for decades. Instead of stating, "the chemist observed the experiment," scientists have usually written, "the experiment was observed," not only writing in the passive voice but also omitting all mention of the person doing the observation. The rationale is that (1) normally the results of the scientific investigation are much more important than the investigator, and (2) passive verbs make the sentence more "objective."

This rationale is only *half* right. Using passive verbs does focus attention on the receiver of a sentence's action. Often the object of the action is more important than the actor and deserves more attention. To say, "The feasibility of ocean surveillance platforms in detecting submarines has repeatedly been demonstrated" focuses attention on that feasibility rather than on who demonstrated it, and that focus may be perfectly appropriate, depending on your purpose.

But realize that such a statement is in no way more objective than a statement that identifies who did the demonstrating. Changing a statement to say "it *was concluded* that low-flying aircraft would not cause mines to detonate" is no more objective than saying "*we concluded* that low flying aircraft would not cause mines to detonate." The way you write the sentence doesn't change the facts or the objectivity; someone must have drawn the conclusion in either case.

Understanding this concept, modern technical writing experts recommend much less use of the passive voice than they once did. So should you rigorously correct the passive voice in technical documents you have to chop or sign off on? That depends. In circumstances where such rewriting won't make much difference, or where it will be highly controversial (say, where your boss was trained to use the passive voice and deems doing otherwise unprofessional), the improvement probably will not be worth the effort. However, wherever passive voice adversely affects the readability of a document in a major way or when you anticipate that the document will have very high visibility, you should at least put the executive summary into mostly active voice and perhaps go on to rework the "Conclusions" and "Recommendations" sections as well.

Another major problem plaguing technical writing is the wide use of noun stacks or noun strings. Noun strings longer than three or four words such as "aircraft car-

> *"Passives are generally weak because they place a mushy emphasis on the thing done rather than on the doer. 'The battle was won by the Marines' is a flabby way of saying, 'The Marines won the battle.' 'I love you' is far more likely to get results than 'You are loved by me.'"*
> —ARGUS TRESIDDER, FORMER PROFESSOR OF ENGLISH, MCDEC, QUANTICO

rier crack arrestor applications" (from one of the abstracts above) or "Commander Navy Region Southwest San Diego Dockside Mail Center" (from another one) frequently occur in technical writing. Although scientists are accustomed to the use of noun stacks, when present in great numbers or stretched out at length, noun strings can also help to make a document almost unreadable and unclear as well. Keep an eye out for this tendency, and if you find many noun strings in your own writing, consider breaking some of them up by the use of prepositional phrases ("crack arrestor applications *in* aircraft carriers," for example, or "the San Diego Dockside Mail Center *of* Commander Navy Region Southwest").

For more on these and other problems that affect technical writing, see the section on Plain English in the opening chapter of this book.

OTHER TECHNICAL DOCUMENTS

Much of the writing in industry and business is very much like the writing in the naval services—letters, memos, and directives prevail in almost all organizations. While formats and styles differ from firm to firm, and one organization may use full-block style and another semi-block for its letters, a writer can usually recognize a letter anywhere and adapt to the required format quickly.

However, some technical documents differ greatly from standard naval correspondence or staff work. Such documents can be very troublesome for those naval personnel who have to compose them. Supply officers and others, for example, often have to write "specifications" for contracts. Also involved in the contracting process are "statements of work," which shipboard officers frequently have to write. While on staffs, many naval personnel will have to draft or revise "position descriptions," and then try to get those positions funded. Naval personnel will have to write many other technical documents from time to time.

You may find the office or lab you work with has put out a style guide to help you. If not, seek guidance for writing such documents from knowledgeable professionals, or from standard technical writing texts and sourcebooks such as those listed below.

REFERENCES ON TECHNICAL WRITING

The following are two very helpful civilian textbooks on technical writing. Both of them cover the basic kinds of technical reports (reports, proposals, progress reports, etc.) as well as abstracts, executive summaries, technical illustrations, and so on. Each has gone through several editions.

- Mike Markel, *Technical Communication* (New York; Bedford: St. Martin's, current edition).

- Paul V. Anderson, *Technical Writing: A Reader-Centered Approach* (New York: Harcourt Brace Jovanovich, current edition).

   Another useful text is this dictionary of technical-writing terms and concepts:

- Charles T. Brusaw, Gerald J. Alred, and Walter E. Oliu, *Handbook of Technical Writing* (New York: St. Martin's, current edition).

   An excellent guide to technical editing is

- Anne Eisenberg, *Guide to Technical Editing: Discussion, Dictionary, and Exercises* (New York: Oxford University Press, current edition). This is a very practical workbook, filled with examples and exercises.

A terrific workbook on editing in general (providing practice on all those rules about punctuation, grammar, and style that we all once learned and but often have forgotten) is

- *The Copyeditor's Guide to Substance & Style* (Alexandria, VA: EEI Press). The third edition of this text (published in 2006) includes almost fifty pages on electronic editing.

Finally, a technical style guide especially designed for those who work as online technical editors is

- *The Microsoft Manual of Style for Technical Publications* (Redmond, WA: The Microsoft Press, current edition).

Beyond this, many naval or other military offices have their own research guides, which can be very helpful. Some of these are oriented specifically toward historical research while others are more technically or operationally oriented. Good ones are put out by the Marine Corps Historical Center, the Naval War College, and the Naval Air Test Center.

An excellent research source for researching military articles is the *Air University Index of Military Periodicals* (its database includes naval as well as general military journals). This index is available online. Also online is the "Staff College Automated Military Periodical Index" (SCAMPI), an index of military periodicals put out by the Joint Forces Staff College.

Finally, one should also become familiar with the resources used widely by naval and defense researchers, specifically the abstracting services put out by the National Technical Information Service (NTIS), the Defense Technical Information Center (DTIC), and (for logistics) the Defense Logistics Agency (DLA). Depending on the topic, there are literally hundreds of abstracting services upon which naval researchers might call. Librarians and subject-matter experts are proficient in this kind of data retrieval.

10

JAG Manual Investigations

General Background

INTRODUCTION

A JAG Manual (JAGMAN) Investigation is basically a *management tool,* a means by which a command can gather the facts needed to make a decision. That decision might concern public or congressional inquiries, loss or compromise of classified material, claims for or against the government, destruction of property, accidents, injuries to personnel, or loss of life. Even minor investigations can have substantial effects.

When doing an investigation, you gather information, express considered opinions, and make careful recommendations that will help a commander (the "convening authority") make intelligent decisions. In some cases, people's careers depend on what appears in a JAGMAN Investigation. These investigations routinely affect medical retirement, disability pay, veteran's benefits, and promotion opportunities. In other cases, many thousands of dollars are at issue. As you can see, doing an investigation is a very important responsibility. Conducting one can also teach a person a good deal about command decision making.

The type of JAGMAN investigation covered in this chapter is the *Command Investigation.* It is the most common type and the one most often assigned to someone who has never done one before.

Another kind of investigation you might have to do is the *Litigation-Report Investigation,* which differs from the Command Investigation in that it targets incidents involving potential claims for or against the government. In many respects this investigation (designed partly to help protect government-privileged information in civil proceedings) resembles a Command Investigation except that the investigating officer in a Litigation-Report Investigation works directly under the supervision of a JAG officer and pays special attention to the rules involving claims. If you can do a Command Investigation, you'll be able to do the litigation one too (especially since you'll personally be given special instructions by a judge advocate). So in this chapter we limit our discussion mainly to the Command Investigation and still refer to it as a "JAGMAN Investigation," which continues to be its informal name.

One other brief legal survey you might be called upon to conduct is the *Preliminary Inquiry.* This is a preliminary search into an incident, designed to discover whether any investigation should be conducted at all, and if so, what kind. A Preliminary Inquiry of some sort (though often an extremely informal one) is supposed to precede most JAGMAN Investigations. A brief discussion of a Preliminary Inquiry (with a sample write-up) can be found at the end of this chapter.

The JAGMAN Investigation—In General

If you are assigned to conduct a JAGMAN Investigation, understand several important points.

First, a JAGMAN Investigation will normally become *your primary duty* until you complete it. Second, doing an investigation is an excellent opportunity to get the attention of your commanding officer because the CO will review and personally endorse your report once you complete it. The CO can ask you to do it over if it isn't as good as he or she thinks it should be. (On the other hand, as investigating officer, you can recommend that the CO enlarge, restrict, or modify the scope of the investigation or change any instruction in the appointing order.) Third, realize that this investigation will often go on up the line, through your boss's boss and maybe even higher, to the Office of the Judge Advocate General. Sometimes the CO will decide the investigation doesn't need to be forwarded—but often it will be.

Another point to remember: Should anyone have criticisms along the way, criticisms either of the report you prepare or of your command's way of doing business as reflected in the report, they won't be private. Your boss will hear of them for sure, and possibly many other officers as well. Those critiques could reflect both on you and on your ship or unit.

These investigations are not kept within the military either. Because of the Freedom of Information Act, they are not proprietary information, and virtually anyone can get copies. Unlike Litigation-Report Investigations, which are kept privileged, Command Investigations are routinely distributed; the office of the Judge Advocate General sends out thousands of copies a year. Next of kin, lawyers, reporters, members of Congress—all can request copies (and can almost always get them), and a JAGMAN Investigation involving the death of a service member goes to the next of kin as a matter of course.

"Our problems are that JAGMAN Investigations are usually shuffled off to people with little Navy experience."

—JAG Commander

Altogether, then, these investigations have very high potential visibility—possibly higher than anything else a junior officer or senior enlisted person will write. Moreover, with other important documents, a junior person will usually only draft them, not sign them, whereas that same person *will* sign the JAGMAN Investigation. All these factors—to say nothing of the most important matter of all, to see that justice and truth are served, both for the service member and for the Navy or Marine Corps itself—suggest you should do your very best with this demanding research/writing task.

What follows below is a quick (and, because of space limitations, necessarily incomplete) primer on doing a JAGMAN Investigation. Reading this section will serve as a starting point. Of course, *do not depend on this section alone, but go to the official sources,* especially the JAG Manual. Also consult official instructions,

Figure 10.1 An Executive Summary of JAGMAN Changes in the Form of a Message.

SURFLANT Message Summary of 1995 JAGMAN Changes

1. SECNAV approved Chg 2 to JAGMAN on 12 Mar 95. Mods are not superficial.

2. Goal is to conduct/review investigations only when value is added.

3. Preliminary Inquiry (PI) is first step, a quick and informal look at facts to see if additional action is required.

4. Based on PI, several options possible:
   A. Take no further action.
   B. Conduct a "Command Investigation" (formerly, "Informal Investigation").
   C. Convene new "Litigation-Report Investigation."
   D. Rarely, forward PI to General Courts-Martial authority for court or board of inquiry.
   —Command will report option chosen to ISIC.

5. "Command Investigation" will be most common type.
   A. Normally done as letter report.
   B. Upon completion, if of no interest outside command and not a mandatory investigation, cmd may treat as internal report.
   C. Guidance on convening authority endorsement is in JAGMAN 0209G, 0218.
   D. Routing of investigations has been changed drastically. Not routinely forwarded to JAG, but routed via chain of command to first flag officer, or higher authority as directed.
      (1) Some to CINCLANTFLT via chain (cf. LANTFLT Regs 2612)
      (2) Reports of fol. incidents to COMNAVSURFLANT to endorse:
          (A) Incidents with potential "lessons learned"
          (B) Collisions, groundings, fires, flooding involving SURFLANT ships
          (C) Aircraft accidents
          (D) Death cases
          (E) Adverse Line of Duty/Misconduct determinations
          (F) Loss or destruction of govt property over $1,000, or when due to negligence or theft
          (G) Incidents involving poss. environmental hazards or pollution
          (H) Possible compromise of classified material
          (I) Any other matter a subordinate GCMA thinks COMNAVSURFLANT should review.
      (3) For reports other than (1) or (2), first GCMA will be final review.
      (4) Copies to be provided IAW JAGMAN 0209G and H, and 0219.
   E. Investigation is final when last reviewing GCMA determines further endorsement not necessary.

                              —an abbreviated form of an unnumbered
                               ALSURFLANTFLT issued to summarize JAGMAN
                               changes and apply them to SURFLANT.
                               Reprinted by permission.

chain of command directives, and the other helpful guides that are available (see the next section). As you'll see, many sources are available to help you both *do* and *write up* this kind of investigation.

REFERENCES ON JAGMAN INVESTIGATIONS

- Article 31, UCMJ.
- Manual of the Judge Advocate General (JAG Manual or JAGMAN). This is, of course, the standard reference on JAGMAN Investigations, as on many other things

    Of special importance for JAGMAN Investigations are the sections in the JAG Manual on:
    — Privacy Act compliance
    — the Appointing Order
    — the Investigative Report itself
    — Line-of-Duty and Misconduct Determinations
    — Injury/Disease Warnings
    — Article 31 Warnings
    — Investigations of Specific Types of Incidents
    — Checklists of Various Kinds
    — Claims for or against the Government
- JAGMAN Investigation Handbook, put out by the Naval Justice School (NJS)— for detailed guidance on investigations, including checklists and sample documents of many kinds.
- OPNAVINST 5510.1 series, Security Manual. See the sections and exhibits discussing JAGMAN Investigations.
- MILPERSMAN, Section 4210100—for death cases.
- Checklists and instructions issued by the local JAG officials and various type and administrative commanders.

PRELIMINARY STEPS WHEN ASSIGNED A JAGMAN INVESTIGATION

Some officers in the fleet and field say that the problem with a JAGMAN Investigation is not writing the report but doing the investigating. They argue that the tough part is digging down to the underlying, determining facts of the case. However, those people who review JAGMAN Investigations insist (from having read dozens) that the writing is a big problem too. So we'll look at both tasks. We'll start by discussing what you should do to begin your investigation.

- First, read the whole section on JAGMAN Investigations in this book, for general familiarity. As you do, pay special attention to the various terms and concepts involved.
- Then, read the appointing order very carefully. It is your basic marching order, and it should address your specific investigation. If you don't understand any item in the appointing order, ask the "convening authority" (which is usually your CO) about it. Further, if during your investigation you feel that you should broaden or narrow the scope of the inquiry, or that you need to change any instructions in the appointing order, submit a request (orally or in writing) to the convening authority. Realize too that any single JAGMAN Investigation should cover *only one* incident. If you find you're really investigating two or three separate incidents, report this early on.

- Get hold of an updated JAG Manual, and review the sections mentioned specifically in the appointing order and those listed under "References," above, especially those sections involving your particular case. For instance, if you must make a line-of-duty/misconduct determination, be sure to review that section of the JAGMAN; if you are investigating a death, review the section on death cases; and so on.

- Take a look at some recently completed JAGMAN Investigations from files at your ship or station, and/or the samples and guidance in the NJS handbook. Reading a few will give you more familiarity with what they look like and, perhaps more important, what they customarily look *into*. The examples later in this chapter will provide a start.

- Talk to an officer (or chief) aboard your ship or station who has done investigations before or who has been to a naval school on this or related subjects. This officer should be able to give you both practical advice and good written guidance.

- However, if this person is also the ship's or station's legal officer, he or she might have to keep a distance from the case. If it goes to mast or trial, this person may be required to get involved in the case later. Beyond this, the legal officer will usually have to draft the first endorsement for the CO.

- Find out where the local staff JAG is, or if that officer is not available locally, seek another naval lawyer (perhaps at a local Naval Legal Services Office) who might be able to give you some help. Most staff JAGs are more than willing to discuss with you how to go about an investigation, and later they will be glad to look at a rough draft. Indeed, *some staff JAGs expect you to visit them first* and then to send them a rough draft before you formally submit your report. Such a review will often save them time later. (Of course, don't communicate with the staff JAG unless your CO first gives consent.)

- Don't forget to take counsel from those in your own chain of command, such as the executive officer. JAG officers are not necessarily attuned to the special sensitivities of operational commands or all the intricacies of shipboard situations.

- Whoever you talk to, make sure you get a good feeling for
  — where to go for information;
  — what to look for;
  — who to talk to;
  — what kind and number of questions to ask;
  — any available checklists concerning the specific kind of incident you are investigating, beyond those discussed below (see the section "Pointers on Conducting the Investigation"); and
  — when to stop investigating and start writing.

IMPORTANT FEATURES OF INVESTIGATIONS

Privacy Act Statements

As the investigating officer, you must ask individuals to sign Privacy Act Statements whenever you request them to disclose private (personal) information about themselves. Such situations, however, are *not* the rule, and you should *avoid unnecessary use of the Privacy Act Statement.*

During an investigation into a loss of funds, for example, if you ask an accountable individual to disclose his or her personal financial status, this disclosure is subject to the Privacy Act. But asking a service member to account for actions when on watch, to recount actions in the course of official duties, or to relate events observed

> *"Line officers think that to ask for help is a sign of weakness."*
>
> —Chief Legalman

> *"Once a lawsuit is filed, it is likely the investigating officer will have been transferred and witnesses will have left the area. It is time-consuming, frustrating, and often counter-productive to try to reconstruct an incident or correct a slip-shod investigation after months or years have passed."*
>
> —JAGMAN Investigations Handbook, Naval Justice School

in the course of routine activities is *not* a request for private information and does not require a Privacy Act warning statement.

The requirement for a Privacy Act Statement is spelled out in the JAGMAN, and a format for one can be found in a JAGMAN appendix. Very good formats appear in an appendix to the NJS handbook and in many local instructions.

Social Security Numbers

Watch how you use social security numbers (SSNs). As a rule, don't solicit SSNs from individuals. In most cases, including SSNs in JAGMAN Investigations is simply not necessary.

Injury/Disease Warnings

"We have only seven officers, so chiefs do a lot of JAGMANS."
—XO, Naval Station

Don't ask service members about the origin or aggravation of any disease or injury or disability they have suffered without first advising them of their statutory rights not to make such a statement. Have them sign JAGMAN Warnings that they have read and understood their rights before proceeding with interviews. Again, a proper warning form is in an appendix of the NJS handbook.

Article 31 Warning

Whenever a person is suspected of committing an offense under the UCMJ, you must advise that person of his or her rights under Article 31, UCMJ, before proceeding with any questions. These so-called Article 31 Rights include the right to remain silent, the right to consult with a lawyer, and the right to terminate the interview at any time, as well as the warning that any statements made might be used against that person in trial by court-martial. (A proper warning form is in an appendix of the JAG Manual and also in the NJS handbook.)

Line-of-Duty/Misconduct Determinations

Perhaps the most common JAGMAN Investigations are cases of injury and disease. Here a major part of your responsibility is to help your commanding officer make a "line-of-duty/misconduct" determination, that is, to help the chain of command determine (1) if an injury incurred "in the line of duty" and (2) whether it involved misconduct—two separate determinations. Many rights and benefits depend on these determinations.

What constitutes "line of duty," and what is "misconduct"? Put briefly, the service presumes you've incurred any injuries or diseases "in the line of duty" unless clear and convincing evidence exists otherwise. What would such evidence be? If a service member incurred an injury as a result of misconduct, while deserting, or while an unauthorized absentee in excess of 24 hours, then the injury might be regarded as "not in the line of duty."

A finding of "misconduct," on the other hand, would come about if an investigation clearly showed that (1) a service member intentionally incurred an injury or (2) that it was "the proximate result of such gross negligence as to demonstrate a reckless disregard of the consequences." These rules are pretty clear, but of course pinning down individual cases can be tricky.

Specific relationships exist between misconduct and line of duty. For example, a determination of misconduct always requires a determination of "not in the line of duty." To put the whole issue simply, the finding must be one of these three:

1. In the line of duty, not due to own misconduct.
2. Not in the line of duty, not due to own misconduct.
3. Not in the line of duty, due to own misconduct.

Consult the JAGMAN section on "Line-of-Duty and Misconduct Determinations." In particular, study the special rules on intoxication, on mental responsibility, and on suicidal acts and gestures to make sure you fully understand these determinations.

You should realize also that a determination of misconduct is not a punitive measure. While it may directly affect such compensations as VA benefits, medical retirement, and disability pay, a favorable or unfavorable determination has no binding power on any issue of guilt or innocence in a disciplinary proceeding. Of course, an investigator has the responsibility to draw up specific charges if the investigation suggests they are warranted. But the determinations of "line of duty" and "misconduct" are administrative rather than judicial determinations.

Indeed, once having had an injury investigated, a commander may report the LOD/misconduct determination informally by an entry in a health record, on a form 5800/15, or in a letter report. The commander does not have to have to send the JAGMAN Investigation up the chain. Many investigators forget this possibility. As a senior judge advocate once remarked:

> My advice to commands/investigating officers is to use the documentation vehicle that requires the least amount of work and that is sufficient to protect the rights of the service member and the interests of the government. I am not suggesting that we look for ways to avoid work. What I mean is that you should use health or dental record entries and forms or letter reports (in accordance with JAGMAN) when appropriate. I see too many JAG Manual Investigations that did not need to be done.

See the decision tree on LOD/misconduct reporting in figure 10.2 for a step-by-step approach to deciding whether a JAGMAN Investigation is actually required.

GENERAL GUIDELINES FOR LOD/ MISCONDUCT DETERMINATIONS

The following are guidelines to follow concerning LOD/misconduct determinations. These guidelines are in addition to other guidelines for JAGMAN Investigations.

- Ensure you understand fully line of duty, misconduct, the relationship between these concepts, and all special rules involved.
- Make sure you make a finding of fact as to the leave, liberty, or duty status of any injured person.
- See that the investigation clarifies the nature and extent of all injuries and includes the place, extent, and cause of any hospitalization. Especially ensure that you differentiate periods of alcohol or drug impairment and periods of psychiatric treatment.
- Ensure that you state clearly the *amount of lost work time,* if any, as a finding of fact. If the injured person is still disabled when you submit the report, *include a medical officer's prognosis.*
- The convening authority will afford a JAGMAN hearing to any service member who is thought to have been injured or diseased either "not in the line of duty" or "due to his own misconduct" and will append the hearing results as an enclosure

"Always remember—
Mom *is the ultimate recipient of a death investigation. The family's anguish of death is compounded by your stating in the investigation that 'SN Smith was a scumbag.' There's no reason to say that even if it's true."*

—Chief Legalman

Figure 10.2 A Decision Tree on Line-of-Duty/Misconduct Reporting. This decision tree aids an investigating officer in determining what kind of report is required.

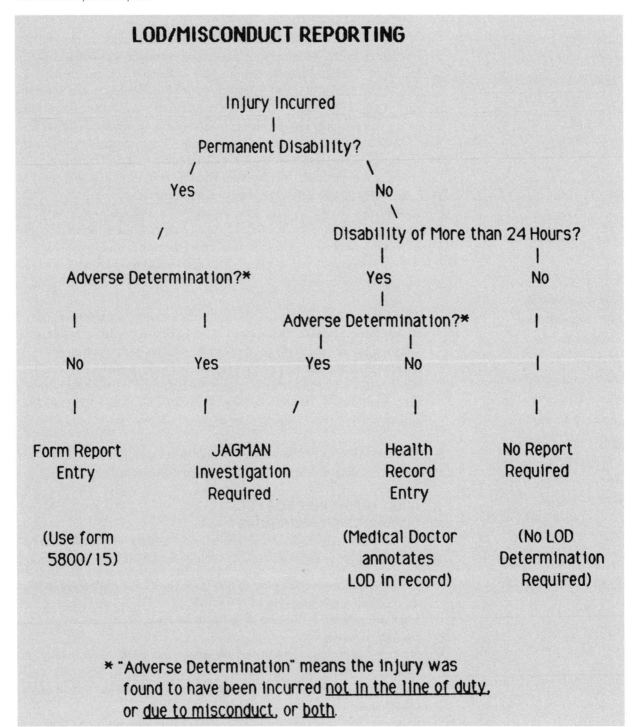

LOD/MISCONDUCT REPORTING

Injury Incurred
|
Permanent Disability?
/   \
Yes   No
\
/   Disability of More than 24 Hours?
| |
Adverse Determination?*   Yes   No
|
| | Adverse Determination?* |
| | | | |
No   Yes   Yes   No |
| | / | |
Form Report   JAGMAN   Health   No Report
Entry   Investigation   Record   Required
               Required   Entry

(Use form   (Medical Doctor   (No LOD
5800/15)   annotates   Determination
                                             LOD in record)   Required)

* "Adverse Determination" means the injury was
found to have been incurred <u>not in the line of duty,</u>
or <u>due to misconduct,</u> or <u>both</u>.

"I remember doing one JAGMAN investigation in my career; I was a lieutenant. Supply reported they had lost a clear plastic canopy for an F-18. How do you lose a canopy? The canopy had cost the Navy $273,000.

"So I began the investigation, and started a round of interviewing. I was still working on it two days later, when Supply called me up: 'We found it!' It's remarkable how quickly you can find something when they begin to take it out of your pay. . . ."

—NAVY CAPTAIN

"The Convening Authority will prescribe when the report is due, normally 30 days from the date of the convening order."

—JAGMAN
INVESTIGATIONS
HANDBOOK, NAVAL
JUSTICE SCHOOL

to the first endorsement to the investigation. Appropriate hearing forms are in the appendixes to the JAGMAN.

- Fill out a line-of-duty/misconduct checklist as you conduct your investigation. See JAGMAN, NJS publications, or local directives.
- Finally, place your opinion as to the LOD/Misconduct determination in the *Opinions* section of the investigation.

POINTERS ON CONDUCTING THE INVESTIGATION

Get the Right Checklists

Assemble all the relevant checklists. There are the two standard ones—the first is the JAGMAN section on the "Investigative Report," which is an overall guide on doing the investigation; the second, the JAGMAN "Checklist for Fact-Finding Bodies," which is a line-of-duty/misconduct checklist. Then there are many special checklists. Several— "aircraft accidents," "vehicle accidents," "explosions," "postal violations," and many more—can be found in the JAGMAN section on "Investigations of Specific Types of Incidents" and in the NJS Handbook.

There are also locally prepared checklists, some of which deal with events that commonly occur in a particular type of ship or unit, and others that cover standard situations even more thoroughly than the JAG Manual. You should ask about these lists as you talk to your XO, local JAG, and other JAG officers. Indeed, sometimes you will find you are *required* to follow a special checklist. In any case, local lists may help you greatly in figuring out what to look for and in making sure you've researched all the right data. They'll tell you what witnesses to interview and the kinds of documents to seek out, and sometimes they'll suggest physical evidence to look for too.

If a single incident you are investigating involves more than one of the categories specifically listed in the JAG Manual section entitled "Investigations of Specific Types of Incidents," you should go through the checklist for *each category* that is involved.

Make Careful Plans before Interviewing Witnesses

- Have a plan for going about your interviews. Do them in a reasonable order. Again make sure you know what warnings to give (see JAGMAN on warnings and Article 31, UCMJ), and be sure you give them in each case.
- You should ordinarily collect relevant information from all other sources prior to interviewing persons suspected of an offense or improper performance of duty, though don't delay interviewing when people are likely to transfer or deploy soon. When the interview begins, make sure you give the proper warning (see above), and afterward document your warnings.
- Also, for witnesses suspected of an offense or other difficult witnesses, make sure you have done your homework. Research the case as best you can before you see them, write down some questions ahead of time, check with lawyers, and so on. The more complex the case, the more homework you'll want to do before you talk to the key people.
- Conducting interviews in person is best—but for witnesses out of town or otherwise hard to reach, you can conduct telephone, mail, message, or even e-mail interviews (though remember that mail will take a while). For each oral interview, prepare a written memorandum for record, setting down the substance of

the conversation, the time and date it took place, full identification of the inter-viewees, and any rights or warnings provided.

- Begin an in-person investigation by sitting down with the person, giving out a voluntary statement form, and asking the person to write down all relevant facts surrounding the incident. Then ask specific questions orally if you want to make sure you cover particular points. Work any oral responses into a final draft of the person's statement, and have the individual review the statement as soon as possible.

- When taking a statement from anyone, be sure to phrase it in the actual language of the witness. Try to have the witness sign it, but if the witness cannot or will not, certify it yourself to be an accurate summary or the verbatim transcript of oral statements the witness made.

- Most importantly, be sure the witnesses speak as factually and specifically as pos-sible. Vague statements such as "pretty drunk," "a few beers," and "pretty fast" do not specify events clearly enough to be very helpful. Try to pin the witness down. For example, instead of accepting "pretty drunk," use a series of questions:
  — How long did you observe this person?
  — How clear was his speech?
  — Did you observe him walk?
  — What was the condition of his eyes?
  — What did he smell like?
  — What was he drinking?
  — Exactly how much had he drunk?
  — Over what period of time? etc.

Look for Relevant Documents and Physical Evidence

General

In general, include whatever of the following may be useful as real or documentary evidence: photographs, records, operating logs, directives, watch lists, pieces of damaged equipment, sketches, military or civilian police accident reports, autopsy reports, hospitalization or clinical records, etc. (although watch out for Privacy Act problems with the last). The NJS handbook contains good guidelines for collecting each kind of evidence. Below are a few guidelines for particular types of cases. See the JAGMAN checklists for additional pointers on your specific case. Also see the section "Documents and Enclosures," following, for further guidance on documen-tary evidence.

Automobile Accidents

In cases involving an automobile accident, include maps, charts, diagrams, or photo-graphs of an accident scene or of a vehicle or other evidence, as needed. Identify the date and subject matter of any photographs. You can write notes and refer to directions, objects, or elevations, and attach those references to the reverse of the photo, if helpful. Note that photos used as enclosures, like the rest of the investiga-tion, are subject to public release under the Freedom of Information Act. So normally don't include gruesome photos of dead bodies or bloody weapons, beds, floors, and the like.

Death

In the case of a death, make sure that the death certificate supports a finding of fact as to the *time* and *cause* of death. (However, don't wait to submit a death investigation beyond the mandatory processing time if you still haven't obtained the death certificate; instead, send the investigation on, noting "death certificate to follow." When the certificate comes, send it on to whomever holds the investigation at the time.)

LOD/Misconduct

In LOD/misconduct cases, locate and include documentary evidence that substantiates the member's duty status at the time of any injury, disease, or death. This evidence could be an email or message report of the member's duty status, certified copies of service record documents, or a written statement from the division officer, platoon leader, personnel officer, or other person authorized to grant liberty or record leave status. *Note:* An unsupported statement by the investigating officer as to the duty status of the individual is not an acceptable substitute for documentary evidence of such status.

Don't Combine JAGMAN Investigations with Other Investigations

More than one kind of investigation may go on with respect to any one incident. Make sure your JAGMAN Investigation is completely separate from (and has no reference to) any Aircraft Mishap Investigation Reports, Inspector General Reports, or Medical Quality Assurance Investigations that are under way. Do not include any reference at all to polygraph examinations. Do not make any use of the narrative of any Naval Criminal Investigative Service (NCIS) investigation that may be going on.

However, you may use the *exhibits* of an NCIS investigation in your report. NCIS investigators are usually extremely thorough and professional about giving warnings, questioning, and so on. If you know the NCIS is talking to someone you would also like to talk to (say, about misconduct), you might go on with other aspects of your investigation, and then ask to see (and use in your report, if pertinent) advance copies of applicable statements by witnesses or like NCIS exhibits. This way you might find that part of your work is already done. Of course, you may then have to conduct additional interviews on your own. On this whole subject, see JAGMAN on "Noncombinable Investigations" or "Investigations Required by Other Regulations."

Follow These Additional Guidelines

- Get started quickly. Witnesses will be more likely to be on hand and to have fresh memories, ships or units may still be in the area, and damaged equipment/materials are more apt to be in the same relative position and condition if you get to them quickly.
- Be careful to observe the time limits typically specified, that is, thirty days to complete an investigation from the date of the investigator's appointment.
- Be far-seeing, and request any delay as soon as you see a need for one. But try your best to get the investigation done quickly. Some investigations stretch over months because of unforeseen ship movements, TAD, or other such interruptions. If you are not alert, important witnesses may suddenly turn out to be hundreds of miles away or even out of the country because of transfer or deployment.
- You may acquire evidence in any reasonable manner, and the formal rules of evidence required for courts-martial do not bind investigating officers. The reason is that a JAGMAN Investigation is purely administrative in nature and not judicial. Its report is strictly advisory, and its opinions are not final determinations or legal judgments. On the other hand, if investigating officers uncover good evidence for use in criminal actions related to the investigation, you may invalidate the evidence if, in acquiring it, you have ignored rules of evidence. So keep your wits about you here too.

On two different audiences for a JAGMAN Investigation: "There are two dragon's mouths to avoid, and they read the investigation in different ways. The staff JAG, the attorney, looks to see if you followed the regulations, if you jumped through all the hoops. Was the checklist completed, was the specific language used? The flag, on the other hand, looks for readability and the bottom line. And he doesn't appreciate legalese."

—Marine JAG Major

- Remember, the overall purpose of your investigation is to tell a *complete story,* to answer the standard questions who, what, where, when, how, and why. As you go through your investigation, keep brainstorming with these six basic questions in mind until you're sure you've answered them all.
- Realize, of course, that investigations containing sensitive matter must be classified. See OPNAVINST 5510.1 and appropriate sections of the JAGMAN.
- Remember that if at any time in your work you find you are investigating possible claims for or against the government, you should probably be doing a Litigation-Report Investigation (rather than a Command Investigation). Immediately inform your CO and be guided by his or her direction.
- Having considered all the above, begin your investigation.

Writing the JAGMAN Investigation—Section by Section

"Investigators need to simplify, think logically, spell out acronyms, and use Plain English. Otherwise, readers can get awfully frustrated."

—JAG Captain

Because these reports have a stipulated format, the paragraphs below contain a detailed discussion of how to write *each section* of the JAGMAN Investigation. You shouldn't begin writing immediately, however. Instead, first work on grouping the facts. By making use of outlines or note cards, you can work to see the main structures in your material. You can fit all the facts together, separating them from the opinions and recommendations. If you have many facts, you can try different patterns for them.

First focus on the big picture that your report will present. Then proceed to paint in all the details according to the requirements of each individual section of the report, as discussed below. Look to the examples for guidance; although all the personal names included are fictional, the examples have been carefully crafted to resemble actual JAGMAN Investigations.

One other thing. When you read JAGMAN Investigations and other legal writing, you'll notice that writers use the passive voice widely (alongside other legalisms). Normally there is no need to. As much as possible, write in active voice here as in other naval writing.

SUBJECT LINE

Subject lines for JAGMAN Investigations differ from other subject lines chiefly in their length; don't be concerned if you need three to five lines to identify the incident thoroughly. Usually, the subject line will be the same one specified in the appointing order—but you may find it needs to be amended. In any case, the subject line should use ALL CAPS, begin with the word "INVESTIGATION," and then go on to cite:

1. The *basic nature* of the incident, i.e., an accident, a collision;
2. The *identity* of the unit or ship that was involved in the incident, or of the service member who was involved, or both;
3. The *date* the incident occurred or was discovered.

Examples of Subject Lines

Here are two good subject lines. Each of them identifies the *nature* of the incident, the *identity* of the unit or individual involved, and the *date.*

Subject: INVESTIGATION INTO THE CIRCUMSTANCES SURROUNDING THE SHORTAGE OF FUNDS IN THE SHIP'S STORE ON BOARD

USS COONTZ (DDG 40) WHICH WAS DISCOVERED IN JANUARY 1988

Subject: INVESTIGATION TO INQUIRE INTO THE CIRCUMSTANCES CONNECTED WITH THE PHYSICAL INJURY/ACCIDENT THAT OCCURRED ON 13 FEBRUARY 1992 INVOLVING SERGEANT GEORGE F. W————, USMC

LIST OF ENCLOSURES

The JAG Manual requires that the appointing order be the first enclosure to a JAG-MAN Investigation, and it should usually be followed by any requests for extension. List subsequent enclosures in the order mentioned in the investigation. See the complete JAGMAN Investigation later in this chapter for an example of a list of enclosures.

PRELIMINARY STATEMENT

In the preliminary statement you inform the convening authority of the nature of the investigation and of any difficulties you had in complying with the appointing order or in procuring evidence. Also call attention to any other difficulties encountered in this particular investigation. First refer to the appointing order, and then comment on as many of the following as are pertinent:

- the general nature of the investigation
- whether you carried out the appointing order and all other directives of the convening authority (some may prove to be impossible)
- any difficulties encountered, including difficulties in gathering information or in ascertaining a particular fact
- conflicts in evidence, if any, and how you resolved them
- reasons for any delay (you should have requested one earlier, and the written request and approval will be enclosures, but still mention the reasons in the preliminary statement)
- the name and organization of any judge advocate consulted
- whether you have advised persons of various rights, as required
- a note of any refusal by a service member to sign or make a statement concerning disease or injury
- any other preparatory information necessary for a complete understanding of the case

DO NOT include a synopsis of the facts here—the findings of facts should tell the basic story. DO NOT include opinions or recommendations. DO NOT include your own itinerary for doing the investigation.

Examples of Preliminary Statements

The preliminary statement below explains several of the items mentioned above:

PRELIMINARY STATEMENT

1. Following reference (a) and enclosure (1), a command investigation was conducted to inquire into the circumstances surrounding injuries sustained by Petty Officer Second Class Jack M. Sweetman in an automobile accident on 25 October 1995.

2. I encountered difficulties obtaining the police report from the Orleans Parish Police Department and the medical bills from Mercy Hospital. An extension was granted to 21 November (Encl (2) and (3)).

"We had one guy who went through all of a unit's instructions and reported all their typos in the findings of fact. Tailor the report, filter the information, stay focused. If you feel this information needs to be said, say it briefly in the preliminary statement: 'The instructions, incidentally, were riddled with errors.'"

—JAG EXPERT

3. Although several enclosures indicate that Petty Officer Sweetman had been drinking, the report on his blood alcohol analysis was not available at the time of this report.

Most preliminary statements are shorter; the one below specifically mentions the advising of rights:

"I approach each investigation with this attitude: I don't know what happened—this investigation is supposed to explain it to me."

—JAG Lieutenant Commander

PRELIMINARY STATEMENT

1. As directed by enclosure (1) and in accordance with reference (a), an investigation was conducted to inquire into the circumstances surrounding the damage sustained by SH-3H BUNO 152131 (also described in this report by its MODEX number, 519) on board USS KITTY HAWK at or about 2200, 17 March 1984. There were no difficulties encountered in obtaining evidence or information required to complete the investigation; all parties interviewed provided testimony or cooperated fully in all respects. The investigating officer consulted LCDR Jeffrey A. T——, USN, Command Judge Advocate, USS KITTY HAWK, on several occasions.

2. Based upon testimony received, AA John R. J—— and AA Earl F. R —— were warned that they might be suspected of dereliction of duty and were advised of their rights under Article 31, UCMJ.

FINDINGS OF FACT

In the findings-of-fact section, the investigating officer assembles all pertinent evidence. Strive to present the reviewer with an accurate picture of *exactly what happened* —the specifics as to times, places, and events—in the most logical and clear manner possible.

Although the JAG Manual states that you may group facts into narrative form, most JAG officers find this format cumbersome to work with and recommend that you *list each fact separately.* Once you're sure you have all the facts, assembling the information *chronologically* is usually best; normally a chronological order is more coherent for the reader.

Admittedly more than one series of events may have been taking place simultaneously, and you'll have to adjust by first narrating one series of events and then going back chronologically to describe another. Don't jump around aimlessly, leaving facts in haphazard order, or you will confuse the reader as to exactly what did happen. Do your best to be as coherent as possible. As an 0-5 JAG on a major type command's staff remarked, "I can tell a good investigation if, after reading the findings of fact, I can tell what happened. The biggest problem is that often investigators don't tell a narrative story."

For each finding of fact you must reference an enclosure. However, your treatment should be so clear that the reader doesn't need to look up an enclosure to understand what happened.

Follow these additional guidelines:

- State each fact with definiteness.
- Number each finding of fact, and make sure you support each fact with one or more specified enclosures (one of which might be the observations of the investigating officer).

- Include a specific finding of fact as to the time of any death and cause of the death, supported by a certificate of death or statement by a doctor or medical officer. (Again, don't hold the investigation to wait for the certificate.)
- If a finding of fact is based upon your personal knowledge as investigating officer, provide the basis for your personal knowledge in a signed memo for record.
- Make sure you've questioned all material witnesses. (If not, explain why not in the preliminary statement.)
- Don't include extraneous information. While investigators often err by *leaving information out* of an investigation, you can also *include too much*. Officials at one major command recounted a report that was virtually unreadable because it had 2,300 findings of fact—many of them simply unnecessary.
- On the other hand, make sure to record the right kinds of data for the kind of investigation at hand—road and visibility conditions in an automobile accident, alertness of the watch team in a collision, etc. Again, *checklists* for each kind of investigation will help you know exactly what to look for in each case. *Double check these checklists* as you draw up your findings of fact.

Examples of Findings of Fact

Example of a Poor Findings of Fact Section from a Report on a Vehicle Accident

The excerpt below is representative of reports that *fail to tell a coherent story*. The writer lists facts randomly, showing neither chronological nor logical order, so it's very hard to tell exactly what happened by reading the report. As it turns out, endorsers had to add several additional findings of fact (speed of the vehicles, the speed limit, etc.) to this report.

FINDINGS OF FACT

1. That LCDR W—— did not hold U.S. Government Motor Vehicle Operator's Identification Card (CT-14) in his possession at the time of the accident. (encls (2), (5))
2. That immediately following the accident, the Fort Polk Military Police were notified. (encl (2))
3. That Mrs. Mary J —— was within posted speed limits on Magnolia Avenue. (encl (2))
4. That LCDR W—— did fail to yield right-of-way to westbound traffic on Magnolia Avenue after having made a complete stop on General Lee Boulevard. (encls (2), (5))
5. That LCDR W—— was on official business at the time of the accident. (encls 121,151)
6. That LCDR W—— holds a valid state driver's license. (encl (2))
7. That LCDR W—— observed pavement markings (stop line) on General Lee Boulevard. (encls (2), (5))
8. That LCDR W—— made a sworn statement to Fort Polk Military Police concerning the accident. (encls (2), (5))

Example of a Good Findings of Fact Section on an Accident

The report below follows rough chronological order and tells a coherent story. When it has to shift from the events to describe one of the drivers and a vehicle, it follows a logical train in that discussion too.

7. That Lance Corporal A—— was involved in a motor vehicle accident at 1600 on 22 March 1988. (encl (6))

8. That the accident occurred on the Elysian Expressway, Shreveport, Louisiana. (encl (6))

9. That Lance Corporal A—— was driving eastbound on the Elysian Expressway when he lost control of his vehicle. (encl (6))

10. That Lance Corporal A—— lost control of his vehicle because of a blowout in a tire on his vehicle. (encls (5), (6), and (8))

11. That the blowout caused the vehicle Lance Corporal A—— was driving to cross the cement median and collide head-on with Ms. J——'s vehicle. (encls (6) and (8))

12. That there were only two vehicles in the subject accident. (encl (6))

13. That Lance Corporal A—— was driving a 1976 Ford Mustang bearing Louisiana license plate number 579X203. (encl (6))

14. That the vehicle identification number for the vehicle that Lance Corporal A—— was driving is 4D05V465698. (encl (6))

15. That there is no record that Lance Corporal A—— is the registered owner of the vehicle he was driving. (encl (6))

16. That the Police Officer who investigated the subject accident ran a check on the license plate on Lance Corporal A——'s vehicle to determine if the vehicle was stolen or had any outstanding citation. Officer M—— discovered that the license tag on Lance Corporal A——'s vehicle was assigned to a 1980 Volkswagen Rabbit owned by a Mr. Ralph A. T——. (encl (6))

17. That when questioned by Officer M——, Lance Corporal A—— indicated that he had found the license plate and placed it on his vehicle. (encl (6))

18. That Lance Corporal A—— was cited for a total of six traffic law violations, consisting of no driver's license on person, no brake tag, no proof of liability insurance, switched license plates, no license plate, and no registration papers. (encl (6))

Especially in longer reports, you can divide the findings of fact up into sections that are logically complete in themselves. In a report on damage to an aircraft, damage that occurred while it was being towed about the hangar spaces of an aircraft carrier, for example, the investigating officer divided the findings of fact into these coherent sections:

Environmental Conditions
Personnel Qualifications
Equipment Condition and Documentation
Circumstances Surrounding the Damage

OPINIONS

Opinions are logical inferences that flow from the findings of fact. List only those opinions required by the appointing order—that is, those required by regulations (such as the various "Line-of-Duty and Misconduct" and "Investigation of Specific Types of Incidents" sections of the JAG Manual)—or opinions naturally pertinent to the case. A good opinions section will seem to flow so naturally from the findings of fact that the opinions seem virtually self-evident.

The biggest mistake made in this section is to begin with preconceived opinions and try to prove them despite evidence to the contrary. Be sure to be open-minded in your investigation, follow where the facts lead, and dig deeply enough to get those *key* facts that bear *significant inferences.* Beyond those basics,

"Don't take the investigation personally—lots of times the opinions are not supported by the findings of fact, and are emotionally charged. Don't let such things as your bias against alcohol affect the tone of your report."

—JAG EXPERT

- Number each opinion separately.
- Support each opinion by explicit reference to one or more findings of fact (abbreviated "FF").
- Don't confuse facts with opinions. (This confusion is unfortunately very common; too often, opinions appear as findings of fact.)
- Remember that you must include an opinion on line-of-duty/misconduct in a case involving injury or disease, but that you never include line-of-duty/misconduct opinions in an investigation into the death of a service member (see the section on LOD misconduct, above).

Examples of Opinions Sections

The following opinions section is from a line-of-duty/misconduct investigation; note the reference to specific findings of fact in each opinion.

OPINIONS

1. That, due to the length of LCpl K——'s unauthorized absence prior to his injuries (seven days), his absence materially interfered with the performance of his required military duties. (FF (1), (2), (4))
2. That LCpl K——'s injuries were not sustained in the line of duty. (FF (1), (2), (4))
3. That LCpl K—— was under the influence of alcohol. (FF (6))
4. That the minor injuries received by LCpl K—— during the motor vehicle accident were proximate results of the influence of alcohol and demonstrated a reckless disregard of the consequences. (FF (4), (5), (6))
5. That the minor injuries received by LCpl K—— in the motor vehicle accident were due to his own misconduct. (FF (4), (5), (6))
6. That LCpl K—— handled a firearm in a grossly negligent manner and demonstrated a reckless disregard of the consequences. (FF (6), (8), (9))
7. That LCpl K—— willfully violated a law of the state of North Dakota by assaulting a police officer with a firearm. (FF (9), (15))
8. That the injuries received by LCpl K—— from gunshots were due to his own misconduct. (FF (6), (8), (9), (11), (13), (14), (15))

"They try to do the JAGMAN too quickly. They shouldn't be thinking of opinions and recommendations before they've got all the Findings of Fact."

—CHIEF LEGALMAN

The following example is from a report on contamination of an enlisted dining facility. Note the clear, conclusive statement of opinions and the use of underlining to point those summary opinions. (*Note:* This example was taken from an investigation written prior to Change 2 to the JAGMAN, which introduced the Litigation-Report Investigation. Clearly, since this case involves claims by the government, it would now properly be the subject of the litigation investigation and would be done under the direction of a JAG officer.)

OPINIONS

1. During the course of authorized work to remove sealant from the deck tiles of the Enlisted Dining Facility's galley, the Contractor deviated from the approved plan. He introduced an unapproved chemical (muriatic acid),

and used that chemical in a careless manner by failing to follow the directions of LT B—— or the labels on the boxes and jugs. Muriatic acid mist spread from the work sites throughout the galley, contaminating and damaging the building and equipment in the building. The Contractor's unapproved use of muriatic acid was the direct cause of the damage. (FF (4), (5), (11), (12), and (15))

2. LT B—— advised the Contractor of at least three precautions to take while using muriatic acid. The boxes and jugs had instructions, precautions, and warnings on their labels. The Contractor failed to heed any of these precautions, precautions that might have prevented the damage or reduced its scope. The Contractor's failure contributed directly to the damage. (FF (6), (8), (13), and (14))

3. The General Provisions of the Construction Contract state, in part, that the Contractor "will repair or restore any damage . . . resulting from . . . failure to exercise reasonable care in the performance of the work." The Contractor poured large quantities of undiluted muriatic acid over large areas of the galley, allowing the mist to damage and contaminate equipment and surfaces throughout the building. The Contractor did not exercise reasonable care in the use of muriatic acid and is responsible to repair or restore any damage. (FF (16) and (18))

See also figure 10.3, which is a page from a long JAGMAN Investigation. That investigation was reviewed (endorsed) at the highest levels before being released in a redacted version (at last notice, the whole investigation could be found on the Internet). A "lesson learned" message concerning the same event discussed in figure 10.3 can be found in figure 5.2.

RECOMMENDATIONS

Make recommendations only if the appointing order or the JAG Manual specifically directs you to do so. These recommendations should flow clearly from the expressed opinions and findings of facts, and they may suggest corrective, disciplinary, or administrative action. In addition,

- Make your recommendations as *specific as possible.*
- Make sure your recommendations are *reasonable* and *just.*
- See that your recommendations are *practicable,* that is, that *they can be carried out.*
- Realize that your recommendations are not binding on any reviewing authorities; those recommendations will undergo a thorough review. As investigating officer, you won't bear the whole weight of the judgment in any particular case.
- If you recommend punitive charges or letters of reprimand, see the next section on follow-up documents to prepare.

Examples of Recommendations Section

Recommendations Involving Personnel

Below is a straightforward, clear section from an automobile accident report:

RECOMMENDATIONS

1. That Petty Officer M—— be the subject of some form of punitive action, either NJP or a Summary Court-Martial.

Figure 10.3 Page from a JAGMAN Investigation. This page is from the Opinions section of a long Command Investigation into a tragic "man overboard" event. The opinions expressed here were later slightly modified by an endorsement from Submarine Group 8 (in the first of four endorsements).

```
Subj:  COMMAND INVESTIGATION INTO THE DEATHS OF SENIOR CHIEF
       THOMAS HIGGINS AND PETTY OFFICER MICHAEL HOLTZ ONBOARD
       USS MINNEAPOLIS-ST PAUL (SSN 708) ON 29 DECEMBER 2006

5. Despite visual observations of sea conditions outside and
beyond the end of the breakwater, personnel did not detect the
impending hazard, probably due to the presence of wind driven chop
that obscured underlying swells. (Expert local mariners noted that
this inability to assess swell size from inside the lee of the
breakwater was typical for Plymouth Sound.) [FF (13), (14), (108),
(123), (136)]

6. Nevertheless, based on the harbor's geometry, prevailing
weather conditions, and common understanding of the purpose for a
breakwater, the ship should have been able to foresee the presence
of hazardous seas beyond the breakwater's lee. [FF (14), (15),
(17), (136)]

7. The direct cause for the two fatalities was personnel
remaining tethered to the ship's deck when washed overboard in
heavy seas. This precluded their expeditious recovery either on
deck or by escort vessels. Of the five personnel who were washed
overboard in this event, those who were not tethered were
recovered quickly by supporting small boats and suffered few -
and minor - injuries. [FF (160)-(242)]

8. Of the three who remained tethered, only one survived. Due
to seas and the shock of falling overboard, the surviving man was
not able to regain the ship's deck on his own - rather, he was
fortunate to be tossed on deck by a wave and able to crawl to the
FET hatch. [FF (160) - (188)]

9. Ship's personnel had adequate information and experience
necessary to avoid this incident. Based on the charted geography
of Plymouth Sound, the reports of approaching heavy weather from
the south, the presence of waves breaking over the breakwater, the
appearance of waves on the northern shore of Plymouth Sound beyond
the lee of the breakwater compared to those on the northern shore
behind the breakwater's lee, and the high southerly winds observed
by the ship during the outbound transit, a professional mariner
should have been able to anticipate the rough seas experienced by
the ship past the end of the breakwater. [FF (14), (15),
(17)-(19), (77-80), (106), (136)]

                       -From pp. 35-36 of Command Investigation
```

2. That steps be taken to ensure that Petty Officer M—— completes a safe driver's training course.
3. That Petty Officer M—— be held responsible for all medical expenses incurred as a result of this accident.
4. That Petty Officer M—— be charged lost time for the period of time he was hospitalized at County Hospital.
5. That Petty Officer M—— be processed for administrative separation for misconduct, either for civil conviction (MARCORSEPMAN 6210.7), pattern of misconduct (MARCORSEPMAN 6210.3), or both.

Recommendations for Changing Procedures
The recommendations below suggest how to avoid another occurrence of a laundry fire such as has just taken place in the ship's laundry.

<u>RECOMMENDATIONS</u>

1. As stated by the Fire Marshal, it does not appear that lint removal every two hours is sufficient to allow proper circulation of air in the dryers. Recommend that NAVEDTRA 414-01-45-81, Chapter 6 be amended to reflect this change. Until this change is made, recommend lint removal be conducted hourly to preclude any further difficulties.
2. Recommend the ship continue to wash and dry laundry in laundry bags, because washing and drying laundry for several hundred personnel without laundry bags could pose a severe accountability problem. When using the open-mesh laundry bags, recommend the following precautions:
   a. Do not overload the dryers.
   b. Do not place recently dried clothes in nylon bags; avoid concentrating the heat.
3. Recommend that laundry personnel be instructed to keep the dryer thermostats at the recommended level (140–160 degrees). Further, recommend that laundry personnel be required to man the space for a minimum of four hours after the completion of the drying cycle to ensure detection of any other fires of the sort that occurred.
4. Recommend including all the above recommendations in the laundry training program and in the daily operation of the laundry.
5. Recommend no disciplinary action be taken, as apparently no deliberate actions caused the fire.

DOCUMENTS AND ENCLOSURES

Make the written appointing order the first enclosure. Subsequent enclosures should contain all the evidence developed in the investigation, as well as charge sheets and punitive letters of reprimand, if recommended. In addition,

- Make each statement, document, or exhibit a separate enclosure.
- Ensure you've completely identified each document.
- Number the pages of a lengthy enclosure to help the reviewer. This way you can specifically reference the relevant passage (by page number) in the finding of fact, as in: "15. The Ferguson vehicle was traveling in excess of 50 mph. Enclosure (10), p. 7; Enclosure (14), p. 3; Enclosure (15), p. 1." You can also tab and highlight pertinent passages in any enclosure that is particularly bulky.
- If your personal observations provide the basis for any findings of fact, attach as an enclosure a memo for record of those observations.

"I was involved with JAGMANs in the medical field. When doctors were called for, we sometimes assigned a doctor from a different specialty than the field involved in the incident being investigated.

"Yes, general expertise helps, but a non-specialist will often have fewer preconceptions."

—JAG LIEUTENANT

- For every witness's statement, consider laying a foundation in that statement, either by preface or in the questions asked, to explain to the reviewer why the witness can speak competently on a particular subject.
- Because handwritten documents are often illegible, have witnesses' statements printed or typed. Whenever possible obtain signed, sworn statements. Sworn statements carry greater weight with readers and reviewers than unsworn statements.
- When you cannot obtain a witness's signature, draft your own summaries of a witness's oral statements. Make sure to sign this summary, certifying it is a valid account or an accurate transcript of the interview, if it is.
- Include as an enclosure the Privacy Act Statement for each witness from whom you obtained personal information by direct inquiry. Attach it to the respective witness's statement.
- Include as an enclosure any prior request (and its approval, too) for exceeding time requirements in conducting the investigation.
- Make sure all copies of the report itself and all enclosures are clear and readable.

You may also want to take the following steps:

- Preparing a signed, sworn charge sheet if you recommend punitive action, and including it as an enclosure. This step is part of completed staff work.
- Preparing a punitive letter of reprimand or admonition if you're recommending that the command issue such a letter, and including it as an enclosure. This step also shows completed staff work.
- Preparing a nonpunitive letter of reprimand, if your recommendation is to issue one. You should *not* include this letter in the investigation but forward it separately to the appropriate authority for issuance.

Signature and Security Classification

Sign your report.

Omit classified material unless inclusion is essential. Assign the whole report the classification of the highest classified material in it. Staff Judge Advocates and reviewers will often declassify enclosures and investigations whenever possible; still, some reports will have to remain classified. If yours must be, see that you classify and label *the whole report* appropriately, and ensure that you appropriately classify and label each individual finding of fact, opinion, recommendation, and enclosure. Remember to include the proper downgrading instructions. See OPNAVINST 5510.1.

Addresses and Copies

- Normally address the report to the convening authority (usually the commanding officer). The convening authority will forward the investigation via the chain of command. For details as to all addressees, see your convening authority and the JAGMAN sections on "Action by Convening and Reviewing Authorities" and "Disposition of the Record of Proceedings and Copies."
- Provide an *advance copy* directly to OJAG in admiralty cases (Code 11), death cases, or other serious cases so OJAG will not have to wait for all officers in the chain to act before reviewing the initial findings.
- Provide a copy for each intermediate addressee.
- Make sure that copies to all addressees include all the enclosures.
- Ensure all photocopies are legible and securely fastened.
- Keep a copy for yourself, unless especially sensitive or classified.

EXAMPLE OF A COMPLETE JAGMAN INVESTIGATION
Below is a decent example of a complete investigation. All of the names in this example are fictional.

---

23 February 1988

From: LT Joseph L. Wilson, USNR, 2305
To: Commanding Officer, USS PIEDMONT (AD 17)

Subj: INVESTIGATION TO INQUIRE INTO THE CIRCUMSTANCES SURROUNDING THE FAINTING OF ET2 SYDNEY LEE SAILOR, USN, ON BOARD USS PIEDMONT (AD 17) DURING GENERAL QUARTERS ON OR ABOUT 1415, 10 FEBRUARY 1988

Ref: (a) JAGMAN
        (b) OPNAVINST 5100.20C

Encl: (1) Appointing Order dated 20 Feb 88
        (2) CIC Watchbill for 7–27 February 1988
        (3) Deck log of USS PIEDMONT (AD 17) 701R09 time 1326 to 1427
        (4) Statement of ET2 Sydney Sailor, USN
        (5) Statement of IT R. B. Rome, USN, Operations Officer, USS PIEDMONT (AD17) TAO
        (6) Statement of ENS E. F. Snyder, USNR
        (7) Statement of ENS E. C. Johnson, USN, CIC Officer, USS PIEDMONT (AD 17)
        (8) Statement of ET3 V I. Shirley, USN, JA Phone Talker
        (9) Statement of LTJG R. S. Reynolds, USNR
        (10) Statement of HMC R. C. Jefferson, USN
        (11) Statement of HM2(SW) Y. B. Murfree, USN
        (12) Statement of HM2 C. C. Bruce, USN
        (13) Statement of IT D. T. Daniel, MC, USNR, Medical Officer, USS PIEDMONT (AD 17)
        (14) Medical Department Log Book 0730, 10 February 1988 to 0800, 11 February 1988
        (15) SF600 Chronological Record of Medical Care ET2 Sailor on 10 February 1988
        (16) NAVMED 6500/1 Report of Heat/Cold Casualty ET2 Sailor

<u>PRELIMINARY STATEMENT</u>

1.   Following enclosure (1) and in accordance with references (a) and (b), an informal investigation was conducted to inquire into the circumstances surrounding the fainting of ET2 Sydney Sailor, USN, on board USS PIEDMONT (AD 17) during General Quarters on or about 1415, 10 February 1988. All relevant evidence was collected. The investigator met all directives and special requirements set out in enclosure (1).

<u>FINDINGS OF FACT</u>

1.   On 10 February 1988 ET2 Mary Lee Sailor, USN, was on active duty and assigned to the USS PIEDMONT (AD 17). (encl (2))

2.   On 10 February 1988 the USS PIEDMONT was steaming from Mayport, Florida, to Norfolk, Virginia. (encl (3))

3.   On 10 February 1988 ET2 Sailor was standing underway log watch at her General Quarters station in the Combat Information Center. (encls (2) and (4))

4.   Ventilation had been secured because of the drill, and CIC was described as "very uncomfortable." (encls (4) and (5))

5.   Material condition "Circle William" was improperly set in that the recirc system R-03-43-2, classified "William," was also secured at the time of the incident. (encl (6))

6.   ET2 Sailor "became overheated and was perspiring profusely . . . and felt weak and sick. Because of the importance of the drill and because everyone else was uncomfortable . . . [she] was reluctant to take off the MK V gas mask and anti-flash any earlier." (encl (4))

7.   ET2 Sailor was instructed by LT Rome to take off her MK V gas mask but became unconscious before being able to do so. (encl (4))

8.   ET2 Sailor was caught as she became unconscious and lowered to the deck. Her MK V gas mask was removed. (encls (5) and (7))

9.   ET3 Shirley, JA phone talker, relayed "Medical emergency in CIC, not a drill" to D.C. Central. Medical emergency was called away on the 1MC at 1411. (encls (2) and (8))

10.   When medical emergency was called away, LTJG Reynolds, HMC Jefferson, and HM2 (SW) Murfree responded from the Forward Decontamination Station with a stretcher team. IT Daniel, Medical Officer, also responded. (encl (9))

11.   ET2 Sailor was lying on the deck, alert and conscious. (encls (9), (10), and (11))

12.   ET2 Sailor had her feet elevated and was conscious and responsive when the medical officer arrived at the scene. (encl (13))

13.   ET2 Sailor was evaluated for injuries and was able to walk from CIC with some assistance by medical personnel. (encls (9), (10), (12), and (13)) 14. ET2 Sailor again lost consciousness at the bottom of the first ladder. She was transported to Medical in a Neil-Robertson stretcher. (encls (9), (10), (11), and (12))

15.   ET2 Sailor arrived at sick bay in a Neil-Robertson stretcher at 1415. (encls (14) and (15))

16.   ET2 Sailor's vital signs were normal. (encl (15))

17.   ET2 Sailor was diagnosed and treated for heat exhaustion, i.e., VASOVAGAL SYNCOPE SECONDARY TO HEAT STRESS. (encl (15))

18.   Medical Officer's notes state: "Past medical history unremarkable except that patient states that she and other members of her family have a tendency to 'pass out easily.'" (encls (15) and (16))

19.   ET2 Sailor had eaten lunch before General Quarters, had had some 9 hours of sleep in the past 24 hours, and had drunk 4 to 5 cups of coffee and 6 glasses of water in the 12 hours prior to her illness. (encl (16))

OPINIONS

1.   That ET2 Sailor became unconscious as a result of mild heat exhaustion. (FF (17))

2.   That ET2 Sailor was motivated to participate in the drill and would not have fainted if she had spoken up sooner. (FF (6))

3.   That the combination of material condition and battle dress probably precipitated the illness, but that ET2 Sailor is prone to fainting and might have fainted as a result of battle dress alone. (FF (4), (5), and (18))

4.   That the illness occurred in the line of duty and not as a result of her own misconduct. (FF (3), (6), and (7))

5.   That there is no likelihood of permanent or recurring illness or disability as a result of the single episode, and that claims against the government are not warranted. (FF (16–19))

6. That first aid rendered by personnel at the scene was correct, that the medical emergency was promptly and correctly called away, and that medical department response was prompt and correct. (FF (9-15))

<u>RECOMMENDATIONS</u>

1. That ET2 Sailor be counseled not to tax herself to the point of illness during a drill scenario.

2. That supervisory personnel in CIC and the Communications Center ensure that recirc system R-03-43-2 remain energized so long as electrical power is available to the controller.

JOSEPH L. WILSON

WHAT AN INVESTIGATING OFFICER OUGHT TO KNOW ABOUT AN ENDORSEMENT

How will the chain of command review your report? *Thoroughly* and *repeatedly.* That's why you have to be sure that you've done it all as well as you can.

The purpose of an endorsement is to give the reviewer's point of view on the matter under investigation and to make sure that you've followed all technical procedures (e.g., that you've observed all the rights and given the appropriate warnings). In other words, an endorsement is at once a check or review and an opportunity for the reviewing authority (the first of which is usually the commanding officer) to make comments.

The reviewing authority will comment on the soundness of the findings, opinions, and recommendations in the report and will also advise what follow-on actions have been taken in relation to the case. A commanding officer will typically state what recommendations have been approved and acted on, what further steps beyond the recommendations have been taken, what disciplinary action the unit has initiated, and what administrative improvements the command has decided on.

Below is a fictionalized version of an actual endorsement. If the report it endorses were written today, it probably still would not be a Litigation-Report Investigation despite the alleged damage to private property involved because claims against the government seem very unlikely. However, before making such a determination in a case like this, the original investigating officer should consult a Judge Advocate.

Incidentally, because this document uses comparatively little passive voice, it reads much more like plain English than many endorsements.

5800
Ser 12/0037
15 SEP 88

FIRST ENDORSEMENT on LT John L. Wilson, USNR, 1310, ltr dtd 11 SEP 88

From: Commanding Officer, USS ROBERT A. OWENS (DD 827)
To: Commanding Officer, Naval Legal Service Office (Claims Department), U.S. Naval Station, San Diego, California

Subj: INVESTIGATION TO INQUIRE INTO THE CIRCUMSTANCES SURROUNDING OVERSPRAYING OF VEHICLES IN THE VICINITY OF USS ROBERT A. OWENS DURING THE PERIOD OF 10 AUGUST THROUGH 15 AUGUST 1988

1. Readdressed and forwarded.

2. The Deck Department, USS ROBERT A. OWENS, and Port Services, U.S. Naval Station San Diego, did take reasonable precautions to place drivers in the vicinity of the ship on notice of spray-painting operations. Although most claimants knew or should have known about the potential for damage to their vehicles, it is apparent that some vehicles incurred damage after reasonable preventative steps had been taken.

3. Spray painting is a fact of life for Navy ships. This ship must be painted regularly, and the methods of accomplishing this evolution during the month of August were appropriate. In addition, significant efforts were taken to provide information to those who park and work in the vicinity of USS ROBERT A. OWENS.

4. During the period in question the ship was fully engaged in Selected Restricted Availability, which required extensive refurbishing, repairs, and painting. The Availability was the primary mission of all personnel assigned to USS ROBERT A. OWENS at the time.

5. Typical paint overspray consists of a light mist that is normally removed from a vehicle with a rubbing compound and an hour or two of buffing. It was this method that I used successfully on my own black sports car to remove overspray from the same painting operations.

6. Subject to the foregoing, the findings of fact, opinions, and recommendations of the investigating officer are approved.

GEORGE Z. WATSON

Copy to:
OJAG (Code 11, Admiralty)
Naval Station San Diego
LT John L. Wilson

Each authority to whom you route a JAGMAN Investigation forwards it by endorsement. If an authority decides the investigation has major errors, that endorser can turn the report back down the chain for further inquiry or for corrections. However, unless the errors are especially severe, each endorser will normally correct the mistakes in the report (and those in any prior endorsements), add any additional necessary findings of fact or opinions, approve or disapprove of the conclusions and recommendations (perhaps adding others), and *send the package on.* Otherwise, the delay could be extensive.

This process doesn't mean you're completely off the hook for any errors you may have made in the investigation. After forwarding the report, the endorser will send a copy of the endorsement *back down the chain* to your commanding officer's reporting senior(s), first. On a staff, an endorsement will usually go on the read board, so that many eyes will see seniors' criticisms of the report you've written. The endorsement will eventually get back to your own commanding officer and finally to you. You can be sure that your boss will notice (and certainly not appreciate) any mistakes you've made.

For instance, a few years back, a loss of $150 was discovered aboard a destroyer, an event that caused the relief of the ship's store operator (a petty officer third class) and some considerable embarrassment to the supply officer. But that's not where the embarrassment ended. The third endorsement to this investigation, signed by the commander of a cruiser-destroyer group, had this to say:

The overall lack of quality of the basic investigation, particularly the absence of written statements from the principals, is noted with concern. . . . Commanding Officer, USS VESSEL (DD XX) is directed to ensure compliance with reference (a) in future investigations.

This critique was sent on to the Judge Advocate General via two other major naval organizations (standard practice at the time), with copies to the ship's DESRON commander, the ship's commanding officer, and the lieutenant who wrote and signed the original investigation.

As the O-6 JAG at a major type command commented, too often an investigating officer will call up the staff JAG when first seeing such an endorsement and ask, "Why didn't you call me? Why did you have to put the gig in print? My skipper is going to hit the overhead when he sees this!" You have to remember that once it's in print, it's official, and that the staff JAG works for the O-6 or flag, not for you. (The process is slightly different in the Marine Corps. Marine legal officers commented that they make a policy of doing the same review for the battalion officer as they do for the general, thus solving perceived problems before an investigation reaches the general's desk.)

What will the endorser look at? Anything and everything suggested above, and perhaps other details too. Before submitting your report, check it over one last time to make sure you've met all the requirements. If you can say yes to all the questions in the checklist below, you can be pretty sure you have a decent report.

FINAL CHECKLIST ON JAGMAN INVESTIGATIONS
- Does your report "answer the mail"? Have you carried out what the appointing order directed you to do?
- Do all the parts mesh? Does the preliminary statement properly introduce the rest of the report? Do the findings describe the basic facts? Do the opinions and recommendations logically follow through?
- Does every fact have an enclosure and every opinion a reference?
- Are the opinions and recommendations reasonable?
- Has the investigation been as thorough as you could reasonably expect?
- Is the report technically complete and correct in all its details? Have you classified it correctly? Have you identified all the witnesses? Are all the enclosures in place, properly marked, and highlighted? Are all the copies (including reproduced copies of enclosures) readable? Have you made enough copies of the report?
- Have you shown this report to someone else (a knowledgeable reader and good critic)? Can that person follow it all? Does it make sense to him or her?
- Does the report needlessly present a poor image of your command or any individuals involved in the investigation?
- If you were the officer charged with seeing to it that the government's interest had been looked after, would you think all required duties and responsibilities had been carried out?
- On the other hand, if you were the person whose acts were under investigation, would you think you had gotten a complete hearing and a fair shake?

A Preliminary Inquiry

One last section is called for, about one other legal report you might have to do. Preceding any formal investigation, a command will often conduct a *Preliminary Inquiry.*

This is a preliminary and informal survey, a "quick look" at an incident, basically designed to determine whether any official investigation ought to be conducted at all, and if so, what kind. In this inquiry, a CO may choose any means at all to search into an incident, may conduct such a search personally or delegate someone else to do it, and may decide whether or not to document the inquiry in writing.

If he or she decides to assign it to you, the CO will direct that you complete the inquiry *within three days*. If you find you can't finish it within that time, you might be trying to do too much, and you should go back to your CO for further guidance.

When assigned to do a Preliminary Inquiry, begin immediately, using (if available) the Preliminary Investigation Checklist from the JAGMAN Investigation Handbook (put out by the Naval Justice School and briefly summarized here). Check first to see if the incident is under investigation by other civilian or military agencies, or if it should be considered a "major" incident—in either of these cases, follow the respective guidelines in chapter 2 of the JAGMAN. Otherwise:

- Obtain available documentation pertaining to the inquiry;
- Locate and preserve evidence;
- Draw up a list of possible witnesses;
- Interview those witnesses in person, by phone, or by message (advising each witness of rights and obtaining Privacy Act Statements as necessary—all of this as outlined earlier in this chapter);
- Pursue all the above just so far as necessary to make an informed recommendation as to what specific course the Convening Authority should pursue, that is,
  — No further action,
  — A Command Investigation (normal JAGMAN),
  — A Litigation-Report Investigation, or
  — A recommendation to convene a Court or Board of Inquiry;
- Then report back to the Convening Authority with your recommendation, meanwhile preserving all documentation, evidence, and witness statements for any eventual investigation.

Although written documentation of the Preliminary Inquiry is not mandatory, your boss may ask you to write up your findings. If so, follow the format in the JAGMAN. The fictionalized sample below follows that format and is based upon actual events. Neither the names nor the ship is those of the actual incident.

A Preliminary Inquiry—Sample Write-Up

10 November 1996

From: LTJG Paul Robichaux, USNR, 1115
To: Commanding Officer, USS WHIDBEY ISLAND (LSD 41)

Subj: PRELIMINARY INQUIRY INTO THE RUMORED COLLISION OF LCM 8-1 AND PRIVATELY OWNED FISHING VESSELS AT MOREHEAD CITY, NC, ON 8 NOVEMBER 1996

Ref: JAGMAN Section 0204

1.   On the evening of 8 November 1995, WHIDBEY ISLAND personnel overheard rumors that charges were to be made against the ship because of an alleged collision of one of the ship's LCMs with some fishing boats that supposedly had occurred that morning.

I was assigned to conduct a preliminary investigation into this rumored incident. This is the report of my investigation.

2. <u>Personnel Contacted:</u>

a.   BM2 R. F. DOUGHERTY, USN, USS WHIDBEY ISLAND (LSD 41). Dougherty was the Boat Officer aboard LCM 8-1 at the time of the incident.

b.   BM2 H. D. SHENK, USN, USS WHIDBEY ISLAND (LSD 41). Shenk was the Boat Coxswain aboard LCM 8-1 at the time of the incident.

c.   Mr. C. O. Smith, owner of a fishing boat moored at the Morehead City docks, telephone 804-111-1111. Mr. Smith was a witness to the incident.

3. <u>Materials reviewed:</u>

a.   Bow and port side of LCM 8-1.

b.   Fishing boats "Jennifer," "Faring Well," and "Jennifer II"

c.   Pilings nearby these fishing boats.

4. <u>Summary of findings:</u>

a.   At about 0900 on 8 November 1995, LCM 8-1 was towing another assault craft in the vicinity of private boat docks at Morehead City, NC. The port engine became fouled with a tow rope, and strong winds and current made it difficult to maneuver the craft. The lead LCM came into brief contact with dock pilings near the privately owned fishing craft named in paragraph 3(b).

b.   BM2 Daugherty and BM2 Shenk report that LCM 8-1 did not contact or damage any of the fishing boats. Mr. C. O. Smith (who was working on his boat at the time and who witnessed the event) agreed that although the lead LCM came as close as ten feet to one of the fishing boats, no contact actually occurred. Moreover, he reports that two of the fishing boats mentioned above ("Jennifer" and "Faring Well") were taken to sea soon afterward. The third ("Jennifer II") was moored well away from the pilings, too far away to have been involved.

c.   My observation of the fishing boats from the dock indicated no obvious recent damage. No gray paint from LCM 8-1 or other indication of a possible collision was visible.

d.   The owner of the fishing boats mentioned above is Mr. J. R. Turner, telephone 804-222-2222. I did not speak to Mr. Turner.

5. <u>Recommendation:</u>

That no action be taken at this time. If someone makes a formal complaint, I recommend Commanding Officer, USS WHIDBEY ISLAND, immediately initiate a Litigation-Report Investigation of this incident.

PAUL ROBICHAUX, LTJG, USNR

I keep six honest serving men (They taught me all I knew); Their names are What and Why and When and How and Where and Who.

—RUDYARD KIPLING

11

Writing for the News Media

Who besides official journalists or public affairs officers needs to know about news writing? Quite a number of people, as it turns out: COs who want to tell the good story of their commands and get their people recognition; COs, XOs, and CDOs who may have to approve and release news stories; Marine Corps Unit Information Officers (UIOs) who put out information on their units; and many Navy officers who, on their ships, air squadrons, or other stations, are assigned as collateral duty public affairs officers (PAOs).

Some of the latter part-time PAOs have a great deal to say about the importance of writing good news releases, along with other aspects of their jobs. For example, the educational services officer on an amphibious assault ship commented on how his PAO work affected those aboard. He began putting an article in the base newspaper every month—the CO loved it. Coming back from Beirut, three hundred award recipients spelled out the ship's hull number on the flight deck for a photo, which appeared in the Norfolk and Little Creek base newspapers—the awardees loved it. He went into the engine rooms during an inspection and got another article with photos into the base paper—and the snipes (who *never* had recognition) loved it too.

Besides enhancing crew morale and pleasing the CO, news or feature writing can do real service in informing the public, not only the public of families and friends served by base newspapers but also the wider naval audience reached by such papers and magazines as *Navy Times, All Hands, Naval Aviation News, Naval Reservist News, Leatherneck,* and *Marines.* Navy Newstand is the premier distribution service for Navy news. Of course there are also many civilian outlets for naval news, from the local paper and other local media on up. Articles that reach the publics that these forums serve do inestimable benefit for us all.

News writing is distinctly different from most of the other writing spoken of in this book. It requires a "wholly different style," according to the CO of a training command. Part of the difference lies in the nature of the subject matter. While there are different kinds of news writing, and some elements are more important to one kind than another, any genuine news item should contain all or most of these basic ingredients:

- Something must HAPPEN!
- It must be timely.
- It must be significant.
- It must have local interest.

The item will be even more valuable as news if it contains

- Humor
- Conflict
- Human interest
- Well-known personalities
- Suspense

Recognizing news is one thing; finding it is another. Some stories will come to a writer as gifts. But you will obtain most of your significant news only by lots of leg work, a little ingenuity, some imagination, and an organized routine. Don't wait for news to find you. Go seek it out.

Military writers make use of two standard kinds of journalistic writing: (1) news releases and (2) features. These writings differ primarily in the way they deal with *reader interest.*

The news release follows the order of *decreasing* interest, the so-called inverted pyramid, in which you assume a reader might stop anywhere in the story. A writer begins the story with a basic summary of an event—the most crucial facts—and then expands on those facts.

In contrast, the feature story generally tries to intrigue readers by dangling incidental facts or using special techniques, and then leads them to and through the more important information. The feature story assumes level or *increasing* interest. A simple diagram will illustrate the difference.

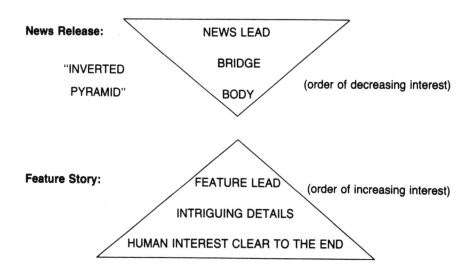

The news release and feature require sharply different techniques, each of them having been perfected over decades of journalistic practice. Both are very useful for naval writers to learn, not only for use in news writing but also for the spin-offs they have in day-to-day staff and organizational writing. Let's look at each of them in some detail.

THE NEWS RELEASE

News releases have three parts—the lead, the bridge, and the body. Most important of these is the lead.

Write an Accurate Summary Lead

Although reader interest is always a consideration, you don't design a lead primarily to get a reader to read a story. Headlines have more of that function, and subject matter itself is probably the most important factor in determining which news stories any particular person reads. Rather than being an enticement, a lead is better defined as an effective summary that spills all the basic facts at once, allowing the reader to scan the paper and decide which stories to read through for more details.

A good lead, then, offers the basic information of the story in quick summary form—like this:

> Eight Sailors on two fifty-foot Navy shuttle boats rescued two people from the Mississippi River at 6 A.M. this morning. (from NSA New Orleans Release 95-0838)

Writing leads like this one is an art that requires much practice.

A lead is usually a single sentence of some twenty to thirty words and can be of several types, each of which has special usefulness. You categorize a lead by which of the five *W*s and one *H* it emphasizes (although more than one of these should appear in it, just one receives special emphasis). Is it a *who, what, where, when, why,* or *how* lead? The lead above is a *what* lead.

Before writing a lead, list the *who, what, where, when, why,* and *how* of a story. Then consider the story from your audience's viewpoint. Which emphasis will likely have most impact on your reader? Which might be most interesting, or hardest hitting? Theoretically, by emphasizing any one of these aspects, you could compose six different summary leads. However, "when" and "where"—important as they are to a news story—don't usually provide the best leads. On the other hand, there are two different kinds of "who" leads. Altogether, you have five strong possible leads for a story:

A WHAT Lead—usually the most important element in hard news stories:

> The destroyer USS Deyo (DD 989) arrived in its new home port of Norfolk May 22, relocated from Charleston, S.C., as a result of the base closure and realignment decisions announced in 1993.

A WHO Lead—especially useful if the *who* is well known or holds an important position:

> The Assistant Secretary of Defense for Reserve Affairs, Deborah R. Lee, will meet with senior leaders of the Marine Corps Reserve in New Orleans Friday at 2:00 P.M.

An IMPERSONAL WHO Lead—used if the "who" is not well known or not important; the person is identified in the bridge or the body of the story:

Navy wrestlers won four of the 17 medals taken by U.S. wrestlers at the Conseil International du Sport Militaire in December.

A WHY Lead—"why" is sometimes the most interesting element:

Because of a shortage of instructors in the Naval Dental School, the student–instructor ratio will be increased to 16–1 next month.

A HOW Lead—occasionally the "how" is the strongest possible lead:

By dropping a bomb down the chimney, an escaped arsonist blew up the town judge's home yesterday.

Remember—don't get bogged down in secondary details or get tangled in the chronology of events in a lead; let those elements follow in the body.

Compose a "Bridge" as an Effective Link

The bridge is a sentence or two that links the summary information in the lead to the detailed information of the body. Although not always required, it helps a writer avoid cluttering the lead with secondary facts. The bridge serves the lead, because the kind of lead usually determines the type of bridge that follows.

For example, a bridge following an "impersonal who" lead provides complete identification of the individuals mentioned in the lead:

Lead: An off-duty Marine gate guard stationed here saved a 10-year-old boy from drowning just off the seawall near the base gym.

Bridge: By jumping off the seawall and swimming 50 yards, Corporal Sam Jones saved the life of the unidentified youngster, who had fallen off a sailboat.

Another common purpose is to tell the source of information given in the lead and to supply additional information.

Lead: Vandals in the students' barracks destroyed nearly $12,000 worth of fire protection equipment in the last six months, leaving their fellow students at the risk of injury or death.

Bridge: According to Base Fire Chief Charles W. Smith, vandals have torn down smoke detectors, bells, and pull stations that contractors installed in the barracks about six months ago. In addition, 211 fire extinguishers had to be replaced, the chief said.

A bridge following a lead that omits some of the five Ws simply adds other information.

Lead: The harbor tug Wobegon (YTB 472) rescued two men from a disabled motorboat that was drifting to sea on the ebb tide early Saturday morning.

Bridge: The motorboat had been without power for three hours when the Wobegon appeared about 4:30 A.M. a half-mile southeast of Fort Sumter, Charleston, S.C. The two men in the boat, who were not identified, got the tug's attention by a flashlight SOS.

Other bridges tie a lead back to earlier stories on the same subject or simply add additional facts.

In the Body, Add Details in Descending Order of Importance

In the body, elaborate on the elements given in the lead and bridge by adding details, in-depth discussion, chronology of events, or quotes on what occurred. In essence, the body *retells in detail and descending order of importance* the summary facts given in the lead.

Remember these important principles when writing the body of a news release. First, an editor with limited space who wants to use your story will *cut from the bottom.* Make sure no essential material is left to the end, and place the most important information in paragraphs immediately succeeding the lead and bridge. Again, write in descending order of importance, with minor details left for the end.

Second, remember that newspaper columns are very narrow. Dense blocks of type inhibit reading wherever encountered, but narrow columns of news type can make reading even more difficult than usual. Limit your paragraphs to two or three sentences in length.

Don't Forget the Heading

Once you've composed a news release complete with lead, bridge, and body, don't overlook one other part—a news release *heading.* A good heading can mean the difference between good material being used, lost, or thrown out. Include in this heading five basic items:

1. The *name of the command.* Identifies the releasing authority.
2. The *contact individual* within the command. Your name, phone, and fax numbers are very important—they tell the editor how to reach you to clarify information, to confirm some aspect of the release, etc.
3. The *telephone and fax numbers and email* of the command or contact individual.
4. A *"slug"* or *title* to give the editor an idea of the story content.
5. The *release date and time.* Note the following common terms:
    - FOR IMMEDIATE RELEASE—for hot items
    - FOR GENERAL RELEASE—for feature and other items with no time element
    - HOLD FOR RELEASE UNTIL—for items mailed in advance of the time/date when the public can be informed
    - DO NOT USE AFTER—for items not accurate or pertinent after a certain date (such as publicizing an open house, etc.)

Don't include a cover letter for your release—that's too much official clout, and editors don't have time to read a cover letter anyway. The paper will recognize you're submitting a news release by reading the heading and the title "News Release."

Figure 11.1 is a good short news release, heading and all.

THE FEATURE STORY

Many naval stories—especially those written in weekly base papers—are feature stories. Commercial newspapers usually cover hard news while base newspapers, which have limited staff resources, simply can't be as up-to-date as other news sources.

Timeliness is still important in some instances. A story about a ship returning from deployment should come out in the base paper within a week of the event; the same for changes of command and so on. But in most cases the interest in such stories is

Figure 11.1 A News Release from a Navy Ship. This release, complete on one page, tells the story quickly and well.

USS THEODORE ROOSEVELT (CVN-71)

PUBLIC AFFAIRS OFFICE
FPO NEW YORK 09599-2871
(A) 546-7402
(C) 804-444-7402

For Immediate Release   10 January 1988

                    TWO MEN RESCUED FROM ATLANTIC

     ABOARD USS THEODORE ROOSEVELT (CVN-71)...The nuclear aircraft carrier

USS THEODORE ROOSEVELT rescued two 24-year-old men from the Atlantic Ocean 10

January after they had drifted with the wreckage of their trimaran for four-and-a-half days.

     Joseph Donald Buffkin, Jr., and John Wirth Frederico were rescued 20 nautical miles

from San Salvador Island at 7:06 pm after being spotted from the 98,000-ton THEODORE

ROOSEVELT by the ship's starboard lookout, Seaman Rodney Jackson.

     "I saw a light off the starboard side and reported it to the bridge," said Jackson, an

Alabama native who has been in the Navy for a year-and-a-half. "The officer of the deck

identified the signal as an SOS so we turned the ship around."

     The trimaran sailboat overturned and broke apart in heavy weather according to

Buffkin. "We had sold our cars and bought the boat to island hop. We set out from

Jacksonville and have been sailing around down here since October."

     Buffkin and Frederico spent 96 hours holding on to the crippled hull. By diving down

and entering the compartment they located food and water. On the last of their

excursions they found the flashlight that helped save their lives.

     After being brought aboard the Navy's newest aircraft carrier they were examined by

the ship's medical staff, fed and allowed to rest. Suffering only minor cuts and bruises in

their ordeal, they were flown to Guantanamo Bay, Cuba.

no longer on the event itself but on some special aspect of it. So instead of a "hard news" release, you would write a "feature story" and send it either to a base newspaper, or, if it is good enough, to a journal like *All Hands, Surface Warfare,* or *Marines.* These magazines aren't interested in "hard news" but rather in human interest, humor, technical information, and military or institutional facts of life. As one writer put it, "Feature stories are the readers' gravy in the meat and potato world of news. They add a human dimension to what is sometimes perceived as an impersonal approach to reporting the news of the day" (JOC Jon Cabot, *Direction,* Spring 1983).

Feature stories on Navy and Marine Corps subjects can help humanize the services for nonnaval audiences. This type of reporting helps citizens relate to and understand men and women in the service. On the other hand, feature stories that specifically target service members and their families—most of the features in base newspapers—help us relate to and understand one another. They deal with our tasks, jobs, environments, desires, loves, challenges, and predicaments. Moreover, by giving fitting recognition to the dedication and deeds of service members and their families, news features help boost individual and unit morale.

The task of the feature writer, then, is first to find that special story worth telling, and then to tell it in a way that will prick interest. As a result, the whole approach of a feature story differs from that of the news release.

Writing Feature Leads

The feature lead serves a different purpose than the news lead. Unlike the news lead, it does not deliver all the basic facts at once—instead, it attempts above all to get readers interested, to grip them and make them want to learn more. Many different leads can introduce feature stories—there is no standard formula based upon the five Ws. Nor is there a necessary "lead-bridge-body" structure, but instead (1) a lead to intrigue followed by (2) secondary interest, often leading to (3) a story and reader climax. Maybe such a formula is impractical in all cases, but at the least material of sustained interest should follow the lead, and a well-crafted ending should wrap up the story. (The emphasis on the ending is distinctive of the feature; in contrast, the hard news release just ends. You shouldn't spend any special time on its ending, for an editor is likely to cut off the last few paragraphs to save space anyway.)

The following paragraphs illustrate several popular kinds of feature leads— leads connected with several different kinds of stories. These examples are just a few of many possibilities.

The SUMMARY lead leads off with fascinating facts. It resembles a news lead but is more interesting. This example is from a story on what the Navy is doing to control the cost of spare parts.

> A 4-cent diode cost the Navy $110. A 67-cent bolt was priced at $17.59. A $15 claw hammer was marked up to $435.
>
> Such overcharging seems impossible, but the Navy and other military services did pay the inflated prices for these and many other items.

The NARRATIVE or DESCRIPTIVE lead sets the mood, stirs emotions, and gets a reader into the story. The following lead is adapted from a story written by Sgt. David J. Ferrier:

> Not able to sleep, Lance Corporal Zachary Mayo put on his blue coveralls, green T-shirt, and boots and walked out on the catwalk—a place he often went

to get fresh air. Mayo remembered later that he had forgotten to firmly shut the ship's heavy, steel, watertight door. As the aircraft carrier USS America patrolled the North Arabian Sea, she turned to port. Swinging open, the hatch slammed into Mayo's back, knocking him through the safety rails, and he plummeted nearly six stories into the ocean.

The Osburn, Idaho, Marine survived nearly 36 hours alone and adrift on the high seas. . . .

The TEASER lead captures a reader's interest by promising something interesting, without telling the reader what the story is about. The reader learns more of the subject as the story continues. The following story is about the Navy's first aircraft, the A-1, but it doesn't name the aircraft until later.

It was a light delicate aircraft, but in its short life it survived several crashes. And like most pioneers, it had its share of failures and accomplishments.

The QUOTATION lead is suitable for historical stories or recent events. Use it rarely, and only with dynamic and short quotes.

"You really don't know what freedom is until you have had to escape from Communist captivity" said Navy Lt. Deiter A. Dengler, an escapee from a Viet Cong prison camp.

The DIRECT ADDRESS lead states or implies the word "you" somewhere in the first paragraph.

If you write a rubber check at a stateside commissary, you'll have to pay a $10 service charge and stand the chance of facing a judge, either civil or military.

On Writing the Rest of the Feature

As with the news release lead, authorities often advise that you write the feature lead first, before writing a story. The lead will often set the stage for the rest of the article, suggesting a logical structure.

How you go about writing the rest of the story varies. "The bottom line in feature writing," said JOC Jon Cabot in the Spring 1983 *Direction,* "is adding personality or character to any given subject. The easiest way to take a topic and make it a feature is to think in terms of putting the topic on a stage, much like an actor. You then move the topic across the stage through the effective use of quotes and anecdotes until you come to the end of the stage or your summary."

Colorful writing and freedom of composition are not only permissible but encouraged in feature writing. This subjectivity differs from writing news releases, in which journalists do their best to be (and to appear to be) objective. "Straight news" writers see to it that no opinions remain unattributed, and they scrutinize their adjectives to ensure no bias has crept in. They do their best to disappear from the story.

In contrast, writers of feature stories are allowed, even encouraged, to state opinions (they usually receive bylines, not only to give them credit for their stories but also to identify the source of whatever opinions appear). They are also encouraged to write colorfully to keep the interest up. Writers can use several techniques—looking at events from differing points of view, making intriguing comparisons and contrasts, using striking quotations—the possibilities are endless. The best way to learn to write features is probably to read features and to study the techniques in stories that especially interest you.

The end of a good feature shows as much craft as the beginning. One good way to end is with a choice quotation from an interview; another favorite method is to summarize the key points of the story and comment on their impact. A good feature story keeps the interest of the reader to the very end and if possible surprises or delights the reader even in the conclusion itself.

Here's an example of a feature story written years ago by a collateral-duty PAO aboard a destroyer. Published in *Soundings,* the base newspaper in Norfolk, it is a good example of a standard feature that a part-time PAO would write. After the heading, the story begins with a quotation lead, and then proceeds to tell its story, keeping up interest with details about the Cape Verde Islands and an adept use of several quotations, including a good one to end the story. (Remember that this release would be *double spaced* on an actual news release form.)

NEWS RELEASE

USS COMTE DE GRASSE (DD 974)
Lt. Joe DiRenzo III, Public Affairs Officer Phone 804-444-7552
"Comte de Grasse Makes Port Visit to the Cape Verde Islands"
FOR GENERAL RELEASE

"It is a distinguished pleasure and privilege to host the USS Comte de Grasse (DD 974) here in the islands," commented U.S. Ambassador Vernon D. Penner, Jr., during a luncheon on board the ship as it rested at anchor in the Cape Verde Islands. "We have had other ships, but nothing like this magnificent vessel," continued Penner.

The USS Comte de Grasse, having just left the Mediterranean Sea and duties with the U.S. Sixth Fleet, had traveled more than 1,500 miles to this tiny group of islands 385 miles west of Senegal.

Under the command of Cmdr. Russell J. Lindstedt II, the officers and crew were treated to a port visit vastly different from any they had seen during their five and one-half months in the Mediterranean.

With several small fishing boats on either side, the Comte de Grasse anchored off the port city of Mindelo. "Mindelo's ties with the U.S. are rich ones," commented the ambassador.

"Mindelo is the sister city of Bedford, Massachusetts, and has many exchanges with Bedford," continued Ambassador Penner. "Overall, our ties to this country extend over 900 years and have been strengthened by visits like this." Many Cape Verdeans were part of the U.S. armed forces in World War I and World War II, he added.

The ambassador's visit was one of the several official calls Cmdr. Lindstedt made and received. "These people have awaited your arrival for a while," added Penner. "The embassy received a lot of calls to host the captain. I only wish your stay could be longer."

Cape Verde became an independent nation on July 5, 1978. Until granted independence, the country was a Portuguese colony. The new government of Cape Verde is working hard to improve the standard of living for all Cape Verdeans. "They are developing, getting more trade and more currency," continued Penner. "Just last year several new hotels opened."

In addition to the ambassador's luncheon, the ship hosted Cmdr. Amancio Lopez, commander of the Cape Verde Navy, and his flag deputy Subtente Amante Da Rosa, and gave them a tour of the ship.

The commander remarked through an interpreter, "I have always wanted to see a U.S. warship and meet the crew. It was a pleasurable experience and one I will remember for a long time." Added Lopez, "This one ship is longer than our whole Navy."

The two news articles in figure 11.2 appeared in successive Fall 1995 issues of the *Continental Marine,* a journal published by the Pubic Affairs Office of the Marine Forces Reserve. A public affairs specialist wrote the release on the MIT Marine; an officer who had participated in the Colorado 10-K wrote the other. Photographs accompanied both stories. While the MIT story follows news style more directly (query lead, very short paragraphs, interesting twist at the end), both articles tell their stories well.

NEWS STYLE VERSUS OFFICIAL STYLE

Whether you compose hard news releases or features, and whether you write for civilian or military sources, remember to write in "news" style, not official. Here are a few pointers on news style.

Avoid Acronyms

Far too many people send out press releases full of unidentified acronyms. Proper news style is to use as few acronyms as possible, whether identified or unidentified. Even if a story is intended for a Navy or Marine Corps audience, spell out all acronyms the first time—but then *use them as little as possible.* To save space (and help the reader), look for a generic term: for example, "the wing" instead of COMASWWINGPAC, or "the training group" in place of FASOTRAGRUPAC.

Remember, many readers may have just joined the service, and others are civilian employees or dependents with little service knowledge. Even among long-time service members, will a submariner understand aviation acronyms? Will an infantry Marine follow Pentagon budget terms?

Stay Away from Jargon

Of course, avoid Navy and Marine Corps jargon, and technical terms like "displacement," but realize that Navy ratings can be jargon too. What would the public think of a "mess management specialist"? It's best to call that person MS2 Jones, and briefly explain the job he does. Better yet, quote MS2 Jones explaining his own rating.

At the same time, sometimes (if rarely) there may be a use in ambiguity. The author of this book had occasion to write an editorial about his son's enlisted service in the Navy for the New Orleans *Times-Picayune* right after September 11. In that article he happened to mention that his son was "hot-bunking" (or "hot-racking") aboard his submarine. The editorial editor of the paper made several changes to the article to make it more understandable to nonmilitary readers, but when she came to the term "hot-bunking," although she did not understand it, she nevertheless left it in. "It sounds exotic and interesting," she remarked.

Use Media Abbreviations for Military Ranks and Other Titles

Another characteristic of news style is that it uses special abbreviations for military ranks—Rear Adm. instead of RADM, for example, and Lt. Cmdr. instead of LCDR. Navy personnel should refer to *JO 3&2* for a complete listing of military ranks; virtually the same list appears in *The Associated Press Stylebook and Libel Manual* under "Military Titles."

Figure 11.2 Two Marine Corps Feature Articles. These releases found their way into the *Continental Marine*.

Building a diverse Corps
MIT student takes a break from school for a new challenge

Stories and photos by LCpl. Rob Lewis

Colorado Marines double-time for the Corps in 4th largest 10-K run in the U.S.

Story by Maj. P. J. McCarthy

The Marines of Colorado recently made their presence known at the 1995 Bolder Boulder 10-K road race held on Memorial Day in Boulder, Colo. Sixty-five regular and reserve Marines from various air and ground units in Colorado, completed the 6.2 mile course in formation. The Bolder Boulder run is the fourth largest road race in the United States, drawing international, world-class participants such as Arturo Barrios, Uta Pippig, Dellilah Asiago and Josphat Machuka. This year's 18th running of the race attracted over 38,000 entrants.

With an open invitation offered by the Bank of Boulder, Marines throughout Colorado volunteered to run with the "Colorado Marines" team. On the morning of the race, a heavy drizzle and 45 degree temperatures discouraged 4,800 of the entrants from participating. However, despite the steady downpour, 65 Marines formed up in three ranks to await the start of the race. Led by Maj. Stephen Manion, site commander of Marine Air Control Squadron-24 TAOC Detachment Forward in Aurora, Colo., the Marines participated as the only registered military formation team.

Inspired by the motto inscribed on their T-shirts, "The more you sweat in peace, the less you bleed in war," the Colorado Marines proudly double-timed in cadence behind the Marine Colors, and received a standing ovation from over 50,000 spectators as they entered the University of Colorado's Folsom Field stadium. The Marines completed the race in one hour and seven minutes. Following the race, seven Marine runners participated in the Memorial Day ceremony, providing a 21-gun salute to honor our fallen veterans.

With CBS live TV coverage of the entire event, the Colorado Marine team received considerable publicity for the Corps and gratitude from veterans and citizens throughout the Rocky Mountain region.

Why pass up the chance to earn a five figure salary to spend 12 weeks chewing on sand and being served as the main course for sand fleas?

Ask that question to PFC James P. White, who graduated from Recruit Training September 22, and you might be surprised.

White not only holds a bachelor of science degree in chemistry from the University of Massachusetts, Amherst, Mass., he was also accepted to the Massachusetts Institute of Technology, where he studied Material's Chemistry in MIT's elite doctoral program.

"There was really no question for me," said the 24-year-old Boston native. "I have the rest of my life ahead of me to start a career, but time was running out for my chance to be a Marine. I knew deep inside that I wouldn't be happy unless I made this change.

"I was good at chemistry, but I had that feeling that I think most Marines get before going to visit a recruiter -- the feeling that there is a challenge out there made for me," White said.

White went to Recruiting Sub-Station Boston and told Marine Recruiter, Sgt. Roy Hessner, he wanted to enlist.

"I listened to this young man tell me his background and the whole time I was thinking, 'this guy is overqualified for even the officer programs,'" Hessner said. "He told me he wanted to learn how to lead from the bottom up and then he'd consider Officer Candidate School later."

"I feel it's important to seek enlistment before pursuing a commission," said White. "A captain at my recruiting station told me how much he regretted not enlisting before he earned a commission."

For now, White will serve as a reservist in the heavy equipment mechanic field.

"My recruiter suggested an MOS where I would be able to better use my experience in science, but I wanted a hands-on job."

In the future, White said he wants to use his technical and teaching skills to help the Marine Corps. He said a teaching job, possibly at the United States Naval Academy, would suit him fine.

In the meantime, White wants to help set a positive example for his fellow devil dogs.

He wasted no time getting started on his plan to help the Corps in the future as he took charge of the only post befitting of an MIT graduate in recruit training - "knowledge recruit" -- of course.

Capitalize Much Less

Realize that you capitalize much less in news writing than in official documents. When writing for a newspaper or magazine, lowercase such occupational titles as "commanding officer," and capitalize the rank or job of "captain" only when immediately preceding a name. News style doesn't use all caps, underlines, or italics for the names of vessels, either.

Be Particularly Careful with Quotation and Attribution

Besides adopting slightly different styles, news writers have to pay particular attention to the use of quotations. Clearly, there are good times to use quotations (when there are unique, surprising, or striking statements; important quotes by important officials; etc.) and other times when it's best not to (when you're dealing with simple, factual material, for instance, or when the quote does nothing to enliven the story). The important point to cover here is the issue of attribution, or how to state the source of information.

Of course you need not cite a source for everything that is common knowledge, but for information that is subject to argument or involves policy, you must keep yourself out of trouble by citing specific sources. Use "he said" or the equivalent at least once per paragraph when citing such data. For variety, insert such attribution between sentences or phrases.

Incidentally, do not be reluctant to use that specific word "said" (as in "he said" or "she said" or "they said") as many times as you wish. Perhaps you can occasionally substitute an equally neutral word like "remarked," "stated," "added," or "commented," but be on your guard. Some substitute terms ("charged," "asserted," or "argued," for instance) can imply a particular emotional stance on the part of the person quoted that you do not intend. Similarly, if you report that a commanding officer "claimed" or "maintained" something, the reader may infer you don't quite believe him. Be very sensitive to the nuances of the words you use.

Direct quotes always need attribution, and of course any direct quotes should be *absolutely accurate.* Make sure you know *exactly* what was said, especially when quoting directly. You'll be surprised how much trouble a slight misquoting can cause, and how much it can upset the person misquoted.

Be aware of one slight exception to this rule of accuracy: if a speaker uses improper English (sentence fragments; bad grammar; lots of "ands," "ifs," or "buts"; agreement errors, etc.)—the accepted practice is to clean up the syntax for the speaker. Indeed, some COs even let you make up comments for them—as long as they can review the story before release.

Here are some examples of various ways to attribute quotes. Besides noting the method of attribution, also pay careful attention to the punctuation and capitalization in the passages below.

• The Basic Information:

Captain Charles B. Stevens made the following statement: "For 20 years we have provided the Navy with the best possible communications officers and radiomen."

• With Direct Attribution in a Complete Sentence:

"For 20 years we have provided the Navy with the best possible communications officers and radiomen," the captain said.

or

Captain Charles B. Stevens, commanding officer of the communications school, said, "For 20 years we have provided the Navy with the best possible communications officers and radiomen."

or

"For 20 years," the captain said "we have provided the Navy with the best possible communications officers and radiomen."

• With Direct Attribution, but Using Just Part of the Quote:

The captain said the school has "provided the Navy with the best possible communications officers and radiomen."

or

The school has provided the Navy with "the best possible officers and radio-men," the captain said.

- Using Indirect Quotation (Minor Rewriting but Same Meaning):

The communications school has aimed at providing top communication officers and radiomen for the Navy, the captain said.

or

The captain said the school has always aimed at providing the Navy with the best communications officers and radiomen.

For Further Style Guidance

For further guidance, see *The Associated Press Stylebook and Libel Manual,* the guide that all Navy and Marine Corps journalists and public affairs officers use for news style. That book is the best quick reference on the style of news writing available; it also has excellent advice on punctuation, word usage, capitalization in news writing, and many other news writing matters.

Many peculiarities of journalistic style pertaining to Navy and Marine Corps writers are found in the "Navy Style Guide," available online at the Navy NewsStand.

Useful as it is, however (and much of the guidance is excellent), this pamphlet-length document is *not* an official guide for general naval style as its title might indicate, but only for Navy and Marine Corps *journalists.*

For instance, its overall guidance that "Navy editors and writers should follow the most recent edition of the Associated Press Stylebook" simply is not standard for Navy correspondence style. Many standard rules for naval documents are to be found in the Naval Correspondence Manual; for a more thorough treatment, see the handbook at the end of this book.

DISTRIBUTING THE STORY

Obviously, writing a story does no good if it doesn't get to the right outlets or doesn't get there in time. Your story will likely get only as far as a well-thought-out distribution list. Determine the public you are targeting, and release information to the media that service that public.

Besides the local daily and weekly press (including base newspapers), don't overlook radio and TV outlets. Also consider sending releases to the house organs of various industrial and service organizations. Often Navy and Marine Corps subjects will be of great interest to these publications.

Many press releases compete at the editorial offices of service-wide publications. When considering whether to send an article to such official magazines as *All Hands, Wifeline, Leatherneck,* or the commercial newspaper *Navy Times,* you need to ask yourself, "If I were in the Indian Ocean on deployment and saw this story appear in a publication, would it whet my interest?" If so, send it in.

Two other possible outlets for items that have especially wide interest are the Navy NewsStand and Headquarters Marine Corps News (MCNEWS)—both now available online. These weekly "wire services" of the Navy and Marine Corps include much service-wide news as well as some public affairs guidance. You've seen products of one or both of these wire services posted on bulletin boards or in the message files, and base newspapers often run stories from these services. Both encourage submission of releases that have Navy-wide or Corps-wide interest.

At last report, collateral duty PAOs are encouraged to establish Navy NewsStand Management accounts through the navy.mil Web site. Stories should then be approved through your PA chain of command and submitted to your accounts. You can find support from Navy Public Affairs Centers (PACENs) on both coasts. When deployed, contact your fleet public affairs officer for help.

Realize that commercial papers are extremely time sensitive. Often a town paper will publish a fairly mediocre article that arrives well before the deadline before a top-notch one that arrives just barely on time. You might consider tailoring releases to specific markets (highlighting special local interest, for example). Although probably not worthwhile for all your releases, taking special care to craft a release for a particular publication, group of publications, or geographic area can sometimes get articles placed that would otherwise reach only the circular file.

A NOTE ON PHOTOS

Send black-and-white photographs with a story whenever possible. Photos (especially good quality pictures) will often convince an editor to publish a story.

Remember that in public affairs photography, the *individual* is the important subject. Strive for *an identity* first; then the job, equipment, or background of the individual can usually appear in a photo without overshadowing the subject.

On the other hand, editors always look for pictures full of action and interest. Stress to your photographer that you want *action* shots. Instead of the ship's Sailor of the year receiving a certificate from the commanding officer, have your photographer shoot the Sailor on the job.

Before you release a photo, ask yourself if anything in it detracts from the main subject. Does equipment or heavy shadow obstruct the faces? Could the photo be taken from a better angle? Is it in poor taste? Is it unflattering to the subject? If the answer to any of these questions is yes, throw it out and have it reshot. Not having a photo at all is better than using one of poor quality.

Be especially careful that the service members depicted present a positive image of the military, including its grooming and uniform standards. Any success you feel from having a story published will quickly disappear when the CO notices one of his Sailors has appeared before the world with an inch of hair over his collar.

Also avoid:

- flag poles, trees, and other objects growing out of a subject's head
- human limbs cut off at unnatural spots
- idle hands: don't let them hang motionless at the subject's sides
- people staring at the camera
- dark backgrounds, especially when the subjects have dark hair
- still and formal poses, or "line-up" shots
- "hand-shakers," also known as "grip 'n' grins": look instead for action and the unusual in your photos

Finally, be sure the prints are no smaller than 5 × 7 inches. Use pieces of cardboard for backing, and place the prints in a sturdy envelope. Follow current PA guidance on submitting digital photos. When possible include four or five different views and both horizontal and vertical formats to give layout editors some leeway when designing the page for your story. Make sure to include a *double-spaced caption* just under the photo (or taped to the back). The caption should include the full names (and ranks/rates or titles if appropriate) of depicted individuals, and explain what is going on in the photo. Give the photographer a photo credit here too. Follow this example:

CAPTION

SN Mike W. Adams catches up on some damage control maintenance while USS Bunker Hill (CG 52) is in port. A leading seaman in the ship's first division, Adams often performs duties required of a petty officer third or second class. (Photo by JO2 Mark Murphy)

OTHER POINTERS

Short items in magazines or newspapers often have surprising impact—a top-notch paragraph by itself may catch the eye, or a striking photo with a deep caption (long cutline). Remember that the release itself should be easily readable—stay away from unreadable typeface on your releases.

When you are deployed, base papers back home will be glad to get your copy. Friends and families will be delighted to see what you're doing. Indeed, for them, getting information published when you're deployed is probably more important than when you're at your home station.

Identify all the people in your stories (full rank or title, first name, middle initial, and last name), and be sure the names are accurate. Some commands insist that the CO's name be in the story you write, along with the full name of the command. On the other hand, remember that people, not ranks, make news. A lieutenant has no more news value than a seaman. Don't feel you have to mention the division officer and chief of every seaman you talk to. If you use quotes to enliven your story (not a bad idea), don't feel you must restrict your quotes to the CO or others in authority. The Sailor can have something of interest to say too—often something of *more* interest.

Finally, make sure the appropriate officials have reviewed and okay'd your story before it goes anywhere. At a minimum, ask the PAO who should see your story; if there is no PAO, consult your XO for releasing guidance.

RESOURCES FOR NEWS WRITING

The electronic resources for gathering information available via the Navy Public Affairs Library, etc. (see p. 206), can be of great help in news writing. Also, get familiar with the pertinent sources below if you aren't already.

- SECNAVINST 5720.44. The basic Public Affairs Officer regulation for both the Navy and Marine Corps.
- "U.S. Navy Style Guide." A short pamphlet discussing a variety of matters of style, from when to use "aboard" versus "on board," to how to abbreviate ships' names, to a discussion of standard journalistic reference to Navy ranks. Pertains chiefly to Navy journalists. Found on Navy NewsStand.
- Fleet Instructions. Almost every fleet or type commander issues written guidance on news writing (and has full-time PAOs who will be glad to give you advice and written guidance).
- *Journalist 3& 2* and *Journalist 1& C.* These rate-training manuals for Navy journalists are comprehensive guides for writing news releases and feature stories, for distributing those stories, and for much, much more. Begin with these books; they are excellent general guides and can be of great help to anyone working part-time or full-time in the area of news writing.
- *The Associated Press Stylebook and Libel Manual.* This book is *the* standard guide to news style for most American magazines and newspapers. It is also the universally accepted PAO style guide, though U.S. Navy public affairs officials

have outlined Navy journalist-specific usage in the "U.S. Navy Style Guide," mentioned above.

- *The Word: Associated Press Guide to Good News Writing,* Rene T. Cappon, current edition. Rather than a dictionary, this writing text is especially good on news writing.
- *The Art of Editing,* Floyd K. Baskette, Jack Z. Sissors, and Brian S. Brooks, current edition. The authors cover copyediting skills, headline-writing skills, and editing for other media.
- *The Editorial Eye,* Karen Brown Dunlap and Jane T. Harrigan (New York: St. Martin's Press, current edition). A highly readable discussion of editing for the newsroom. Packed with guidance on journalism in general.
- *Online Journalism: Reporting, Writing and Editing for New Media,* Richard Craig (Wadsworth, 2005).

ONE LAST EXAMPLE

Most official Navy and Marine Corps magazines are written by staff members. However, this does not seem to be the case with *Approach,* the Navy and Marine Corps "aviation safety" magazine. Its articles are solicited from fliers and maintenance people in both services who have usually had some kind of close call. Because of the frank acknowledgment of difficulties, the typical lively writing style (no doubt enhanced by the editorial staff), and fleetwide interest in naval aviation, the magazine's articles perhaps have more inherent interest than those of any other official publication. Certainly the "lessons learned" found in *Approach* are quite effective.

The very short article below was written by a Marine Corps captain, and was accompanied by a photograph in which he displayed his left hand with its missing finger. Given the arresting photograph, one almost *had* to read the article. Note the effective use of four short imperative sentences at the article's very end.

DANGER LURKS

The morning brought with it my annual egress drill from the AV-Harrier. I was wearing all survival gear required for flight, as briefed by the safety officer. Upon strapping into the aircraft, I realized I wasn't wearing gloves. Further, I was wearing my wedding ring. The egress was going fine until I went to release my grip from the aircraft's canopy rail to get down. My ring caught on the large, rearward facing canopy hook, and held fast as the rest of my body continued descending. I felt a jerk, heard a ripping sound, and looked down to discover my ring finger was totally severed and hanging by a thread perpendicular to its normal position.

It looked as if a sock had been rolled off the finger and left only a bloody bone remaining; my top knuckle was completely torn off.

The emergency room doctors and hand specialists determined that all tendons, nerves and blood vessels of the finger had been destroyed and were beyond repair. A few hours after the accident my finger was amputated a half-inch above its base.

An important and costly lesson learned is that no task in naval aviation is routine. A simple egress drill for me turned into a finger amputation. No matter your experience level, there is always an unforeseen danger lurking in the shadows to take advantage of the unsuspecting aviator or maintenance person. Fight complacency. Wear the required safety gear. Remove all jewelry before work. Spread the word.

—by Capt. Matt Vogt, USMC (at the time he was flying with VMA-542)
Approach, May–June 2006, p. 11.

Contributions with the pen have been significant for even the busiest military professionals. . . . The written word represents another "weapon" for use in achieving professional objectives and making an impact on society at large. For patriots, it remains a valuable tool, readily accessible for use and powerful in effect.

—WILLIAM K. RILEY, EDITOR,
ARMED FORCES STAFF COLLEGE

12

The Professional Article

So you're thinking of writing an article for a professional journal. Perhaps your spouse has remarked, as one commander's did, "Why grouse so much to me? Why not write for *Proceedings* if you're so bothered by this?" Or maybe a shipmate has commented on one of your notions, "You know, that's an excellent idea, and I've never seen it spelled out anywhere. You ought to write it up." With such encouragement, should you take some extra hours over the next several weeks to dig into this subject and write an article? The time and effort are a big sacrifice—and what real good will it do?

Of course, you'd like to see your name in print—always a motive for authors. Then there's the remote possibility that writing this article would do your career some good. Someone up the line might see it and think, "There's someone who might make a good administrative assistant, speechwriter, or aide." There's simply a professional advantage to being identified as a service member who expresses ideas well. A pattern of authorship sometimes has even larger consequences. Reportedly, Lieutenant Colonel Rommel "wrote his way to the command of a Panzer division and an eventual field marshal's baton with his *Infantry Attacks*" (Lt. Col. J. W. Hammond, Jr., "The Responsibility to Write," *Marine Corps Gazette,* January 1970, p. 28).

However, when researching this book, I found very few Navy or Marine Corps authors who thought their publishing would significantly help their careers. On the contrary, the number of times officers commented about the *dangers* of publishing (with warnings like "Be careful when publishing. . . . It's hard for officials to look at what you write with objectivity," or "You can say almost anything—but get it clear in your own mind the *price you may have to pay*") suggests that you should get straight the main reason for writing for publication. These officers didn't write articles primarily for personal prestige, career advancement, or monetary reward. Instead, they wrote for the good of the profession.

THE BEST PLACE FOR SPEAKING OUT

From my own limited perspective, *Proceedings* has been the only vehicle consistently available to articulate the truths about the limitations in our medical readiness posture. In fact, there is no other avenue for collegial discourse among professionals about our observations and suggestions short of surreptitious calls to "Hot Lines," abbreviated letters to the editor in *Navy Times* or going through the stifling point paper process via chains of command.

—CAPT Arthur M. Smith, MC, USNR, in a letter to the editor of the January 1996 issue of *Proceedings,* p. 19.

"Writing is the way to reach those people when they are not at hand and you have no way of getting to them. Talking is like a 24-pdr muzzle loader: terrifically effective at very short range. Writing is like an airplane or a missile: It permits you to be effective over the horizons of space and of time."

—FRANK UHLIG,
FORMER PUBLISHER
OF *NAVAL WAR
COLLEGE REVIEW,*
UNPUBLISHED SPEECH

"Never underestimate the power of a crank letter."
—NAVY CAPTAIN

WHY WE NEED PROFESSIONAL JOURNALS

Because of the nature of naval service, we may need professional argument and open forums more than other professions. Why not just live by official doctrine and official reports? By their very nature, official reports tend to limit expression of views. As Marine officer Gordon D. Batcheller once pointed out in an essay published in the *Marine Corps Gazette* ("For the Sake of the Corps, Write!" February 1984), all official reports "go through the chain of command. This [review process] has an inhibiting effect on all participants. . . . Critical candor becomes the first casualty. A satisfactory answer to 'Whose ox does this gore?' is a hurdle that any critical comment must clear if it is to survive the editorial ax. The more senior the ox, the less goring allowed" (p. 56).

Batcheller went on to argue that because reports are usually staff efforts signed by committees, and because the signers become liable for the product, putting critical views forward is difficult. "Something you may feel with great conviction may not be shared by the officer who has to sign the document. You may be reluctant to ask him to buy into your misery; he may be unwilling to do so" (p. 56).

As a result, the official information received at the top of the chain of command may be limited in value. As Admiral Rickover once commented, "Always rely on the chain of command to transmit and implement your instructions; but if you rely on the chain of command for your information about what's going on, you're dead" (Admiral Rickover was quoted by R. James Woolsey, former Undersecretary of the Navy; the quote was published in the April 1984 *Marine Corps Gazette*). Clearly, many senior officials are insulated from criticism by their positions, and therefore badly need to hear some unofficial views on occasion. One place to hear forthright personal opinions is in professional journals.

Not only commanders but all naval professionals need to have as informed a perspective as possible. True, we all read official publications that help us stay informed of late developments. But unofficial sources help greatly here too. Most naval personnel at sea would know very little about larger developments in the services without such forums as U.S. Naval Institute *Proceedings, Marine Corps Gazette, Navy Times,* and *Naval War College Review.*

Informational articles in such forums keep readers abreast of new developments in hardware, strategy, tactics, logistics, and many personnel-related topics. Journals publish persuasive articles to plant ideas, open discussion, and help readers to think of their jobs in new ways. Some pieces are "seminal" articles; they initiate whole programs and courses of action. Others do good work by "nudging" policy or thought. As Frank Uhlig, longtime publisher of the *Naval War College Review,* pointed out,

OPPORTUNITIES FOR NEW AUTHORS TO WRITE

Should you hesitate to write because of lack of seniority? Absolutely not. Most military journals—and particularly *Proceedings* and the *Gazette*—actively encourage junior authors and go out of their way to help those with promising ideas to improve their articles. They open their pages to enlisted service members, civil servants, and young officers. They even hold contests to stimulate new authors to try their hands at writing essays.

If anything, because of editors' encouragement of junior authors, someone who is not senior will have a marked advantage in getting an article published, especially the very first one. After that, you're an old hand, and will have to sweat and struggle like the rest of us.

even if you don't convince your readers immediately, you get readers to begin thinking about what you're thinking about.

So do your service a favor, and put your good ideas or experience in print. How should you proceed? The following pages present brief guidance gleaned from conversations with many military authors and editors and from published articles on this subject.

Besides reading these pages, if you think either now or later in your career you might have something of value to say, then the very best way you can prepare is to start *reading*. Read books on naval topics; read naval and other military journals; and read beyond strictly military subjects too. The most thoughtful authors know the wide contexts of their subjects. They speak across boundaries of disciplines, and they draw analogies from widely varying fields and eras. In short, the best naval *writers* are good general *readers* first.

WRITING A PROFESSIONAL ARTICLE

Like most writing, professional writing involves a series of discrete processes.

Decide on Your Focus

The basic question is one of focus. First decide whether you know something that your reader doesn't and that is significant or interesting enough to attract attention. Writing well depends above all on having something to say.

One good piece of advice to authors is to concentrate on a specific area—limit your subject. Don't try to refight the First Gulf War in two thousand words or attempt to explain the Navy and Marine Corps budget process even in five thousand. Not only are such subjects impossible to cover in such short space, but narrowing the subject to something you *really are an expert in* will help you to speak authoritatively. Stay in your area of expertise, and write on a subject with which you're familiar.

That doesn't mean you have to have twenty years of experience before you write. As a senior military journal editor pointed out, midshipmen sometimes have held their own with officers ten years their seniors by writing about what it's like to be led by good or bad leaders, or by revealing their thoughts upon first stepping into leadership roles. The midshipmen could speak with credibility and sharpness when they stayed close to their own certain knowledge. Of course, as you gain experience, you can range much further afield. But new authors should start with what is close to home.

"Stake out intellectual territory. Put forward a clear, forceful point of view. Leave no doubt of what you think."
—CAPT JOHN BYRON, USN (RET.), "TEN COMMANDMENTS FOR PROCEEDINGS WRITERS"

Look at What Kinds of Articles Journals Publish

Having selected a subject, consider the kind of forum for which you're trying to write. Locate at least three or four possibilities—journals will often send you back copies as well as a writing guide or information sheet for authors (and most of this information is also available online). If you can, analyze several back issues, taking a careful look at what each journal publishes, especially the kind of articles it has put out recently. What are the style, length, and content of the articles? For whom do they seem to be written? Not only will such analysis help you decide whether your article can fit into that journal, but it may also give you several ideas on good methods of support, ways to begin and end, the best use of anecdotes and quotations, and so on.

Remember that a journal normally has several different sections. *Proceedings,* for instance, has "Professional Notes," and "Nobody Asked Me But," as well as feature articles. The *Marine Corps Gazette* is similar—each issue has several sections, and besides full-length articles of about 2,000–3,000 words, it publishes shorter ones of 750–1,500. Some of the latter involve opinion or argument ("Commentary on the Corps") while others are professional notes ("Strategy and Tactics," "Weapons and Equipment," etc.), or short historical vignettes. Typically the editorial review process differs for different sections of a journal; getting a piece into the shorter sections is sometimes a bit less difficult.

Letters to the editor, by the way, can add much to the professional perspective. The 2007 online guidance to people interested in writing letters to the *Marine Corps Gazette* pointed out that such letters "correct factual mistakes, reinforce ideas, outline opposing points of view," and identify additional needed considerations. The guidance concluded by saying that "the best letters are sharply focused on one or two specific points."

Do Any Necessary Research

Of course, you must have excellent support for whatever kind of article you write. Your reader rightly expects you to have rich and detailed knowledge or experience—assets that make you worth listening to.

Regardless how much you think you already know about your subject, become familiar with its wider context by reading published sources, including past articles related to your topic. Besides giving you more information and assuring you of the quality of your ideas, these sources will help you orient your article in the current professional discussion.

You may find that you need to do additional research, or you may conclude you already have sufficient arguments and data at hand. Whether you need to do further research is a judgment call on your part. The test of whether you have enough to present your topic fully is often the very first draft.

Draft the Article—Get the Content Down

Content is, of course, the key to any article. Journal editors have great patience with authors who have dynamic ideas, even if those authors can't write very well. As the *Gazette's* "Writing Guide" once commented, "We'll gladly accept a good idea written with a pencil stub on wrapping paper." Not everyone would go quite *that* far ("It's much easier to edit if it's typed, double-spaced, with one-inch margins," responded one harassed *Proceedings* editor), but if the content is good enough, almost all editors will go out of their way to help.

On the other hand, if you have problems with the content, whatever catchy introductions and other stylistic dressing-up you add won't help. One prominent military journal editor complained about bad content even in articles submitted from war colleges. Though an article by definition is conceptual and not "completed staff work," still, he argued, it must at least nod toward real-world issues like cost, manpower, priorities, and so on.

Therefore, when writing a professional article, concentrate on the *basic idea* and *its proof* (if yours is an argumentative essay) or on a *sharp presentation of content and data* (if it is an informative piece). Here are some of the questions that *Proceedings* editors often ask of an article that crosses their desks:

- Is the subject relevant?
- Is its focus sharp and the topic limited?
- Is the topic timely?
- Does the author know what he or she is talking about?
- Is the logic sound?
- Has the research been thorough?
- Is the thought sequence easy to follow?
- Do the main points emerge clearly from the details?
- Are the explanations clear and convincing?
- Are the details interesting?
- Has the writer had experts criticize this paper?

Editors can fix the grammar, and they can help an author with an introduction, a closing, and the whole style of a piece. But a miner mines raw materials only to recover some precious metal within. Make sure your essay has good *substance* to begin with.

Revise Your Article for Content

After getting a good draft down, work it over again (wait a couple of days first—you'll be surprised how different it all looks). Flesh out your ideas and generally rework the piece. You may find your thesis has to be modified or that your organization needs rethinking. Much of your effort will be adding details, examples, and illustrations, and looking at your logic. All of this work can be tedious, but if your first draft was successful, you can often revise a section at a time till you've substantially revised the whole article.

Of course, *double check all your facts.* Remember, yours is the final responsibility for what you say. Except in relatively unknown fields, magazines will usually rely on your subject-matter expertise; they do not check the basic accuracy of all that they publish.

Here are some other tests for the content of your article, once you're in the revision stage:

- Is your idea sound? Is it so clearly presented that it seems self-evident to the reader?
- In an argumentative article, have you taken a strong stand, adopted a definite point of view?
- Do you have sufficient support? Do you present justification for all superlatives and evidence for all generalizations? Evidence can be facts, descriptions, graphs, tables, anecdotes, and many other things. When deciding how much to say, follow this general rule: Don't say *everything you know* about the subject, but do say *everything the reader needs to know* in order to understand and to buy your main point.
- Have you included quotations (if available)? Quotes can add both interest and credibility to your article. Look for expressions that perfectly capture the issue

"Edit ruthlessly. Nobody gets it just right the first time. Keep editing until you can't make the piece better."
—CAPT JOHN BYRON, USN (RET.), "TEN COMMANDMENTS FOR *PROCEEDINGS* WRITERS"

"The memories of [event] participants often clouds with the passage of time, so individual recollections should be checked against other sources. Try to find at least two witnesses to confirm visual evidence."
—CAPT PAUL RYAN, USN (RET.), "HOW TO WRITE FOR *PROCEEDINGS*"

TAKING THE EMOTION OUT

You may find yourself very much emotionally engaged in your argument. Such involvement in itself can be either good or bad, depending on how you address your readers. Colonel John Greenwood of the *Marine Corps Gazette* once suggested that writers should make the assumption that those to whom they are writing are intelligent and as patriotic and conscientious as they. That attitude will take any viciousness or pent-up frustration out of your argument. Put the audience on the same side as you are; assume that readers are reasonable and open to argument, and you'll avoid being too strident or on edge in your tone.

Admittedly, sometimes even this attitude isn't enough. The emotion that affects you can be very powerful, not only clouding your view but inhibiting you altogether from writing with a reasonable tone. An officer was so greatly worked up over the "Women in the Military" issue as to be literally unable to write on the topic *at all* without sounding vindictive, or defensive, or both. Apparently the bare mention of any word involving gender triggered a deep emotional reaction. It was only by altering the very terms being dealt with—so that instead of saying "men" and "women" the officer spoke in terms of "the incoming group" and "the current group"—that this writer was able to get the emotion out and successfully complete the article.

Don't refrain from writing an article just because you're charged up about it. Emotion has a great deal of psychic power, energy that you can channel into highly effective (and vitally needed) communication. *Do* recognize that you may be overwrought and, because of your emotional engagement, may be seeing only one side of the issue. Besides doing what you can to see the matter objectively, get several outside reviews from professionals who are not steamed up like you are. Going through a review process can not only make your article better, but it can also provide a learning experience as to how to communicate with others.

---

at hand, or supporting statements that carry weight because of the authority of the person who uttered them. Don't clutter your manuscript with long quotes that only restate what you are trying to prove, but look for the *telling* comment, the *penetrating* phrase.

- Have you documented all special sources and data? Editors are wary of any unsupported assertions.
- Are your examples clear? Have you taken into account the specific audience you are writing for and its level of understanding? Make sure you explain difficult concepts and technical terms.
- Have you clarified your argument's *relevance?* That is, have you also made clear your argument's consequences and put those consequences in terms with which your readers can identify?
- Have you refuted any opponents' likely arguments (usually after adducing positive support)?
- Finally, if you have criticized a policy or program, have you also offered constructive recommendations? Avoid criticizing a policy or procedure without suggesting an alternative—unless you are simply saying, *Stop it! Right now!*

Revise Your Article for Style

Once satisfied with the basic content, work on your style. Although journals edit articles before publishing them, an editor is more likely to publish a polished article than a dull, awkward, and mistake-riddled one. Here are some points to remember:

- Is the writing vivid, or does it sound like a training manual or an official instruction? If the latter, try *writing the way you speak.* That approach will freshen up your language. Virtually no one *talks* bureaucratese—so if you talk out your article, the writing will usually be clearer, simpler, and more natural.
- Make sure you use the *active voice.* Virtually all military journals mention this point. None of them wants all that impersonal and longwinded discourse so common to navalese—"it is recommended that," "the suggestion is made to," "the argument is offered that," and so on.
- Don't repeat yourself unnecessarily. Military authors tend to repeat themselves overmuch in their writing, and also to add too much background and context. As a result, military journals often cut two or three pages *from both ends* of an article.
- Watch for long sentences and cut them back (an average of about seventeen words per sentence is ideal, according to some experts). Keep the paragraphs short, too. Cut out all words, sentences, or paragraphs that are dull, repetitive, or unnecessary.
- Work on rhythm and phrasing, reading aloud to listen to your prose. Strive for exactly the right word.
- Try using subheads in your article, perhaps every five to seven paragraphs or so, depending on the content. Subdivision will help keep the reader oriented and might attract readers who are just browsing through.
- Finally, avoid jargon. Define all important terms. Avoid unnecessary abbreviations and acronyms. Define what acronyms you absolutely must use the first time you use them, as in tactical action officer (TAO), remotely piloted vehicle (RPV), or airborne early warning (AEW). Then you can use these acronyms in succeeding sentences, as long as they aren't several paragraphs apart. Vary subsequent references by interspersing other, simpler nouns ("the officer," "the vehicle," "the concept", etc.) to keep from overusing the acronym.

Consider Including Graphics

See if you can add any graphics support. Good graphics can make your argument much more readable and interesting and can incline the editorial board in your favor. Photos, charts, tables, maps, and diagrams are all good possibilities—and sometimes a staff artist can fix your rough sketches. Of course, think in terms of lively illustrations meant for magazines, not dull charts from a training manual. Although not all articles include illustrative material, it may help sell your article. If you have an idea for artwork but can't get it yourself, let the editors know. A magazine (like *Proceedings* or *Marine Corps Gazette,* particularly) can often illustrate your article with photographs from its own files.

Get Good Critiques, and Then Revise Again

Once you have a good draft, get some good criticism. How much, and from whom? One frequent contributor to *Proceedings* argues that you should find ten people who know a lot about your subject and have them tear your article apart. He always does. As a result, he finds that his material sails through editorial staffs—and he looks a lot smarter, too.

ON PUBLISHING AND PROMOTION—TWO OPINIONS

As a LT or LCDR, an article in *Proceedings* or *Approach* can find a place in a fitrep bullet, and be bragged on during a local ranking board. "Hey, my lieutenant was published in *Approach*—my lieutenant is better than yours!"

—Naval aviator, CAPT

Can professional articles help get you promoted? Say a board were briefed that a particular officer in the 'crunch zone' had published two articles in *Proceedings*. Well, if he's so far down in professionalism that he needs *this* argument, I wouldn't vote for him.

—Naval aviator, CDR

Maybe you can't get ten—but get some experts to review your work. To make sure you are not speaking over your readers' heads, have some nonexperts read your article as well.

Then revise your essay once more.

Get the Required Security and Policy Review

Normally, service members and Department of Defense civilians must clear articles for security through their local public affairs offices prior to submission and must include a signed statement of clearance with the article. Although some journals will assume responsibility for a security review, the author must usually get the article cleared. Don't regard a security review as antagonistic; do your homework ahead of time.

Not only security but policy may be an issue. For one thing, be careful about using the privileged information your job gives access to, even if it is unclassified. Such information may not be intended for public distribution. Wise authors make a practice of getting the material they use from some standard naval source and then citing that source in their articles.

For another thing, recognize that readers may have difficulty separating your own view from that of the office that you occupy. Even with a useful disclaimer on your part—"Opinions, conclusions, and recommendations expressed or implied within are solely those of the author and do not necessarily represent the views of . . ."—people will often assume that the stance you take is official because of your official position. Talk to experienced authors around your duty station or community if you envision any problems in this area.

Another difficult subject is how to handle legitimate dissent within such a hierarchical and honor-bound institution as the military. On this subject, a senior officer once gave this even-handed advice:

Your oath of office doesn't cease when sitting at the typewriter. You have a professional obligation (1) not to reveal any classified information, (2) to be responsible and objective, and not harmful to the service, (3) to learn the current rules for getting articles cleared for policy as well as security, and

"A Marine willing to terminate his career in a firefight should be no less willing to terminate it through the candid expression of his professional convictions, constructively offered. . . . The real issue is not the risk to the critic, but the risk to the Corps if there are no critics."

—COL. GORDON D. BATCHELLER, *MARINE CORPS GAZETTE* (MAY 1987). REPRINTED BY PERMISSION; COPYRIGHT RETAINED BY *MARINE CORPS GAZETTE*

(4) never to sandbag your boss (send a courtesy copy to your boss when your article has been prepared for publication).

On the other hand, remember that it is not possible to say "good morning" without some fellow in Washington objecting to it. Yes, follow the rules, but there are times to put your blind eye to the telescope.

A magazine editor suggested, "Try to stay within the regs, but don't be slavish to them. If you run into review problems, contact the editor. Maybe he can help."

Final Review

As a final review, check all figures, dates, names, titles, footnotes, quotations (especially quotations—and against the original source), and other material to make sure you have not made inadvertent errors. Also check grammar, mechanics, spelling, and punctuation.

Format the Article, Type It, and Send It In

- Double-check the exact format required by the journal to which you're sending the article. (As stated above, most journals describe on their Web sites what they look for, including format and number of copies. Also, a journal will usually list its specific format requirements in each issue, somewhere near the title page.) Some journals require footnotes; others ask you to work documentation into your text as done in this chapter. Technical journals will often ask you to submit an abstract.
- Some journals will accept articles as attachments to emails. Otherwise, submit your article typewritten and double-spaced on white 8½″ × 11″ bond paper (one side of the page only). Don't use script or all caps. Make your margins at least one inch at top, bottom, and right, and an inch and a half at the left (some journals require a three-inch top margin on the first page). List your name, rank, office, and phone at the beginning or end of your article, and number your pages. The production of most journals is now fully computerized, so you should also send your article in on disk. Always mail manuscripts of more than five pages flat, with a paper clip. Include a cover letter of no more than a page in length. Remember to include a self-addressed, stamped return envelope.
- Send tables or graphs to illustrate your article, and make sure they are in black ink, not photocopy. Check with each particular magazine for whether they prefer black and white or color photos (and what size), or if they want slides or digital photos. Identify pictured individuals on a separate sheet (writing on the back of a photo can damage it). For all illustrations, include a suggested caption. The caption should explain the illustration, relate it to the text as appropriate, but not repeat the exact words of the text.
- Remember that most journals ask authors not to submit material to more than one journal at a time, regarding multiple submissions as unprofessional. However, check each journal's policy on this.

Consider These Naval and Other Military Journals

Below are the four major professional magazines or journals that provide forums for expression of opinion on the naval profession:

- U.S. Naval Institute *Proceedings*
- *Marine Corps Gazette*

- *Naval War College Review*
- *Naval History*

Here are some other official Navy magazines that might also be worth looking to, if you have suitable material (they are written mostly by staff):

- *Leatherneck*
- *Naval Aviation News*
- *Submarine Review*
- *Seapower*
- *Surface Warfare*
- *Navy Civil Engineer*

CONVERTING A PAPER INTO AN ARTICLE

Many professional military articles originate in a classroom, but what makes a good student paper is not what makes a good article. The paper typically has a particular instructor as the intended audience (an expert who is already interested in the topic), and part of the paper's purpose is to show off the student's research. So the paper burgeons with buzzwords and stumbles with weighty footnotes. To interest journal readers who have never so much as thought about the subject before, the author must spread a much wider net by cutting back mere documentation and enlivening crucial support.

Typically, those who've written a good paper at Newport, Quantico, Monterey, or some other service school must describe their subjects much more simply (and visually) than they did in the original essay. They must also change the terms they use; the terminology and acronyms that work for experts are often gibberish for others.

In fact, so specialized has military terminology become that when writing for a broad military audience, an author does best to assume that the readers aren't in the service at all. As Frank Uhlig of the *Naval War College Review* once put it, "Assume that the people reading your article are intelligent and interested *laymen. A destroyer officer and a fighter pilot both belong to the same navy, but neither is likely to know very much about the other's business. The same is true if you are aiming at people in other services, or civilians, only more so."

Adding intriguing introductions, simpler and fuller explanations, descriptive language, simplified terms, and striking conclusions may help to transform a paper into a journal article. Readers can always put the magazine down when what you have written does not engage them—so you must work for relevance, interest, even charm.

What follow are examples of openings or "leads," exemplifications or illustrations, and conclusions or "sign-offs." These examples are somewhat artificial; they have been taken out of context and are necessarily brief. Nevertheless, they show the principles in action.

Openings, or "Leads"

A good beginning not only attracts the reader's attention but also draws the reader immediately into important material. A "lead" can be a sentence, a phrase, or a paragraph. On a professional note, the lead will often be very short, for when describing new programs or recent developments you can sometimes count on ready reader interest. In contrast, the lead for a feature article will occasionally extend over several paragraphs. Even there you shouldn't lose motion. Craft the lead to draw the reader quickly into the meat of the article. See the examples.

Open with an anecdote that pertinently introduces your topic:

Attention-getting anecdote

A scientist and an engineer were put in a room across from a bag of gold. They were told they could have the bag when they moved across the room. They could go as fast as they wanted provided they went no more than half the remaining distance with each move. The scientist, recognizing the impossibility of the situation, left the room. The engineer, on the other hand, moved across the room until he was within arm's reach of the bag. At this point, he declared that he had gone far enough for an engineering approximation, grabbed the bag, and left.

introduces the topic.

In developing its weapons, the Navy's goal frequently is to build a state-of-the-art system on the cutting edge of technology, rather than a simpler system that is good enough to get the job done. The result is that developmental work is always halfway finished, and its goals are never reached.

—LCDR Eric Johns, USN, "Perfect is the Enemy of Good Enough," U.S. Naval Institute *Proceedings* (October 1988): 37.

Open with a striking statement:

Arresting statement

leads to

the central issue.

Are Army infantry soldiers more important than Marines as human beings or as components of U.S. defense strategy? If this strikes you as a preposterous and insulting notion in 2006, more than six decades after Iwo Jima, consider the fact that Marines still do not have a dedicated medevac helicopter—a nicety of war that is all about saving limbs and lives and that Soldiers have had for many years.

—CAPT Michael Vengrow, MC, USN, "Saving Limbs and Lives," U.S. Naval Institute *Proceedings* (February 2007): 20.

. . . or open with an arresting question:

Arresting question

Because one missile may sink a ship, naval officers often ask:

I know I can use force in self-defense if my ship is actually attacked. *But do I have to take the first hit?*

leads to subjects

This paper discusses how international law, Navy Regulations and naval rules of engagement (ROE) answer this question for the on-scene

of discussion.

commander. It also deals with the more general question sometimes asked by the President and other national command authorities: Are there circumstances when the United States may use force first?

—George Bunn, "International Law and the Use of Force in Peacetime: Do U.S. Ships Have to Take the First Hit?" *Naval War College Review* (May–June 1986): 69.

Open professional articles by getting right to the point. The main point of this article is in the very first sentence:

Main Point

The Marine Corps loses the talent of innovative and capable Marines because of the poor leadership they experience during the first four years. After their first contract they're gone and are never coming back."

—Cpl. Michael K. Adams, USMC, "Leadership and the Private's Agenda," U.S. Naval Institute *Proceedings* (July 2006): 86.

This professional article also opens with its thesis:

Thesis . . .

exemplified.

The information superhighway—the proposed National Information Infrastructure—is under construction and the Navy had better build some on-ramps. Information can be more valuable than money; already, when it comes to combat, safety of flight, or linking remote medical facilities with experts around the world, some information has become priceless.

—CDR T. D. Goodall, USN, "Getting Navy on the Information Highway," U.S. Naval Institute *Proceedings* (November 1994): 92.

And here the author locates the context in recent published work:

One problem's solution

has other benefits.

The problem of continuity units assigned to the northern NATO commitment has been discussed in recent *Gazette* articles. The Marine Corps Reserve could take a major step in solving the problem of continuity by establishing a Marine amphibious brigade (MAB) dedicated to a cold weather environment. Establishing such a cold weather unit would increase preparedness to fight a Soviet invasion and at the same time greatly enhance the individual reservist's sense of mission. . . . If properly trained and organized, the Reserves could greatly enhance the Marine

> Corps' ability to deploy and fight on short notice
> in the arctic environment.
>
> —Capt. Eric J. Green, USMC, "Continuity in Arctic Units,"
> *Marine Corps Gazette* (February 1986): 36. Reprinted by permission;
> copyright retained by *Marine Corps Gazette.*

Illustrations and Examples

Making bare facts or general statements meaningful can require special methods, such as visualization, comparison, exemplification, and so on. The possibilities are countless, but the techniques below are common.

Use statistics creatively to make your point. Strategic use of statistics may prove conclusive. Do your best to make your figures comprehensible to your reader, with comparisons, multiplications, or other such manipulation (as long as you do it honestly). Also make sure to list your source, as in the example below.

A selection board scenario

seen in its financial ramifications

> There is great pressure to reduce defense expenses. People in powerful positions are more and more often heard commenting that "something has got to give"—the tremendous cost of maintaining our modern defense establishment must somehow be reduced. Consequently, they look askance at the fact that each of the Navy captains who must be retired from active duty at 26–30 years of service is entitled to a pension (on the average) of about $40,000 per year for perhaps as long as 27.1 more years. By the Bureau of Naval Personnel (BuPers) official estimate, this totals $1,087,468 over the remainder of his life. Multiplying this number by the 250 senior captains who retired in 1986 (again, a BuPers estimate), it appears that their flag selection board added about $280,000,000 to our national debt.
>
> —CAPT Edward L. Beach, USN (Retired), "Up Or Out: A Financial Disaster," U.S. Naval Institute *Proceedings* (June 1987): 54.

Here statistics are used to refute a widespread contention:

Important contention

refuted by one

> Universal "Truth" Number Two:
> *Service academy graduates do not stay longer.*
>
> This perception does not come from any data officials at the service academies are familiar with. Retention rates for Naval Academy graduates exceed all other officer accession sources at every major career decision point. For example, to produce 40 career-designated officers—those with at least ten years of service and selected for

set of statistics . . .

and by another.

lieutenant commander—requires an initial accession of 100 Naval Academy graduates, 140 from NROTC, and 153 from Officer Candidate School (OCS). Furthermore, the last class that was tracked to reach the 20-year point had a retention rate of 41% for the Naval Academy, 24% for NROTC, and 21% for OCS. So that universal truth has absolutely no factual basis.

—ADM Charles R. Larson, USN, "Service Academies—Critical to Our Future," U.S. Naval Institute *Proceedings* (October 1995): 34.

Use examples to support your assertions. Examples that support your points will both illustrate what you mean and tend to convince by accumulation. In the example below, the authors drive home their points by narrating telling incidents with the same general import from three different armed services.

Author's point, proved by . . .

Navy example,

Army example,

Royal Navy example.

In addition, a disturbing set of events occurred which seemed to reflect doubt on the advisability of using polyester materials for naval uniforms. A chief petty officer wearing double-knit khakis was severely burned when exposed to flash fire in a ship's fireroom. Safety Center experiments showed that corfam shoes burned and melted when subjected to flame. A U.S. Army aviator wearing a Nomex flight suit received fatal burns following a crash traceable to the melted nylon undershorts and undershirt he was wearing. (His Nomex flight suit was intact and his copilot, wearing Nomex with cotton undergarments, was only slightly injured.) In more recent experience, Royal Navy crewmen wearing polyester coveralls suffered severely aggravated polyester slag burns during the Falklands Conflict.

—LT David M. Kennedy, USN, and LT William R. C. Stewart III, Medical Corps, USNR, "That Dangerous Polyester Look," U.S. Naval Institute *Proceedings* (January 1984): 97.

Use comparisons and contrasts to make your points clear. Using implicit contrast, here an author criticizes a modern movie for being unrepresentative of actual Marines:

Description of the Marines in the movie . . .

The Marine infantrymen depicted in this movie are not the same warriors that Lieutenant General James N. Mattis and others led into Iraq in 2003 under the credo of "No Better Friend, No Worse Enemy." The men in *Jarhead* are enemies of each other, held prisoner by a barrage of phallic references, boredom and their

omits a typical Marine's dedication

own inability to make sense of their decisions. Collectively, they are driven by nothing more than a base lust to kill. Honor, courage, and commitment mean nothing to the Marines in *Jarhead.* They only want to fight, frolic, and fornicate.

—"Jarhead: A Tale Better Left Untold," Reviewed by David J. Danelo, U.S. Naval Institute *Proceedings* (December 2005): 78.

. . . and here another author also uses contrast:

Other agencies' claims

I hear that the Army Corps of Engineers thinks it can manage aids to navigation better than we can. Maybe the Navy thinks it can blockade the Mona Passage more efficiently than we can. The Environmental Protection Agency wants the strike teams and oil-pollution-control budget. Maybe Amtrak wants a piece of the Coast Guard, too.

the essence of the Coast Guard's mission

But nobody else has stepped up to say that they can maintain a 24-hour-a-day watch along our entire coastline. Nobody else has offered to put three young men and women into a small boat, in high seas, time and time again, in all weather, and in all conditions. Nobody else has stepped up to say that they will go out again and again when everyone else is coming in.

—Thomas W. Gross, "For Those in Peril," U.S. Naval Institute *Proceedings* (December 1994): 59.

And of course you can use bullet format in articles as well as point papers, as in this argument against the multitude of rules governing captain's mast in the Coast Guard:

Author's thesis

For example, if a Coast Guard non-rated enlisted member is awarded non-judicial punishment, the following administrative measures are required:

supported by several specific instances.

- Member is no longer eligible for transfer without CG Personnel Command approval.
- Supervisor must prepare a special, adverse evaluation.
- Supervisor must assign an "unsatisfactory" mark in conduct on the member's evaluation, with automatic loss of Good Conduct eligibility.
- Member cannot be advanced during the remainder of the marking period.

- Member is ineligible to apply for officer commissioning programs for 36 months.
- Member must be removed from any "A" school waiting list and is ineligible to reapply for 6 months.
- Member is ineligible for special duty assignments for 4 years . . . (and the list goes on).

—CDR Kevin E. Lunday, USCG, "Repeal the 16-Pound Sledgehammer," U.S. Naval Institute *Proceedings* (February 2007): 41.

Closings, or "Sign-Offs"

A good closing or "sign-off" to an article will usually lead back in some way either to the heart of the article or to some special high point in it. It may summarize, call to action, or challenge the reader. Whatever the approach, the best closing provides a "sense of an ending," releasing the reader's attention gracefully but with a final flick of the wrist. At the very end (the last sentence or words), you might hark back to the introduction, cite a historical quotation, or make some kind of appeal.

Close **with a summary:**

Summary is put in terms of waging war.

When a virulent epidemic emerges, commanders must restrict, sequester, and cohort personnel in time and space. The main effort must be to protect and support combatant commanders and units that are disease free. Assuming a strong defensive posture in the face of a lethal epidemic deprives the disease of the initiative. Captains must recall the away parties, pull up the gangplank, and prepare to repel boarders.

Generalization

A new war is upon us, and how we respond will determine if we are able to serve our Sailors, loved ones, ships, and country.

—LCDR Thomas Luke, LCDR Timothy Halenkamp, and CAPT Edward Kilbane, all MC, USN, "Naval Quarantine: Impervious to Epidemics of Virulent Disease," U.S. Naval Institute *Proceedings* (July 2006): 53.

Close **with a conclusion:**

Summary

Much damage has already been done from religious commentary by commanders. However well-intentioned, it is rarely received that way.

Elaboration

When subordinates are antagonized by the missionary zeal of their commanders, there can be few positive results. It is time for this conduct to

Call to action

cease—whether by self-imposed restraint or by official prohibition.

—Maj. David S. Jonas, USMC, "Gratuitous Religious Comment," U.S. Naval Institute *Proceedings* (August 1994): 82.

Close by **citing an authority:**

Summary

Citing of authority

Conclusive last sentence

The story of our POW experience in Vietnam, accepting a modicum of failure, is one of undaunted, unremitting courage. Even a fleeting profile of POW opinion demonstrates that the Code of Conduct proved to be sound doctrine. Capt Jim Mulligan put the Code in final perspective:

> It can't answer everything, but it sets the rules. If you don't have any moral guts or personal integrity, the Code is not going to give them to you. But most military people have them someplace inside, and the Code of Conduct brings them out.

—Maj. Terrence P. Murray, USMC, "Code of Conduct—A Sound Doctrine," *Marine Corps Gazette* (December 1983): 62. Reprinted by permission; copyright retained by *Marine Corps Gazette.*

. . . or by **citing historical precedent:**

Return to article's beginning,

pointing out historical mistakes.

Present actions to take

to prevent future mistakes.

In the early days of World War II, we failed to anticipate the actions of our enemies. Thousands of Americans died as a result. Among these legions were many merchant mariners and civilians who lost their lives in an obscure operational backwater—ironically, a backwater that lies on the very shores of our continental United States. It would be painful to relearn these lessons from a new generation of enemy sailors by repeating the mistakes of our history. Through creative planning and use of our Reserve forces, we can prepare for a future enemy campaign in the Gulf of Mexico. This strategic imperative is crucial for our Nation's ability to maintain the industrial tempo that wartime will demand: a major loss of the vast resources of the Gulf coast could spell tragedy in any future, major conflict.

—LT William J. Cox, USNR, "The Gulf of Mexico: A Forgotten Frontier in the 1980s," *Naval War College Review* (Summer 1987): 75.

Close by illustrating **how success is close at hand:**

Summary

Intriguing cost as conclusion

History clearly shows us the utility of smaller vessels in support of major fleet elements; we can have this small boat capacity at a cost which does not force us to weaken other vital defense projects, and we can have it quickly. For less than $175 million, the Navy could have 24 new patrol combatants by early 1985.

—LCDR R. D. Jacobs, USNR, "In Search of . . . Patrol Combatants,"
U.S. Naval Institute *Proceedings* (September 1983): 127.

Close **with a comparison:**

*Need for
biological change*

*Need for
naval change*

In biological evolution, species that can do more with less, better than their competitors can, thrive. They narrow the niche of other species competing for the same resources, sometimes to extinction. Evolution, also, is punctuated by sudden environmental changes. Species that cannot adapt quickly enough, perish. The U.S. submarine force faces today a sudden change toward an environment in which the resources it needs for new growth are being consumed by competitors that are more efficient in satisfying national security concerns. Unless the submarine force can compete for construction resources more effectively, SSNs will go the way of the dreadnoughts.

—John T. Hanley, "Implications of the Changing Nature of Conflict for the Submarine Force," *Naval War College Review* (Autumn 1993): 26.

Or close by **calling to action:**

*Summary precedes
call for action*

A system that requires individual Sailors to cover governmental obligations until it is convenient for the government to pay is fundamentally flawed and unreasonable. . . . We owe it to our Sailors to investigate other options and make the travel process more reasonable and less onerous to those least able to bear the burden. For our Sailors' sake, the DoD travel card must go.

—LCDR Chris Davis, USN, "The DoD Travel Card Must Go,"
U.S. Naval Institute *Proceedings* (February 2007): 67.

Handbook

The guidelines suggested here reflect current military and professional writing practices and were developed with reference to both official and unofficial sources. The Department of the Navy Correspondence Manual, Marine Corps documents of various sorts, and the Air Force pamphlet *Tongue and Quill* are chief sources for this section. Note: This handbook does *not* cover Navy journalism. See pages 270–73 in this book for a discusssion of journalistic style and references.

Because practices differ from place to place within the services, naval writers should also follow whatever guides have been developed locally and are standardized throughout a command, service, or service community.

This short section, of course, can't cover everything. Besides this handbook, every professional should have close at hand a college-level (hardbound) dictionary and a complete handbook. Other useful books might include a thesaurus and a short reference manual. Most of these resources are available at the local Servmart. You should also have ready access to the Correspondence Manual, any desktop guide your command may have put out, and handy desk planners such as the Navy Leader Planning Guide (NAVPERS 15255 series). See "The Well-Stocked Desk" at the end of this section.

NUMBERS

In general, **write all numbers as figures** (3, 10, 17, 347). However, note exceptions as follows:

Spell Out . . .

Numbers that begin a sentence:

> Eight stevedores loaded the vessel.
> Twenty-five games remain.

Numbers used in connection with serious or dignified subjects, especially in formal writing:

> The Thirteen Colonies
> The Ten Commandments
> The Eighty-second Congress
> Fourscore and seven years . . .

Numbers of one hundred or less preceding a compound modifier containing a figure (spell out to avoid confusion):

> Two ¼-inch pipes
> three 30-year-old destroyers
> seventeen 8-inch guns
> > *but*
> 155 20-year-old aircraft

Indefinite expressions of round numbers:

> a thousand and one reasons
> thirteenth-century architecture
> the early eighties
> > *but*
> the 1990s (or the '90s)

Numbers of a million and up (for easy grasp of large numbers):

> $15 million
> $1.9 million
> 300 billion
> > *but*
> $15,000
> 316,965

Fractions that stand alone:

> one-third the cost
> > *but*
> ¾-inch boards

The plurals of numbers used with other plurals:

> two fours
> sixty fifteens

Write in Figures Any Numbers Expressing . . .

Age:

> a 5-year-old child
> She is 18 years old.
> > *but*
> He's in his eighties. (*not* his '80s or 80s)

Time:

> before 10:00 AM
> 0900 (*not* 0900 hours)
> 4 o'clock in the afternoon (*not* 4 o'clock PM)
> after 9:30 PM
> 15 years 4 months 13 days

Dates:

> 15 October 1997 *or* 15 Oct 97 *[if you abbreviate the year, also abbreviate the month]*

June 1989 or June 22, 1989 (*not* June, 1989 *or* June 22nd, 1989)

10 January to 24 May 1995

Class of 1943 or Class of '43

23rd of February

1st, 2nd, 3rd, and 4th of the month

   but

Fourth of July—the holiday

Money:

Give the cabbie $20.

They sent a bill for $55,787.00.

a $50 bill

It costs $8.65.

65 yen, 2.5 francs, etc.

Measurements:

8 meters wide

about 15 yards long

8 by 12 inches

9 gallons

15.5 bushels

3,500 acres

7 feet by 7 feet 8 inches

¼ to ½-inch margin

Numbers used as numbers:

You have to multiply by 4.

Pick a number between 1 and 10.

Miscellaneous numbers:

speed: The ship can do 35 knots.

        The aircraft can fly at 525 miles per hour.

sizes: He has a size 34 waist.

temperature: It reached 102 degrees today.

degrees: The ship had a 5-degree list, and it rolled 25 degrees to port.

percentages: The number of voters increased by 200 percent.

ratio: a ratio of 3 to 2 *or* a 3-to-2 ratio

vote: a vote of 15 to 13

scores: They won by a score of 7 to 4.

     or She bowled a score of 225.

     or Navy beat Air Force by 12 points.

     or It was Navy 75, Army 0.

Various numerical abbreviations:

No. 152

£22 4s. 6d.

No. 77

212 B.C. or 212 B.C.E.

Genesis 24:8

lines 6 and 7

pages 137–138

paragraph 13

A.D. 13–15 or C.E. 13–15

Chapter 15

In Any Case

Treat related numbers in the same set alike:

The $800,000 increase in income taxes followed a $2,000,000 boost in property taxes. *[Because the thousands are written out, so are the millions.]*

Two out of twenty-five Marines were wounded. *[The second number is spelled out because the first one is.]*

He wrote checks of $10.50, $121.00, and $.50.

Designate plurals by adding –s, and form numerical form of first, second, third, fourth, etc., by adding –st, –nd, –rd, –th, etc.

built in the 1970s

temperature in the 20s

1st, 2nd, 3rd, 4th, and 5th

their 25th year of marriage

the 100th aircraft

NUMBERS USED IN TITLES OF MILITARY UNITS

Navy Units

Spell out all numbers in the address element of naval messages:

— 1 to 19 as one word (SEVEN or TWELVE or NINETEEN):

COMCARDIV FIVE

CRUDESGRU TWELVE

— 20 and up as:

COMDESRON FIVE ZERO

TASK UNIT ONE FIVE THREE PT FOUR PT TWO

Spell out naval fleets:

Sixth Fleet

Spell out naval districts:

Twelfth Naval District

Spell out unit numbers in a letterhead, especially if the numbers are small:

Naval Reserve Readiness Command Region Ten

Mobile Technical Unit Nine

Helicopter Anti-Submarine Squadron Eighty Five

But note that increasingly in correspondence numbers of units are written as figures:

Naval Security Group 1

Submarine Development Group 1 Detachment Alameda

Write as figures hull numbers of ships*:

USS GEORGE C. MARSHALL (SSBN 654)

USS SHREVEPORT (LPD 12)

USS JOHN C. STENNIS (CVN 74)

Write as figures task unit designations*:

Task Force 62

Commander, Task Group 62.3 (CTG 62.3)

But see the rule for the address elements of naval messages.

Marine Corps Units

U.S. Marine Corps units are designated by using letters for companies and batteries; Arabic numerals for divisions, regiments, battalions, platoons, and squads; and Roman numerals for forces:

Company B
1st Marine Division (1st MarDiv)
Marine Fighter Squadron 212 (VMF-212)
III Marine Expeditionary Force (III MEF)
2d Squad
See HQO 5216.6 for more examples.
Normally, use figures for all Marine Corps units rather than spelling out the numbers:
2d Marine Expeditionary Brigade
III Marine Expeditionary Force (3d MarDiv)
Marine Aircraft Group 42 (MAG-42)
Marine Heavy Helicopter Squadron
772 Detachment A (HMH 772 Det A)
4th Marine Aircraft Wing
Exception: Spell out a numbered unit if the number begins a sentence:
First Platoon will be inspected on Thursday.
Third Marine Expeditionary Force (III MEF) will embark for Africa.

Army Units

Use figures for all army units except corps and numbered armies. Use Roman numerals for corps, and spell out numbered armies:
82d Infantry Regiment
7th AAA Brigade
2d Infantry Division
III Corps
2d Army Group
First Army

Air Force Units

Use figures for units up to and including air divisions. Use figures for numbered air forces only if using the abbreviation AF.
31st Combat Support Group; 31 CSG
22d Tactical Fighter Wing; 22 TFW
934th Air Division; 934 AD
Ninth Air Force; 9 AF
Fifth Air Force; 5 AF

CAPITALIZATION

The First Word

Capitalize the first word of every sentence and other expression used as a sentence:
The umpire called the batter out.
Stop! First get the gun. The M-16 in the locker.
The case is solved. Without a question.
Capitalize the first word in quoted sentences and in direct quotations or questions within sentences:
That was his argument. "No two ships could be on exactly the same bearing at the same distance at the same time."
The chief said, "Bring the two seamen up here."
Both recruits had one worry: What could they tell the drill sergeant?

Don't capitalize fragmentary or incomplete quotations:
— She argued with the stipulation that military personnel "must be covered even while exercising."
— Lincoln asked "whether that nation, or any nation so conceived and so dedicated, can long endure."

Capitalize the first word of each item in a series of sentences that is introduced by a complete sentence:

Two results follow on the decision to send combatants to such a distant location: First, food will have to be obtained locally. Second, all the other pipelines—ammunition, repair parts, crew reliefs for personnel, mail, etc.—will be greatly extended.

Do not capitalize if the series completes the sentence that introduces it:
— The decision means that
  • some foodstuffs will have to be obtained locally, and
  • all the other pipelines will be greatly extended.
— Officers present raised several issues: per diem, BOQ space, and transportation back to base.

Capitalize the first word of a parenthetical sentence that stands on its own (and place the period within the final parenthesis):

The three surface line officers discussed the DD's capabilities. (It was old but carried lots of guns.)

Do not capitalize the first word of such a sentence if the sentence does not stand on its own:
— The three midshipmen (who had failed English 101) reported for extra instruction Wednesday afternoon.

Also do not capitalize the first word in a parenthetical expression that is not a sentence (unless you have some other reason to capitalize it):
— The admiral started up the hallway (out to E Ring) but stopped suddenly.
— The course instructor (Professor Gilliland) took the roll.

Capitalize the first word of an independent clause following a colon if the expression following is clearly the more dominant element, or if it is introduced by a word such as Note, Warning, Caution, etc. Otherwise, use lowercase.

The rule is: Check every third automobile.

Warning: This drum contains highly corrosive material.

But

Whatever the case, the enemy will not retreat: this line is critical to their supplies and communications.

Proper versus Common Nouns

Capitalize proper nouns, that is, the names of specific persons, offices, places, and things:

Athens
New York
Martin Luther King
The Bowery
Messenger of the Watch
Officer Candidate School
Egypt
Anita Roberts-Long
Master at Arms

THE CAPITAL SAILOR

Along with the dates of [Arleigh Burke's] birth and passing is a very simple inscription that says: *Admiral Arleigh A. Burke, Sailor, United States Navy.* He thought of himself as a Sailor . . . and he was. In his honor, from this day forward, the title "Sailor" will be written in our Navy with a capital "S" to reflect the fact that those of us, from seaman recruit to admiral, remember this special Sailor and are proud to be in the Navy he loved so much and served so well.

—ADM Mike Boorda, Chief of Naval Operations,
in *Navy News,* January 1996.

Capitalize a common noun or adjective that forms an essential part of a proper noun. Normally use lower case for the common noun alone when used as a substitute for the name of a place:

Naval War College; the college
Jefferson Memorial; the memorial
University of Kansas; the university
Suez Canal; the canal
Golden Gate Bridge; the bridge

Military and Naval Terms
Capitalize the following widely used terms in the Navy and Marine Corps; lowercase common nouns as indicated:

Department of the Navy; Navy Department; DON
United States Navy; the Navy (always capitalized if used in reference to the U.S. Navy); a Navy regulation; a Navy officer; a Sailor *but* foreign navies; an officer, a chief, a lieutenant, etc.
Marine Corps; the Marines; the Corps; a Marine Corps officer; a Marine; *but* a sergeant, a corporal, etc.
Armed Forces; *but* armed services
Naval Academy; the Academy; *but* service academies Brigade of Midshipman; the Brigade; *but* the midshipman
Naval Reserve; Marine Corps Reserve; the Reserves; *but* a reserve officer
Pensacola Naval Air Station; Naval Military Personnel Command; *but* naval air stations; naval personnel; naval aviation; naval terms
The term "naval" has reference to both the Navy and the Marine Corps. See General Simmons's explanation on pages 47–48.

Names of Naval Ships
Use all capitals for naval vessels, except in journalism and professional articles.

USS CALIFORNIA (CGN 36)
USS GEORGE WASHINGTON CARVER (SSBN 656)

Military and Naval Ranks and Titles
Capitalize military ranks when used with a proper noun. Do not capitalize when they stand alone:

Captain Jeffries gave the order; *but* the captain ordered
Sergeant Gonzalez was cited; *but* the sergeant was commended
Senior Chief Oko gave the orders; *but* the senior chief took charge

Airman Adams worked hard; *but* the airman handled the details

Note 1: Capitalize the word "captain" when referring to the captain of a ship, whatever the officer's rank:

— The Captain ordered us to . . .

— According to the Captain, the beach is . . .

Note 2: When referring to a particular military member in official documents, first identify by full grade and full name (usually first name, middle initial, and last name), and subsequently just by short title and last name, both capitalized:

— Lieutenant Jennifer J. Johnson brought up school quotas. Concerned with timely application, LT Johnson argued . . .

— Sergeant Major George R. Wood . . . SgtMaj Wood

— Chief Boatswain's Mate George Sand . . . BMC Sand or Chief Sand

Capitalize billet or organizational titles when used with a proper name, when used in place of a proper name, or when such usage is customary. But don't capitalize generic job descriptions.

The Administrative Officer will escort you to your quarters.

Few of them had negative things to say about the Leading Petty Officer, SKI Lemoine.

She earned the designation "Naval Flight Officer."

We need good courses if we're going to train good communications officers.

Capitalize the names of departments within an organization, such as specific departments or divisions aboard ship or departments in a Marine combat unit. Do not capitalize the common nouns that refer to them.

I think he works in the Weapons Department of the frigate that's in port.

Requisition all supplies through the Supply Department in the Headquarters and Service Battalion.

We'll want to get the department heads and division officers in on this.

National Government Offices and Titles

Always capitalize the reference to a head of state or assistant head of state:

President Bush; the President; *but* presidents

Vice President Gore; the Vice President

Prime Minister Tony Blair; the Prime Minister

Capitalize the titles of U.S. Government officials, and the names of U.S. Government bodies, buildings, and documents:

U.S. Government; the Federal Government; the Government

U.S. Congress; Congress; Congressman Smith; *but* a congressman from Wyoming; congressional matters

U.S. Senate; the Senate; Senator Arthur; *but* a senator on the committee; U.S. House of Representatives; the House; Representative Macuso; the Speaker; *but* a representative from Minnesota

Supreme Court; Justice Powell; *but* a justice

U.S. Constitution; the Constitution; *but* constitutional

the Capitol; the White House; the Jefferson Memorial; the memorial; the Department of Defense; Defense Department; DOD

Local Government Terms and Titles

Capitalize the full names of state or local organizations, but not the short names for them.

the New Orleans City Council; *but* the city council's task
the Ohio State Legislature convened; *but* the legislature adjourned
The capital of Maryland is Annapolis.

Capitalize the titles of state or local officials when the titles are used with the name, but when used alone, lowercase them.

Mayor Stephanie Alison addressed the meeting; *but* the mayor spoke
Lieutenant Governor Jefferson presided; *but* the lieutenant governor's job
they contacted Sheriff Delahoussaye; *but* the sheriff arrived

Capitalize the terms "state," "city," "county," "ward," etc., only if part of the corporate name, with this exception: also capitalize a traditional name for a state or city:

New York State; the state of New York
New York City; the city of New York
Kansas City; the city
Oswego County; the county
Third Ward; the ward
   traditional names:
the Empire State
the Sunflower State
the Windy City
   also:
the Fifty States
it was good to get back to the States

Educational Terms

Capitalize the proper names of schools, colleges, and academic departments. *Do not capitalize common nouns that refer to them:*

University of New Orleans; *but* the university
Department of Mathematics; *but* the math department
Officer Indoctrination School; OIS; *but* the school

Capitalize the name of a class, but not the member of the class; capitalize specific course titles, but not the common noun referring to them, and not areas of study:

the Third Class; *but* third classman
the Junior Class; *but* a junior
English 410, Classics of Greece and Rome; but the classics course
Mary is studying physics at UCLA.

Capitalize academic degrees (including abbreviations) that follow a person's name, or whenever using the complete title of the degree:

he has a Ph.D. in Engineering; *but* he holds a doctoral degree
Amy Johnson, M.A.; *but* Amy holds a master's degree
A Naval Academy graduate is awarded a Bachelor of Science (B.S.) even if he
   or she majors in history.
George Gray, M.D.; *not* Mr. George Gray, M.D. *nor* Dr. George Gray, M.D.

History

Capitalize names of important historical events, periods, or documents:

the Korean War
the Tet Offensive
the Battle of the Bulge
the Renaissance
the Sixteenth Century; *but* the sixteen hundreds
Magna Carta

Laws, Acts, Documents, Bills, and Treaties

Capitalize the official names of laws but not the common nouns that refer to them:

Public Law 165; *but* the law

Sherman Antitrust Act; *but* the act

Marine Corps Manual; *but* the manual

the Unequal Treaties; *but* the treaties

Article 31 of Naval Regulations; *but* the article

Days, Months, Holidays, and Seasons

Capitalize all but seasons:

Wednesday, Thursday

February, March

Memorial Day; Easter; New Year's Day; Fourth of July (the Fourth)
but
fall, winter, spring, summer, autumn

Compass Directions

Capitalize compass directions used to indicate geographical regions, or when part of names:

the Midwest

the West Coast

Northwestern Mutual

The Democrats want to carry the South.

The battalion deployed to the Middle East.

He enrolled at East Texas State University.

> *Do not capitalize compass directions used just to indicate direction or position:*
> — The fleet was northwest of Hawaii.
> — Proceed south to Point Alfa; then go southeast.
> — The enemy patrols in the northern sector are thin.

Races, Peoples, Languages, Nations, and Religions

Capitalize all:

Caucasian; Japanese; European

French; Indo-European; Russian

the Soviet Union; Venezuela; Angola; the Virgin Islands

Roman Catholic; Methodist; Buddhist

Organizations, Corporations, and Commercial Products

Capitalize the name of an organization, but not the common noun that refers to it:

Rand Corporation; the corporation; the company

the Veterans Administration; the VA; the administration; veterans' benefits

the Republican party; the party; Republicans

> *A concept such as "democracy" is not capitalized, except when part of a proper noun such as "the Democratic party." Someone who believes in democracy is a democrat (not in caps) and may also be a member of the party by that name, i.e., a Democrat (capitalized). However, that person might also be a Republican. The word "party" is always lowercased, e.g., the Socialist party.*

Capitalize the name of departments within an organization, but not the common noun that refers to them:

Cassius Jones of the Accounting Department; *but* Mr. Jones of accounting will speak to you.

I'm applying for a position in maintenance.

Capitalize trade names, variety names, and names of market grades and brands, but don't capitalize the common nouns that follow these names:

Nabisco crackers

a Pendleton shirt

Seth Thomas clock

Zenith television set

> *Don't capitalize one-time trade names, proper names, or place names that through usage have become generic. But check a dictionary if in doubt.*

> venetian blinds

> pasteurize

> neoprene

PUNCTUATION

Use the Apostrophe

In contractions where letters have been omitted:

can't

isn't

won't

it's

she'll

should've

To form possessives of nouns:

> *Add –'s to all singular nouns.*

> the officer's stateroom

> CDR Jones's schedule

> yesterday's menu

> the boss's office

> *Add –'s to plural nouns not ending in –s:*

> men's gymnasium

> alumni's gathering

> *Add only the apostrophe to plural nouns ending in –s:*

> engineers' estimates

> officers' formation

> boys' and girls' rooms

To form plurals of letters and figures:

ten a's

four m's

two 4's

> *It is becoming increasingly common to omit the apostrophe following figures and acronyms (multiple letters). In this case:*

> > *Omit the apostrophe to indicate plurals of figures or acronyms:*

> > the 1980s

> > three Boeing 747s

> > two MEUs

> > many PAOs

"In the Navy, speed usually trumps correctness."
—Commander

"So much of the Correspondence Manual is just for the yeoman."
—Navy Commander

Use an apostrophe with such letters and figures—singular or plural—to show possession:

> The 727's front wheels blew out. [One 727 had its wheels blow out.]
>
> The F-18s' wings iced up. [Several F-18s had their wings ice up.]
>
> The DD's bow was buckled. [One DD had a buckled bow.]
>
> The BTs' schooling had proved inadequate. [Several BTs had poor schooling.]
>
> *Whichever style you use, make sure you are consistent within any one document.*

As single quotation marks to indicate a quote within a quote:

> The survivor said, "I thought the gig had gone until I heard someone say, 'Let's look one more time around the anchor chain.'"

Do not use the apostrophe with the possessive forms of personal pronouns, but do use the apostrophe with the possessive forms of indefinite pronouns:

> ours
>
> hers
>
> yours
>
> its
>
> theirs
>
> ours
>
> anybody's
>
> everyone's
>
> someone's
>
> *Watch possible confusion between it's (it is) and the pronoun its:*
>
> **Wrong:** *Its* clear that the patrol boat has turned off *it's* searchlights.
>
> **Right:** *It's* the only way we can get the telescope to *its* destination.

Use the Asterisk

To refer readers to footnotes at the bottom of a page:*

> * Like this. Asterisks follow all punctuation marks (including quotation marks).

To mark the omission of one or more paragraphs:

> A line of asterisks (seven per line) or periods, usually centered on the page, can be used to indicate the omission:
>
> * * * * * * *

Use Brackets

To insert brief editorial comments or explanations in direct quotations:

> "The French Admiral [Darlan] disagreed."
>
> "Order those troops [the Marines] to return to the front."

With *sic* to mark an error of spelling, usage, or fact within a quotation:

> "Practically speaking, the Navy and Marine Corps have lived, worked, and fought together since their enception [*sic*]."
>
> *The* sic *tells the reader that what may seem an error on your part is a faithful copy of the original material. A* sic *can imply a strong criticism, saying in effect, "See the errors this guy makes?" In some circumstances you may want to correct a minor error in a quotation and leave out the* sic.

To signify parentheses within parentheses:

> The board president then ended the meeting (although only after the officers [LCDR Arthur and LTJG Gregg] had departed).

Use the Colon

After a main clause to introduce a list or some other summation, if "as follows" or "the following" is expressed or implicit in the clause before the colon:

The order of entry will be the following: Colonel McDaniel, Major Mazzeno, and Professor White. ("The following" is explicit.)

The inspection party found two discrepancies: loose wiring in the overhead and a leaking faucet. ("As follows" is implicit.)

Do not use a colon between a verb and its object or complement, or between a preposition and its object.

Right: They visited three new ports: Marseilles, Barcelona, and Cadiz.

Wrong: They traveled through: Denver, Colorado Springs, and Pueblo.

Wrong: Public hearings have been scheduled on: August 26, September 3, and October 8.

To join two independent clauses when the second illustrates or explains the first:

After plebe year, you begin to feel like a prisoner on good conduct: all those privileges they had once taken away they now begin to give back one by one.

It was cold that night; the mercury dropped to thirty below.

Note the difference between the colon and the semicolon: the colon introduces items to follow; a semicolon separates coordinate sentence elements, that is, two complete clauses or phrases whose ideas are very closely tied together.

To express the preposition *to* in a ratio:

2:1

5:3

To punctuate the salutation in a business letter:

Dear Mrs. Parsons:

Dear Corporal Smith:

To separate hours from minutes in 12-hour clock time:

3:01

12:15

10:45

To separate the place of publication from the name of the publisher in a bibliography entry:

New Orleans: Pelican Press, 2007.

Use the Comma

To separate an introductory subordinate clause or a long prepositional phrase from the clause it modifies:

If the Major approves, we will send out the briefing package this afternoon.

When you come to Poydras Street, turn right.

During the extended firefights near My Tho, the boats were not reinforced.

To set off words that introduce quotations, as long as the word "say" (or a substitute) is included:

The steward said, "Dinner is served." He replied, "Give her the orders."

The admiral asked, "Does anyone have a question?"

Note 1: Use a colon instead of a comma if the word "say" or a substitute is omitted, or if that word takes an object prior to the quotation:

— The captain turned: "Who gave that order?"

— The captain said these words distinctly: "Who gave that order?"

Note 2: No comma is necessary if the quotation functions as an integral part of the sentence:

— The argument "might makes right" is immoral.

To set off introductory words such as "Yes," "No," or "Oh":

No, we didn't fly that low.

Oh, you must mean the ship's boat.

To separate a series of modifiers:

The recruits were young, scared, and homesick.

To separate three or more words in a series, including the word before the final "and," "or," or "nor":

She issues food, equipment, and clothing.

Move the people in any way you can—on cars, planes, trains, or buses.

To separate parallel phrases or clauses:

She has excellent writing skills, works hard, and is a very quick study.

To separate parallel adjectives:

a hard, cold winter

a shiny, brittle material

If the order of the adjectives can be reversed, or if and *can stand between them, then the adjectives are parallel and a comma should separate them. Do* not *use a comma if the second adjective and the noun form a single concept:*

— a light blue dress

— a new video recorder

To separate two or more independent clauses in a compound sentence if they are joined by a simple conjunction such as *or, nor, and,* or *but.* (You can omit the comma when the statements are short and closely related.)

There are several districts, and each district has its own commandant.

"Either I'll go by plane, or I won't go at all."

The shooting started and all the ships reversed course.

Do not use a comma before a coordinating conjunction *that joins compound subjects, compound verbs, or phrases.*

Wrong: The Congressman, and his staff, walked up the gang plank.

Wrong: The inspection team tested the procedures, and found no discrepancies.

Right: The aviators and their maintenance staffs looked on, smugly.

To follow transitional words and phrases such as *however, that is, namely, therefore, for example, moreover,* and *i.e.* Use a comma after these terms when they interrupt the flow of the sentence. The type of punctuation used *before* such transitional words and phrases is determined by the strength of the interruption.

She bought all the groceries; however, she forgot to go to the bank.

He had been decorated in battle—nevertheless, he still opposed the war.

Moreover, the sea state was very high.

When such words are used to be emphatic, do not set them off *with commas.*

— There are therefore no missiles at all left in the magazine.

Before *for,* when *for* is used as a conjunction:

He did not issue the order, for the troops had not yet rested.

To set off a noun or phrase in direct address:

Mr. Chairman, the committee has voted.

Congresswoman Phillips, we ask your assistance.

I enjoyed my tour of the ship, Ensign Alfred, and I appreciate your hospitality.

To set off words or phrases that are appositives (explanatory equivalents):

Captain Robichaux, the skipper of the ship, has been in the Navy for ten years.

Peter Elshire, the courteous professor, explained the phrase.

To set off words or phrases in contrast when introduced by *not* or *but:*

The women, not the men, have offered leadership here.

Classes are not held in the portables, but in the main building.

The sergeant is known for his successes, not his failures.

To set off parenthetic words, phrases, or clauses (commas in pairs have the force of weak parentheses):

There is, my friend, no alternative.

Plan B, on the other hand, may have some merit.

The recommendations, developed months ago, have not yet been implemented.

Use the comma with "nonrestrictive clauses"—clauses that are parenthetical are called nonrestrictive. Clauses that limit or modify the meaning of a sentence in a way that is not parenthetical –which are essential to the sentence's meaning—are called "restrictive" and are not *set off by commas.*

Nonrestrictive—use commas:

The lieutenant, who was wounded, was left behind. *There was only one lieutenant in the area. The phrase is not essential to the sentence, but just adds information.*

Restrictive—no commas:

The lieutenant who was wounded was left behind. *Tells which lieutenant of several was left behind. The phrase is necessary to identify which lieutenant is being referred to.*

To set off interrupting words, phrases, or clauses when they break the flow of a sentence:

The price they paid, in fact, was twice as much as advertised elsewhere.

The senior chief, you know, has the ear of the CO.

She knew that the butcher, too, was likely to quit his job.

To indicate the omission of an understood word or words:

Before those encounters, we used the tactic again and again; afterward, never.

The second comma takes the place of we used it.

To set off afterthoughts:

It will get out of the channel by 1700, won't it?

The general has been given the VIP suite, I hope.

To separate words or figures that might otherwise be misread or misunderstood:

To Charles, Jeffrey was friendly.

Out of 50, 22 actually graduated.

What the target is, is now clear.

Just before, the boat docked successfully.

To separate repeated words:

It was a deep, deep depression.

Now, now. Settle down.

To separate thousands, millions, etc., in numbers of four or more digits:

17,854

4,880,000

2,900

After the date of the month when the date is expressed in conventional civilian terms (military style uses no commas in dates):

Civilian Style: November 17, 1988

Military Style: 17 November 1988

In a sentence: He lived in Boulder from December 13, 1967, to March 22, 1969.

To separate parts of an address (but no comma precedes the ZIP Code):

The telegram was delivered to 1177 Louisiana Street, Lawrence, Kansas 66044.

To separate parts of the titles of bases, stations, or other military installations:

He was to report to Naval Air Station, Memphis, on October 1st.

The ship left Naval Station, Charleston, at 2000.

> *Omit the comma with the shortened name of a military facility or installation:*
> — MCAS Beaufort
> — NAS Key West
> — MCB Camp Lejeune

To set off names of states and foreign countries when used with other place names (use the comma before and after):

She moved from Dalhart, Texas, to Kansas City.

The squadron arrived in Atsugi, Japan, on 15 December.

To separate some titles and following personal names: Jr. and Sr. are set off by commas, and so are academic degrees. But 2nd, 3rd and II, III are not.

Henry Ford II

Rolando Smith, Jr.

George Thomas Kennedy, Esq.

Jennifer Dunn, M.A.

John Houston, Ph.D.

Between a title and the name of an organization, and between different levels within an organization:

Sandra Estoff, Corporal, USMC

Henry Dean, Lieutenant Commander, JAGC, USN

Director, Strategic Sealift

Chairman, House Armed Services Committee

Commanding Officer, Company A, 1st Battalion, 2d Marines

Use the Dash

To indicate a sudden break or abrupt change in thought:

Order two copies of the document—no, on second thought, order a whole case.

The change to the Awards Manual should be—no, will be—published by year's end.

To set off emphatically (stronger than commas) words or phrases of explanation that you want to emphasize:

The boat crew—every petty officer—acted competently in the crisis.

> *Make sure if you set off a word or phrase in the middle of a sentence that you put dashes on both sides of it.*

To set off nonessential explanatory clauses when those clauses contain internal commas:

All of these subjects—English, history, and philosophy—are in the humanities.

To set off single words:

He's after just one thing—guns.

Before a clause that summarizes a series of words or phrases:

The Navy and the Marine Corps—together, these services comprise the Department of the Navy.

Before the source of a quotation or credit line:

> I have not yet begun to fight.
>
> —John Paul Jones

Occasionally, to indicate emphasis:

> The F-16s must be moved—but to somewhere else in Europe.
>
> *If your typewriter or word processor has no dash, make the dash with two hyphens and no space before or after--like this.*

Use the Exclamation Point

To mark surprise, incredulity, admiration, appeal, irony, or other strong emotion:

> What a beautiful sight!
>
> Great! I don't have to go.
>
> Get going!
>
> The ship leaves the pier in five minutes!
>
> *Use a comma after* mild *interjections; end mildly exclamatory sentences with a period:*
>
> > — Oh, it seems the ship got under way early.
> >
> > — I wish you success.

To mark a statement made with particular emphasis or force, including an order or command:

> "Cease fire! Cease fire!"
>
> "All stop! All back full! Sound the collision alarm!"

Place an exclamation point within a closing quotation mark only if it belongs to the quoted material:

> He shouted, "All aboard!"
>
> "I never, never heard the captain say, 'Return to port'!"
>
> *Remember that exclamation marks and dashes quickly lose effectiveness if overused.*

Use the Hyphen

To join two or more words serving as a single adjective before a noun:

> two-story house
>
> well-bred person
>
> up-to-date report
>
> *Such words are not hyphenated when they follow the noun:*
>
> > — Charles is well bred.
> >
> > — This report is up to date.
>
> Do not *use a hyphen to connect an adverb ending in –ly and an adjective, or the adverb* very *and an adjective.*
>
> > — an easily mastered task
> >
> > — a very attractive person

When describing family relationships involving great- and -in-law:

> brother-in-law
>
> great-grandfather

To join compound numbers, and when writing out a fraction:

> sixty-six
>
> one-fifth of the crew
>
> twenty-eight
>
> six and one-third kilometers

With the prefixes ex- (meaning former), self-, all-, quasi-, and the suffixes -elect and -designate:

    ex-governor

    all-American

    quasi-complete

    self-made

    president-elect

    ambassador-designate

To avoid mispronunciation, or to make clear what word you mean:

    His re-creation of the old village was complete.

    The draftsman re-marked the plans.

    The two engineers co-operated the plant.

To connect geographically descriptive terms:

    Latin-American

    Anglo-Irish

To link two numbers that represent a continuous sequence when they are not introduced by the words "from" or "between":

    the 1980–88 time frame *but* between the years 1980 and 1988

    pages 1–55 *but* from page 1 to page 55.

To join single capital letters to nouns or participles:

    A-bomb

    X-ray

    U-shaped

To indicate continuation of a word divided at the end of a line:

    The ships fall into three categories: com-
    bat, repair, and supply ships.

    Always consult a dictionary if you are not sure where the syllable breaks are, and attempt to place at least three letters on each line.

To connect numerals with their units of measure (watch possible confusion here):

    Right: The Sailors maintained an extraordinary 80-hour work week.

    Right: They required 10-inch-thick metal plates. (The number comprises part of a unit of measure, is a part of the compound adjective 10-inch-thick.)

    Right: They required 10 inch-thick metal plates. (The number modifies plates. Inch-thick is the compound adjective.)

    Wrong: They required 10 inch thick metal plates. (The meaning is unclear.)

When carrying a modifier over to a later word (this is called a "suspended hyphen"):

    two-, four-, and six-gun vessels

    low-, moderate-, and high-income families

In military usage, link the numerical designation of aviation squadrons and groups to the abbreviated title of the unit by a hyphen:

    VF-33

    HM-15

    MAG-32

Do not use a hyphen when the full name for the unit is written out, or with ground units, or with the hull designators for Navy ships, or to separate the names of an exercise from the year in which it occurs:

    Fighter Squadron Thirty Three

    USS WISCONSIN (BB 64) 4th MEB

    Marine Attack Squadron 223

USS FULTON (AS 11)
Bold Eagle 86

Use Parentheses

To set off explanatory material (a single word, phrase, or entire sentence) that is not essential to the main point of the sentence. If constructed properly, the material between parentheses can always be deleted without harming the logical or grammatical structure of the sentence.

> A ship's gig (from the CARL VINSON, it turned out) had just cast off from the landing.

> The result (see fig. 15) is impressive.

To enclose a parenthetical clause where the interruption is too great to be indicated by commas:

> His boat (the fastest in the country, no doubt) won three prizes last year.

> *Parentheses signal a stronger interruption than commas. On the other hand, dashes give much more emphasis than either commas or parentheses to interrupting material:*

> > — Let's make sure that *all* the military services—don't forget the Marine Corps—get invited to the conference.

To enclose numbers or letters designating items in a series:

> You will observe that the sword is (1) old fashioned, (2) still sharp, and (3) unusually light for its size.

> Normally the stations on the phone line will be (a) port lookout, (b) starboard lookout, (c) after lookout, (d) QMOW, and (e) combat.

Place a period outside parentheses at the end of a sentence unless the words within the parentheses comprise a complete sentence:

> Individual incomes in the northeast (chart 7), which have not been discussed, are greater than those in the southeast (chart 8).

> Inspecting officers listened to all the petty officers' complaints. (In fact, they even talked to some nonrated men.)

Place periods, commas, and other punctuation within the parentheses if they belong to the parenthetical clause or phrase; place them outside the parentheses if they belong to the words of the rest of the sentence:

> Certain types of vessels (destroyers, cruisers, carriers, frigates, etc.) are known as "combatants."

> You've met the senior admiral (Admiral Heyward), I believe?

Use the Period

To end declarative and mildly imperative sentences. Use exclamation points where greater emphasis is desired.

> The Marines stood at attention. Stand at attention.

> Get the rifle up here. Hurry!

To end an indirect question:

> She asked if the tax reduction was an illusion.

To follow abbreviations, unless by usage the period is customarily omitted (as with organizations, agencies, and terms known by their initials):

> etc.

> O.A.S.

> Rev.

> Gal.

Mr.

but

DOD

ICC

UFO

CONUS

EAOS

Normally abbreviate United States as U.S.

To form an ellipsis—three spaced periods (with a space between each) that indicate omission of one or more words within a quoted passage:

Fourscore and seven years ago our fathers brought forth upon this continent a new nation . . . dedicated to the proposition that all men are created equal.

If the omission ends with a period, use four spaced periods (three to show the omission, and one to mark the end of the sentence).

— We have come to dedicate a portion of that field as a final resting place. . . .

If only a fragment of a sentence is quoted within another sentence, you need not use ellipses to signify the omission of words:

— The speaker cited the principle of "government of the people, by the people and for the people" at the conclusion of her talk.

As a decimal point:

.05

$9.40

10.7%

Use the Question Mark

After a sentence that asks a direct question:

Who gave that order?

When did the broadcast go down?

Punctuate indirect *questions as you would direct statements, that is,* without *question marks:*

Right: Would you have time for me to stop by the exchange? (direct question)

Wrong: He asked her if she would have time to stop by the exchange? (indirect question)

Right: The petty officer asked Lieutenant Humphrey if he could go on liberty at 1300. (indirect question)

When a question is involved in a quotation, follow this rule: If the quotation alone comprises the question, leave the question mark within *the quotation marks. But if the whole sentence that encloses the quotation is a question, place the question mark* outside *the quotation marks.*

— The lieutenant asked, "Who gave the order?"

— Did the lieutenant say, "the screen commander"?

To indicate doubt or uncertainty as to the correctness of the preceding word, figure, or date:

This ship is 125 (?) feet long.

John Johnston, 1556 (?)–1633

Use Quotation Marks

To enclose a direct quotation, the exact words of a speaker or writer:

He said, "Hold your fire."

"I say again," shouted the captain into the mike, "come aboard."

General Lejeune argued, "The relation between officers and enlisted men should in no sense be that of superior and inferior . . . but rather that of teacher and scholar."

If the passage is five or more lines, set it off from the rest of the text and indent it as a block quotation without quotation marks. Also see page 314 for the use of periods as ellipses to indicate omission of short passages. See page 306 on using asterisks for longer omissions.

To enclose slang expressions, nicknames, words used ironically, slogans, humor, or poor grammar:

They resented being regarded as the "fall guys."

We have heard lots about "Flower Power" since the Sixties.

To indicate the titles of short works (such as poems, songs, essays, articles) and parts of longer works (chapters, lessons, topics, sections):

He remembered reading Kipling's "If."

Sybil Stockdale's part of *In Love and War* begins with chapter 2, "The Navy Wife."

Dvorak made the spiritual "Goin' Home" the theme of *The New World Symphony.*

His essay, "The Classics, the Military, and the Missing Modern Element," has just been published by the journal *Observer.*

As seen above, longer works (such as books, names of newspapers, magazines, symphonies, and operas) are underlined or italicized.

To enclose titles of completed but unpublished works like reports, dissertations, and manuscripts:

Evidently, none of the members of the committee had read "The State of the Shipyards after the Building of the 600-ship Navy."

Although her dissertation, "John Milton and the Concept of Right Reason," was excellent, she had difficulty getting it published.

With any matter following expressions such as "the word," "the term," "marked," "endorsed," "titled," "designated," "classified," and "signed," when the exact title or other message is quoted:

The directive, titled "Revised Damage Control Policy," has been revised.

The envelope was marked "Top Secret"; he feared to open it.

His letter was signed "With Best Wishes, Tom."

Classified just "For Official Use Only," the document seemed unimportant.

The petty officer was designated "Jack of the Dust."

Use single quotation marks to enclose a quotation within a quotation:

"The airman was heard to say, 'Let's forget the inspection and take off early.'"

Always place commas and periods inside the quotation marks:

"The colonel may say 'We can't afford it,' and he ought to know."

Always place colons and semicolons outside:

Mrs. Joseph argued, "The professor isn't in yet"; she obviously didn't want the student to go into the office.

Place question marks and exclamation points inside or outside, depending on whether they apply just to the quotation or to the whole sentence:

"Is this the correct form?" he asked.

What is the meaning of the "balance of payments"?

She exclaimed, "You can't pay them that much!"

Use the Semicolon

To separate independent clauses in a compound sentence when you don't want to use a coordinating conjunction (and, or, nor, for, but, or yet):

The repair is finished; the ship sails today.

To connect two independent clauses that are closely related and joined by a conjunctive adverb such as *however, consequently, therefore, nevertheless, thus, moreover,* etc.:

They argued as hard as they could; however, the contractor remained unconvinced.

The admiral had attended the briefing; therefore, he had his aides gather the charts.

Normally, a comma follows the linking adverb, as above.

To separate elements in a complex series if the elements themselves include commas:

Included in the battle group were NEW JERSEY, a battleship; TOPEKA, a cruiser; and several destroyers and other escorts.

To precede words or abbreviations that introduce a summary or explanation of what has gone before in the sentence:

The regatta included a wide variety of vessels; for example, sailboats, launches, and yachts mingled in the holiday atmosphere of a race.

Use Italics (or the Underscore)

For the names of trains, aircraft, and spacecraft:

The Orient Express (or <u>The Orient Express</u>)

Enola Gay (or <u>Enola Gay</u>)

Challenger (or <u>Challenger</u>)

Note: Using the underscore in manuscripts to indicate italics is a holdover from typewriter days, when typewriters did not have an italic font. When used in manuscripts, the underscore is converted to italics in preparation for printing. Modern naval practice is to use italics in most cases although one occasionally still sees the underscore.

Also: Civilian practice is to use italics for ships' names:

U.S.S. *Saratoga;* S.S. *Titanic*

However, consistent Navy and Marine Corps practice is to use all caps and no periods in USS or USNS:

USS ENTERPRISE (CVN 65)

USNS H. H. ARNOLD

USS DAVID R. RAY (DD 971)

For the titles of whole published works: books, pamphlets, magazines, newspapers, plays, movies, symphonies, operas, long poems, essays, lectures, sermons, and reports:

U.S. Naval Institute Proceedings

Richard McKenna's *The Sand Pebbles*

the *Washington Post*

For sections or parts of published works (chapters, parts, etc.), for short stories and short plays, and for titles of unpublished works (like manuscripts and dissertations), use quotation marks:

— I liked the article in *Money,* "Affording College."

— One of Frank O'Connor's finest stories is "My Oedipus Complex."

To refer to words, numbers, symbols, and words used as such:

The word *omitted* has only one *m.*

The verbs *attribute* and *contribute* are often confused.

Quotation marks are also used for the same purpose, but be consistent in your usage.

The verbs "attribute" and "contribute" are often confused.

For emphasizing (sparingly) certain words, phrases, or sentences:
What do we need to focus all our efforts on? <u>Damage control</u>.

ABBREVIATIONS AND ACRONYMS

"In the last BOQ I went into, there were almost no bachelors, very few officers, and it's question-able it could be defined as quarters. But still it's called a BOQ. . . ."

—LIEUTENANT COMMANDER

Several sources for guidance on abbreviations exist. Chapter 9 of the GPO *Style Manual* contains some general guidelines, but common military practices differ significantly from GPO rules. For the Marine Corps, chapter G of the Individual Records and Administration Manual (IRAM) is the principal reference for abbreviations. For the Navy, the most comprehensive guide is the *Dictionary of Naval Abbreviations,* ed. Deborah W. and Thomas J. Cutler (Annapolis, MD: Naval Institute Press, current edition). See later in this handbook for abbreviations of Navy and Marine Corps forces, exercises, and ranks; abbreviations of days, months, and states; and abbreviations commonly used in naval messages.

General Rules on the Use of Abbreviations and Acronyms

- Do not introduce an abbreviation or acronym *at all* unless you will use it more than once. *Put clarity before economy.*
- If you do plan to use an acronym several times, spell out the complete term on first use and follow it by the acronym in parentheses, like this: Marine Corps Development and Education Command (MCDEC). Use the acronym consistently from then on in place of the full term.
- Don't use an acronym or other abbreviation once on page one, and then not again until pages later. The reader may have forgotten its meaning.
- Except in task organization designations (e.g., Task Unit 15.3.2 or Task Element 5.3.2.1), do not use periods with military abbreviations and acronyms. Instead, run the letters together without separation, as in SECNAV or HQMC. However, do separate the unit title from the numerical designation, as in COMCARDIV THREE or COMCRUDESGRU EIGHT.
- Designate the plural of an acronym by a lower case *s* following the acronym, as in "several DDs" (several destroyers) or "twenty RMs" (twenty radiomen). In the case of possessives, use apostrophes according to standard rules, e.g., "CNO's desires are . . ." or "FLETRAGRU's position was . . ." or "the DDs' line of bearing was . . ." (CNO and FLETRAGRU are singular, but there are several destroyers, all on a line of bearing).

Typical Abbreviations of Navy Forces

Below are common abbreviations of U.S. Navy forces. Note the consistent use of ALL CAPS in Navy abbreviations.

SECNAV, ASSTSECNAV, UNSECNAV
OPNAV
CNO and VCNO and DCNO
COMNAVMILPERSCOM
COMNAVSURFLANT
COMCRUDESGRU FOUR
USS THEODORE ROOSEVELT

Typical Abbreviations of Marine Corps Forces

Here are common abbreviations of U.S. Marine Corps forces. Note the practice of using both lowercase and uppercase letters except where the abbreviation is made up entirely of the initial letters of major words. Note also the use of numbers. See HQO 5216.6 for further instruction.

> HQMC
> USMC
> FMFLant
> MedEvac
> CG III MAF
> BLT 2/3
> 7th Mar
> CG lst MarDiv
> 24th MAU
> 2d MAW
> CG FMFPac

Abbreviation of Exercises

Both the Navy and Marine Corps abbreviate the names of exercises, but typically the Navy uses all caps while the Marine Corps capitalizes only the first word in each noun:

> *Navy:* EXERCISE BRIGHT STAR 95
> PACSUBICEX 1-96
> *Marine Corps:* Exercise Bold Eagle
> Team Spirit 93

Abbreviations of Navy and Coast Guard Enlisted Ranks

Pay Grade E-1 through E-3 Titles	*Abbreviation*
Airman Recruit, Airman Apprentice, Airman	AR, AA, AN
Constructionman Recruit, Constructionman Apprentice, Constructionman	CR, CA, CN
Dentalman Recruit, etc.	DR, DA, DN
Fireman Recruit, etc.	FR, FA, FN
Hospitalman Recruit, etc.	HR, HA, HN
Seaman Recruit, etc.	SR, SA, SN

Higher Pay Grades	*Title*	*Abbreviation*
E-4	Petty Officer Third Class	PO3
E-5	Petty Officer Second Class	PO2
E-6	Petty Officer First Class	PO1
E-7	Chief Petty Officer	CPO
E-8	Senior Chief Petty Officer	SCPO
E-9	Master Chief Petty Officer	MCPO
E-9	Master Chief Petty Officer of the Navy/Coast Guard	CPON or MCPOCG

Abbreviations of Marine Corps Enlisted Ranks

E-1	Private	Pvt
E-2	Private–First Class	PFC
E-3	Lance Corporal	LCpl
E-4	Corporal	Cpl
E-5	Sergeant	Sgt
E-6	Staff Sergeant	SSgt

E-7	Gunnery Sergeant	GySgt
E-8	Master Sergeant	MSgt
E-8	First Sergeant	1stSgt
E-9	Master Gunnery Sergeant	MGySgt
E-9	Sergeant Major	SgtMaj
E-9	Sergeant Major of the Marine Corps	SgtMaj

Abbreviations of Navy and Coast Guard Officer Ranks

W-1	Warrant Officer	WO
W-2	Chief Warrant Officer	CWO2
W-3	Chief Warrant Officer	CWO3
W-4	Chief Warrant Officer	CWO4
W-5	Chief Warrant Officer	CWO5
O-1	Ensign	ENS
O-2	Lieutenant Junior Grade	LTJG
O-3	Lieutenant	LT
O-4	Lieutenant Commander	LCDR
O-5	Commander	CDR
O-6	Captain	CAPT
O-7	Rear Admiral (Lower Half)	RDML
O-8	Rear Admiral (Upper Half)	RADM
O-9	Vice Admiral	VADM
O-10	Admiral	ADM

Abbreviations of Marine Corps Officer Ranks

W-1	Warrant Officer	WO
W-2	Chief Warrant Officer	CWO2
W-3	Chief Warrant Officer	CWO3
W-4	Chief Warrant Officer	CWO4
W-5	Chief Warrant Officer	CWO5
O-1	Second Lieutenant	2ndLt
O-2	First Lieutenant	1stLt
O-3	Captain	Capt
O-4	Major	Maj
O-5	Lieutenant Colonel	LtCol
O-6	Colonel	Col
O-7	Brigadier General	BGen
O-8	Major General	MajGen
O-9	Lieutenant General	LtGen
0-10	General	Gen

Abbreviations of Days and Months

Days	Months	
Mon	Jan	Jul
Tues	Feb	Aug
Wed	Mar	Sep
Thurs	Apr	Oct
Fri	May	Nov
Sat	Jun	Dec
Sun		

State Abbreviations

Alabama	AL	Alaska	AK
Arizona	AZ	Arkansas	AR
California	CA	Colorado	CO
Connecticut	CT	Delaware	DE
Florida	FL	Georgia	GA
Hawaii	HI	Idaho	ID
Illinois	IL	Indiana	IN
Iowa	IA	Kansas	KS
Kentucky	KY	Louisiana	LA
Maine	ME	Maryland	MD
Massachusetts	MA	Michigan	MI
Minnesota	MN	Mississippi	MS
Missouri	MO	Montana	MT
Nebraska	NE	Nevada	NV
New Hampshire	NH	New Jersey	NJ
New Mexico	NM	New York	NY
North Carolina	NC	North Dakota	ND
Ohio	OH	Oklahoma	OK
Oregon	OR	Pennsylvania	PA
Rhode Island	RI	South Carolina	SC
South Dakota	SD	Tennessee	TN
Texas	TX	Utah	UT
Vermont	VT	Virginia	VA
Washington	WA	West Virginia	WV
Wisconsin	WI	Wyoming	WY

Territories and Districts

District of Columbia	DC	Guam	GU
Puerto Rico	PR	Virgin Islands	VI

THE WELL-STOCKED DESK

Just as no carpenter would be without saw, hammer, and nails, so every naval writer should have at his or her fingertips tools essential to writing, tools in addition to this text. Many of them are in the supply system—some, in fact, may be picked up at the local Servmart. But we often forget to do so.

Experienced writers learn they can dispense with one or two of them after years at the trade, but they'll still want them somewhere about the office. What follows is a good general list—add to your short bookshelf with gouges or useful tips as you find them. See specialized sections of this text for reference to good books or articles on news writing, professional writing, speaking and briefing, JAGMAN Investigations, etc.

For Every Desk
Correspondence Manual

- Department of the Navy Correspondence Manual, SECNAVINST 5216.5 (current edition). Have a copy on hand, or ready access to one.

Dictionary. Use a standard collegiate (hardbound) dictionary, not a pocket dictionary. The following are excellent:

- *Webster's Eleventh New Collegiate Dictionary* (or latest edition)
- *Random House Dictionary,* current edition
- *The American Heritage Dictionary,* current edition

Handbook of Grammar and Mechanics. The short handbook in this text doesn't cover everything. Besides grammar and usage (punctuation, capitalization, use of numbers, etc.), handbooks usually cover style, general writing guidance, résumé writing, and other things having to do with writing. See such handbooks, too, for guidance on documentation, including footnotes or endnotes, the number-reference method, and bibliographies. Here are some good ones:

- *Harbrace College Handbook,* current edition, eds. John C. Hodges and Mary Whitten
- *New English Handbook,* current edition, ed. Hans Guth
- *Scott, Foresman Handbook for Writers,* current edition, eds. Hairston and Ruszlciewicz
- *GPO Style Manual.* Although this book is primarily a typesetter's and printer's manual, some naval writers still swear by its sections on proofreader's marks, capitalization, spelling, compound words, hyphenation, punctuation, abbreviations, number usage, and signs and symbols. Note that naval practice in some areas differs from GPO guidance.
- *Chicago Manual of Style.* Chicago: University of Chicago Press, current edition. Another classic reference text for the same kinds of things as listed above under *GPO Style Manual.* The *Chicago Manual of Style* governs, for example, the style of most book publishing companies. However, in case of conflicts, military offices should generally go by the *GPO Style Manual.*

Guides to Naval Abbreviations and Naval Terms
- *Dictionary of Naval Abbreviations,* ed. Deborah W. and Thomas J. Cutler, Naval Institute Press, current edition.
- *Dictionary of Naval Terms,* ed. Deborah W. and Thomas J. Cutler. Naval Institute Press, current edition.

For Some Desks
Word Division Guide
- *Word Division Supplement* to the *GPO Style Manual,* current edition. Tells you how to divide words at the end of a line.

Short Reference Manual
- *Gregg Reference Manual,* current edition, ed. W. A. Sabin. Some authors swear by this one.

Desk Planner
- Navy Leader Planning Guide, NAVPERS 15255 series, published annually. Contains a yearly calendar with pertinent administrative dates, an index to instructions on personnel, and some phone numbers. Automatically distributed to most Navy commands annually.

Thesaurus (dictionary of synonyms and antonyms)
- *Random House Thesaurus*
- *Roget's: The New Thesaurus, No. II*
- *Webster's Collegiate Thesaurus*

Permissions

Grateful acknowledgment is made to all those who provided letters, memos, evaluations, and so on, from which text examples have been drawn or upon which they have been modeled. In addition to examples from individuals, and examples from official government publications, thanks are extended for permission to reprint the following previously published materials that have been obtained from journals or publishing houses:

- Adams, Daniel T. HMC, USN. "We're Short-Changing Wounded Marines." U.S. Naval Institute *Proceedings* (July 2008): 86.
- Beach, Edward L., CAPT, USN (Ret.). "Up or Out: A Financial Disaster." U.S. Naval Institute *Proceedings* (June 1987): 54.
- Blair, Carvel, CAPT, USN. "Effective Writing, Navy or Civilian." U.S. Naval Institute *Proceedings* (July 1968): 131.
- Broome, Jack. *Make Another Signal.* London: William Kimber, 1973.
- Coonts, Stephen. *Flight of the Intruder.* Annapolis: Naval Institute Press, 1986.
- Danelo, David J. Review. "*Jarhead:* A Tale Better Left Untold." U.S. Naval Institute *Proceedings* (December 2005): 78.
- Davis, Chris, USN. "The DoD Travel Card Must Go." U.S. Naval Institute *Proceedings* (February 2007): 67.
- Goodall, T. D., CDR, USN. "Getting Navy on the Information Highway." U.S. Naval Institute *Proceedings* (November 1994): 92.
- Green, Eric J., Capt., USMC. "Continuity in Arctic Units." *Marine Corps Gazette* (February 1986): 36.
- Gross, Thomas W. "For Those in Peril." U.S. Naval Institute *Proceedings* (December 1994): 59.
- Jacobs, R. D., LCDR, USNR. "In Search of . . . Patrol Combatants." U.S. Naval Institute *Proceedings* (September 1983): 127.

- Johns, Eric, LCDR, USN. "Perfect Is the Enemy of Good Enough." U.S. Naval Institute *Proceedings* (October 1988): 37.
- Jonas, David, SMaj., USMC. "Gratuitous Religious Comment." U.S. Naval Institute *Proceedings* (August 1994): 82.
- Kennedy, David M., IT, USN, and IT William R.C. Stewart III, Medical Corps, USNR. "That Dangerous Polyester Look." U.S. Naval Institute *Proceedings* (January 1984): 97.
- Larson, Charles, RADM, USN. "Service Academies—Critical to Our Future." U.S. Naval Institute *Proceedings* (October 1995): 34.
- Luke, Thomas, LCDR, Medical Corps, USN; Timothy Halenkamp, LCDR, Medical Corps, USN; and Edward Kilbane, CAPT, Medical Corps, USN. "Naval Quarantine: Impervious to Epidemics of Virulent Disease." U.S. Naval Institute *Proceedings* (July 2005): 53.
- Lunday, Kevni E., CDR, USCG. "Repeal the 16-Pound Sledgehammer." U.S. Naval Institute *Proceedings* (February 2007): 41.
- Mixson, Riley D., RADM, USN. "Where We Must Do Better." U.S. Naval Institute *Proceedings* (August 1991): 38–39.
- Morison, Samuel Eliot. "Notes on Writing Naval (Not Navy) English." *The American Neptune* (January 1949): 10.
- Murray, Terence P., Maj., USMC. "Code of Conduct—A Sound Doctrine." *Marine Corps Gazette* (December 1983): 62.
- Vernon, Michael Vengrow, MC, USN. "Saving Limbs and Lives." U.S. Naval Institute *Proceedings* (February 2007): 20.

Index

About the Author

Robert Shenk saw his initial Navy duty during the Vietnam War, serving as communications officer of the destroyer *Harry E. Hubbard* (DD 748) during two deployments to Southeast Asia, and as senior patrol officer for a year with River Patrol Division 535, mainly in the Mekong Delta of South Vietnam. After leaving the Navy, he earned a Ph.D. from the University of Kansas, serving meanwhile in various naval reserve units. He returned to active duty with the Navy in 1979 to teach English at the U.S. Air Force Academy, and continued on active duty from 1982 to 1985 in the English department at the U.S. Naval Academy. Currently professor of English at the University of New Orleans, Shenk retired from the Naval Reserve as a captain in 1993.

Shenk's several books include *Authors at Sea: Modern American Writers Remember Their Naval Service* (Naval Institute Press, 1996), *The Left-Handed Monkey Wrench: Stories and Essays by Richard McKenna* (Naval Institute Press, 1986), and *The Sinners Progress: A Study of Madness in English Renaissance Drama* (Universität Salzburg, 1978). He introduced Richard McKenna's *The Sand Pebbles,* Kenneth Dodson's *Away All Boats,* and Gordon Forbes's *Goodbye to Some* for the Naval Institute's Classics of Naval Literature series. With Professor C. Herbert Gilliland of the Naval Academy, Shenk published a biography titled *Admiral Dan Gallery: The Life and Wit of a Navy Original* with the Naval Institute Press in 1999, and his *Playships of the World,* an edition of Admiral Gallery's early naval diaries, is to be published by South Carolina Press in spring 2008. Shenk has also published some twenty articles on naval writing, technical writing, rhetoric, and literature.